OXFORD **READERS**

Nationalism

John Hutchinson is a Senior Lecturer in the Faculty of Humanities at Griffith University, Brisbane, where he teaches modern European history. He has specialized in the cultural and political history of Britain and Ireland, but his forthcoming book, *Modern Nationalism* (1994), explores a wide range of issues in the field of ethnicity and nationalism. He is also the author of *The Dynamics of Cultural Nationalism* (1987).

Anthony D. Smith is Professor of Sociology at the London School of Economics. He has specialized in the study of ethnicity and nationalism, especially the theory of the nation. His work has focused particularly on the historical and social origins of nations; he is the author of *Theories of Nationalism* (1971), *The Ethnic Revival* (1981), *The Ethnic Origins of Nations* (1986), and *National Identity* (1991).

OXFORD **READERS**

Nationalism

Edited by

John Hutchinson *and* Anthony D. Smith

Oxford · New York

OXFORD UNIVERSITY PRESS

Oxford University Press, Walton Street, Oxford OX2 6DP
Oxford New York
Athens Auckland Bangkok Bogota Bombay
Buenos Aires Calcutta Cape Town Dar es Salaam
Delhi Florence Hong Kong Istanbul Karachi
Kuala Lumpur Madras Madrid Melbourne
Mexico City Nairobi Paris Singapore
Taipei Tokyo Toronto
and associated companies in
Berlin Ibadan

Oxford is a trade mark of Oxford University Press

British Library Cataloguing in Publication Data
Data available

Library of Congress Cataloging in Publication Data
Nationalism / edited by John Hutchinson and Anthony D. Smith.
p.   cm.—(Oxford readers)
Includes bibliographical references.
1. Nationalism.
I. Hutchinson, John, 1949–
II. Smith, Anthony D.
III. Series.
JC311.N295   1994   320.5'4—dc20   94-17708
ISBN 0-19-289260-6

10 9 8 7 6 5

Printed in Great Britain
on acid-free paper by
Bookcraft (Bath) Ltd.
Midsomer Norton
Avon

Preface

This reader on **nationalism** is an attempt to provide students with some idea of the many contributions that have been made by scholars from several disciplines in this rapidly expanding field of learning. For a long time the study of ethnicity and nationalism has been treated with reserve, especially in the Anglo-Saxon world. But the situation is now being swiftly remedied, and we are witnessing a remarkable growth of rich and penetrating works on every aspect of ethnicity and nationalism in all parts of the world. Given the explosion of ethno-nationalist sentiment and activity everywhere, the need for intensive study based on comparative analysis has become pressing. It is in this spirit that the present collection of some of the key texts in the field to date is offered.

Any attempt to encompass so vast a field as nations and nationalism is bound to be highly selective. We are all too conscious of the fact that limited space has made it necessary to prune our extracts and omit important material and contributions. The field of ethnicity and nationalism is expanding at an exponential rate and it is impossible to bring together in a single volume all the relevant new (as well as older) findings and explorations in this vast terrain. Where we have not been able to include important writers, we refer the reader to the Select Bibliography for each section, though even here it has proved impossible to include the writings of all those scholars whom we should have liked to acknowledge.

We are also conscious of the fact that some aspects of the field are undergoing radical change. This is especially true of the new work on gender and ethnicity, cultural studies and post-modern conceptions of the nation, and globalization and nationalism. To do justice to these and other issues would require a second volume. We are also aware that we have not paid sufficient attention to the important areas of nationalism and religion, race and nation, language and nation, and war and nationalism. All of these deserve separate intensive treatment.

We should like to record our thanks to Diana Solano for her thorough work in assembling the texts of the readings and in compiling the Index, and to Seeta Persaud for her patient assistance in reproducing the texts and handling the correspondence. Our thanks are also due to Catherine Clarke and Oxford University Press for their encouragement and help throughout.

J. H. and A. D. S.

London
February 1994

Contents

Nationalism

Introduction

....

Nationalism is one of the most powerful forces in the modern world, yet its study has until recently been relatively neglected. As an ideology and movement, nationalism exerted a strong influence in the American and French Revolutions, yet it did not become the subject of historical enquiry until the middle of the nineteenth century, nor of social scientific analysis until the early twentieth century. Sustained investigation of nationalism had to wait until after the First World War, and it is really only since the 1960s, after the spate of anti-colonial and ethnic nationalisms, that the subject has begun to be thoroughly investigated by scholars from several disciplines.

There are several reasons for this state of affairs. To begin with, the field of nationalist phenomena, which includes the growth of nations and the national state, as well as ethnic identity and community, is vast and ramified. It spills over into any number of cognate subjects: race and racism, fascism, language development, political religion, communalism, ethnic conflict, international law, protectionism, minorities, gender, immigration, genocide. The forms that nationalism takes have been kaleidoscopic: religious, conservative, liberal, fascist, communist, cultural, political, protectionist, integrationist, separatist, irredentist, diaspora, pan, etc. The fluidity and variety of national sentiments, national aspirations, and national cultural values create another obstacle to systematic research, as do the many differences in national identities.

Then there is the problem of interdisciplinarity. The study of nations and nationalism cannot be confined to a single disciplinary perspective. Historians long dominated the field, but latterly they have been joined by anthropologists, political scientists, sociologists, social psychologists, students of linguistics, international relations scholars, geographers, philosophers, regional economists, international lawyers, and many others. The sheer variety of components of national identities and of possible causal factors has made it impossible for scholars of any one discipline to study more than a few aspects and examples of the subject.

Add to this the fact that other fields of enquiry, and other concepts and phenomena, long held the attention of most scholars—class, capitalism, the market, industrialization, the state, Marxism, parties, kinship, tribes, and communications—and we begin to grasp why the systematic study of nations and nationalism has only recently begun to develop.

Central Concepts

Perhaps the central difficulty in the study of nations and nationalism has been the problem of finding adequate and agreed definitions of the key concepts, nation and nationalism.

The concept of the *nation* has, in fact, been contested on two fronts: in terms of rival scholarly definitions, and as a form of identity that competes with other kinds of collective identity. While it is recognized that the concept of the nation must be differentiated from other concepts of collective identity like class, region, gender, race, and religious community, there is little agreement about the role of ethnic, as opposed to political, components of the nation; or about the balance between 'subjective' elements like will and memory, and more 'objective' elements like territory and language; or about the nature and role of ethnicity in national identity. What is often conceded is the power, even primacy, of national loyalties and identities over those of even class, gender, and race. Perhaps only religious attachments have rivalled national loyalties in their scope and fervour. At the same time, national attachments can intermingle with, even slide into, other forms of collective identity, or alternate with them in terms of power and salience (Rustow 1967; Connor 1978).*

The situation is only a little improved when we turn to the other major concept, that of *nationalism*. Once again, there are important differences in ways of defining the concept, some equating it with 'national sentiment', others with nationalist ideology and language, others again with nationalist movements. There is also a difference between those who stress the cultural rather than the political aspects of nationalism. Here it seems that a synthesis is possible, in that the ideology and movement incorporate political and cultural dimensions (Hutchinson 1987: ch. 1; Smith 1971: ch. 7). That, at any rate, is how the founding fathers—Rousseau, Herder, Fichte, Korais, and Mazzini— saw the ideological movement of nationalism. In their view, and that of most subsequent nationalists, the movement brought together the vital aspirations of the modern world: for autonomy and self-government, for unity and autarchy, and for authentic identity (Kemilainen 1964).

Nationalism was, first of all, a doctrine of popular freedom and sovereignty. The people must be liberated—that is, free from any external constraint; they must determine their own destiny and be masters in their own house; they must control their own resources; they must obey only their own 'inner' voice. But that entailed fraternity. The people must be united; they must dissolve all internal divisions; they must be gathered together in a single historic territory, a homeland; and they must have legal equality and share a single public culture. But which culture and what territory? Only a homeland that was 'theirs' by historic right, the land of their forebears; only a culture that was 'theirs' as a heritage, passed down the generations, and therefore an expression of their authentic identity.

---

* Details of works extracted in this volume, but not included in the Select Bibliography, are to be found as sources at the end of the relevant extract.

Autonomy, unity, identity: these three themes and ideals have been pursued by nationalists everywhere since Rousseau, Herder, Fichte, Korais, and Mazzini popularized them in Western and Central Europe. They have also under-pinned the more specific goals of nationalist movements, most of which have been founded and inspired by intellectuals. In most of these movements it has been possible to discern a pattern of mobilization, which has been described by Miroslav Hroch in the Eastern European case. Starting with an élite of intellec-tuals, the movement has subsequently fanned out to include the professional classes, who have often acted as political agitators, and finally has been broadened to other sectors of society—the masses of clerks, artisans, workers, and even peasants. Of course, not all movements have reached this final phase. Sometimes the middle sectors have been wary of involving the lower strata. Hence we cannot say, with Tom Nairn, that nationalism is always an inter-class and populist movement, though it usually seeks to present itself that way (Nairn 1977: ch. 2; Hroch 1985).

The Origins of Nationalism

Many historians would agree that, as an ideology and discourse, nationalism became prevalent in North America and Western Europe in the latter half of the eighteenth century, and shortly thereafter in Latin America. The dates that are often singled out as signalling the advent of nationalism include 1775 (the First Partition of Poland), 1776 (the American Declaration of Independence), 1789 and 1792 (the commencement and second phase of the French Revolu-tion), and 1807 (Fichte's *Addresses to the German Nation*). This early ideological phase was permeated by neo-classicism, the conscious return in letters, poli-tics, and the arts to classical antiquity and, above all, to the patriotism and solidarity of Sparta, Athens, and republican Rome, the models and exemplars of the public, and often heroic, virtues. It was quickly succeeded by more varied currents, generally subsumed under the rubric of romanticism, which emphasized the role of intellectuals and artists, humanity's yearning for the infinite, the centrality of human emotion and self-expression, the need to find one's own identity through a return to authentic experience, the importance of discovering one's roots and true nature and, in the case of national com-munities, of rediscovering their pristine origins and golden ages. In fact, we can see in neo-classicism an early, pre-romantic phase of these concerns: both Rousseau and Herder mingled their admiration for classical virtue with a love of nature and the simple life of authentic experience and sentiment (Kedourie 1960).

Nationalism, as an ideological movement, did not emerge without ante-cedents. For some, millennial Christianity prepared the way, for others it was the printing press and especially newspapers. It is also possible to trace some of the key nationalist motifs to the classical humanism of some Northern

Italian cities, notably fifteenth- and early sixteenth-century Florence, from Bruno Latini to Machiavelli. Certainly, a strong and consciously classical emphasis on civic virtue and solidarity became an important component of later civic nationalism, duly transposed to larger territories and populations. This in turn drew on ancient Greek and Roman models, notably the patriotism of the *polis* and its ideological contrast between Greek liberties and barbarian servitude. Perhaps more important was the legacy derived from ancient Israel by the Puritans after the Reformation. The parallel they drew between the election and persecution of the children of Israel and their own lot, their Old Testament interpretation of their sufferings at the hands of hostile state authorities, gave a powerful impetus to the growth of national sentiment among the middle strata in England and Holland in the sixteenth and seventeenth centuries. Through these theological channels, there flowed into modern nationalism the doctrine of ethnic election which, originating perhaps with the ancient Israelites, became widely diffused in the Middle East, Europe, and East Africa, though analogues can be found as far afield as Japan (Greenfeld 1992: ch. 2).

Social and political developments during this period were increasingly conducive to the rise of nations, national states, and nationalism. For one thing, a classically educated intelligentsia was, as McNeill points out, steeped in the peculiar virtues of civic patriotism. The eighteenth century also witnessed the new phenomenon of widespread alienation of the intellectuals from society and politics; in Germany Schiller was only the most eloquent to complain of the artificiality of society and the machine-like nature of bureaucratic politics. Such disenchantment was the product of both urban life and absolutism. The growth of free towns as centres of capitalism and the rapid expansion of population in Europe was matched by the failure of its élites to make use of the talents of the more educated sons who languished in dull provincial towns, a life of waste so vividly conveyed for nineteenth-century Russia by Turgenev and Chekhov. At the same time, urban wealth encouraged new generations to seek secular education, engage in various branches of scientific and humanistic learning, and enter the expanding professions. Yet, because the numbers of the educated were small enough to form reading publics who could communicate and associate with each other through salons, coffee-houses, and clubs, the possibility of concerted political action by radically minded circles of the intelligentsia gave these new ideas about the nation and autonomy a social base that could translate them into political movements (Barnard 1969; Anderson 1983: ch. 5; McNeill 1986: ch. 2).

Politically, too, the failure to reunite Europe on the model of the Roman empire, and the rise of competing absolutist states, meant that the territorial and economic basis for national states had been well prepared as far back as the later fifteenth century, if not earlier. The disentangling of 'England' from 'France' at the end of the Hundred Years War (1337–1453), and the rise of separate ethnically based states in Spain, Switzerland, Holland, Sweden, and

Poland by the sixteenth century, broke the unity of Christendom even before the Wars of Religion and the Counter-Reformation, and forged an interstate system based on a complex web of alliances and balances of power. Commercial competition and wars between these states, as well as the later absolutisms of Prussia, Austria, and Russia, increased the links between urban capitalism and the monarchies and forced rulers to mobilize and standardize their populations in terms of religion, education, and even language. Loyalty to the ruler was increasingly accompanied by patriotism, a sense of identification with a particular state and its territory and people. Though eighteenth-century wars continued to be fought largely by professionals, the younger generations were fired as much by love of country and people as by any sense of obedience to rulers (Tilly 1975: Introduction; Tivey 1980).

Varieties of Nationalism

It was in and during the American and French Revolutions that these various social, political, and intellectual developments found powerful and explosive expression in radical politics. The causes of the revolutionary movements in America and Europe were many and varied, but their emotional and intellectual content were increasingly nationalist, and their consequences led to a dramatic transformation of absolutism into the mass national state. After 1792 the French Revolution, with its tricolour, 'Marseillaise', assemblies, oaths, processions, fêtes, and the like, began exporting its patriotic ideals all over Europe, and in this respect Napoleon's conquests, and the strong reactions they provoked in England, Spain, Germany, Poland, and Russia, intensified and diffused the civic ideas of national autonomy, unity, and identity across Europe and throughout Latin America (Kohn 1967).

The period of royalist reaction from 1815 to 1848 brought into sharper focus the ethnic character of several of these nationalisms, together with what Hans Kohn has called the organic 'eastern' forms of nationalism, in contrast to the civic and rational 'western' versions current in France, England, and the United States—though not in Ireland. Perhaps the most obvious case was that of Greece, though it was also a complex one, being at once a 'rational' and westernizing movement of merchants and intelligentsia for a revived Hellas along the lines of ancient Athens, and a yearning for an ethno-religious revival of the Orthodox Byzantine empire in Constantinople among the clergy and peasant communities. In Poland, too, nationalism in the late eighteenth century had begun as an aristocratic aspiration for the return of lands lost in the partitions, to be followed by a romantic movement of intellectuals for the myth of redemption of a Catholic Poland. This vein was also mined by the Slavophile intellectuals in Russia, who harked back to pre-Petrine Muscovy and its Orthodox monastic ways, at a time when westernization and incipient capitalism had severed Russia from its feudal past. And in India, too, the same note of romantic yearning for a return to an idealized ethnic and religious past which was being eroded by westernization and capitalism was to be found in late nineteenth-century intellectuals like Tilak and Aurobindo and in movements like the Arya Samaj (Kohn 1960; Taylor and Yapp 1979; Kitromilides 1989).

All these were movements of intelligentsia and opposition groups calling for the vernacular mobilization of 'the people' against a variety of evils: autocracy, bureaucracy, capitalism, and western ways. But such was the chameleon-like character of nationalism that it could be appropriated by the autocrats, bureaucrats, and capitalists. The classic instances are Germany and Japan. In Germany the 1848 revolutions of the intellectuals were divided and crushed; the Prussian chancellor, Bismarck, swiftly appropriated and tamed German linguistic nationalism in the service of a Prussian-led *Kleindeutschland* and a Lutheran Prussian monarch. Popular German nationalism accordingly migrated into Pan-German expansionism and the *volkisch* fantasies of an academic proletariat who dreamed of German conquest and agricultural settlement in the East, in the footsteps of Teutonic Knights and medieval German merchants. It was from these fringe groups of intelligentsia that the Nazi movement developed, even if its racism was to leave far behind the original linguistic bases of German romantic nationalism (Mosse 1964; Breuilly 1982).

In Japan the Meiji Restoration of 1868 put a swift end to the declining Tokugawa era and instituted a modern bureaucratic state under the aegis of the restored emperor. The reformers quickly realized the importance of mass public education as the key to a civic nationalism on the French model, and, using the imperial authority, proceeded to inculcate the virtues of a specifically Japanese culture mixed with western arts and technology. The Japanese nationalist model proved highly successful, both in terms of modernizing Japanese society and of establishing a strong nation-state, unlike the Ottoman attempt at reform in the mid-nineteenth-century Tanzimat period, which foundered on the multi-ethnic character and the economic and military weakness of the empire. In the West, too, state-based nationalism spilled over easily into imperialism and colonialism; French, British, Dutch, and Portuguese annexations during the nineteenth century were as much the products of nationalist interstate competition being transposed across the seas as of any desire to exploit markets and export capital (Lewis 1968; Yoshino 1992).

State-based nationalisms were not confined to the 'official' ideologies of empire. They were also characteristic of the twentieth-century 'anti-colonial' movements that sought to oust imperial rulers and set up new states in the ex-colonial territories. Thus Arab nationalisms in the Middle East and North Africa accepted the imperialist territorial units and applied western civic concepts of the nation (*watan*) to these often artificial divisions. At the same time, they drew on romantic popular notions of ethno-religious ties stemming from shared myths of Arab origin and the Islamic golden age of the Caliphates, even though several early Arab nationalists were Christian and many Arab states could boast separate pre-modern histories and traditions. Pan-Arabism also drew on ethnic, religious, and political antagonism to Zionist claims in Palestine; the latter similarly combined a westernized (even socialist) civic and territorial anti-colonialism with a pan-Jewish ethno-religious nationalism of the diaspora harking back to the ancient kingdoms of Israel and subsuming wide differences among Jewish communities, particularly after the immense demographic losses of the Holocaust (Haim 1962).

In India and Africa similar fusions and tensions could be found: on the one hand, a civic, territorial, anti-colonial nationalism, and, on the other hand, various ethnic and pan cultural movements, among which Hindu nationalism and pan-Africanism have exerted the most powerful influence. Pan-Africanism, indeed, combined a search for a specifically African history with elements of racial consciousness and pride, in the face of western cultural devaluation and political subjection; from Blyden to Senghor and Nkrumah, the 'natural' spiritual and social heritage of Black Africans has been counterposed to a materialist, atomist West (Kedourie 1971: Introduction; Geiss 1974).

For several historians and political scientists, the injection of racism brought nationalism to its mid-twentieth-century apogee. They have tended to see in fascism and especially in Nazism the logical culmination of nationalist ideas and practices; common to both were a belief in heroic struggle, the idea of the *Volk*, racial imperialism and agrarian settlement, the appeal to collective will and brutal instincts, and obedience to charismatic leaders. These are the nationalisms of late development, and they mark the evolution of the inner 'subjective' tendencies inherent in nationalism as it interacts with a modern political economy. For other scholars, fascism and Nazism were products of a specific phase of modern European history; they were essentially totalitarian movements, tied to a particular period of industrialization and democratization. Though they had nationalist harbingers and historical links with specific nationalisms, fascist movements and Nazism owed more to social Darwinian ideas of racial struggle and eugenics and to doctrines of state power and authoritarian militarism, which flourished especially among the lower middle classes in the wake of the Great War and the failures of orthodox nationalisms and parliamentary democracy after 1918 (Smith 1979; Hobsbawn 1990).

On a more general level, the early twentieth century confirmed for many the intimate connection between nationalism and war. This was already apparent in September 1792: the battle of Valmy, fought for the first time by a mass citizen army of conscripts, the *levée en masse*, was seen as a war in defence of *la patrie en danger*. Since that time, many nationalists have seen in heroic struggle both a test of collective fitness and the true route to independence from oppression. This was given a further European dimension in the resistance to Napoleon, by philhellenes in the Greek War of Independence (1821–30), by the Italian Risorgimento, and by the Hungarian uprising of 1849.

In Latin America the Liberator Bolívar and San Martín also exemplified the generous spirit of freedom through military revolt from Spain, while the 'primary resistance' of Africans in the Gold Coast, Southern Africa, and the Sudan furnished the myths of national awakening for later generations, including later anti-colonial guerrilla wars in Algeria, Kenya, and Angola (Humphreys and Lynch 1965; Rotberg and Mazrui 1970; Howard 1976).

The links between war and nationalism were amply underlined by the central part played by nationalism in the two world wars. Historians still differ over the extent to which Balkan nationalism was a major causal factor in the Great War, but it clearly dominated the aftermath of Germany's defeat, especially as a result of the role assigned to national self-determination in President Wilson's Fourteen Points of 1918. Even if Wilson's vision was severely curtailed, it did provide a standard for many of the successor states and their ethnic minorities in the interwar period, as well as for the ill-fated League of Nations. The Second World War also served to underline the centrality of nationalism. This was apparent in the European and non-European resistance movements against German and Japanese attempts to create empires; and in Bolshevik Russia Stalin appealed to neo-Slavophile Russian nationalism in the Great Patriotic War. The United Nations, paradoxically created in the aftermath of the co-operation of the many national resistance movements, has also experienced major problems over the application of the principle of national self-determination enshrined in its charter to non-colonial, stateless, and ethnically defined units which are raising the banner of national independence (Wiberg in Lewis 1982).

The Revival of Nationalism

The horrors of Nazism and the world wars were thought to have rendered ethnic ties and national ideals obsolete, largely because of their associations with discredited racist ideas. To many it came as something of a surprise, therefore, that in the wake of the spate of anti-colonial movements in Africa and Asia during the 1940s and 1950s, and of the Black movement in America, the affluent, stable, democratic western states should experience something of an 'ethnic revival'. Perhaps this *revival* was really only a *survival*, making its reappearance in the revolutionary 1960s; perhaps, too, it owed much to the examples of liberation movements inspired by Mao, Fanon, and Che Guevara and to the close links forged by 'national communism' between the two great revolutionary ideologies in Yugoslavia, China, Vietnam, Kampuchea, the Yemen, Somalia, and Angola. In either case, the appearance of movements demanding ethnic autonomy (sometimes outright independence) in Quebec, Scotland, Wales, Flanders, Brittany, Corsica, Euzkadi, Catalonia, and other 'ethno-regions' in old-established western states undermined many common assumptions about modernization and democracy and unleashed a veritable flood of scholarly and political explanations (Hechter 1975; Esman 1977; Smith 1981).

Recent events in Eastern Europe and the former Soviet Union have only deepened this unease, raising once again the spectre of a Europe wracked by more than localized ethnic conflicts. The Bolshevik strategy to supersede nationalism through the merging of nations in a socialist society unravelled with astonishing rapidity once the central control of the party and its security organs was loosened. The break-up of Yugoslavia and the Soviet empire may not have been caused by ethnic nationalisms, but ethnically defined nations have certainly become their heirs, and the conflict in Bosnia and the anxious relations with significant Russian and other minorities in several of the former Soviet republics are likely to add to international destabilization. The 'dark side' of nationalism, too, has been revealed in the rapid rise of ultra-nationalism, neo-Nazism, and anti-Semitism among a vociferous minority in both Western and Eastern European states. This has led to questions about the civic-political or ethnic-linguistic character of nationalism, and the social conditions which give rise to these different types (Bremmer and Taras 1993).

At the same time, in a multipolar world following the end of the Cold War, the transformations, instability, and populist nationalism within Russia, the long-standing conflicts in the Middle East, the renewed ethno-religious violence in the Indian subcontinent, the risings of indigenous peoples, from the Aborigines and Mohawks to the Chiapas Zapatistas, and the deep antagonisms in East and Southern Africa, have placed 'the national question' once again firmly at the centre of world affairs. Issues of ethnic secession and irredentism, of sovereignty, identity, and self-determination, have again become the cockpit for international suspicions and rivalries, and the greatest burden and brake on international co-operation. This has led to sustained discussion about the causes, and conditions of success, of ethnic secession in a world that has seen the creation of at least fifteen new states since 1990. Though other issues vie for world attention—poverty, crime, disease, gender, ecological problems—ethnic conflicts and nationalisms remain the most ubiquitous, explosive, and intractable problems at the end of the twentieth century, and the greatest challenge to the framing of an international order based on justice and parity (Horowitz 1985; Mayall 1990).

Can we realistically forecast any diminution, let alone supersession, of nationalism? A number of scholars have discerned signs that we are moving into a 'post-national' era, dominated by the globalizing forces of an international division of labour, transnational companies, great power blocs, an ideology of mass consumerism, and the growth of vast networks of communications. In the face of these massive 'movements of history', ethnic conflicts and nationalism are becoming a secondary concern and increasingly irrelevant. They may trouble the surface of world developments for a time, but they will soon disappear as people come to appreciate the massive problems of planetary survival. Against these forecasts must be set the current proliferation and intensity of ethnic conflicts, and the continuing dangers they pose for regional and global peace and security. There is also the continuing impact of nationalist ideals, which can be, and are being, applied to their own situations by large numbers of politically unrecognized or unsatisfied *ethnies* (ethnic communities), using the new channels of mass communications; and the persistent interstate rivalries, often bolstered by gross economic inequalities, which can so easily use (and be used by) mass nationalist legitimizations (Richmond 1984; Hobsbawm 1990: ch. 6).

All these problems are to be found in the debates on ethnic immigration into western states and on the unification of Europe. The vast population movements this century which have strained many economies have also rendered the borders of western states porous and are helping to redefine their sense of national identity; how far the influx of *Gastarbeiter*, asylum-seekers, and immigrants has furthered an everyday practical process of national reconstruction which is negating the more traditional, national, 'pedagogical' narratives of the nation in the old metropolitan centres, as some cultural critics suggest, is a question for further investigation. As for Europe, rapid economic integration has undoubtedly produced strong political and institutional drives for greater continental centralization; but these have recently been resisted by significant sections of the population in some European states, and the trend towards European Union enlargement, while still popular in Eastern Europe, has occasioned increasing doubts in Scandinavia. On the cultural level, while there are some shared European traditions, and while there is evidence of a growing élitist identification with 'Europe', the degree to which a European identity has emerged at the cost of national identities or commands a popular following in most European states remains largely uncharted, as have the meanings which different populations attribute to any such larger identity. Once again, placing the unification of Europe on the political agenda has only served to heighten the salience of *national* identity as a popular political issue (McNeill 1986; Bhabha 1990: ch. 16; Smith 1991: ch. 7).

These are only some of the main empirical issues raised by a study of nations and nationalisms. There are, of course, many others in a rapidly expanding field. There has not been space to include them all. Undoubtedly, more could have been said about issues of ethnicity and gender, about race relations, about post-modernist discourses of the nation, about post-colonialism and immigration, as well as about the whole field of ethnic conflict regulation and various forms of power-sharing between élites of ethnic communities in a polyethnic state. These are vital and pressing issues, but they are well treated elsewhere, and could easily divert attention from the central debates on nations and nationalism. Instead, we have concentrated on what we think are the main lines of general and theoretical debate, as they have developed over several disciplines, and have therefore had to exclude many important problems, areas, and issues that would have been included in a larger volume (Rex and Mason 1986; Anthias and Yuval-Davis 1989).

In what follows, we have sought to present the key texts in the study of nations and nationalism. Wherever possible, we have tried to balance different viewpoints. Inevitably, but with regret, space has compelled us to compress many of the selected texts. Given the variety and conflict which abound in the field, particular emphasis has been laid on the rival theoretical approaches to ethnicity and nationalism, and the problems of definition. These debates are briefly described, and contextualized, in the introductions to these sections. The later sections deal in more detail with some of the empirical issues outlined above, including the rise of nations in Europe, nationalism and nation-building in Africa, Asia, and Latin America, relations between nationalism and the international community, and the transcendence of nations and nationalisms. We have tried to avoid the temptation to be 'radical' and fashionable, since one decade's fashions are the next's *bêtes noires*. Instead, we have aimed for a broad selection of the most influential and profound studies of the complex issues in this field. In this way, we hope to provide students embarking on courses in this field, as well as more advanced students, with an informed, critical, and balanced introduction to the theoretical and empirical problems in the study of nations and nationalism. An introduction is no substitute for deeper immersion in the texts themselves and in the problems they raise. But we hope that this introduction will stimulate students to undertake this exploration of a field which is both fundamental to our grasp of modern society and politics and richly rewarding for a more profound understanding of humanity.

Section I

The Question of Definition

INTRODUCTION

Questions of definition have bedevilled our field of study, and there is no agreement among scholars about 'subjective' and 'objective' factors in the definition of nations, or about the relationship of nations and nationalism to ethnicity on the one hand, and statehood on the other.

Three classic statements are those of Renan, Stalin, and Weber. They cover a wide spectrum. Ernest Renan rejects the statist concept of the nation in order to identify the nation as a form of morality. It is a solidarity sustained by a distinctive historical consciousness. The nation, he declares, is a daily plebiscite. Stalin's influential definitions, by contrast, contain a mix of objective and subjective elements. Differentiating nations from races and tribes on the one hand, and imperial states on the other, he argues that a nation comes into existence only when several elements have come together, especially economic life, language, and territory. Max Weber examines the nation as a 'prestige community', endowed with a sense of cultural mission. Nations, he claims, are too various to be defined in terms of any one criterion, but he affiliates nations to ethnic communities as populations unified by a myth of common descent. What distinguishes the nation is a commitment to a political project.

Karl Deutsch's socio-demographic approach offers a functional definition of the nation which avoids single-factor characterizations of the nation, and proposes 'the presence of sufficient communication facilities with enough complementarity to produce the overall result'. Deutsch argues that the objective of nationalist organizations is to strengthen and extend the channels of communication which can ensure a popular compliance with national symbols and norms.

Clifford Geertz, from an anthropological perspective, indicates that there are two competing yet complementary components—ethnic and civic—in the nationalism of post-colonial states. The ethnic dimension is portrayed as a commitment to 'primordial' loyalties which endow individuals with a distinctive identity; the civic as a desire for citizenship in a modern state. Since state and ethnic boundaries often clash, the result is endemic conflict.

In contrast, Anthony Giddens presents an unambiguously statist definition of the nation, described here as a 'bordered power-container'. This and much else is the subject of a critique by Walker Connor, who rejects tendencies to equate nation with state, and nationalism with state patriotism. Like Weber, he defines the nation as a community of descent, but distinguishes it from ethnic communities by its degree of self-consciousness; whereas an ethnic group may be other-defined, a nation must be self-defined.

1 Qu'est-ce qu'une nation?

A nation is a soul, a spiritual principle. Only two things, actually, constitute this soul, this spiritual principle. One is in the past, the other is in the present. One is the possession in common of a rich legacy of remembrances; the other is the actual consent, the desire to live together, the will to continue to value the heritage which all hold in common. Man, sirs, does not improvise. The nation, even as the individual, is the end product of a long period of work, sacrifice and devotion. The worship of ancestors is understandably justifiable, since our ancestors have made us what we are. A heroic past, of great men, of glory (I mean the genuine kind), that is the social principle on which the national idea rests. To have common glories in the past, a common will in the present; to have accomplished great things together, to wish to do so again, that is the essential condition for being a nation. One loves in proportion to the sacrifices which one has approved and for which one has suffered. One loves the house which he has built and which he has made over. The Spartan chant: 'We are what you make us; we are what you are' is simply the abbreviated hymn of the Fatherland.

In the past, a heritage of glory and a reluctance to break apart, to realize the same program in the future; to have suffered, worked, hoped together; that is worth more than common taxes and frontiers conforming to ideas of strategy; that is what one really understands despite differences of race and language. I have said 'having suffered together'; indeed, common suffering is greater than happiness. In fact, national sorrows are more significant than triumphs because they impose obligations and demand a common effort.

A nation is a grand solidarity constituted by the sentiment of sacrifices which one has made and those that one is disposed to make again. It supposes a past, it renews itself especially in the present by a tangible deed: the approval, the desire, clearly expressed, to continue the communal life. The existence of a nation (pardon this metaphor!) is an everyday plebiscite; it is, like the very existence of the individual, a perpetual affirmation of life. Oh! I know it, this is less metaphysical than the concept of divine right, less brutal than the so-called historic right. In the order of ideas that I submit to you, a nation has no more right than a king of a province to say: 'You appear to me, I take you.' A province for us is its inhabitants; if anyone in this matter has a right to be considered, it is the inhabitant. A nation never has a real interest in being annexed or holding on to a country despite itself. The desire of nations to be together is the only real criterion that must always be taken into account.

We have traced the politics of metaphysical and theological abstractions. What remains after that? Man remains, his desires, his needs. . . . Human desires change; but what does not change on this earth? Nations are not something eternal. They have begun, they will end. They will be replaced, in all probability, by a European confederation. But such is not the law of the century in which we live. At the present time the existence of nations happens to be good, even necessary. Their existence is a guarantee of liberty, which would be lost if the world had only one law and only one master.

Through their varied, frequently opposing, abilities, nations serve the common cause of civilization; each holds one note in the concert of humanity, which, in the long run, is the highest ideal to which we can aspire. Isolated, they have their weaknesses. I often say to myself that a person who has these defects in quality that nations have, who nourishes himself on vainglory, who is jealous, egotistic and quarrelsome, who could support nothing without fighting; he would be the most intolerable of men. But all these unharmonious details disappear when we are united. Poor humanity! How you have suffered! What ordeals await you yet! Can the spirit of wisdom guide you to prevent the many dangers that line your path?

I continue, sirs. Man is not enslaved, nor is his race nor his language, nor his religion, nor the course of the rivers, nor the direction of the mountain ranges. A great aggregation of men, with a healthy spirit and warmth of heart, creates a moral conscience which is called a nation. When this moral conscience proves its strength by sacrifices that demand abdication of the individual for the benefit of the community, it is legitimate, and it has a right to exist.

[*Qu'est-ce qu'une nation*, trans. Ida Mae Snyder (Calmann-Levy: Paris, 1882), 26–9.]

JOSEPH STALIN

2 The Nation

What is a nation?

A nation is primarily a community, a definite community of people.

This community is not racial, nor is it tribal. The modern Italian nation was formed from Romans, Teutons, Etruscans, Greeks, Arabs, and so forth. The French nation was formed from Gauls, Romans, Britons, Teutons, and so on. The same must be said of the British, the Germans and others, who were formed into nations from people of diverse races and tribes.

Thus, a nation is not a racial or tribal, but a historically constituted community of people.

On the other hand, it is unquestionable that the great empires of Cyrus and Alexander could not be called nations, although they came to be constituted historically and were formed out of different tribes and races. They were not nations, but casual and loosely-connected conglomerations of groups, which fell apart or joined together according to the victories or defeats of this or that conqueror.

Thus, a nation is not a casual or ephemeral conglomeration, but a stable community of people.

But not every stable community constitutes a nation. Austria and Russia are also stable communities, but nobody calls them nations. What distinguishes a national community from a state community? The fact, among others, that a national community is inconceivable without a common language, while a state need not have a common language. The Czech nation in Austria and the Polish in Russia would be impossible if each did not have a common language, whereas the integrity of Russia and Austria is not affected by the fact that there are a number of different languages within their borders. We are referring, of course, to the spoken languages of the people and not to the official governmental languages.

Thus, *a common language* is one of the characteristic features of a nation.

This, of course, does not mean that different nations always and everywhere speak different languages, or that all who speak one language necessarily constitute one nation. A *common* language for every nation, but not necessarily different languages for different nations! There is no nation which at one and the same time speaks several languages, but this does not mean that there cannot be two nations speaking the same language! Englishmen and Americans speak one language, but they do not constitute one nation. The same is true of the Norwegians and the Danes, the English and the Irish.

But why, for instance, do the English and the Americans not constitute one nation in spite of their common language?

Firstly, because they do not live together, but inhabit different territories. A nation is formed only as a result of lengthy and systematic intercourse, as a result of people living together generation after generation. But people cannot live together for lengthy periods unless they have a common territory. Englishmen and Americans originally inhabited the same territory, England, and constituted one nation. Later, one section of the English emigrated from England to a new territory, America, and there, in the new territory, in the course of time, came to form the new American nation. Difference of territory led to the formation of different nations.

Thus, *a common territory* is one of the characteristic features of a nation.

But this is not all. Common territory does not by itself create a nation. This requires, in addition, an internal economic bond to weld the various parts of the nation into a single whole. There is no such bond between England and America, and so they constitute two different nations. But the Americans themselves would not deserve to be called a nation were not the different parts of America bound together into an economic whole, as a result of division of labour between them, the development of means of communication, and so forth.

Take the Georgians, for instance. The Georgians before the Reform[1] inhabited a common territory and spoke one language. Nevertheless, they did not, strictly speaking, constitute one nation, for, being split up into a number of disconnected principalities, they could not share a common economic life; for centuries they waged war against each other and pillaged each other, each inciting the Persians and Turks against the other. The ephemeral and casual union of the principalities which some successful king sometimes managed to bring about embraced at best a superficial administrative sphere, and rapidly disintegrated owing to the caprices of the princes and the indifference of the peasants. Nor could it be otherwise in economically disunited Georgia. . . . Georgia came on the scene as a nation only in the latter half of the nineteenth century, when the fall of serfdom and the growth of the economic life of the country, the development of means of communication and the rise of capitalism, introduced division of labour between the various districts of Georgia, completely shattered the economic isolation of the principalities and bound them together into a single whole.

The same must be said of the other nations which have passed through the stage of feudalism and have developed capitalism.

Thus, *a common economic life, economic cohesion*, is one of the characteristic features of a nation.

But even this is not all. Apart from the foregoing, one must take into consideration the specific spiritual complexion of the people constituting a nation. Nations differ not only in their conditions of life, but also in spiritual complexion, which manifests itself in peculiarities of national culture. If England, America and Ireland, which speak one language, nevertheless constitute three distinct nations, it is in no small measure due to the peculiar psychological make-up which they developed from generation to generation as a result of dissimilar conditions of existence.

Of course, by itself, psychological make-up or, as it is otherwise called, 'national character,' is something intangible for the observer, but in so far as it manifests itself in a distinctive culture common to the nation it is something tangible and cannot be ignored.

Needless to say, 'national character' is not a thing that is fixed once and for all, but is modified by changes in the conditions of life; but since it exists at every given moment, it leaves its impress on the physiognomy of the nation.

Thus, *a common psychological make-up*, which manifests itself in a common culture, is one of the characteristic features of a nation.

We have now exhausted the characteristic features of a nation.

A nation is a historically constituted, stable community of people, formed on the basis of a common language, territory, economic life, and psychological make-up manifested in a common culture.

It goes without saying that a nation, like every historical phenomenon, is subject to the law of change, has its history, its beginning and end.

It must be emphasized that none of the above characteristics taken separately is sufficient to define a nation. More than that, it is sufficient for a single one of these characteristics to be lacking and the nation ceases to be a nation.

It is possible to conceive of people possessing a common 'national character' who, nevertheless, cannot be said to constitute a single nation if they are economically disunited, inhabit different territories, speak different languages, and so forth. Such, for instance, are the Russian, Galician, American, Georgian and Caucasian Highland *Jews*, who, in our opinion, do not constitute a single nation.

It is possible to conceive of people with a common territory and economic life who nevertheless would not constitute a single nation because they have no common language and no common 'national character.' Such, for instance, are the Germans and Letts in the Baltic region.

Finally, the Norwegians and the Danes speak one language, but they do not constitute a single nation owing to the absence of the other characteristics.

It is only when all these characteristics are present together that we have a nation.

['The Nation', in *Marxism and the Natural Question*, from *The Essential Stalin: Major Theoretical Writings 1905–1952*, ed. Bruce Franklin (Croom Helm: London, 1973), 57–61.]

MAX WEBER

3   The Nation

The fervor of this emotional influence does not, in the main, have an economic origin. It is based upon sentiments of prestige, which often extend deep down to the petty bourgeois masses of political structures rich in the historical attainment of power-positions. The attachment to all this political prestige may fuse with a specific belief in responsibility towards succeeding generations. The great power structures *per se* are then held to have a responsibility of their own for the way in which power and prestige are distributed between their own and foreign polities. It goes without saying that all those groups who hold the power to steer common conduct within a polity will most strongly instill themselves with this ideal fervor of power prestige. They remain the specific and most reliable bearers of the idea of the state as an imperialist power structure demanding unqualified devotion.

In addition to the direct and material imperialist interests, discussed above, there are partly indirect and material and partly ideological interests of strata that are in various ways intellectually privileged within a polity and, indeed, privileged by its very existence. They comprise especially all those who think of themselves as being the specific 'partners' of a specific 'culture' diffused among the members of the polity. Under the influence of these circles, the naked prestige of 'power' is unavoidably transformed into other special forms of prestige and especially into the idea of the 'nation.'

If the concept of 'nation' can in any way be defined unambiguously, it certainly cannot be stated in terms of empirical qualities common to those who count as members of the nation. In the sense of those using the term at a given time, the concept undoubtedly means, above all, that one may exact from certain groups of men a specific sentiment of solidarity in the face of other groups. Thus, the concept belongs in the sphere of values. Yet, there is no agreement on how these groups should be delimited or about what concerted action should result from such solidarity.

In ordinary language, 'nation' is, first of all, not identical with the 'people of a state,' that is, with the membership of a given polity. Numerous polities comprise groups among whom the independence of their 'nation' is emphatically asserted in the face of the other groups; or, on the other hand, they comprise parts of a group whose members declare this group to be one homogeneous 'nation' (Austria before 1918, for example). Furthermore, a 'nation' is not identical with a community speaking the same language; that this by no means always suffices is indicated by the Serbs and Croats, the North Americans, the Irish, and the English. On the contrary, a common language does not seem to be absolutely necessary to a 'nation.' In official documents, besides 'Swiss People' one also finds the phrase 'Swiss Nation.' And some language groups do not think of themselves as a separate 'nation,' for example, at least until recently, the white Russians. The pretension, however, to be considered a special 'nation' is regularly associated with a common language as a culture value of the masses; this is predominantly the case in the classic country of language conflicts, Austria, and equally so in Russia and in eastern Prussia. But this linkage of the common language and 'nation' is of varying intensity; for instance, it is very low in the United States as well as in Canada.

'National' solidarity among men speaking the same language may be just as well rejected as accepted. Solidarity, instead, may be linked with differences in the other great 'culture value of the masses,' namely, a religious creed, as is the case with the Serbs and Croats. National solidarity may be connected with differing social structure and mores and hence with 'ethnic' elements, as is the case with the German Swiss and the Alsatians in the face of the Germans of the Reich, or with the Irish facing the British. Yet above all, national solidarity may be linked to memories of a common political destiny with other nations, among the Alsatians with the French since the revolutionary war which represents their common heroic age, just as among the Baltic Barons with the Russians whose political destiny they helped to steer.

It goes without saying that 'national' affiliation need not be based upon common blood. Indeed, everywhere the especially radical 'nationalists' are often of foreign descent. Furthermore, although a specific common anthropological type is not irrelevant to nationality, it is neither sufficient nor a prerequisite to found a nation. Nevertheless, the idea of the 'nation' is apt to include the notions of common descent and of an essential, though frequently indefinite, homogeneity. The nation has these notions in common with the sentiment of solidarity of ethnic communities, which is also nourished from various sources. But the sentiment of ethnic solidarity does not by itself make a 'nation.' Undoubtedly, even the white Russians in the face of the Great Russians have always had a sentiment of ethnic solidarity, yet even at the present time they would hardly claim to qualify as a separate 'nation.' The Poles of Upper Silesia, until recently, had hardly any feeling of solidarity with the 'Polish Nation.' They felt themselves to be a separate ethnic group in the face of the Germans, but for the rest they were Prussian subjects and nothing else.

Whether the Jews may be called a 'nation' is an old problem. The mass of the Russian Jews, the assimilating West-European-American Jews, the Zionists—these would in the main give a negative answer. In any case, their answers would vary in nature and extent. In particular, the question would be answered very differently by the peoples of their environment, for example, by the Russians on the one side and by the Americans on the other—or at least by those Americans who at the present time still maintain American and Jewish nature to be essentially similar, as an American President has asserted in an official document.

Those German-speaking Alsatians who refuse to belong to the German 'nation' and who cultivate the memory of political union with France do not thereby consider themselves simply as members of the French 'nation.' The Negroes of the United States, at least at present, consider themselves members of the American 'nation,' but they will hardly ever be so considered by the Southern Whites.

Only fifteen years ago, men knowing the Far East still denied that the Chinese qualified as a 'nation'; they held them to be only a 'race.' Yet today, not only the Chinese political leaders but also the very same observers would judge differently. Thus it seems that a group of people under certain conditions may attain the quality of a nation through specific behavior, or they may claim this quality as an 'attainment'—and within short spans of time at that.

There are, on the other hand, social groups that profess indifference to, and even directly relinquish, any evaluational adherence to a single nation. At the present time, certain leading strata of the class movement of the modern proletariat consider such indifference and relinquishment to be an accomplishment. Their argument meets with varying success, depending upon political and linguistic affiliations and also upon different strata of the proletariat; on the whole, their success is rather diminishing at the present time.

An unbroken scale of quite varied and highly changeable attitudes toward the idea of the 'nation' is to be found among social strata and also within single groups to whom language usage ascribes the quality of 'nations.' The scale extends from emphatic affirmation to emphatic negation and finally complete indifference, as may be characteristic of the citizens of Luxembourg and of nationally 'unawakened' peoples. Feudal strata, strata of officials, entrepreneurial bourgeois strata of various categories, strata of 'intellectuals' do not have homogeneous or historically constant attitudes towards the idea.

The reasons for the belief that one represents a nation vary greatly, just as does the empirical conduct that actually results from affiliation or lack of it with a nation. The 'national sentiments' of the German, the Englishman, the North American, the Spaniard, the Frenchman, or the Russian do not function in an identical manner. Thus, to take only the simplest illustration, national sentiment is variously related to political associations, and the 'idea' of the nation may become antagonistic to the empirical scope of given political associations. This antagonism may lead to quite different results.

Certainly the Italians in the Austrian state-association would fight Italian troops only if coerced into doing so. Large portions of the German Austrians would today fight against Germany only with the greatest reluctance; they could not be relied upon. The German Americans, however, even those valuing their 'nationality' most highly, would fight against Germany, not gladly, yet, given the occasion, unconditionally. The Poles in the German State would fight readily against a Russian Polish army but hardly against an autonomous Polish army. The Austrian Serbs would fight against Serbia with very mixed feelings and only in the hope of attaining common autonomy. The Russian Poles would fight more reliably against a German than against an Austrian army.

It is a well-known historical fact that within the same nation the intensity of solidarity felt toward the outside is changeable and varies greatly in strength. On the whole, this sentiment has grown even where internal conflicts of interest have not diminished. Only sixty years ago the *Kreuzzeitung*[1] still appealed to the intervention of the emperor of Russia in internal German affairs; today, in spite of increased class antagonism, this would be difficult to imagine.

In any case, the differences in national sentiment are both significant and fluid and, as is the case in all other fields, fundamentally different answers are given to the question: What conclusions are a group of people willing to draw from the 'national sentiment' found among them? No matter how emphatic and subjectively sincere a pathos may be formed among them, what sort of specific joint action are they ready to develop? The extent to which in the diaspora a convention is adhered to as a 'national' trait varies just as much as does the importance of common conventions for the belief in the existence of a separate 'nation.' In the face of these value concepts of the 'idea of the nation,' which empirically are entirely ambiguous, a sociological typology would have to analyse all sorts of community sentiments of solidarity in their genetic conditions and in their consequences for the concerted action of the participants. This cannot here be attempted.

Instead, we shall have to look a little closer into the fact that the idea of the nation for its advocates stands in very intimate relation to 'prestige' interests. The earliest and most energetic manifestations of the idea, in some form, even though it may have been veiled, have contained the legend of a providential 'mission.' Those to whom the representatives of the idea zealously turned were expected to shoulder this mission. Another element of the early idea was the notion that this mission was facilitated solely through the very cultivation of the peculiarity of the group set off as a nation. Therewith, in so far as its self-justification is sought in the value of its content, this mission can consistently be thought of only as a specific 'culture' mission. The significance of the 'nation' is usually anchored in the superiority, or at least the irreplaceability, of the culture values that are to be preserved and developed only through the cultivation of the peculiarity of the group. It therefore goes without saying that the intellectuals, as we have in a preliminary fashion called them, are to a specific degree predestined to propagate the 'national idea,' just as those who wield power in the polity provoke the idea of the state.

By 'intellectuals' we understand a group of men who by virtue of their peculiarity have special access to certain achievements considered to be 'culture values,' and who therefore usurp the leadership of a 'culture community.'[2]

*   *   *

In so far as there is at all a common object lying behind the obviously ambiguous term 'nation,' it is apparently located in the field of politics. One might well define the concept of nation in the following way: a nation is a community of sentiment which would adequately manifest itself in a state of its own; hence, a nation is a community which normally tends to produce a state of its own.

The causal components that lead to the emergence of a national sentiment in this sense may vary greatly. If we for once disregard religious belief—which has not yet played its last role in this matter, especially among Serbs and Croats—then common purely political destinies have first to be considered. Under certain conditions, otherwise heterogeneous peoples can be melted together through common destinies. The reason for the Alsatians' not feeling themselves as belonging to the German nation has to be sought in their memories. Their political destiny has taken its course outside the German sphere for too long; their heroes are the heroes of French history. If the custodian of the Kolmar museum wants to show you which among his treasures he cherishes most, he takes you away from Grünewald's altar to a room filled with tricolors, *pompier*, and other helmets and souvenirs of a seemingly most insignificant nature; they are from a time that to him is a heroic age. [. . .]

If one believes that it is at all expedient to distinguish national sentiment as something homogeneous and specifically set apart, one can do so only by referring to a tendency toward an autonomous state. And one must be clearly aware of the fact that sentiments of solidarity, very heterogeneous in both their nature and their origin, are comprised within national sentiments.

['The Nation', in *From Max Weber: Essays in Sociology*, trans. and ed. H. H. Gerth and C. Wright-Mills (Routledge & Kegan Paul: London, 1948), 171–7, 179.]

4 Nationalism and Social Communication

The community which permits a common history to be experienced as common, is a community of complementary habits and facilities of communication. It requires, so to speak, equipment for a job. This job consists in the storage, recall, transmission, recombination, and reapplication of relatively wide ranges of information; and the 'equipment' consists in such learned memories, symbols, habits, operating preferences, and facilities as will in fact be sufficiently complementary to permit the performance of these functions. *A larger group of persons linked by such complementary habits and facilities of communication* we may call a *people*.

The test of *complementarity* of any set of communications equipment is communicative effectiveness. How fast and how accurately do messages get through? How complex and voluminous is the information that can be so transmitted? How effectively are operations on one part of the net transmitted to another? The extent of complementarity for any set of facilities, or any community, will be indicated by the answers to these questions.

Complementarity or communicative efficiency is a function, an overall result. The same or a closely similar result may be reached by several different combinations of elements, or even by the entire replacement of some elements by others. [. . .] The communicative facilities of a society include a socially standardized system of symbols which is a language, and any number of auxiliary codes, such as alphabets, systems of writing, painting, calculating, etc. They include information stored in the living memories, associations, habits, and preferences of its members, and in its material facilities for the storage of information, such as libraries, statues, signposts, and the like; and a good deal more. Some of these facilities, individual and social, also deal with the treatment of information, its recall from storage or memory, its transmission and recombination to new patterns. Taken all together, they include, therefore, in particular the elements of that which anthropologists call culture. If these elements are in fact sufficiently complementary, they will add up to an integrated pattern or configuration of communicating, remembering, and acting, that is, to a culture in the sense of the citations quoted earlier in our discussion; and the individuals who have these complementary habits, vocabularies, and facilities are what we call a people.

It is now clear why all the usual descriptions of a people in terms of a community of languages, or character, or memories, or past history, are open to exception. For what counts is not the presence or absence of any single factor, but merely the presence of sufficient communication facilities with enough complementarity to produce the overall result. The Swiss may speak four different languages and still act as one people, for each of them has

enough learned habits, preferences, symbols, memories, patterns of landhold-
ing and social stratification, events in history, and personal associations, all of
which together permit him to communicate more effectively with other Swiss
than with the speakers of his own language who belong to other peoples.[1] 'I
found that my German was more closely akin to the French of my [French-
Swiss] friend than to the likewise German (*Ebenfallsdeutsch*) of the foreigner,'
says the editor of a prominent German-Swiss paper in his reminiscences. 'The
French-Swiss and I were using different words for the same concepts, but we
understood each other. The man from Vienna and I were using the same
words for different concepts, and thus we did not understand each other in the
least.'[2]

What is proposed here, in short, is a functional definition of nationality.
Membership in a people essentially consists in wide complementarity of social
communication. It consists in the ability to communicate more effectively, and
over a wider range of subjects, with members of one large group than with
outsiders.[3] This overall result can be achieved by a variety of functionally
equivalent arrangements.

This function of nationality differs from the old attempts to specify nationality in terms of some particular ingredient, somewhat as modern technological trends towards evaluating materials in terms of their performance differ
from the older practice of evaluating materials in terms of their composition.
In both cases, 'composition specifications' are replaced by 'performance tests,'
based on more detailed analysis of the functions carried out.[4]

Peoples are held together 'from within' by this communicative efficiency,
the complementarity of the communicative facilities acquired by their members. Such 'ethnic complementarity' is not merely subjective. At any moment,
it exists as an objective fact, measurable by performance tests. Similar to a
person's knowledge of a language, it is relatively independent of the whim of
individuals. Only slowly can it be learned or forgotten. It is a characteristic of
each individual, but it can only be exercised within the context of a group.[5]

Ethnic complementarity, the complementarity that makes a people, can be
readily distinguished by its relatively wide range from the narrow vocational
complementarity which exists among members of the same profession, such
as doctors or mathematicians, or members of the same vocational group, such
as farmers or intellectuals. Efficient communication among engineers, artists,
or stamp collectors is limited to a relatively narrow segment of their total
range of activities. In most other things they do, in their childhood memories,
in courtship, marriage, and parenthood, in their standards of beauty, their
habits of food and drink, in games and recreation, they are far closer to mutual
communication and understanding with their countrymen than with their
fellow specialists in other countries. [. . .]

Here we find that a *people* forms a social, economic, and political alignment
of individuals from different social classes and occupations, around a center

and a leading group. Its members are united by more intensive social communication, and are linked to these centers and leading groups by an unbroken chain of connections in communications, and often also in economic life, with no sharp break in the possibilities of communication and substitution at any link, and hence with a somewhat better probability of social rise from rank to rank.[6]

The primary basis of this alignment is the complementarity of communication habits. Its secondary basis is the complementarity of acquired social and economic preferences which involve the mobility of goods or persons. These are the widespread preferences for things or persons of 'one's own kind' (that is, associated with one's particular communication group) in such matters as buying and selling, work, food and recreation, courtship and marriage. A third factor has made all such alignments more important: the rise of industrialism and the modern market economy which offer economic and psychological rewards for successful group alignments to tense and insecure individuals—to men and women uprooted by social and technological change, exposed to the risks of economic competition, and taught to hunger for success. For almost any limited group within a competitive market, both security and success can be promoted by effective organization, alignment of preferences, and coordination of behavior. Vast numbers have felt a need for such a group and have answered it by putting their trust in their nation.

In the political and social struggles of the modern age, *nationality*, then, means an alignment of large numbers of individuals from the middle and lower classes linked to regional centers and leading social groups by channels of social communication and economic intercourse, both indirectly from link to link and directly with the center.[7] [. . .]

In the age of nationalism, *a nationality* is a people pressing to acquire a measure of effective control over the behavior of its members. It is a people striving to equip itself with power, with some machinery of compulsion strong enough to make the enforcement of its commands sufficiently probable to aid in the spread of habits of voluntary compliance with them. As the interplay of compliance habits with enforcement probabilities, such power can be exercised through informal social arrangements, pressure of group opinion, and the prestige of national symbols. It can be exercised even more strongly through formal social or political organizations, through the administration of educational or economic institutions, or through the machinery of government. Whatever the instruments of power, they are used to strengthen and elaborate those social channels of communication, the preferences of behavior, the political (and sometimes economic) alignments which, all together, make up the social fabric of the nationality.

All group power thus acquired by members of the nationality leads them to ask for more. Formally or informally, dissenters find themselves pressed into line, while a significant part of the members of the nationality begin to demand control of the state or part of it.

Once a nationality has added this power to compel to its earlier cohesiveness and attachment to group symbols, it often considers itself a *nation* and is so considered by others. In this sense, men have spoken of a Polish, Czech, or Irish nation, even after these groups had lost their earlier political states, or before they had yet acquired control of any state at all.

In all these cases, nationalities turn into nations when they acquire power to back up their aspirations. Finally, if their nationalistic members are successful, and a new or old state organization is put into their service, then at last the nation has become sovereign, and a *nation-state* has come into being. At this moment, if not earlier, the successful nation may face a new immediate problem: how to use its new panoply of power against the claims of other nationalities. The more successful it has been in promoting its own members into privileged or controlling positions in society, the more it will now have to fear from the rise of other peoples and other nationalist movements.

[*Nationalism and Social Communication*, 2nd edn. (MIT Press: Cambridge, Mass., 1966), 96–8, 101, 104–5.]

CLIFFORD GEERTZ
....

5 Primordial and Civic Ties

The stultifying aura of conceptual ambiguity that surrounds the terms 'nation,' 'nationality,' and 'nationalism' has been extensively discussed and thoroughly deplored in almost every work that has been concerned to attack the relationship between communal and political loyalties.[1] But as the preferred remedy has been to adopt a theoretical eclecticism that, in its attempt to do justice to the multifaceted nature of the problems involved, tends to confuse political, psychological, cultural, and demographic factors, actual reduction of that ambiguity has not proceeded very far. Thus a recent symposium on the Middle East refers indiscriminately to the efforts of the Arab League to destroy existing nation-state boundaries, those of the Sudan Government to unify a somewhat arbitrary and accidentally demarcated sovereign state, and those of the Azerin Turks to separate from Iran and join the Soviet Republic of Azerbaijan as 'nationalism.'[2] Operating with a similarly omnibus concept, Coleman[3] sees Nigerians (or some of them) as displaying five different sorts of nationalism at once—'African,' 'Nigerian,' 'Regional,' 'Group,' and 'Cultural.' And Emerson[4] defines a nation as a 'terminal community—the largest community that, when the chips are down, effectively commands men's loyalty, overriding the claims both of the lesser communities within it and those that cut across it or potentially enfold it within a still greater society . . .,' which simply shifts the ambiguity from the term 'nation' to the term 'loyalty,' as well as seeming to leave such questions as whether India, Indonesia, or Nigeria are nations to the determination of some future, unspecified historical crisis.

Some of this conceptual haze is burned away, however, if it is realized that the peoples of the new states are simultaneously animated by two powerful, thoroughly interdependent, yet distinct and often actually opposed motives—the desire to be recognized as responsible agents whose wishes, acts, hopes, and opinions 'matter,' and the desire to build an efficient, dynamic modern state. The one aim is to be noticed: it is a search for an identity, and a demand that that identity be publicly acknowledged as having import, a social assertion of the self as 'being somebody in the world.'⁵ The other aim is practical: it is a demand for progress, for a rising standard of living, more effective political order, greater social justice, and beyond that of 'playing a part in the larger arena of world politics,' of 'exercising influence among the nations.'⁶ The two motives are, again, most intimately related, because citizenship in a truly modern state has more and more become the most broadly negotiable claim to personal significance, and because what Mazzini called the demand to exist and have a name is to such a great extent fired by a humiliating sense of exclusion from the important centers of power in world society. But they are not the same thing. They stem from different sources and respond to different pressures. It is, in fact, the tension between them that is one of the central driving forces in the national evolution of the new states; as it is, at the same time, one of the greatest obstacles to such evolution.

This tension takes a peculiarly severe and chronic form in the new states, both because of the great extent to which their peoples' sense of self remains bound up in the gross actualities of blood, race, language, locality, religion, or tradition, and because of the steadily accelerating importance in this century of the sovereign state as a positive instrument for the realization of collective aims. Multiethnic, usually multilinguistic, and sometimes multiracial, the populations of the new states tend to regard the immediate, concrete, and to them inherently meaningful sorting implicit in such 'natural' diversity as the substantial content of their individuality. To subordinate these specific and familiar identifications in favor of a generalized commitment to an overarching and somewhat alien civil order is to risk a loss of definition as an autonomous person, either through absorption into a culturally undifferentiated mass or, what is even worse, through domination by some other rival ethnic, racial, or linguistic community that is able to imbue that order with the temper of its own personality. But at the same time, all but the most unenlightened members of such societies are at least dimly aware—and their leaders are acutely aware—that the possibilities for social reform and material progress they so intensely desire and are so determined to achieve rest with increasing weight on their being enclosed in a reasonably large, independent, powerful, well-ordered polity. The insistence on recognition as someone who is visible and matters and the will to be modern and dynamic thus tend to diverge, and much of the political process in the new states pivots around an heroic effort to keep them aligned.

A more exact phrasing of the nature of the problem involved here is that, considered as societies, the new states are abnormally susceptible to serious disaffection based on primordial attachments.[7] By a primordial attachment is meant one that stems from the 'givens'—or, more precisely, as culture is inevitably involved in such matters, the assumed 'givens'—of social existence: immediate contiguity and kin connection mainly, but beyond them the givenness that stems from being born into a particular religious community, speaking a particular language, or even a dialect of a language, and following particular social practices. These congruities of blood, speech, custom, and so on, are seen to have an ineffable, and at times overpowering, coerciveness in and of themselves. One is bound to one's kinsman, one's neighbor, one's fellow believer, *ipso facto*; as the result not merely of personal affection, practical necessity, common interest, or incurred obligation, but at least in great part by virtue of some unaccountable absolute import attributed to the very tie itself. The general strength of such primordial bonds, and the types of them that are important, differ from person to person, from society to society, and from time to time. But for virtually every person, in every society, at almost all times, some attachments seem to flow more from a sense of natural—some would say spiritual—affinity than from social interaction.

In modern societies the lifting of such ties to the level of political supremacy—though it has, of course, occurred and may again occur—has more and more come to be deplored as pathological. To an increasing degree national unity is maintained not by calls to blood and land but by a vague, intermittent, and routine allegiance to a civil state, supplemented to a greater or lesser extent by governmental use of police powers and ideological exhortation. The havoc wreaked, both upon themselves and others, by those modern (or semi-modern) states that did passionately seek to become primordial rather than civil political communities, as well as a growing realization of the practical advantages of a wider-ranging pattern of social integration than primordial ties can usually produce or even permit, have only strengthened the reluctance publicly to advance race, language, religion, and the like as bases for the definition of a terminal community. But in modernizing societies, where the tradition of civil politics is weak and where the technical requirements for an effective welfare government are poorly understood, primordial attachments tend, as Nehru discovered, to be repeatedly, in some cases almost continually, proposed and widely acclaimed as preferred bases for the demarcation of autonomous political units. [. . .]

It is this crystallization of a direct conflict between primordial and civil sentiments—this 'longing not to belong to any other group'—that gives to the problem variously called tribalism, parochialism, communalism, and so on, a more ominous and deeply threatening quality than most of the other, also very serious and intractable problems the new states face. Here we have not just competing loyalties, but competing loyalties of the same general order, on the same level of integration. There are many other competing loyalties in the new states, as in any state—ties to class, party, business, union, profession, or whatever. But groups formed of such ties are virtually never considered as possible self-standing, maximal social units, as candidates for nationhood. Conflicts among them occur only within a more or less fully accepted terminal community whose political integrity they do not, as a rule, put into question. No matter how severe they become they do not threaten, at least not intentionally, its existence as such. They threaten governments, or even forms of government, but they rarely at best—and then usually when they have become infused with primordial sentiments—threaten to undermine the nation itself, because they do not involve alternative definitions of what the nation is, of what its scope of reference is. Economic or class or intellectual disaffection threatens revolution, but disaffection based on race, language, or culture threatens partition, irredentism, or merger, a redrawing of the very limits of the state, a new definition of its domain. Civil discontent finds its natural outlet in the seizing, legally or illegally, of the state apparatus. Primordial discontent strives more deeply and is satisfied less easily. If severe enough, it wants not just Sukarno's or Nehru's or Moulay Hasan's head it wants Indonesia's or India's or Morocco's.

The actual foci around which such discontent tends to crystallize are various, and in any given case several are usually involved concurrently, sometimes at cross-purposes with one another. On a merely descriptive level they are, nevertheless, fairly readily enumerable:[8]

1) *Assumed Blood Ties.* Here the defining element in quasi-kinship. 'Quasi' because kin units formed around known biological relationship (extended families, lineages, and so on) are too small for even the most tradition-bound to regard them as having more than limited significance, and the referent is, consequently, to a notion of untraceable but yet sociologically real kinship, as in a tribe. Nigeria, the Congo, and the greater part of sub-Saharan Africa are characterized by a prominence of this sort of primordialism. But so also are the nomads or seminomads of the Middle East—the Kurds, Baluchis, Pathans, and so on; the Nagas, Mundas, Santals, and so on, of India; and most of the so-called 'hill tribes' of Southeast Asia.

2) *Race.* Clearly, race is similar to assumed kinship, in that it involves an ethnobiological theory. But it is not quite the same thing. Here, the reference is to phenotypical physical features—especially, of course, skin color, but also facial form, stature, hair type, and so on—rather than any very definite sense of common descent as such. The communal problems of Malaya in large part focus around these sorts of differences, between, in fact, two phenotypically

very similar Mongoloid peoples. 'Negritude' clearly draws much, though perhaps not all, of its force from the notion of race as a significant primordial property, and the pariah commercial minorities—like the Chinese in Southeast Asia or the Indians and Lebanese in Africa—are similarly demarcated.

3) *Language.* Linguism—for some yet to be adequately explained reasons—is particularly intense in the Indian subcontinent, has been something of an issue in Malaya, and has appeared sporadically elsewhere. But as language has sometimes been held to be the altogether essential axis of nationality conflicts, it is worth stressing that linguism is not an inevitable outcome of linguistic diversity. As indeed kinship, race, and the other factors to be listed below, language differences need not in themselves be particularly divisive: they have not been so for the most part in Tanganyika, Iran (not a new state in the strict sense, perhaps), the Philippines, or even in Indonesia, where despite a great confusion of tongues linguistic conflict seems to be the one social problem the country has somehow omitted to demonstrate in extreme form. Furthermore, primordial conflicts can occur where no marked linguistic differences are involved, as in Lebanon, among the various sorts of Batak-speakers in Indonesia, and to a lesser extent perhaps between the Fulani and Hausa in northern Nigeria.

4) *Region.* Although a factor nearly everywhere, regionalism naturally tends to be especially troublesome in geographically heterogeneous areas. Tonkin, Annam, and Cochin in prepartitioned Vietnam, the two baskets on the long pole, were opposed almost purely in regional terms, sharing language, culture, race, etc. The tension between East and West Pakistan involves differences in language and culture too, but the geographic element is of great prominence owing to the territorial discontinuity of the country. Java versus the Outer Islands in archipelagic Indonesia; the Northeast versus the West Coast in mountain-bisected Malaya, are perhaps other examples in which regionalism has been an important primordial factor in national politics.

5) *Religion.* Indian partition is the outstanding case of the operation of this type of attachment. But Lebanon, the Karens and the Moslem Arakenese in Burma, the Toba Bataks, Ambonese, and Minahassans in Indonesia, the Moros in the Philippines, the Sikhs in Indian Punjab and the Ahmadiyas in Pakistani, and the Hausa in Nigeria are other well-known examples of its force in undermining or inhibiting a comprehensive civil sense.

6) *Custom.* Again, differences in custom form a basis for a certain amount of national disunity almost everywhere, and are of especial prominence in those cases in which an intellectually and/or artistically rather sophisticated group sees itself as the bearer of a 'civilization' amid a largely barbarian population that would be well advised to model itself upon it: the Bengalis in India, the Javanese in Indonesia, the Arabs (as against the Berbers) in Morocco, the Amhara in—another 'old' new state—Ethiopia, etc. But it is important also to point out that even vitally opposed groups may differ rather little in their

general style of life: Hindu Gujeratis and Maharashtrians in India; Baganda and Bunyoro in Uganda; Javanese and Sundanese in Indonesia. And the reverse holds also: the Balinese have far and away the most divergent pattern of customs in Indonesia, but they have been, so far, notable for the absence of any sense of primordial discontent at all.

['The Integrative Revolution: Primordial Sentiments and Civil Politics in the New States', in Clifford Geertz (ed.), *Old Societies and New States: The Quest for Modernity in Asia and Africa* (Free Press: New York, 1963), 107–13.]

ANTHONY GIDDENS

6 The Nation as Power-Container

A 'nation', as I use the term here, only exists when a state has a unified administrative reach over the territory over which its sovereignty is claimed. The development of a plurality of nations is basic to the centralization and administrative expansion of state domination internally, since the fixing of borders depends upon the reflexive ordering of a state system. We can follow Jones in recognizing four aspects of the transformation of frontiers into borders.[1] These he calls allocation, delimitation, demarcation and administration.

The first refers to a collaborative political decision taken among states about the distribution of territory between them. Delimitation concerns the identification of specific border sites.[2] Demarcation in Jones's scheme—written as a guide for policy-makers and not just an academic study—refers to how borders are actually marked on the physical environment. Many borders, even within the heart of Europe today, are not demarcated. That apparent modern equivalent of the walls built by traditional states, the Berlin Wall, is an anomaly because it symbolizes the failure of a modern state to exert the level of administrative control over its population which its governing authorities deem proper and necessary. The border between East and West Germany must be one of the most highly 'administered', in Jones's terms, in the world. That is to say, a high degree of direct surveillance is maintained along it. Traditional states sometimes constructed frontier posts, demanding payment, and occasionally documentation, of those who travelled through. But where these existed they were usually, in fact, at divisions between provinces rather than between states as such. The coupling of direct and indirect surveillance (customs officials and frontier guards, plus the central co-ordination of passport information) is one of the distinctive features of the nation-state.

A nation-state is, therefore, a bordered power-container—as I shall argue, the pre-eminent power-container of the modern era. [. . .] [A]mong other

things it involves processes of urban transformation and the internal pacification of states. These are phenomena that go together with the creation of
generalized 'deviance' as a category and with processes of sequestration. All
traditional states have laid claim to the formalized monopoly over the means
of violence within their territories. But it is only within nation-states that this
claim characteristically becomes more or less successful. The progress of
internal pacification is closely connected with such success—they are, as it
were, different sides of the same process.

The objection may be raised that there are very many instances, even in
current times, of states whose monopoly of the means of violence is chronic-
ally threatened from within by armed groups; that insurgent movements,
often poorly armed and organized compared with state authorities, have
sometimes challenged and overthrown those authorities; and that there are
diffuse levels of violence in minor contexts of even the most politically quiescent societies (crimes of violence, domestic violence and so on). None of these,
however, compromise the point at issue, which concerns a comparison between nation-states and traditional states. There are circumstances in which
civil war, involving chronic confrontations between armed movements or
coalitions of more or less equal strength, have been quite protracted. However, not only are such circumstances highly unusual, the very existence of
'civil war' presumes a norm of a monopolistic state authority. By contrast,
conditions which in a modern state would be defined as examples of 'civil war',
that is, divisive 'internal' armed struggles, have been typical of all class-divided
societies for very long periods. Again, armed groups or movements today are
almost always oriented to the assumption of state power, either by taking over
an existing state's territory or by dividing up a territory and establishing a
separate state. Such organizations do not and cannot 'opt out' from involvement in state power one way or another as frequently happened in traditional
states. Finally, I have no wish to underplay the importance or extent of
violence that takes place in small-scale contexts in modern societies. But I am
principally concerned with the means of violence associated with the activities
of organized armed forces, not with violence as a more blanket category of the
doing of physical harm to others.

Collecting together the implications of the foregoing observations, we can
arrive at the following concept of the nation-state, which holds for all variants
and is not intrinsically bound to any particular characterization of nationalism.
[. . .] The nation-state, which exists in a complex of other nation-states, is a set
of institutional forms of governance maintaining an administrative monopoly over a territory with demarcated boundaries (borders), its rule being
sanctioned by law and direct control of the means of internal and external
violence.[3]

[A Contemporary Critique of Historical Materialism, ii. The Nation-State and Violence (Polity
Press: Cambridge, 1985), 119–21.]

7 A Nation is a Nation, is a State, is an Ethnic Group, is a . . .

One of the most common manifestations of terminological license is the interutilization of the words *state* and *nation*. This tendency is perplexing because at one level of consciousness most scholars are clearly well aware of the vital distinctions between the two concepts. The state is the major political subdivision of the globe. As such, it is readily defined and, what is of greater moment to the present discussion, is easily conceptualized in quantitative terms. Peru, for illustration, can be defined in an easily conceptualized manner as the territorial—political unit consisting of the sixteen million inhabitants of the 514,060 square miles located on the west coast of South America between 69° and 80° West, and 2° and 18°, 21° South.

Defining and conceptualizing the nation is much more difficult because the essence of a nation is intangible. This essence is a psychological bond that joins a people and differentiates it, in the subconscious conviction of its members, from all other people in a most vital way. The nature of that bond and its well-spring remain shadowy and elusive, and the consequent difficulty of defining the nation is usually acknowledged by those who attempt this task. Thus, a popular dictionary of International Relations defines a nation as follows:

A social group which shares a common ideology, common institutions and customs, and a *sense* of homogeneity. 'Nation' is difficult to define so precisely as to differentiate the term from such other groups as religious sects, which exhibit some of the same characteristics. In the nation, however, there is also present a strong group *sense* of belonging associated with a particular territory considered to be peculiarly its own.[1]

Whereas the key word in this particular definition is *sense*, other authorities may substitute *feeling* or *intuition*, but proper appreciation of the abstract essence of the nation is customary *in definitions*. But after focusing attention upon that essential psychological bond, little probing of its nature follows. Indeed, having defined the nation as an essentially psychological phenomenon, authorities [. . .] then regularly proceed to treat it as fully synonymous with the very different and totally tangible concept of the state.

Even when one restricts *nation* to its proper, non-political meaning of a human collectivity, the ambiguity surrounding its nature is not thereby evaporated. How does one differentiate the nation from other human collectivities? The above cited definition spoke of 'a sense of homogeneity.' Others speak of a feeling of sameness, of oneness, of belonging, or of consciousness of kind. But all such definitions appear a bit timid, and thereby fail to distinguish the nation from numerous other types of groups. Thus, one can conceive of the Amish, Appalachian hill people, or 'down Mainers' as all fitting rather neatly within any of the preceding standards.

With but very few exceptions, authorities have shied away from describing the nation as a kinship group and have usually explicitly denied that the notion of shared blood is a factor. Such denials are supported by data illustrating that most groups claiming nationhood do in fact incorporate several genetic strains. But such an approach ignores the wisdom of the old saw that when analysing sociopolitical situations, what ultimately matters is not *what is* but *what people believe is*. And a subconscious belief in the group's separate origin and evolution is an important ingredient of national psychology. When one avers that he is Chinese, he is identifying himself not just with the Chinese people and culture of today, but with the Chinese people and their activities throughout time. The Chinese Communist Party was appealing to just such a sense of separate origin and evolution in 1937:

[W]e know that in order to transform the glorious future into a new China, independent, free, and happy, all our fellow countrymen, every single, zealous descendant of Huang-ti [the legendary first emperor of China] must determinedly and relentlessly participate in the concerted struggle.

. . . Our great Chinese nation, with its long history is inconquerable.[2]

Bismark's famous exhortation to the German people, over the heads of their particular political leaders, to 'think with your blood' was a similar attempt to activate a mass psychological vibration predicated upon an intuitive sense of consanguinity. An unstated presumption of a Chinese (or German) nation is that there existed in some hazy, prerecorded era a Chinese (or German) Adam and Eve, and that the couple's progeny has evolved in essentially unadulterated form down to the present. It was recognition of this dimension of the nation that caused numerous writers of the nineteenth and early twentieth centuries to employ *race* as a synonym for *nation*, references to a German race or to the English race being quite common.

Since the nation is a self-defined rather than an other-defined grouping, the broadly held conviction concerning the group's singular origin need not and seldom will accord with factual data. Thus, the anthropologist may prove to his own satisfaction that there are several genetic strains within the Pushtun people who populate the Afghani-Pakistani border-region and conclude therefrom that the group represents the variegated offspring of several peoples who have moved through the region. The important fact, however, is that the Pushtuns themselves are convinced that all Pushtuns are evolved from a single source and have remained essentially unadulterated. This is a matter which is *known* intuitively and unquestionably, a matter of attitude and not of fact. It is a matter, the underlying conviction of which is not apt to be disturbed substantially even by the rational acceptance of anthropological or other evidence to the contrary. Depending upon the sophistication of the treatise, this type of sensory knowledge may be described as 'a priori', 'an emotional rather than a rational conviction', 'primordial', 'thinking with the heart (or with the blood) rather than with the mind', or 'a "gut" or "knee-jerk" response.' Regardless of the nomenclature, it is an extremely important adjunct of the national idea.[3] It is the intuitive conviction which can give to nations a psychological dimension approximating that of the extended family, i.e. a feeling of common blood lineage.

The word *nation* comes from the Latin and, when first coined, clearly conveyed the idea of common blood ties. It was derived from the past participle of the verb *nasci*, meaning to be born. And hence the Latin noun, *nationem*, connoting *breed* or *race*. Unfortunately, terms used to describe human collectivities (terms such as race and class) invite an unusual degree of literary license, and *nation* certainly proved to be no exception.[4] Thus, at some medieval universities, a student's *nationem* designated the sector of the country from whence he came. But when introduced into the English language in the late thirteenth century, it was with its primary connotation of a blood related group. One etymologist notes, however, that by the early seventeenth century, *nation* was also being used to describe the inhabitants of a country, regardless of that population's ethnonational composition, thereby becoming a substitute for less specific human categories such as *the people* or *the citizenry*.[5] This infelicitous practice continues to the present day, and accounts for often encountered references to the American citizenry as the American nation. Whatever the American people are (and they may well be *sui generis*), they are not a nation in the pristine sense of the word. However, the unfortunate habit of calling them a nation, and thus verbally equating American with German, Chinese, English, and the like, has seduced scholars into erroneous analogies. Indeed, while proud of being 'a nation of immigrants' with a 'melting pot' tradition, the absence of a common origin may well make it more difficult, and conceivably impossible, for the American to appreciate instinctively the idea of the nation in the same dimension and with the same poignant clarity as do the Japanese, the Bengali, or the Kikuyu. It is difficult for an American to appreciate what it means for a German to be German or for a Frenchman to be French, because the psychological effect of being American is not precisely equatable. Some of the associations are missing and others may be quite different.

Far more detrimental to the study of nationalism, however, has been the propensity to employ the term nation as a substitute for that territorial juridical unit, the state. How this practice developed is unclear, though it seems to have become a relatively common practice in the late seventeenth century. Two possible explanations for this development present themselves. One involves the rapid spread of the doctrine of popular sovereignty that was precipitated about this time by the writings of men such as Locke. In identifying *the people* as the font of all political power, this revolutionary doctrine made the people and the state almost synonymous. *L'état c'est moi* became *l'état c'est le peuple*. And therefore the nation and the state had become near synonyms, for we have already noted the tendency to equate nation with the entire people or citizenry. Thus, the French *Declaration of Rights of Man and Citizen* would proclaim that 'the source of all sovereignty resides essentially in the nation; no group, no individual may exercise authority not emanating expressly therefrom.' Though the drafters of the Declaration may not have been aware, 'the nation' to which they referred contained Alsatians, Basques, Bretons, Catalans, Corsicans, Flemings, and Occitanians, as well as Frenchmen.

It is also probable that the habit of interutilizing *nation* and *state* developed as alternative abbreviations for the expression *nation-state*. The very coining of this hyphenate illustrated an appreciation of the vital differences between *nation* and *state*. It was designed to describe a territorial–political unit (a state) whose borders coincided or nearly coincided with the territorial distribution of a national group. More concisely, it described a situation in which a nation had its own state. Unfortunately, however, *nation-state* has come to be applied indiscriminately to all states. Thus one authority has stated that 'a prime fact about the world is that it is largely composed of nation-states.'[6] The statement should read that 'a prime fact about the world is that it is *not* largely composed of nation-states.' A survey of the 132 entities generally considered to be states as of 1971, produced the following breakdown:

1) Only 12 states (9.1%) can justifiably be described as nation-states.

2) Twenty-five (18.9%) contain a nation or potential nation accounting for more than 90% of the state's total population but also contain an important minority.[7]

3) Another 25 (18.9%) contain a nation or potential nation accounting for between 75% and 89% of the population.

4) In 31 (23.5%), the largest ethnic element accounts for 50% to 74% of the population.

5) In 39 (29.5%), the largest nation or potential nation accounts for less than half of the population.

Were all states nation-states, no great harm would result from referring to them as nations, and people who insisted that the distinction between *nation* and *state* be maintained could be dismissed as linguistic purists or semantic nitpickers. Where *nation* and *state* essentially coincide, their verbal interutilization is inconsequential because the two are indistinguishably merged in popular perception. The state is perceived as the political extension of the nation, and appeals to one trigger the identical, positive psychological responses as appeals to the other. To ask a Japanese *kamikaze* pilot or a banzai-charge participant whether he was about to die for *Nippon* or for the Nipponese people would be an incomprehensible query since the two blurred into an inseparable whole. Hitler could variously make his appeals to the German people in the name of state (Deutsches Reich), nation (Volksdeutsch), or homeland (Deutschland), because all triggered the same emotional associations. Similar responses can be elicited from members of a nation that is clearly predominant within a state. But the invoking of such symbols has quite a different impact upon minorities. Thus, 'Mother Russia' evokes one type of response from a Russian and something quite different from a Ukrainian. De Gaulle's emotional evocations of *La France* met quite different audiences within the Île de France and within Brittany or Corsica.

Whatever the original reason for the interutilization of *nation* and *state*, even the briefest reflection suffices to establish the all-pervasive effect that this careless use of terminology has had upon the intellectual–cultural milieu within which the study of nationalism is perforce conducted. The League of Nations and the United Nations are obvious misnomers. The discipline called International Relations should be designated *Interstate* Relations.[8] One listing of contemporary organizations contains sixty-six entries beginning with the word *International* (e.g. the International Court of Justice and the International Monetary Fund), none of which, either in its membership or in its function, reflects any relationship to nations. International Law and International Organization are still other significant illustrations of the common but improper tendency to equate state and nation. National income, national wealth, national interest, and the like, refer in fact to statal concerns. A recently coined malapropism, *transnational* (and even *transnationalism*) is used to describe interstate, extragovernmental relations. *Nationalization* is still another of the numerous misnomers that muddy understanding of the national phenomenon.

With the concepts of the nation and the state thus hopelessly confused, it is perhaps not too surprising that *nationalism* should come to mean identification with the state rather than loyalty to the nation. Even the same International Relations Dictionary whose definition of the *nation* we cited for its proper appreciation of the psychological essence of the nation, makes this error. After carefully noting that 'a nation may comprise part of a state, or extend beyond the borders of a single state,' it elsewhere says of *nationalism* that 'it makes the state the ultimate focus of the individual's loyalty.'[9] It also says of nationalism that 'as a mass emotion it is the most powerful political force operative in the world.'[10] Few would disagree with this assessment of the power of nationalism, *and this is precisely the problem. Impressed with the force of nationalism, and assuming it to be in the service of the state, the scholar of political development has been pre-programmed to assume that the new states of Africa and Asia would naturally become the foci of their inhabitants' loyalties.* Nationalism, here as elsewhere, would prove irresistible, and alternative foci of loyalty would therefore lose the competition to that political structure alternately called the nation, the state, or the nation-state. This syndrome of assumptions and terminological confusion which has generally characterized the political development school is reflected in the early self-description of its endeavors as 'nation-building'. Contrary to its nomenclature, the 'nation-building' school has in fact been

dedicated to building viable states. And with a very few exceptions, the greatest barrier to state unity has been the fact that the states each contain more
than one nation, and sometimes hundreds. Yet, a review of the literature will
uncover little reflection on how the psychological bonds that presently tie
segments of the state's population are to be destroyed. One searches the
literature in vain for techniques by which group-ties predicated upon such
things as a sense of separate origin, development, and destiny are to be
supplanted by loyalty to a state-structure, whose population has never shared
such common feelings. The nature and power of those abstract ties that
identify the true nation remain almost unmentioned, to say nothing of un-
probed. The assumption that the powerful force called nationalism is in the
service of the state makes the difficult investigation of such abstractions
unnecessary.

As in the case of substituting the word *nation* for *state*, it is difficult to
pinpoint the origin of the tendency to equate nationalism with loyalty to the
state. It is unquestionably a very recent development, for the word *nationalism*
is itself of very recent creation. G. de Bertier de Sauvigny believes it first
appeared in literature in 1798 and did not reappear until 1830. Moreover, its
absence from lexicographies until the late nineteenth and early twentieth
centuries suggests that its use was not extensive until much more recently.
Furthermore, all of the examples of its early use convey the idea of identification *not* with the state, but with the nation as properly understood.[11] While
unable to pinpoint nationalism's subsequent association with the state, it
indubitably followed and flowed from the tendency to equate state and nation.
It also unquestionably received a strong impetus from the great body of
literature occasioned by the growth of militant nationalism in Germany and
Japan during the 1930s and early 1940s.

As outstanding illustrations of the fanatical responses that nationalism can
engender, German and Japanese nationalism of this period have come to
occupy an important place in all subsequent scholarship on nationalism. And,
unfortunately, these manifestations of extreme nationalism have been firmly
identified with the loyalty to the state. The most common word applied to
them has been *fascism*, a doctrine postulating unswerving obedience to an
organic, corporate state. The most popular alternative descriptive phrase,
totalitarianism, perhaps even more strongly conveys the idea of the complete
(total) identification of the individual with the state.

The linking of the state to these examples *par excellence* of extreme nationalism suggests the likelihood that other states will also become the object of
mass devotion. If some states could elicit such fanatical devotion, why not
others? Granted, few would wish to see such extreme and perverted dedication
to the state arise elsewhere. But if the concept of a Japanese state could, during
World War II, motivate 'banzai charges,' kamikaze missions, and numerous
decisions of suicide rather than surrender (as well as the many post-war

illustrations of people enduring for years an animal-like existence in caves on Pacific islands) because of a loyalty to the Japanese state that was so unassailable as to place that state's defeat beyond comprehension, then surely the states of the Third World should at least be able to evoke a sufficiently strong loyalty from their inhabitants so as to prevail against any competing group-allegiances. If a loyalty to a German state could motivate Germans to carry on a war long after it became evident that the cause was hopeless and that perseverance could only entail more deprivation, destruction, and death, then surely other states could at least elicit a sense of common cause and identity from their populations that would prove more powerful than any counter-tendencies to draw distinctions among segments of the populace. If the German and Japanese experiences were pertinent elsewhere, then optimism concerning the stability of present state structures would be justified.

But what has been too readily ignored is the fact that Germany and Japan were among the handful of states that clearly qualify as nation-states. As earlier noted, in such cases the state and the nation are indistinguishably linked in popular perception. Japan to the Japanese, just as Germany to the Germans, was something far more personal and profound than a territorial–political structure termed a state; it was an embodiment of the nation-idea and therefore an extension of self. As postulated by fascist doctrine, these states were indeed popularly conceived as corporate organisms, for they were equated with the Japanese and German nations. As Hitler wrote in *Mein Kampf*: 'We as Aryans, are therefore able to imagine a State only to be the living organism of a nationality which not only safeguards the preservation of that nationality, but which, by further training of its spiritual and ideal abilities, leads it to its highest freedom.'[12]

But could such an emotion-laden conception of the state take root where the nation and the state were not popularly equated? The single rubric of fascism was applied to Hitler's Germany, Tojo's Japan, Mussolini's Italy, Franco's Spain, and Peron's Argentina. It is evident, however, that appeals in the name of Spain have not elicited any great emotion from the Basques, Catalans, and Galicians. In polygenetic Argentina, Peron's message was not a unifying appeal to all Argentinians, but was in fact a divisive call in the name of socioeconomic class. Within Italy, a sense of loyalty to the state proved woefully and surprisingly inadequate in the face of its first major test, the invasion by Allied forces. The reason appears to be that the concept of a single people (national awareness) has not yet permeated the subconsciousness of the Italians to the same measure as a similar concept had permeated the German and Japanese people.[13] In equating nationalism with loyalty to the state, scholars had failed to inquire how many cases there have been where fanatical devotion to a state has arisen in the absence of a popular conception of the state as the state of one's particular nation. Rather than suggesting certain victory on the part of new states in the competition for loyalty, the experiences of Germany and

Japan exemplify the potential strength of those emotional ties to one's nation with which the multiethnic state must contend. German and Japanese nationalism were more prophetic auguries of the growth of concepts such as, *inter alia*, Ibo, Bengali, Kikuyu, Naga, Karen, Lao, Bahutu, Kurd, and Baganda, than they were auguries of the growth of concepts such as Nigeria, Pakistan, Kenya, India, Burma, Thailand, Rwanda, Iraq and Uganda.

Mistakenly equating nationalism with loyalty to the state has further contributed to terminological confusion by leading to the introduction of still other confusing terms. With nationalism preempted, authorities have had difficulty agreeing on a term to describe the loyalty of segments of a state's population to their particular nation. Ethnicity, primordialism, pluralism, tribalism, regionalism, communalism, and parochialism are among the most commonly encountered. This varied vocabulary further impedes an understanding of nationalism by creating the impression that each is describing a separate phenomenon. Moreover, reserving nationalism to convey loyalty to the state (or, more commonly, to the word *nation* when the latter is improperly substituted for state), while using words with different roots and fundamentally different connotations to refer to loyalty to the nation, adds immeasurably to the confusion. Each of the above terms has exercised its own particular negative impact upon the study of nationalism.

Ethnicity

Ethnicity (identity with one's ethnic group) is, if anything, more definitionally chameleonic than *nation*. It is derived from *Ethnos*, the Greek word for *nation* in the latter's pristine sense of a group characterized by common descent. Consonant with this derivation, there developed a general agreement that an ethnic group referred to a basic human category (i.e. not a subgroup). Unfortunately, however, American sociologists came to employ *ethnic group* to refer to 'a group with a common cultural tradition and a sense of identity which exists as a subgroup of a larger society.'[14] This definition makes ethnic group synonymous with minority, and, indeed, with regard to group relations within the United States, it has been used in reference to nearly any discernible minority, religious, linguistic, or otherwise.

The definition of ethnic group by American sociologists violates its original meaning with regard to at least two important particulars. In the traditional sense of an ancestrally related unit, it is evident that an ethnic group need not be a subordinate part of a larger political society but may be the dominant element within a state (the Chinese, English, or French, for example) or may extend across several states, as do the Arabs. Secondly, the indiscriminate application of ethnic group to numerous types of groups, obscures vital distinctions between various forms of identity. In a stimulating and often cited introduction to a volume entitled *Ethnicity*, Nathan Glazer and Daniel Patrick

Moynihan, while rejecting the notion that ethnicity refers only to minorities, defended the incorporation of several forms of identity under this single rubric.

Thus, there is some legitimacy to finding that forms of identification based on social realities as different as religion, language, and national origin all have something in common, such that a new term is coined to refer to all of them: 'ethnicity'. What they have in common is that they have all become effective foci for group mobilization for concrete political ends . . .[15]

However, despite the usefulness that such a categorization possesses for the study of the politics of special interest groups, there is little question but that it has exerted a damaging influence upon the study of nationalism. One result is that the researcher, when struggling through thousands of entries in union catalogs, indices to periodicals, and the like cannot be sure whether a so-called ethnic study will prove germane to the study of nationalism. Sometimes the unit under examination does constitute a national or potential national group. Other times it is a transnational (inter- or intrastate) group such as the Amerindians. And, in most instances, it is a group related only marginally, if at all, to the nation, as properly understood (e.g. the Catholic community within the Netherlands). Moreover, a review of the indices and bibliographies found in those ethnic studies that do deal with a national or potential national group, illustrate all too often that the author is unaware of the relationship of his work to nationalism. The student of nationalism and the student of ethnicity seldom cross-fertilize. The American journal, *Ethnicity*, and the *Canadian Review of Studies in Nationalism*, for example, are remarkably free of overlap with regard to (1) the academic background of their contributors and (2) footnoted materials.

Even if the author uses the term *ethnicity* solely in relation to national groups, his equating of nationalism with loyalty to the state will predispose him to underestimate the comparative magnetism of the former.[16] But the much more common practice of employing ethnicity as a cloak for several different types of identity exerts a more baneful effect. Such a single grouping presumes that all of the identities are of the same order. We shall reserve further comment on the adverse consequences of this presumption to a later discussion of *primordialism* and *pluralism*, noting here only that this presumption circumvents raising the key question as to which of a person's several identities is apt to win out in a test of loyalties.

Anthropologists, ethnologists, and scholars concerned with global comparisons have been more prone to use *ethnicity* and *ethnic group* in their pristine sense of involving a sense of common ancestry.[17] Max Weber, for example, noted:

We shall call 'ethnic groups' those human groups that entertain a subjective belief in their common descent . . . , this belief must be important for the propagation of group formation; conversely, it does not matter whether or not an objective blood relationship exists. Ethnic membership (*Gemeinsamkeit*) differs from the kinship group precisely by being a presumed identity . . .[18]

This definition would appear to equate *ethnic group* and *nation* and [. . .] Weber did indeed link the two notions.[19] However, elsewhere Weber made an important and useful distinction between the two:

[T]he idea of the nation is apt to include the notions of common descent and of an essential though frequently indefinite homogeneity. The 'nation' has these notions in common with the sentiment of solidarity of ethnic communities, which is also nourished from various sources, as we have seen before [5]. *But the sentiment of ethnic solidarity does not by itself make a 'nation'.* Undoubtedly, even the White Russians in the face of the Great Russians have always had a sentiment of ethnic solidarity, yet even at the present time they would hardly claim to qualify as a separate 'nation.' The Poles of Upper Silesia, until recently, had hardly any feeling of solidarity with the 'Polish nation.' They felt themselves to be a separate ethnic group in the face of the Germans, but for the rest they were Prussian subjects and nothing else.[20]

Weber is here clearly speaking of pre-national peoples or [. . .] potential nations. His illustrations are of peoples not yet cognizant of belonging to a larger ethnic element. The group consciousness to which he refers—that rather low level of ethnic solidarity that a segment of the ethnic element feels when confronted with a foreign element—need not be very important politically and comes closer to xenophobia than to nationalism. To the degree that it represents a step in the process of nation-formation, it testifies that a group of people must know ethnically what they *are not* before they know what they *are*. Thus, to Weber's illustrations, we can add the Slovaks, Croats, and Slovenes who, under the Habsburg Empire, were aware that they were neither German nor Magyar, long before they possessed positive opinions concerning their ethnic or national identity. In such cases, meaningful identity of a positive nature remains limited to locale, region, clan, or tribe. Thus, members need not be conscious of belonging to the ethnic group. Ernest Barker made this same point with regard to all peoples prior to the nineteenth century:

The self-consciousness of nations is a product of the nineteenth century. This is a matter of the first importance. Nations were already there; they had indeed been there for centuries. But it is not the things which are simply 'there' that matter in human life. What really and finally matters is the thing which is apprehended as an idea, and, as an idea, is vested with emotion until it becomes a cause and a spring of action. In the world of action apprehended ideas are alone electrical; and a nation must be an idea as well as a fact before it can become a dynamic force.[21]

To refine Barker's wording only slightly, and his meaning not at all, a nation is a self-aware ethnic group. An ethnic group may be readily discerned by an anthropologist or other outside observer, but until the members are themselves aware of the group's uniqueness, it is merely an ethnic group and not a nation. While an ethnic group *may*, therefore, be other-defined, the nation *must* be self-defined.[22] Employing ethnic group or ethnicity in relationship to several types of identities therefore beclouds the relationship between the *ethnic group* and the *nation* and also deprives scholarship of an excellent term for referring to both nations and potential nations.

'A Nation is a Nation, is a State, is an Ethnic Group, is a . . .', *Ethnic and Racial Studies*, 1 / 4 (1978), 379–88.

Section II

Theories of Nationalism

INTRODUCTION

Whatever their views about the relationship of nationalism to pre-modern ethnic sentiments, most scholars agree that nationalism, the global political movement that we know today, is a peculiarly modern phenomenon. They differ, however, over such things as the causes of nationalism, its relationship to modernization and to political power, and whether it is a weak or strong agent of change.

Elie Kedourie's approach is that of a historian of ideas. Nationalism is a form of secular millenarianism that has arisen from Kantian conceptions of human beings as autonomous, which, in turn, has led to politics replacing religion as the key to salvation. When synthesized by Fichte with Herder's doctrines about the natural language differences within humanity, these ideas produced the 'mature' romantic doctrine of nationalism. This prescribes that individuals achieve an independent state animated by the unique culture of their natural community. Kedourie regards nationalism as an extremely powerful, if destructive, force. Its appeal is explained by social breakdown occasioned by a collapse in the transmission of traditional values, and the rise of a restless, secular, educated generation, ambitious for power but excluded from its proper estate.

Ernest Gellner turns Kedourie on his head. Whereas Kedourie places weight on the power of ideas which act as a homogenizing force, Gellner argues that it is the need of modern societies for cultural homogeneity that creates nationalism. Nationalism is thus sociologically rooted in modernity, but it itself is a relatively weak force, a product of the transition from 'agro-literate' societies, regulated by structure, to industrial societies, integrated by culture. Important components of his complex explanation include the unevenness of industrialization; the leading role of an excluded intelligentsia in the invention of the nation; mass, public education; and the discrepancy between the romantic aspirations of nationalists and the utilitarian outcomes.

Tom Nairn, a Marxian thinker, combines Gellner's modernization perspective with that of Gramsci in order to provide a 'materialist' explanation of the dynamism of 'romantic' nationalism; its appeal to an educated middle class; and its ability to mobilize large-scale inter-class support. Nationalism arises in threatened and underdeveloped 'peripheral' societies whose intelligentsias 'invite the people into history' and then use and modernize their vernacular cultures. In this way they are able to mobilize the masses around the developmental goals of a local bourgeoisie. Nairn, unlike Gellner, regards the cultural project of nationalism as an important agent of social change. Nationalism is invariably populist, and its effect is to induct the masses into politics.

These theorists provide an 'instrumentalist' approach to nationalism. This is memorably articulated by the Marxist historian Eric Hobsbawm, who argues that the nation was one of many traditions 'invented' by political élites in order to legitimize their power in a century of revolution and democratization. Paul Brass, a political scientist, takes a similar position in the debate with Francis Robinson (see section V) about the relative weight accorded to 'primordial' or 'instrumental' factors. The study of élite competition and manipulation is the key to an understanding of nationalism, but Brass admits that élites are constrained by mass cultures and institutions.

Benedict Anderson also regards the modern nation as an artefact, 'an imagined political community'. Rather than thinking of it as fabricated, one should understand national distinctiveness in terms of its style of imagination and the institutions that make that possible. Pre-eminent among the latter are 'print-capitalism' and the new genres of newspaper and novel which portray the nation as a sociological community moving along 'homogeneous, empty time'. In contrast, Pierre van den Berghe offers a socio-biological interpretation of ethnic and national ties. Nationalism, like racism, is seen as an extension of kinship selection and 'nepotism' which has become salient in the modern world because of large-scale population movements, colonialism, and conquest.

Several theorists identify the rise of the modern bureaucratic state as a central factor in the genesis of nationalism. John Breuilly argues that a conflict began to emerge between the claims of state and civil society in the seventeenth century to which nationalism seemed to offer a superior, historicist solution: the authentic state is an outgrowth of a historical community. Anthony Smith also accords a pivotal role to the modern 'scientific state', but the problem of legitimacy is more far-reaching. Nationalism arises out of a pervasive moral crisis of 'dual legitimation', where divine authority is challenged by secular state power; from this situation, three solutions—neo-traditionalist, assimilationist, and reformist—emerge, all of which are conducive to different forms of nationalism.

Finally, John Hutchinson argues against the identification of nationalism with statist politics, and reveals the dynamics of cultural nationalism as a separate project focused on the moral regeneration of the community. Rejecting the sometimes negative connotations of cultural nationalism, he argues that the evocation of a golden age is used as a modernizing and integrative device which can offer an alternative political model when the statist type of political nationalism has failed.

It is sometimes argued that there are two or more varieties of nationalism, the linguistic being only one of a number, and the Nazi doctrine of race is brought forward to illustrate the argument that there can be racial, religious, and other nationalisms. But, in fact, there is no definite clear-cut distinction between linguistic and racial nationalism. Originally, the doctrine emphasized language as the test of nationality, because language was an outward sign of a group's peculiar identity and a significant means of ensuring its continuity. But a nation's language was peculiar to that nation only because such a nation constituted a racial stock distinct from that of other nations. The French nationalist writer, Charles Maurras (1868–1952), exemplified this connexion between race and language when he remarked that no Jew, no Semite, could understand or handle the French language as well as a Frenchman proper; no Jew, he remarked, could appreciate the beauties of Racine's line in *Bérénice: 'Dans l'orient désert quel devint mon ennui.'* It was then no accident that racial classifications were, at the same time, linguistic ones, and that the Nazis distinguished the members of the German Aryan race scattered in Central and Eastern Europe by a linguistic criterion. [. . .]

In nationalist doctrine, language, race, culture, and sometimes even religion, constitute different aspects of the same primordial entity, the nation. The theory admits here of no great precision, and it is misplaced ingenuity to try and classify nationalisms according to the particular aspect which they choose to emphasize. What is beyond doubt is that the doctrine divides humanity into separate and distinct nations, claims that such nations must constitute sovereign states, and asserts that the members of a nation reach freedom and fulfilment by cultivating the peculiar identity of their own nation and by sinking their own persons in the greater whole of the nation. All these different facets of the doctrine are admirably summed up in an utterance of Schleiermacher's: 'How little worthy of respect,' he exclaims, 'is the man who roams about hither and thither without the anchor of national ideal and love of fatherland; how dull is the friendship that rests merely upon personal similarities in disposition and tendencies, and not upon the feeling of a greater common unity for whose sake one can offer up one's life; how the greatest source of pride is lost by the woman that cannot feel that she also bore children for her fatherland and brought them up for it, that her house and all the petty things that fill up most of her time belong to a greater whole and take their place in the union of her people!' Behind such a passage lie all the assumptions of nationalist metaphysics and anthropology. It may serve to distinguish nationalism from patriotism and xenophobia with which it is often confused. Patriotism, affection for one's country, or one's group, loyalty to its institutions, and zeal for its defence, is a sentiment known among all kinds of men; so is xenophobia, which is dislike of the stranger, the outsider, and reluctance to admit him into one's own group. Neither sentiment depends on a particular anthropology and neither asserts a particular doctrine of the state or of the individual's relation to it. Nationalism does both; it is a comprehensive doctrine which leads to a distinctive style of politics. But far from being a universal phenomenon, it is a product of European thought in the last 150 years. If confusion exists, it is because nationalist doctrine has annexed these universally held sentiments to the service of a specific anthropology and metaphysic. It is, therefore, loose and inexact to speak, as is sometimes done, of British or American nationalism when describing the thought of those who recommend loyalty to British or American political institutions. A British or an American nationalist would have to define the British or the American nation in terms of language, race, or religion, to require that all those who conform to the definition should belong to the British or American state, that all those who do not, should cease so to belong, and to demand that all British and American citizens should merge their will in the will of the community. It is at once clear that political thought of this kind is marginal and insignificant in Britain and America, and that those who speak of British or American nationalism do not usually have such views in mind.

Nationalism is also sometimes described as a new tribalism. The analogy is meant to indicate that like the tribe, the nation excludes and is intolerant of outsiders. But such characteristics, as has been said, are common to all human groups, and cannot serve to define either tribe or nation. But the analogy is not only unable to shed light on the matter, it can also mislead. A tribesman's relation to his tribe is usually regulated in minute detail by custom which is followed unquestioningly and considered part of the natural or the divine order. Tribal custom is neither a decree of the General Will, nor an edict of legislative Reason. The tribesman is such by virtue of his birth, not by virtue of self-determination. He is usually unaware that the destiny of man is progressive, and that he can fulfil this destiny by merging his will into the will of the tribe. Nationalism and tribalism, then, are not interchangeable terms, nor do they describe related phenomena.

Another assertion often made is that nation-states have been in the process of formation at least since the sixteenth century; but this, again, seems a confusion, which results from using nationalist categories in historiography. When the peculiar anthropology and metaphysics of nationalism are used in the interpretation of the past, history takes on quite another complexion. Men who thought they were acting in order to accomplish the will of God, to make the truth prevail, or to advance the interests of a dynasty, or perhaps simply to defend their own against aggression, are suddenly seen to have been really acting in order that the genius of a particular nationality should be manifested and fostered. Abraham was not a man possessed with the vision of the one

God, he was really the chieftain of a beduin tribe intent on endowing his horde with a national identity. Moses was not a man inspired by God in order to fulfil and reaffirm His covenant with Israel, he was really a national leader rising against colonial oppression. Muhammad may have been the seal of the Prophets, but even more important, he was the founder of the Arab nation. Luther was a shining manifestation of Germanism; Hus a precursor of Masaryk. Nationalists make use of the past in order to subvert the present. One instance of this transformation of the past occurs in a letter written against Zionism by an orthodox rabbi of Eastern Europe in 1900. In this letter, the Dzikover Rebbe contrasts the traditional view which the community of Israel had of itself, and the new nationalist interpretation of the Jewish past. Bitterness gives his speech a biting concision, and this letter thus exhibits in a clear and striking manner the operations of nationalist historiography, as well as the traditional interpretation which it has challenged. 'For our many sins,' writes the Rebbe, 'strangers have risen to pasture the holy flock, men who say that the people of Israel should be clothed in secular nationalism, a nation like all other nations, that Judaism rests on three things, national feeling, the land and the language, and that national feeling is the most praiseworthy element in the brew and the most effective in preserving Judaism, while the observance of the Torah and the commandments is a private matter depending on the inclination of each individual. May the Lord rebuke these evil men and may He who chooseth Jerusalem seal their mouths.'[1] Nationalist historiography operates, in fact, a subtle but unmistakable change in traditional conceptions. In Zionism, Judaism ceases to be the *raison d'être* of the Jew, and becomes, instead, a product of Jewish national consciousness. In the doctrine of Pakistan, Islam is transformed into a political ideology and used in order to mobilize Muslims against Hindus; more than that it cannot do, since an Islamic state on classical lines is today an impossible anachronism. In the doctrine of the *Action Française* Catholicism becomes one of the attributes which define a true Frenchman and exclude a spurious one. This transformation of religion into nationalist ideology is all the more convenient in that nationalists can thereby utilize the powerful and tenacious loyalties which a faith held in common for centuries creates. These loyalties can be utilized even when they are not explicitly spoken of. There is little doubt that the appeal of modern Egyptian, or Panarab, or Armenian, or Greek nationalism derives the greater part of its strength from the existence of ancient communal and religious ties which have nothing to do with nationalist theory, and which may even be opposed to it. The Patriarch of Constantinople Gennadius (d.1468) may illustrate the traditional religious attitude towards ties of race and language: 'Though I am a Hellene by speech, yet I would never say that I was a Hellene,' he wrote, 'for I do not believe as the Hellenes believed. I should like to take my name from my Faith, and if anyone asked me what I am answer "Christian".' But today, with the spread of nationalist doctrine, this opposition between Hellenism and orthodoxy is itself rejected. Orthodoxy and Hellenism are thought to go together and imply one another, as witnessed in the civil war of which Cyprus has been the stage.

Similarly, when nationalist historiography applies itself to the European past, it produces a picture of nations slowly emerging and asserting themselves in territorial sovereign states. It is, of course, undoubtedly the case that a number of territorial sovereignties succeeded in establishing themselves in Europe in modern times, and that gradually these sovereignties were strengthened and made durable by centralizing kings who were able to defeat particularisms and to establish everywhere the authority of their agents and of their 'state'. But these sovereignties were far from being 'nations', as the word is understood in nationalist parlance. The Habsburg Empire was a most powerful state, yet it was not a 'nation'; Prussia was the state at its most perfect, but it was not a 'nation'; Venice was a state which lasted for centuries: was it then a 'nation'? And such states have to be cited in illustration of the political development of modern Europe. Yet how easy is the confusion when, not these, but other European states are being considered; for it is but one step from talking about the French state under Philip the Fair, Henry the Fourth, and Louis the Fourteenth, to talking about the French 'nation' and its development under these monarchs. The continuity of the French state, or of the Spanish state, and their territorial stability, make it easy to adduce them as examples of the growth and development of European 'nations': the shift is vital, yet almost imperceptible. How vital it is may be appreciated when we remember that France is a state not because the French constitute a nation, but rather that the French state is the outcome of dynastic ambitions, of circumstances, of lucky wars, of administrative and diplomatic skills. It is these which maintained order, enforced laws, and carried out policies; these which made possible at last the cohesive existence of Frenchmen within the French state. It is such things which make possible the continuous existence of political communities, whether or not they are the 'nations' of nationalist theory. The matter becomes even clearer when nationalist historiography is made to deal, not with certain countries in modern Europe, where it has a kind of plausibility, but with countries in almost any other part of the world at almost any period of history. In the Roman Empire, the Ottoman Empire, Mogul India, pre-Conquest South America, or China the categories of nationalist historiography, taken seriously, must lead to a contorted, paradoxical, untenable picture of the past. What nationalist historiography professes to explain in the case of modern France or Spain or Italy or Germany, it must in so many other cases, immediately hasten to explain away. The Ottoman Empire was not a 'nation', the Roman Empire was not a 'nation', and yet they were able, as few contemporary states have yet shown themselves able, to continue for centuries, to maintain the cohesion of the social fabric and to attract the loyalties of men. This confusion between states and 'nations' is facilitated by a particular feature of European political history, namely the existence of a European society of states in constant intercourse and conflict, who regulated their relations, however unwillingly and imperfectly, by a universally acknowledged *ius gentium*. Since nationalism sees the world as a world of many states, it seems but natural to consider a society of nations as the equivalent and continuation of the European society of states. But in reality the two are far removed. The European society of states knew a great diversity of governments and constitutions; a society of nations must be composed of nation-states, and any state which is not a nation-state has its title and its existence perpetually challenged. The national principle, then, far from providing continuity in European diplomacy, means a radical subversion of the European state system, an endless attempt to upset the balance of power on which the system must rest.

If nationalism cannot provide a satisfactory account of past political developments, neither can it supply a plain method whereby nations may be isolated from one another and constituted into sovereign states. The world is indeed diverse, much too diverse, for the classifications of nationalist anthropology. Races, languages, religions, political traditions and loyalties are so inextricably intermixed that there can be no clear convincing reason why people who speak the same language, but whose history and circumstances otherwise widely diverge, should form one state, or why people who speak two different languages and whom circumstances have thrown together should not form one state. On nationalist logic, the separate existence of Britain and America, and the union of English and French Canadians within the Canadian state, are both monstrosities of nature; and a consistent nationalist interpretation of history would reduce large parts of it to inexplicable and irritating anomalies. The inventors of the doctrine tried to prove that nations are obvious and natural divisions of the human race, by appealing to history, anthropology, and linguistics. But the attempt breaks down since, whatever ethnological or philological doctrine may be fashionable for the moment, there is no convincing reason why the fact that people speak the same language or belong to the same race should, by itself, entitle them to enjoy a government exclusively their own. For such a claim to be convincing, it must also be proved that similarity in one respect absolutely overrides differences in other respects. What remains in the doctrine is an affirmation that men have the right to stand on their differences from others, be these differences what they may, fancied or real, important or not, and to make of these differences their first political principle. Of course, academic disciplines, like philology, can make a powerful auxiliary for such a political doctrine, and enable it to secure conviction and assent, but they do not constitute the ultimate ground on which it takes its stand. Ernest Renan, in his lecture of 1882, *What is a Nation*, saw that this must be the case, and having examined the different criteria which are used to distinguish nations, and having found them wanting, concluded that the will of the individual must ultimately indicate whether a nation exists or not. Even if the existence of nations can be deduced from the principle of diversity, it still cannot be deduced what particular nations exist and what their precise limits are. What remains is to fall back on the will of the individual who, in pursuit of self-determination, wills himself as the member of a nation. The doctrine occasionally appears in its pure state, stripped of academic flannel and accidental accretions. The Jewish nationalist Ahad Ha'am (1856–1927) has a passage in which he discusses the fundamentals of Jewish nationality. It is a mistake, he writes, to think that Jewish nationality exists only when there is an actual collective national ethos. No doubt this national ethos came into being in consequence of a life lived in common over a number of generations. 'Once, however,' he argues, 'the spirit of nationality has so come into being . . . it becomes a phenomenon that concerns the individual alone, its reality being dependent on nothing but its presence in his psyche, and on no external or objective actuality. If I feel the spirit of Jewish nationality in my heart so that it stamps all my inward life with its seal, then the spirit of Jewish nationality exists in me; and its existence is not at an end even if all my Jewish contemporaries should cease to feel it in their hearts.' Here are no superfluous appeals to philology or biology, no laborious attempts to prove that because a group speaks the same language, or has the same religion, or lives in the same territory, it therefore is a nation. All this is casually brushed aside, and the nation, says Ahad Ha'am, is what individuals feel in their hearts is the nation. Renan's own description of the nation is that it is a daily plebiscite. The metaphor is felicitous, if only because it indicates so well that nationalism is ultimately based on will, and shows how inadequate the doctrine is in describing the political process, for a political community which conducts daily plebiscites must soon fall into querulous anarchy, or hypnotic obedience.

National self-determination is, in the final analysis, a determination of the will; and nationalism is, in the first place, a method of teaching the right determination of the will. [. . .]

But the restlessness was the work not only of the revolutionary legend; it proceeded from a breakdown in the transmission of political habits and religious beliefs from one generation to the next. In societies suddenly exposed to the new learning and the new philosophies of the Enlightenment and of Romanticism, orthodox settled ways began to seem ridiculous and useless. The attack was powerful and left the old generation bewildered and speechless; or if it attempted to speak, it merely gave voice to irritated admonition, obstinate opposition, or horror-stricken rejection, which only served to widen the rift and increase the distance between the fathers and the sons. [. . .]

This violent revolt against immemorial restraints, this strident denunciation of decorum and measure, was inevitably accompanied by powerful social strains which may explain the dynamic and violent character of nationalist movements. These movements are ostensibly directed against the foreigner, the outsider, but they are also the manifestation of a species of civil strife between the generations; nationalist movements are children's crusades; their very names are manifestoes against old age: Young Italy, Young Egypt, the Young Turks, the Young Arab Party. When they are stripped of their meta-physics and their slogans—and these cannot adequately account for the frenzy they conjure up in their followers—such movements are seen to satisfy a need, to fulfil a want. Put at its simplest, the need is to belong together in a coherent and stable community. Such a need is normally satisfied by the family, the neighbourhood, the religious community. In the last century and a half such institutions all over the world have had to bear the brunt of violent social and intellectual change, and it is no accident that nationalism was at its most intense where and when such institutions had little resilience and were ill-prepared to withstand the powerful attacks to which they became exposed. This seems a more satisfactory account than to say that nationalism is a middle-class movement. It is the case that the German inventors of nationalist doctrine came from a class which could be called the middle class, and that they were discontented with the old order in which the nobility was predominant. But the term middle class is closely tied to a particular area and a particular history, that of Western Europe. It presupposes and implies a distinct social order of which feudalism, municipal franchises, and rapid industrial development are some of the prominent features. Such features are not found in all societies, and it would therefore be misleading to link the existence of a nationalist movement to that of a middle class. In countries of the Middle and the Far East, for instance, where the significant division in society was between those who belonged to the state institution and those who did not, nationalism cannot be associated with the existence of a middle class. It developed, rather, among young officers and bureaucrats, whose families were sometimes ob-scure, sometimes eminent, who were educated in Western methods and ideas, often at the expense of the State, and who as a result came to despise their elders, and to hanker for the shining purity of a new order to sweep away the hypocrisy, the corruption, the decadence which they felt inexorably choking them and their society.

[*Nationalism* (Hutchinson: London, 1960), 71–81, 99–102.]

ERNEST GELLNER

9   Nationalism and Modernization

The minimal requirement for full citizenship, for effective moral member-ship of a modern community, is literacy. This is the minimum: a certain level of technological competence is probably also required. Only a person possessing these can really claim and exercise his rights, can attain a level of affluence and style of life compatible with current notions of human dignity, and so forth. But only a nation-size educational system can produce such full citizens: only it has the resources to make men of the raw biological material available, resources large enough to keep in being a sufficient number of specialists, of the second-order teachers and intellectuals necessary to produce the ground-level teachers. For this reason, something roughly of the size of a 'nation' is the minimal political unit in the modern world (i.e. one in which universal literacy is recognised to be the valid norm). Time was, when the minimal political unit was determined by the preconditions of defence or economy: it is now determined by the preconditions of education.[1]

But: an educational system must operate in some medium, some language (both in the literal and the extended sense); and the language it employs will stamp its products. If the educational machinery is effective, its products will be, within reason, substitutable for each other, but less readily substitutable for those produced by other and rival machines. Of course, high-powered specialists can still move across educational frontiers: a Werner von Braun is employable internationally, irrespective of whether he can catch on to allusions in English or Russian literature. But in general, when the tasks to be performed are not such as require the highest, rarest and genuine skills (when allowances are made), they tend to be such that they can only be acceptably performed by a person formed by the local educational machine, using the same idiom as the organisation within which the post is located.

The conditions in which nationalism becomes the natural form of political loyalty can be summed up in two propositions: (1) Every man a clerk. (Universal literacy recognised as a valid norm.) (2) Clerks are not horizontally mobile, they cannot normally move from one language-area to another; jobs are generally specific to clerks who are produced by some one particular educational machine, using some one particular medium of expression.

Condition (2) cannot of course be invoked to explain nationalism, for to do so would be circular: in a way, it is a restatement of a crucial aspect of nationalism itself, which is that intellectuals have ceased to be a substitutable commodity, except within the range of any given language or culture. But the importance of (1)—of the fact that only education makes a full man and citizen, and that education must be in some linguistic medium—has been curiously neglected, obvious though it is. It explains why nationalism can and does move such broad masses of humanity. Men do not in general become nationalists from sentiment or sentimentality, atavistic or not, well-based or myth-founded: they become nationalists through genuine, objective, practical necessity, however obscurely recognised.

The contrast for a situation in which conditions (1) and (2) obtain is, of course, a social order such as that of medieval Christendom, or Islam up to the recent impact of modernism: in those conditions, clerks are, and are meant to be, a subclass of the total society, for there is no need, aspiration, or possibility of making them co-extensive with society at large; and at the same time, clerks are horizontally mobile, at any rate within the frontiers of the script and faith within which they are literate. A Muslim lawyer-theologian, literate in written Arabic, or a medieval clerk with his Latin, is employable, and substitutable for another, throughout the region of his religion. Inside the religious zones, there are no significant obstacles to the freedom of trade in intellect: what later become 'national' boundaries, present no serious obstacles. If the clerk is competent in the written language, say Latin or classical Arabic, his vernacular or origin is of little interest; it doesn't matter whether it is one of the languages derived from the written one, say a Romance language or a spoken form of Arabic, or whether it is not recognisably related to it—say a Teutonic or Berber dialect.

Such a world, however, has been replaced by one in which 'national' boundaries constitute a very serious frontier to clerkly mobility and substitutability, and in which the clerk as such disappears, every man being literate— either in fact or in aspiration, this aspiration however being treated with utmost seriousness both by authorities and populations.

There is a certain obvious connection between the two features of the modern situation: if every man is a clerk, it is a great help if the language in which he is literate is identical with, or at least fairly close to, the vernacular in which he was reared in the family context. Continuity between the idioms of home and school facilitate the task of education. A specialised clerkly class can be expected to master a special clerkly language—indeed it has a strong incentive in this direction, in so far as the additional difficulty helps both to restrict entry and greatly augments the mystery and prestige of the occupation. But when a total population achieves or approaches literacy, the restriction and the prestige become irrelevant, and the proximity of the languages of writing and of daily speech become an advantage. This point does, however, call for a qualification. The facilitation of literacy through the use of a vernacular no doubt favoured 'nationalist' tendencies in Europe: for instance, it is clearly easier to turn Hungarian into a written language than to teach all Hungarian peasants Latin. But in extra-European contexts, the vernaculars are often too numerous and diversified, without any one of them having a manifest predominance, to be used as the literate language. If one of them were arbitrarily selected, no advantage would be gained—for most of the population would still suffer from a bifurcation between the language of school and home—and an additional serious disadvantage would be incurred, in so far as the selected vernacular would lack the conveniences of an old-established literate idiom (availability of technical vocabularies, a body of technical literature, etc.). It would be rash to predict precisely what will happen ultimately in these cases, and indeed there is no reason to suppose that the same thing will happen in each case. (The range of alternative is: the arbitrary elevation of one of the vernaculars into the language of a national educational system, turning it into a literate language; the borrowing of a literate language from a colonial power, with the advantage of taking over a language already equipped with all modern linguistic conveniences, but a disadvantage in terms of national pride; or the borrowing of a pre-existing non-European literate language, or regional lingua franca, such as Arabic or Hausa or Swahili.) In these cases, it can be supposed that the tendency towards the congruence of the languages of home and school will operate in the opposite direction, the language of school ultimately also pervading the home. This process is of course not unknown in Europe: the present reasonably neat linguistic blocks of Eastern Europe, replacing the earlier complicated patchwork, are due to such a process (when they are not due to actual forcible transfers of population).

The connection between nationalism and the situation in which fully human men can only be made by educational systems, not by families and villages, underlines an amusing fact—the inverse relationship between the ideology and the reality of nationalism. The self-image of nationalism involves the stress of folk, folklore, popular culture, etc. In fact, nationalism becomes important precisely when these things become artificial. Genuine peasants or tribesmen, however proficient at folk-dancing, do not generally make good nationalists. It is only when a privileged cousin of the same lineage, and later their own sons, and finally even their own daughters, all go to school, that the peasant or tribesman acquires a vested interest in the language that was employed in the school in which that cousin, son or daughter were educated. (Should a rival nationalism prevail—i.e. a nationalism centred on a language other than that of the school in question, and possibly hostile to it—much of the valuable investment in the kinsman's education might well be wasted.) *Ein Zollverein ist keine Heimat*, but an educational system and its medium of instruction do make a homeland. The famous Three Generations law governing the behaviour of immigrants into America—the grandson tries to remember what the son tried to forget—now operates in many parts of the world on populations that have not migrated at all: the son, who arduously acquires a new idiom at school, has no desire to play at being a tribesman, but his son in turn, securely urbanised, may do so.

The pre-existing genuine folk cultures are of course not totally irrelevant to the operation of nationalism. If a nationalism crystallises around language X, the peasants speaking various demotic versions of X do of course form the natural and preferred catchment area for the nationalism in question. But in practice, nationalist leaders and organisations have seldom if ever been very fastidious about this. Although they discern the simple, robust, noble virtues primarily in X-speaking peasants, they do not really object to incorporating Y- or Z-speaking peasants, provided their sons can be X-ified: indeed, the leaders, once in charge of a state machine, do not object to employing forceful persuasion when canalising rustics, previously lacking in national consciousness or even tempted by a 'wrong' one, into the right national trough. In brief, they are perfectly happy to poach on each other's natural catchment areas.

So far, the argument—starting from the erosion of local all-embracing social structures and the consequent importance of culture, and from the role of educational systems and the linguistic media in which they operate in forming acceptable human beings—has taken us *some* of the way towards a schematic explanation of nationalism: these factors explain why in general (abstracting from local complications) modern loyalties are centred on political units whose boundaries are defined by the language (in the wider or in the literal sense) of an educational system: and that when these boundaries are made rather than given, they must be large enough to create a unit capable of sustaining an educational system. In other words, we have explained why modern loyalty-evoking units are not very small (local, like tribal, feudal or classical units), and why they are *cultural* units. But we have not really explained the *upper* limit of these units: the curious fact that loyalty-engendering units are often smaller than those of pre-existing faiths-civilisations (e.g. Islam, Christendom), notwithstanding the fact that these wider civilisations, where they exist at all, would provide a convenient prefabricated 'shared' language. In other words, we have not explained the divisive aspects of nationalism, as opposed to its unifying tendency.

A Model

Consider any arbitrary pre-industrial 'empire', a largish territory under one ultimate political sovereign. (The model can accommodate, with possible minor modifications, both a continuous, land-mass empire, and one separated by seas, of the 'colonial' type.) The chances are that (*a*) the territory comprises a multiplicity of languages; (*b*) that notwithstanding nominally unique sovereignty at the centre, there is in fact a certain diffusion of power, a multiplicity of local, semi-autonomous power centres. The semi-autonomous centres guard their measure of independence thanks to the difficulties encountered by any attempts at really effective centralisation in pre-modern conditions: but in turn, they are probably the best means of controlling the rural populations of the backwoods. In this set-up, language is not an important issue. The language privileged at court may not be identical with the one privileged in religion (e.g. as in Ottoman Turkey); and there may be a multiplicity of both vertical, regional, and of horizontal (occupational, estate, religious) groupings, all of which are of direct concern to people: 'culture' as such however is not, even though the membership of existing groups may and generally will express itself in 'cultural' form.

Now consider the possible forms of the impact of modernity on such a society: increase in the proportion and in the importance of literacy, consequent on the transformation of economic life; greater mobility of various kinds; the emergence of an industrial proletariat; and above all, the fact that *one* of the languages—perhaps the language of the old heartland of the empire—has become *the* language of the modern organisations, of the new industrial, governmental and educational machines. The local structures are being eroded.[2]

This much has already been indicated above: and these factors already imply that henceforth, identification, loyalty and effective citizenship depends on literacy and education in the one favoured language. But the factors indicated so far only suggest that there will be a rush for the acquisition of this particular passport to full citizenship, accompanied by a sentiment of loyalty conceived in terms of it. But why should there also be new divisive nationalism?—why should some territories, and in extreme cases even territorially discontinuous populations, decide to opt for a new citizenship other than that of the one privileged language (and henceforth, 'nation') on the territory of the *ancien régime*? It cannot be stressed enough that the answer is not that the language in question, and hence its 'nation', is not really their own. This is also true of the many, the very many, who do adopt a new language and style of being. Changing one's language is not the heart-breaking or soul-destroying business which it is claimed to be in romantic nationalist literature. Highlanders in Glasgow become Anglophone, Berbers in Marrakesh become Arabophone, Czechs in Vienna, etc., etc., etc.; if switching of language were the only problem, no new divisive nationalism need ever arise.

The reason isn't really far to seek. Sometimes the entry into the dominant nation is very difficult, or almost impossible (though not owing to a difficulty in learning a language, literally); sometimes, even if it is possible, it seems or *is* advantageous to set up a rival 'nation' of one's own instead. There is a type of superficial reason why it is sometimes difficult: it is difficult to change basic cultural traits (i.e. consider the requirement that an Algerian had to abjure Muslim personal law to become a Frenchman), and it is impossible to change one's pigmentation, in cases where the nation to be 'entered' is defined partly in terms of colour. But these factors are themselves consequences rather than causes. There is nothing in the nature of things which decrees that a viable large political unit must contain only members of the same kind of pigmentation, any more than it requires similarity in the colour of hair or eyes. And even nations which subsequently made a fetish of colour, such as the Boers, did not find it difficult at earlier stages to incorporate 'colour'.

Industrialisation and modernisation notoriously proceed in an uneven manner. Just as notoriously, it is the early stages, the first few generations, of these processes which cause the greatest disruption, the greatest misery, and which provide the maximum opportunity for political revolution and for the re-thinking and re-drawing of loyalties. This ghastly tidal wave does not hit various parts of the world simultaneously: on the contrary, it hits them successively (though of course not in any neat and orderly succession). Essentially, nationalism is a phenomenon connected not so much with industrialisation or modernisation as such, but with its uneven diffusion. The uneven impact of this wave generates a sharp social stratification which, unlike the stratifications of past societies, is (a) unhallowed by custom, and which has little to cause it to be accepted as in the nature of things, which (b) is not well protected by various social mechanisms, but on the contrary exists in a situation providing maximum opportunities and incentives for revolution, and which (c) is remediable, and is seen to be remediable, by 'national' secession. Under these circumstances, nationalism does become a natural phenomenon, one flowing fairly inescapably from the general situation.

Consider the tidal wave of modernisation, sweeping over the world, in a devastating but untidy flood, aided or obstructed by pre-existing currents, deflected or canalised by the rocks and sandbanks of the older social world. Suppose it passes, in succession, territories A and B, where both these are initially under the same sovereignty (suppose both, for instance, to be parts of our hypothetical empire). The fact that the wave hit A first and B later, means that at the time when dislocation and misery are at their height in B, A is already approaching affluence or, in Rostow's phrase, the period of mass consumption. B, politically united with A, is a slum area of the total society comprising both A and B. What happens to the men originating from B?

Here two alternatives must be considered: is B fairly homogeneous culturally with A or not? Suppose first of all that it is so. The men of B, less educated, more 'backward', more recently torn from the land or its traditional equilibrium, will provide the lower ranks of the proletariat of the total society A&B; but being reasonably similar to the more 'advanced' and privileged workers of A, it would be difficult to exclude them wholly from the advantages gained by workers from A: some of these perks will spill over. Their exclusion from the moral community, their material disinheritance, will not be complete. Moreover, their potential leaders, including the small group of those from B possessing advanced education, will have no particular difficulty in rising up within A&B. So, all in all, it is likely that region B, though discontented, will remain within the larger society, either awaiting the moment when the high tide of prosperity reaches it as well, or anticipating events by large-scale migration.

But suppose instead that the men of B are fairly radically differentiated from those of A: that they can easily be picked out in the street—in virtue of pigmentation, or deeply rooted and religiously sanctioned customs, say. Their situation is correspondingly worse: far less, if anything, of the benefits accruing to the more 'advanced' proletariat, spills over to them. Above all, their discontent can find 'national' expression: the privileged are manifestly different from themselves, even if the shared 'nationality' of the under-privileged men from B starts off from a purely negative trait, i.e. shared exclusion from privilege and from the 'nation' of the privileged. Moreover, the men from B now do have leaders: their small intellectual class probably cannot easily pass into A, and even if it can, it now has an enormous incentive not to do so; if it succeeds in detaching B-land, by the rules of the new national game, in which intellectuals are not substitutable across frontiers, it will have a virtual monopoly of the desirable posts in the newly independent B-land.

Why should it have been difficult for the low proletarians from B to be incorporated, at least on the level of their native-A fellow workers, in A-land? In general, advanced lands do not have any interest in sharing their prosperity with the ill-trained latest arrivals. The solidarity of the working class is a myth. The tomatoes thrown in Algiers at Monsieur Guy Mollet, to bring home to him the need for an illiberal policy, were not thrown by members of the aristocracy, nor even, I believe, of the *haute bourgeoisie*. In cases when, however, the new entrants in the industrial world aren't markedly distinguishable from the older ones, they cannot really be excluded—it is not practically feasible. This is where culture, pigmentation, etc., become important: they provide means of exclusion for the benefit of the privileged, and a means of identification, etc., for the under-privileged. Distance, seas to be crossed, can serve as well to reinforce chromatic or cultural differences. Nationalism is not the awakening of nations to self-consciousness: it invents nations where they do not exist—but it does need some pre-existing differentiating marks to work on, even if, as indicated, these are purely negative (i.e. consist of disqualifying marks from entry to privilege, without any positive similarity between those who share the disqualification and who are destined to form a new 'nation'). This incidentally shows how mistaken Rostow is, in a way, in crediting 'react-ive nationalism' with the crucial role in economic development.[3] This observa-tion needs to be turned upside-down. It is the need for growth which generates nationalism, not vice versa.

The two prongs of nationalism tend to be a proletariat and an intelligentsia. The proletariat is in general morally uprooted, but it need not always be literally uprooted, i.e. physically removed from its previous rural habitat. For instance, the beginnings of the Algerian national revolution were in the Aures mountains, amongst villagers least removed, in a superficial sense, from the traditional tribal order, who had remained in their old area, and who were geographically furthest removed from the modern urban and industrial centres. Yet, as Germaine Tillion showed, they were disrupted by a kind of sociological action at a distance: they were, in her expressive phrase, *clochar-disées*.[4] Yet this kind of phenomenon should not lead one to generalise and suppose that 'the peasants' must always constitute the 'vanguard' of such movements, and that the industrial proletariat proper has been 'bribed' and has 'sold out', an idea that can be part of a generalised mystique of the *tiers monde* such as can be found, for instance, in the works of the late Frantz Fanon. For instance, no-one bribed the literally uprooted inhabitants of the Moroccan *bidonvilles*, and it was they who effectively carried out the struggle for national independence.

In general, both an intelligentsia and a proletariat is required for an effective national movement. Their fates diverge after the achievement of national independence. For the intellectuals, independence means an immediate and enormous advantage: jobs, and very good jobs. The very numerical weakness of an 'underdeveloped' intelligentsia is its greatest asset: by creating a national unit whose frontiers become in effect closed to foreign talent (except in 'advisory' short-term capacity), they create a magnificent monopoly for themselves. For the proletarians, on the other hand, independence must in the short run bring disillusion: the hardships are not removed, indeed they are likely to be increased by the drive for rapid development and the fact that a national government can sometimes afford to be harsher than a foreign one.[5]

['Nationalism', in *Thought and Change* (Weidenfeld and Nicholson: London, 1964), 158–69.]

ERNEST GELLNER
....

10   Nationalism and High Cultures

[But] nationalism is *not* the awakening of an old, latent, dormant force, though that is how it does indeed present itself. It is in reality the consequence of a new form of social organization, based on deeply internalized, education-dependent high cultures, each protected by its own state. It uses some of the pre-existent cultures, generally transforming them in the process, but it cannot possibly use them all. There are too many of them. A viable higher culture-sustaining modern state cannot fall below a certain minimal size (unless in effect parasitic on its neighbours); and there is only room for a limited number of such states on this earth.

The high ratio of determined slumberers, who will not rise and shine and who refuse to be woken, enables us to turn the tables on nationalism-as-seen-by-itself. Nationalism sees itself as a natural and universal ordering of the political life of mankind, only obscured by that long, persistent and mysterious somnolence. As Hegel expressed this vision: 'Nations may have had a long history before they finally reach their destination—that of forming themselves into states'.[1] Hegel immediately goes on to suggest that this pre-state period is really 'pre-historical' (*sic*): so it would seem that on this view the real history of a nation only begins when it acquires its own state. If we invoke the sleeping-beauty nations, neither possessing a state nor feeling the lack of it, against the nationalist doctrine, we tacitly accept its social metaphysic, which sees nations as the bricks of which mankind is made up. Critics of nationalism who denounce the political movement but tacitly accept the existence of nations, do not go far enough. Nations as a natural, God-given way of classifying men, as an inherent though long-delayed political destiny, are a myth; nationalism, which sometimes takes pre-existing cultures and turns them into nations, sometimes invents them, and often obliterates pre-existing cultures: *that* is a reality, for better or worse, and in general an inescapable one. Those who are its historic agents know not what they do, but that is another matter. [. . .]

The great, but valid, paradox is this: nations can be defined only in terms of the age of nationalism, rather than, as you might expect, the other way round. It is not the case that the 'age of nationalism' is a mere summation of the awakening and political self-assertion of this, that, or the other nation. Rather, when general social conditions make for standardized, homogeneous, centrally sustained high cultures, pervading entire populations and not just elite minorities, a situation arises in which well-defined educationally sanctioned and unified cultures constitute very nearly the only kind of unit with which men willingly and often ardently identify. The cultures now seem to be the natural repositories of political legitimacy. Only *then* does it come to appear that any defiance of their boundaries by political units constitutes a scandal.

Under these conditions, though under these conditions *only*, nations can indeed be defined in terms both of will and of culture, and indeed in terms of the convergence of them both with political units. In these conditions, men will to be politically united with all those, and only those, who share their culture. Polities then will to extend their boundaries to the limits of their cultures, and to protect and impose their culture with the boundaries of their power. The fusion of will, culture and polity becomes the norm, and one not easily or frequently defied. (Once, it had been almost universally defied, with impunity, and had indeed passed unnoticed and undiscussed.) These conditions do not define the human situation as such, but merely its industrial variant.

It is nationalism which engenders nations, and not the other way round. Admittedly, nationalism uses the pre-existing, historically inherited proliferation of cultures or cultural wealth, though it uses them very selectively, and it most often transforms them radically. Dead languages can be revived, traditions invented, quite fictitious pristine purities restored. But this culturally creative, fanciful, positively inventive aspect of nationalist ardour ought not to allow anyone to conclude, erroneously, that nationalism is a contingent, artificial, ideological invention, which might not have happened, if only those damned busy-body interfering European thinkers, not content to leave well alone, had not concocted it and fatefully injected it into the bloodstream of otherwise viable political communities. The cultural shreds and patches used by nationalism are often arbitrary historical inventions. Any old shred and patch would have served as well. But in no way does it follow that the principle of nationalism itself, as opposed to the avatars it happens to pick up for its incarnations, is itself in the least contingent and accidental.

Nothing could be further from the truth than such a supposition. Nationalism is not what it seems, and above all it is not what it seems to itself. The cultures it claims to defend and revive are often its own inventions, or are modified out of all recognition. Nonetheless the nationalist principle as such, as distinct from each of its specific forms, and from the individually distinctive nonsense which it may preach, has very very deep roots in our shared current condition, is not at all contingent, and will not easily be denied.

Durkheim taught that in religious worship society adores its own camouflaged image. In a nationalist age, societies worship themselves brazenly and openly, spurning the camouflage. At Nuremberg, Nazi Germany did not worship itself by pretending to worship God or even Wotan; it overtly worshipped itself. In milder but just as significant form, enlightened modernist theologians do not believe, or even take much interest in, the doctrines of their faith which had meant so much to their predecessors. They treat them with a kind of comic auto-functionalism, as valid simply and only as the conceptual and ritual tools by means of which a social tradition affirms its values, continuity and solidarity, and they systematically obscure and play down the difference between such a tacitly reductionist 'faith', and the real thing which had preceded it and had played such a crucial part in earlier European history, a part which could never have been played by the unrecognizably diluted, watered-down current versions.

But the fact that social self-worship, whether virulent and violent or gentle and evasive, is now an openly avowed collective self-worship, rather than a means of covertly revering society through the image of God, as Durkheim insisted, does not mean that the current style is any more veridical than that of a Durkheimian age. The community may no longer be seen through the prism of the divine, but nationalism has its own amnesias and selections which, even when they may be severely secular, can be profoundly distorting and deceptive.

The basic deception and self-deception practised by nationalism is this: nationalism is, essentially, the general imposition of a high culture on society, where previously low cultures had taken up the lives of the majority, and in some cases of the totality, of the population. It means that generalized diffusion of a school-mediated, academy-supervised idiom, codified for the requirements of reasonably precise bureaucratic and technological communication. It is the establishment of an anonymous, impersonal society, with mutually substitutable atomized individuals, held together above all by a shared culture of this kind, in place of a previous complex structure of local groups, sustained by folk cultures reproduced locally and idiosyncratically by the micro-groups themselves. That is what *really* happens.

But this is the very opposite of what nationalism affirms and what nationalists fervently believe. Nationalism usually conquers in the name of putative folk culture. Its symbolism is drawn from the healthy, pristine, vigorous life of the peasants, of the *Volk*, the *narod*. There is a certain element of truth in the nationalist self-presentation when the *narod* or *Volk* is ruled by officials of another, an alien high culture, whose oppression must be resisted first by a cultural revival and reaffirmation, and eventually by a war of national libera- tion. If the nationalism prospers it eliminates the alien high culture, but it does not then replace it by the old local low culture; it revives, or invents, a local high (literate, specialist-transmitted) culture of its own, though admittedly one which will have some links with the earlier local folk styles and dialects. But it was the great ladies at the Budapest Opera who really went to town in peasant dresses, or dresses claimed to be such. At the present time in the Soviet Union the consumers of 'ethnic' gramophone records are not the remaining ethnic rural population, but the newly urbanized, appartment-dwelling, educated and multi-lingual population,[2] who like to express their real or imagined senti- ments and roots, and who will no doubt indulge in as much nationalist behaviour as the political situation may allow.

So a sociological self-deception, a vision of reality through a prism of illu- sion, still persists, but it is not the same as that which was analysed by Durkheim. Society no longer worships itself through religious symbols; a modern, streamlined, on-wheels high culture celebrates itself in song and dance, which it borrows (stylizing it in the process) from a folk culture which it fondly believes itself to be perpetuating, defending, and reaffirming.

The Course of True Nationalism Never Did Run Smooth

A characteristic scenario of the evolution of a nationalism [. . .] ran something like this. The Ruritanians were a peasant population speaking a group of related and more or less mutually intelligible dialects, and inhabiting a series of discontinuous but not very much separated pockets within the lands of the Empire of Megalomania. The Ruritanian language, or rather the dialects which could be held to compose it, was not really spoken by anyone other than these peasants. The aristocracy and officialdom spoke the language of the Megalomanian court, which happened to belong to a language group different from the one of which the Ruritanian dialects were an offshoot.

Most, but not all, Ruritanian peasants belonged to a church whose liturgy was taken from another linguistic group again, and many of the priests, especially higher up in the hierarchy, spoke a language which was a modern vernacular version of the liturgical language of this creed, and which was also very far removed from Ruritanian. The petty traders of the small towns serving the Ruritanian countryside were drawn from a different ethnic group and religion still, and one heartily detested by the Ruritanian peasantry.

In the past the Ruritanian peasants had had many griefs, movingly and beautifully recorded in their lament-songs (painstakingly collected by village schoolmasters late in the nineteenth century, and made well known to the international musical public by the compositions of the great Ruritanian na- tional composer L.). The pitiful oppression of the Ruritanian peasantry provoked, in the eighteenth century, the guerrilla resistance led by the famous Ruritanian social bandit K., whose deeds are said still to persist in the local folk memory, not to mention several novels and two films, one of them produced by the national artist Z., under highest auspices, soon after the promulgation of the Popular Socialist Republic of Ruritania.

Honesty compels one to admit that the social bandit was captured by his own compatriots, and that the tribunal which condemned him to a painful death had as its president another compatriot. Furthermore, shortly after Ruritania first attained independence, a circular passed between its Ministries of the Interior, Justice and Education, considering whether it might not now be more politic to celebrate the village defence units which had opposed the social bandit and his gangs, rather than the said social bandit himself, in the interest of not encouraging opposition to the police.

A careful analysis of the folk songs so painstakingly collected in the nineteenth century, and now incorporated in the repertoire of the Ruritanian youth, camping and sports movement, does not disclose much evidence of any serious discontent on the part of the peasantry with their linguistic and cultural situation, however grieved they were by other, more earthy matters. On the contrary, such awareness as there is of linguistic pluralism within the lyrics of the songs is ironic, jocular and good-humoured, and consists in part of bilingual puns, sometimes in questionable taste. It must also be admitted that one of the most moving of these songs—I often sang it by the camp fire at the holiday camp to which I was sent during the summer vacations—celebrates the fate of a shepherd boy, grazing three bullocks on the seigneurial clover (*sic*) near the woods, who was surprised by a group of social bandits, requiring him to surrender his overcoat. Combining reckless folly with lack of political awareness, the shepherd boy refused and was killed. I do not know whether this song has been suitably re-written since Ruritania went socialist. Anyway, to return to my main theme: though the songs do often contain complaints about the condition of the peasantry, they do not raise the issue of cultural nationalism.

That was yet to come, and presumably post-dates the composition of the said songs. In the nineteenth century a population explosion occurred at the same time as certain other areas of the Empire of Megalomania—but not Ruritania—rapidly industrialized. The Ruritanian peasants were drawn to seek work in the industrially more developed areas, and some secured it, on the dreadful terms prevailing at the time. As backward rustics speaking an obscure and seldom written or taught language, they had a particularly rough deal in the towns to whose slums they had moved. At the same time, some Ruritanian lads destined for the church, and educated in both the court and the liturgical languages, became influenced by the new liberal ideas in the course of their secondary schooling, and shifted to a secular training at the university, ending not as priests but as journalists, teachers and professors. They received encouragement from a few foreign, non-Ruritanian ethnographers, musicologists and historians who had come to explore Ruritania. The continuing labour migration, increasingly widespread elementary education and conscription provided these Ruritanian awakeners with a growing audience.

Of course, it was perfectly possible for the Ruritanians, if they wished to do so (and many did), to assimilate into the dominant language of Megalomania. No genetically transmitted trait, no deep religious custom, differentiated an educated Ruritanian from a similar Megalomanian. In fact, many did assimilate, often without bothering to change their names, and the telephone directory of the old capital of Megalomania (now the Federal Republic of Megalomania) is quite full of Ruritanian names, though often rather comically spelt in the Megalomanian manner, and adapted to Megalomanian phonetic expectations. The point is that after a rather harsh and painful start in the first generation, the life chances of the offspring of the Ruritanian labour migrant were not unduly bad, and probably at least as good (given his willingness to work hard) as those of his non-Ruritanian Megalomanian fellow-citizens. So these offspring shared in the eventual growing prosperity and general embourgeoisement of the region. Hence, as far as individual life chances went, there was perhaps no need for a virulent Ruritanian nationalism.

Nonetheless something of the kind did occur. It would, I think, be quite wrong to attribute conscious calculation to the participants in the movement. Subjectively, one must suppose that they had the motives and feelings which are so vigorously expressed in the literature of the national revival. They deplored the squalor and neglect of their home valleys, while yet also seeing the rustic virtues still to be found in them; they deplored the discrimination to which their co-nationals were subject, and the alienation from their native culture to which they were doomed in the proletarian suburbs of the industrial towns. They preached against these ills, and had the hearing of at least many of their fellows. The manner in which, when the international political situation came to favour it, Ruritania eventually attained independence, is now part of the historical record and need not be repeated here.

There is, one must repeat, no need to assume any conscious long-term calculation of interest on anyone's part. The nationalist intellectuals were full of warm and generous ardour on behalf of the co-nationals. When they donned folk costume and trekked over the hills, composing poems in the forest clearings, they did not also dream of one day becoming powerful bureaucrats, ambassadors and ministers. Likewise, the peasants and workers whom they succeeded in reaching felt resentment at their condition, but had no reveries about plans of industrial development which one day would bring a steel mill (quite useless, as it then turned out) to the very heart of the Ruritanian valleys, thus totally ruining quite a sizeable area of surrounding arable land and pasture. It would be genuinely wrong to try to reduce these sentiments to calculations of material advantage or of social mobility. The present theory is sometimes travestied as a reduction of national sentiment to calculation of prospects of social promotion. But this is a misrepresentation. In the old days it made no sense to ask whether the peasants loved their own culture: they took it for granted, like the air they breathed, and were not conscious of either. But when labour migration and bureaucratic employment became prominent features within their social horizon, they soon learned the difference between dealing with a co-national, one understanding and sympathizing with their culture, and someone hostile to it. This very concrete experience taught them to be aware of their culture, and to love it (or, indeed, to wish to be rid of it) without any conscious calculation of advantages and prospects of social mobility. In stable self-contained communities culture is often quite invisible, but when mobility and context-free communication come to be of the essence of social life, the culture in which one has been *taught* to communicate becomes the core of one's identity.

So *had* there been such calculation (which there was not) it would, in quite a number of cases (though by no means in all), have been a very sound one. In fact, given the at least relative paucity of Ruritanian intellectuals, those Ruritanians who did have higher qualifications secured much better posts in independent Ruritania than most of them could even have hoped for in Greater Megalomania, where they had to compete with scholastically more developed ethnic groups. As for the peasants and workers, they did not benefit immediately; but the drawing of a political boundary around the newly defined ethnic Ruritania did mean the eventual fostering and protection of industries in the area, and in the end drastically diminished the need for labour migration from it.

What all this amounts to is this: during the early period of industrialization, entrants into the new order who are drawn from cultural and linguistic groups that are distant from those of the more advanced centre, suffer considerable disadvantages which are even greater than those of other economically weak new proletarians who have the advantage of sharing the culture of the political and economic rulers. But the cultural/linguistic distance and capacity to differentiate themselves from others, which is such a handicap for individuals, can be and often is eventually a positive advantage for entire collectivities, or potential collectivities, of these victims of the newly emergent world. It enables them to conceive and express their resentments and discontents in intelligible terms. Ruritanians had previously thought and felt in terms of family unit and village, at most in terms of a valley, and perhaps on occasion in terms of religion. But now, swept into the melting pot of an early industrial development, they had no valley and no village: and sometimes no family. But there *were* other impoverished and exploited individuals, and a lot of them spoke dialects recognizably similar, while most of the better-off spoke something quite alien; and so the new concept of the Ruritanian nation was born of this contrast, with some encouragement from those journalists and teachers. And it was not an illusion: the attainment of some of the objects of the nascent

Ruritanian national movement did indeed bring relief of the ills which had helped to engender it. The relief would perhaps have come any way; but in this national form, it also brought forth a new high culture and its guardian state.

[*Nations and Nationalism* (Blackwell: Oxford, 1983), 48–9, 55–62.]

TOM NAIRN

11 The Maladies of Development

'[N]ationalism' in its most general sense is determined by certain features of the world political economy, in the era between the French and Industrial Revolutions and the present day. We are still living in this era. However, we enjoy the modest advantage of having lived in it longer than the earlier theorists who wrestled with the problem. From our present vantage-point we may be a little more able than they were to discern some overall characteristics of the process and its by-products. Indeed it would not say much for us if we were not able to do this.

Next, we must inquire what are those features of general historical development which give us some clue about nationalism. At this point it may help to dip briefly into the mythology of the subject. If someone were producing an up-dated version of Gustave Flaubert's *Dictionnaire des idées reçues* for the use of politics and social-science students, I think the entry 'Nationalism' might read as follows: '*Nationalism*: infrequently used before the later nineteenth century, the term can nonetheless be traced back in approximately its contemporary meaning to the 1790s (Abbé Baruel, 1798). It denotes the new and heightened significance accorded to factors of nationality, ethnic inheritance, customs and speech from the early nineteenth century onwards. The concept of nationalism as a generally necessary stage of development for all societies is common to both materialist and idealist philosophies. These later theoretical formulations agree that society must pass through this phase (see e.g. texts of F. Engels, L. von Ranke, V. I. Lenin, F. Meinecke). These theories also agree in attributing the causes of this phase to specific forces or impulses resident within the social formations concerned. Nationalism is therefore an internally-determined necessity, associated by Marxists with, for example, the creation of a national market economy and a viable national bourgeois class; by Idealists with the indwelling spirit of the community, a common personality which must find expression in historical development. Both views concur that this stage of societal evolution is the necessary precondition of a subsequent, more satisfactory state of affairs, known as "internationalism" ("proletarian" or "socialist" internationalism in one case, the higher harmony of the World Spirit in the other). This condition is only attainable for societies and individuals who have developed a healthy nationalism previously. While moderate, reasonable nationalism is in this sense praised, an immoderate or excessive nationalism exceeding these historical limits is viewed as unhealthy and dangerous (see entry "Chauvinism", above).' The gist of this piece of global folklore (which unfortunately embraces much of what passes for 'theory' on nationalism) is that nationalism is an inwardly-determined social necessity, a 'growth-stage', located somewhere in between traditional or 'feudal' societies and a future where the factors of nationality will become less prominent (or anyway less troublesome in human history). Regrettably, it is a growth-stage which can sometimes go wrong and run amok. This is mysterious. How can adolescence become a deadly disease?

Whatever the doctors say about this, they agree on the double inwardness attaching to nationalism. It corresponds to certain internal needs of the society in question, *and* to certain individual, psychological needs as well. It supplies peoples and persons with an important commodity, 'identity'. There is a distinctive, easily recognizable subjectivity linked to all this. Whenever we talk about nationalism, we normally find ourselves talking before too long about 'feelings', 'instincts', supposed desires and hankerings to 'belong', and so on. This psychology is obviously an important fact about nationalism.

The universal folklore of nationalism is not entirely wrong. If it were, it would be unable to function as myth. On the other hand, it would be equally unable to function in this way if it were true—that is, true in the sense that concerns us in this place. It is ideology. This means it is the generally acceptable 'false consciousness' of a social world still in the grip of 'nationalism'. It is a mechanism of adjustment and compensation, a way of living with the reality of those forms of historical development we label 'nationalism'. As such, it is perhaps best regarded as a set of important clues towards whatever these forms are really about.

The principal such clue is the powerful connection that common sense suggests between nationalism and the concept of development or social and economic 'growth'. It is true that the distinctively modern fact of national*ism* (as opposed to nationality, national states and other precursors) is somehow related to this. For it is only within the context of the general acceleration of change since about 1800, only in the context of 'development' in this new sense, that nationhood acquired this systemic and abstract meaning.

However, it is not true that the systemic connotation derives *from the fact of development as such*. This is the sensitive juncture at which truth evaporates into useful ideology. It is simply not the case (although humanity has always had plenty of reasons for wishing it were the case) that national-ism, the compulsive necessity for a certain socio-political form, arises naturally from these new developmental conditions. It is not nature. The point of the folklore is of course to suggest this: to award it a natural status, and hence a 'health' label, as if it were indeed a sort of adolescence of all societies, the road we have to trudge along between rural idiocy and 'modernity', industrialization (or whatever).

A second significant clue is that pointing towards social and personal subjectivity. It is true that nationalism is connected with typical internal movements, personnel and persons. These behave in similar ways and entertain quite similar feelings. So it is tempting to say (e.g.) that the Italian nationalism of the 1850s or the Kurdish or Eritrean nationalism of the 1970s rest upon and are generated by these specific internal mechanisms. They express the native peculiarities of their peoples, in a broadly similar way—presumably because the people's soul (or at least its bourgeoisie) needs to.

However, it is not true that nationalism of any kind is really the product *of these internal motions as such.* This is the core of the empirical country-by-country fallacy which the ideology of nationalism itself wishes upon us. Welsh *nationalism*, of course, has much to do with the specifics of the Welsh people, their history, their particular forms of oppression and all the rest of it. But Welsh national*ism*—that generic, universal necessity recorded in the very term we are interested in—has nothing to do with Wales. It is not a Welsh fact, but a fact of general developmental history, that at a specific time the Welsh land and people are forced into the historical process in this fashion. The '-ism' they are then compelled to follow is in reality imposed upon them from without; although of course to make this adaptation, it is necessary that the usual kinds of national cadres, myths, sentiments, etc., well up from within. All nationalisms work through a characteristic repertoire of social and personal mechanisms, many of them highly subjective. But the causation of the drama is not within the bosom of the *Volk*: this way lie the myths of blood and *Geist*. The subjectivity of nationalism is an important objective fact about it; but it is a fact which, in itself, merely reposes the question of origins.

The real origins are elsewhere. They are located not in the folk, nor in the individual's repressed passion for some sort of wholeness or identity, but in the machinery of world political economy. Not, however, in the process of that economy's development as such—not simply as an inevitable concomitant of industrialization and urbanization. They are associated with more specific features of that process. The best way of categorizing these traits is to say they represent the *uneven development* of history since the eighteenth century. This unevenness is a material fact; one could argue that it is the most grossly material fact about modern history. This statement allows us to reach a satisfying and near-paradoxical conclusion: the most notoriously subjective and ideal of historical phenomena is in fact a by-product of the most brutally and hopelessly material side of the history of the last two centuries. [. . .]

The unforeseeable, antagonistic reality of capitalism's growth into the world is what the general title 'uneven development' refers to. It indicates the shambling, fighting, lop-sided, illogical, head-over-heels fact, so to speak, as distinct from the noble uplift and phased amelioration of the ideal. Modern capitalist development was launched by a number of West-European states which had accumulated the potential for doing so over a long period of history. The even-development notion was that this advance could be straightforwardly followed, and the institutions responsible for it copied—hence the periphery, the world's countryside, would catch up with the leaders in due time. This evening-up would proceed through the formation of a basically homogeneous enlightened class throughout the periphery: the international or 'cosmopolitan' élite in charge of the diffusion process. But no such steady diffusion or copying was in fact possible, and neither was the formation of this universal class (though there have been and are caricatural versions of it, in the shape of comprador bourgeoisies allying themselves to metropolitan capital instead of to their own people).

Instead, the impact of those leading countries was normally experienced as domination and invasion. The spirit of commerce was supposed to take over from the traditional forms of rapine and swindle. But in reality it could not. The gap was too great, and the new developmental forces were not in the hands of a beneficent, disinterested élite concerned with Humanity's advance. Rather, it was the 'sordid material interests' (as Marx and Engels relished saying) of the English and French bourgeois classes which were employing the concepts of the Enlightenment and classical political economy as a smokescreen. Even with the best will in the world (which they did not have), Progress could not help identifying herself to some degree with these particular places, classes and interests. And in this way she could not help fomenting a new sort of 'imperialism'.

On the periphery itself, outside the core-areas of the new industrial-capitalist world economy, people soon needed little persuasion of this. They learned quickly enough that Progress in the abstract meant domination in the concrete, by powers which they could not help apprehending as foreign or alien. In practice as distinct from the theory, the acculturation process turned out to be more like a 'tidal wave' (in Ernest Gellner's phrase) of outside interference and control. Humanity's forward march signified in the first instance Anglicization or Frenchification, for as long ahead as the people most conscious of the change could see. As was said later on, more globally: 'Westernization' or 'Americanization'.

There was never either time or the sociological space for even development. The new forces of production, and the new state and military powers associated with them, were too dynamic and uncontrolled, and the resultant social upheavals were far too rapid and devastating for any such gradual civilization-process to take place. There was to be no 'due time' in modern history. All time was undue once the great shock-wave had begun its course. For those outside the metropolis (where in unique and unrepeatable circumstances things had matured slowly) the problem was not to assimilate culture at a reasonable rate: it was to avoid being drowned.

The Enlightenment was borne into wider reality by bourgeois revolutions which shook the older social world around them to pieces. In these less-developed lands the élites soon discovered that tranquil incorporation into the cosmopolitan technocracy was possible for only a few of them at a time. The others, the majority, saw themselves excluded from the action, rather than invited politely to join in; trampled over rather than taught the rules of the game; exploited rather than made partners. It was no consolation to be told that patience was in order, that things would even up in the next generation, or the one after that. Was this true at all? Would not the actual configuration of the new forces of change merely put the English even more firmly in charge of an even more unIndian India; the Germans even more in control of second-class, Slav lands? True or not, the point came to seem academic. Given the violence and rapidity of the changes in act, patience and time were no longer human possibilities anyway.

The Necessary Resort to Populism

Huge expectations raced ahead of material progress itself. The peripheric élites had no option but to try and satisfy such demands by taking things into their own hands. 'Taking things into one's own hands' denotes a good deal of the substance of nationalism, of course. It meant that these classes—and later on sometimes the masses beneath them, whom they felt responsible for—had to mobilize *against* 'progress' at the same time as they sought to improve their position in accordance with the new canons. They had to contest the concrete form in which (so to speak) progress had taken them by the throat, even as they set out to progress themselves. Since they wanted factories, parliaments, schools and so on, they had to copy the leaders somehow; but in a way which rejected the mere implantation of these things by direct foreign intervention or control. This gave rise to a profound ambiguity, an ambivalence which marks most forms of nationalism.

Unable to literally 'copy' the advanced lands (which would have entailed repeating the stages of slow growth that had led to the breakthrough), the backward regions were forced to take what they wanted and cobble it on to their own native inheritance of social forms. In the annals of this kind of theorizing the procedure is called 'uneven and combined development'. To defend themselves, the periphery countries were compelled to try and advance 'in their own way', to 'do it for themselves'. Their rulers—or at least the newly-awakened élites who now came to power—had to mobilize their so-cieties for this historical short-cut. This meant the conscious formation of a militant, inter-class community rendered strongly (if mythically) aware of its own separate identity vis-à-vis the outside forces of domination. There was no other way of doing it. Mobilization had to be in terms of what was there; and the whole point of the dilemma was that there was nothing there—none of the economic and political institutions of modernity now so needed.

All that there *was* was the people and peculiarities of the region: its inherited *ethnos*, speech, folklore, skin-colour, and so on. Nationalism works through *differentiae* like those because it has to. It is not necessarily democratic in outlook, but it *is* invariably populist. People are what it has to go on: in the archetypal situation of the really poor or 'under-developed' territory, it may be more or less all that nationalists have going for them. For kindred reasons, it had to function through highly rhetorical forms, through a sentimental culture sufficiently accessible to the lower strata now being called to battle. This is why a romantic culture quite remote from Enlightenment rationalism always went hand-in-hand with the spread of nationalism. The new middle-class intelligentsia of nationalism had to invite the masses into history; and the invitation-card had to be written in a language they understood.

It is unneccessary here to explore the process in detail. Everyone is familiar with its outline, and with much of its content. We all know how it spread out from its West-European source, in concentric circles of upheaval and reaction: through Central and Eastern Europe, Latin America, and then across the other continents. Uniformed imperialism of the 1880–1945 variety was one episode in this larger history, as were its derivatives, anti-colonial wars and 'decolonization'. We have all studied the phenomena so consistently accompanying it: the 'rediscovery' or invention of national history, urban intellectuals invoking peasant virtues which they have experienced only through train windows on their summer holidays, schoolmasters painfully acquiring 'national' tongues spoken only in remote valleys, the infinity of forms assumed by the battle between scathing cosmopolitan modernists and emotional defenders of the Folk . . . and so on.

But [. . .] let me try to sum up this part of the argument. Real, uneven development has invariably generated an imperialism of the centre over the periphery; one after another, these peripheric areas have been forced into a profoundly ambivalent reaction against this dominance, seeking at once to resist it and to somehow take over its vital forces for their own use. This could only be done by a kind of highly 'idealist' political and ideological mobilization, by a painful forced march based on their own resources: that is, employing their 'nationality' as a basis. The metropolitan fantasy of even development had predicted a swelling, single forward march that would induct backward lands into its course; in reality, these lands found themselves compelled to attempt radical, competitive short-cuts in order to avoid being trampled over or left behind. The logistics of these short-cuts brought in factors quite absent from the universalizing philosophy of Progress. And since the greater part of the globe was to be forced into detours of this kind, these factors became dominant in the history of the world for a long period, one still not concluded.

> [*The Break-up of Britain: Crisis and Neo-Nationalism*, 2nd edn. (New Left Books: London, 1977), 332–6, 337–41.]

ERIC HOBSBAWM
....

12 The Nation as Invented Tradition

In this connection, one specific interest of 'invented traditions' for, at all events, modern and contemporary historians ought to be singled out. They are highly relevant to that comparatively recent historical innovation, the 'nation', with its associated phenomena: nationalism, the nation-state, national symbols, histories and the rest. All these rest on exercises in social engineering which are often deliberate and always innovative, if only because historical novelty implies innovation. Israeli and Palestinian nationalism or nations must be novel, whatever the historic continuities of Jews or Middle Eastern Muslims, since the very concept of territorial states of the currently standard type in their region was barely thought of a century ago, and hardly became a serious prospect before the end of World War I. Standard national languages, to be learned in schools and written, let alone spoken, by more than a smallish élite, are largely constructs of varying, but often brief, age. As a French historian of Flemish language observed, quite correctly, the Flemish taught in Belgium today is not the language which the mothers and grandmothers of Flanders spoke to their children: in short, it is only metaphorically but not literally a 'mother-tongue'. We should not be misled by a curious, but understandable, paradox: modern nations and all their impedimenta generally claim to be the opposite of novel, namely rooted in the remotest antiquity, and the opposite of constructed, namely human communities so 'natural' as to require no definition other than self-assertion. Whatever the historic or other continuities embedded in the modern concept of 'France' and 'the French'—and which nobody would seek to deny—these very concepts themselves must include a constructed or 'invented' component. And just because so much of what subjectively makes up the modern 'nation' consists of such constructs and is associated with appropriate and, in general, fairly recent symbols or suitably tailored discourse (such as 'national history'), the national phenomenon cannot be adequately investigated without careful attention to the 'invention of tradition'.

*   *   *

Nevertheless, the state linked both formal and informal, official and unofficial, political and social inventions of tradition, at least in those countries where the need for it arose. Seen from below, the state increasingly defined the largest stage on which the crucial activities determining human lives as subjects and citizens were played out. Indeed, it increasingly defined as well as registered their civil existence (*état civil*). It may not have been the only such stage, but its existence, frontiers and increasingly regular and probing interventions in the citizen's life were in the last analysis decisive. In developed countries the 'national economy', its area defined by the territory of some state or its subdivisions, was the basic unit of economic development. A change in the frontiers of the state or in its policy had substantial and continuous material consequences for its citizens. The standardization of administration and law within it, and, in particular, state education, transformed people into citizens of a specific country: 'peasants into Frenchmen', to cite the title of an apposite book.[1] The state was the framework of the citizens' collective actions, insofar as these were officially recognized. To influence or change the government of the state, or its policy, was plainly the main objective of domestic politics, and the common man was increasingly entitled to take part in it. Indeed, politics in the new nineteenth-century sense was essentially nation-wide politics. In short, for practical purposes, society ('civil society') and the state within which it operated became increasingly inseparable.

It was thus natural that the classes within society, and in particular the working class, should tend to identify themselves through nation-wide political movements or organizations ('parties'), and equally natural that de facto these should operate essentially within the confines of the nation.[2] Nor is it surprising that movements seeking to represent an entire society or 'people' should envisage its existence essentially in terms of that of an independent or at least an autonomous state. State, nation and society converged. [. . .]

In terms of the invention of tradition, three major innovations are particularly relevant. The first was the development of a secular equivalent of the church—primary education, imbued with revolutionary and republican principles and content, and conducted by the secular equivalent of the priesthood—or perhaps, given their poverty, the friars—the *instituteurs*.[3] There is no doubt that this was a deliberate construction of the early Third Republic, and, given the proverbial centralization of French government, that the content of the manuals which were to turn not only peasants into Frenchmen but all Frenchmen into good Republicans, was not left to chance. Indeed the 'institutionalization' of the French Revolution itself in and by the Republic has been studied in some detail.[4]

The second was the invention of public ceremonies.[5] The most important of these, Bastille Day, can be exactly dated in 1880. It combined official and unofficial demonstrations and popular festivities—fireworks, dancing in the streets—in an annual assertion of France as the nation of 1789, in which every French man, woman and child could take part. Yet while it left scope for, and could hardly avoid, more militant, popular manifestations, its general tendency was to transform the heritage of the Revolution into a combined expression of state pomp and power and the citizens' pleasure. A less permanent form of public celebration were the occasional world expositions which gave the Republic the legitimacy of prosperity, technical progress—the Eiffel Tower—and the global colonial conquest they took care to emphasize.[6]

The third was the mass production of public monuments [. . .]. It may be observed that the Third Republic did not—unlike other countries—favour massive public buildings, of which France already had a large supply—though the great expositions left some of these behind them in Paris—nor gigantic statuary. The major characteristic of French 'statuomania'[7] was its democracy, anticipating that of the war memorials after 1914–18. It spread two kinds of monuments throughout the cities and rural communes of the country: the image of the Republic itself (in the form of Marianne which now became universally familiar), and the bearded civilian figures of whoever local patriotism chose to regard as its notables, past and present. Indeed, while the construction of Republican monuments was evidently encouraged, the initiative, and the costs of, such enterprises were undertaken at a local level. The entrepreneurs catering for this market provided choices suitable for the purses of every Republican commune from the poorest upwards, ranging from modest busts of Marianne, in various sizes, through full-figure statues of varying dimensions, to the plinths and allegorical or heroic accessories with which the more ambitious citizenry could surround her feet.[8] The opulent ensembles on the Place de la République and the Place de la Nation in Paris provided the ultimate version of such statuary. Such monuments traced the grass roots of the Republic—particularly in its rural strongholds—and may be regarded as the visible links between the voters and the nation.

Some other characteristics of the official 'invented' traditions of the Third Republic may be noted in passing. Except in the form of the commemoration of notable figures from the local past, or of local political manifestos, it kept away from history. This was partly, no doubt, because history before 1789 (except perhaps for 'nos ancêtres les Gaulois') recalled church and monarchy, partly because history since 1789 was a divisive rather than unifying force: each brand—or rather degree—of Republicanism had its own corresponding heroes and villains in the revolutionary pantheon, as the historiography of the French Revolution demonstrates. Party differences were expressed in statues to Robespierre, Mirabeau or Danton. Unlike the USA and the Latin American states, the French Republic therefore shied away from the cult of Founding Fathers. It preferred general symbols, abstaining even from the use of themes referring to the national past on its postage stamps until long after 1914, though most European states (other than Britain and Scandinavia) discovered their appeal from the mid-1890s onwards. The symbols were few: the tricolour (democratized and universalized in the sash of the mayor, present at every civil marriage or other ceremony), the Republican monogram (RF) and motto (liberty, equality, fraternity), the 'Marseillaise', and the symbol of the Republic and of freedom itself, which appears to have taken shape in the last years of the Second Empire, Marianne. We may also note that the Third Republic showed no official hankering for the specifically invented ceremonies so characteristic of the First—'trees of liberty', goddesses of reason and ad hoc festivals. There was to be no official national day other than 14 July, no formal mobilizations, processions and marches of the civilian citizenry (unlike the mass régimes of the twentieth century, but also unlike the USA), but rather a simple 'republicanization' of the accepted pomp of state power—uniforms, parades, bands, flags, and the like.

The Second German Empire provides an interesting contrast, especially since several of the general themes of French Republican invented tradition are recognizable in its own. Its major political problem was twofold: how to provide historical legitimacy for the Bismarckian (Prusso-Little German) version of unification which had none; and how to deal with that large part of the democratic electorate which would have preferred another solution (Great Germans, anti-Prussian particularists, Catholics and, above all, Social Democrats). Bismarck himself does not seem to have bothered much about symbolism, except for personally devising a tricolour flag which combined the Prussian black–white with the nationalist and liberal black–red–gold which he wished to annex (1866). There was no historical precedent whatever for the Empire's black–white–red national banner.[9] His recipe for political stability was simpler: to win the support of the (predominantly liberal) bourgeoisie by carrying out as much of its programme as would not jeopardize the predominance of the Prussian monarchy, army and aristocracy, to utilize the potential divisions among the various kinds of opposition and to exclude political democracy as far as possible from affecting the decisions of government. Apparently irreconcilable groups which could not be divided—notably the Catholics and especially the post-Lassallean Social Democrats—left him somewhat at a loss. In fact, he was defeated in his head-on confrontations with both. One has the impression that this old-fashioned conservative rationalist, however brilliant in the arts of political manoeuvre, never satisfactorily solved the difficulties of political democracy, as distinct from the politics of notables.

The invention of the traditions of the German Empire is therefore primarily associated with the era of William II. Its objects were mainly twofold: to establish the continuity between the Second and First German Empires, or more generally, to establish the new Empire as the realization of the secular national aspirations of the German people; and to stress the specific historical experiences which linked Prussia and the rest of Germany in the construction of the new Empire in 1871. Both, in turn, required the merger of Prussian and German history, to which patriotic imperial historians (notably Treitschke) had for some time devoted themselves. The major difficulty in the way of achieving these objects was firstly the history of the Holy Roman Empire of the German nation was difficult to fit into any nineteenth-century nationalist mould, and secondly that its history did not suggest that the denouement of 1871 was historically inevitable, or even likely. It could be linked to a modern nationalism only by two devices: by the concept of a secular national enemy against whom the German people had defined their identity and struggled to achieve unity as a state; and by the concept of conquest or cultural, political and military supremacy, by means of which the German nation, scattered across large parts of other states, mainly in central and eastern Europe, could claim the right to be united in a single Greater German state. The second concept was not one which the Bismarckian empire, specifically 'Little German', cared to stress, though Prussia itself, as its name implied, had been historically constructed largely by expansion into Slavonic and Baltic areas outside the range of the Holy Roman Empire.

Buildings and monuments were the most visible form of establishing a new interpretation of German history, or rather a fusion between the older romantic 'invented tradition' of pre-1848 German nationalism and the new régime: the most powerful symbols being those where the fusion was achieved. Thus, the mass movement of German gymnasts, liberal and Great German until the 1860s, Bismarckian after 1866 and eventually pan-German and antisemitic, took to its heart three monuments whose inspiration was basically not official: the monument to Arminius the Cheruscan in the Teutoburg Forest (much of it constructed as early as 1838–46, and inaugurated in 1875); the Niederwald monument above the Rhine, commemorating the unification of Germany in 1871 (1877–83); and the centenary memorial of the battle of Leipzig, initiated in 1894 by a 'German Patriotic League for the Erection of a Monument to the Battle of the Peoples at Leipzig', and inaugurated in 1913. On the other hand, they appear to have showed no enthusiasm for the proposal to turn the monument to William I on the Kyffhäuser mountain, on the spot where folk myth claimed the Emperor Frederick Barbarossa would appear again, into a national symbol (1890–6), and no special reaction to the construction of the monument to William I and Germany at the confluence of the Rhine and the Moselle (the 'Deutsches Eck' or German Corner), directed against French claims to the left bank of the Rhine.[10]

Leaving such variations aside, the mass of masonry and statuary which went up in Germany in this period was remarkably large, and made the fortunes of sufficiently pliable and competent architects and sculptors.[11] Among those constructed or planned in the 1890s alone, we may mention the new Reichstag building (1884–94) with elaborate historical imagery on its façade, the Kyffhäuser monument already mentioned (1890–6), the national monument to William I—clearly intended as the official father of the country (1890–7), the monument to William I at the Porta Westfalica (1892), the William I monument at the Deutsches Eck (1894–7), the extraordinary Valhalla of Hohenzollern princes in the 'Avenue of Victory' (Siegesallee) in Berlin (1896–1901), a variety of statues to William I in German cities (Dortmund 1894, Wiesbaden 1894, Prenzlau 1898, Hamburg 1903, Halle 1901) and, a little later, a spate of Bismarck monuments, which enjoyed a more genuine support among nationalists.[12] The inauguration of one of these monuments provided the first occasion for the use of historical themes on the postage stamps of the Empire (1899).

This accumulation of masonry and statuary suggests two comments. The first concerns the choice of a national symbol. *Two* of these were available: a vague but adequately military 'Germania', who played no notable role in sculpture, though she figured extensively on postage stamps from the start, since no single dynastic image could as yet symbolize Germany as a whole; and the figure of the 'Deutsche Michel', who actually appears in a subordinate role on the Bismarck monument. He belongs to the curious representations of the nation, not as country or state, but as 'the people', which came to animate the demotic political language of the nineteenth-century cartoonists and was intended (as in John Bull and the goateed Yankee—but *not* in Marianne, image of the Republic) to express national character, as seen by the members of the nation itself. Their origins and early history are obscure, though, like the national anthem, they are almost certainly first found in eighteenth-century Britain.[13] The point about the 'Deutsche Michel' is that his image stressed both the innocence and simple-mindedness so readily exploited by cunning foreigners, and the physical strength he could mobilize to frustrate their knavish tricks and conquests when finally roused. 'Michel' seems to have been essentially an anti-foreign image.

The second concerns the crucial significance of the Bismarckian unification of Germany as the *only* national historical experience which the citizens of the new Empire had in common, given that all earlier conceptions of Germany and German unification were in one way or another 'Great German'. And within this experience, the Franco-German war was central. Insofar as Germany had a (brief) 'national' tradition, it was symbolized in the three names: Bismarck, William I and Sedan.

This is clearly exemplified by the ceremonials and rituals invented (also mainly under William II). Thus the chronicles of one Gymnasium record no less than ten ceremonies between August 1895 and March 1896 recalling the twenty-fifth anniversary of the Franco-Prussian war, including ample commemorations of battles in the war, celebrations of the emperor's birthday, the official handing-over of the portrait of an imperial prince, illuminations and public addresses on the war of 1870–1, on the development of the imperial idea (*Kaiseridee*) during the war, on the character of the Hohenzollern dynasty, and so on.[14]

A more detailed description of one such ceremony may elucidate their character. Watched by parents and friends, the boys marched into the school yard singing the 'Wacht am Rhein' (the 'national song' most directly identified with hostility to the French, though, interestingly, neither the Prussian nor the German national anthem).[15] They formed up facing representatives of each class who held flags decorated with oak leaves, which had been bought with money collected in each class. (The oak had associations with Teutonic-German folklore, nationalism and military virtues—still remembered in the oak leaves which marked the highest class of military decoration under Hitler: a suitably Germanic equivalent to the Latin laurel.) The head boy presented these banners to the headmaster, who in turn addressed the assembly on the glorious days of the late Emperor William I, and called for three ringing cheers for the reigning monarch and his empress. The boys then marched under their banners. Yet another address by the headmaster followed, before the planting of an 'imperial oak' (Kaisereiche) to the accompaniment of choral singing. The day concluded with an excursion into the Grunewald. All these proceedings were merely preliminaries to the actual commemoration of Sedan Day two days later, and indeed to a scholastic year amply punctuated by ritual gatherings, religious and civic.[16] In the same year an imperial decree was to announce the construction of the Siegesallee, linking it with the twenty-fifth anniversary of the Franco-Prussian war, which was presented as the rising of the German people 'as one man', though 'following the call of its princes' to 'repel foreign aggression and achieve the unity of the fatherland and the *restoration* of the Reich in glorious victories' (my italics).[17] The Siegesallee, it will be recalled, represented exclusively the Hohenzollern princes back to the days of the Margraves of Brandenburg.

A comparison of the French and German innovations is instructive. Both stress the founding acts of the new régime—the French Revolution in its least precise and controversial episode (the Bastille) and the Franco-Prussian war. Except for this one point of historic reference, the French Republic abstained from historical retrospect as strikingly as the German Empire indulged in it. Since the Revolution had established the fact, the nature and the boundaries of the French nation and its patriotism, the Republic could confine itself to recalling these to its citizens by means of a few obvious symbols—Marianne, the tricolour, the 'Marseillaise', and so on—supplementing them with a little ideological exegesis elaborating on the (to its poorer citizens) obvious if sometimes theoretical benefits of Liberty, Equality and Fraternity. Since the 'German people' before 1871 had no political definition or unity, and its relation to the new Empire (which excluded large parts of it) was vague, symbolic or ideological, identification had to be more complex and—with the exception of the role of the Hohenzollern dynasty, army and state—less precise. Hence the multiplicity of reference, ranging from mythology and folklore (German oaks, the Emperor Frederick Barbarossa) through the shorthand cartoon stereotypes to definition of the nation in terms of its enemies. Like many another liberated 'people', 'Germany' was more easily defined by what it was against than in any other way.

['Introduction: Inventing Traditions', and 'Mass-Producing Traditions: Europe, 1870–1914', in *The Invention of Tradition*, ed. Eric Hobsbawn and Terence Ranger (CUP: Cambridge, 1983), 13–14, 264–5, 271–8.]

PAUL R. BRASS

13   Élite Competition and Nation-Formation

The study of the processes by which ethnic groups and nations are formed has been beset by a persistent and fundamental conceptual difference among scholars concerning the very nature of the groups involved, namely, whether they are 'natural', 'primordial', 'given' communities or whether they are creations of interested leaders, of élite groups, or of the political system in which they are included.[1] The primordialist argues that every person carries with him through life 'attachments' derived from place of birth, kinship relationships, religion, language, and social practices that are 'natural' for him, 'spiritual' in character, and that provide a basis for an easy 'affinity' with other peoples from the same background. These 'attachments' constitute the 'givens' of the human condition and are 'rooted in the non-rational foundations of personality.'[2] Some go so far as to argue that such attachments that form the core of ethnicity are biological and genetic in nature.[3] Whatever differences in detail exist among the spokesmen for the primordialist point of view, they tend to unite upon the explicit or implicit argument that ethnicity, properly defined, is based upon descent.[4] Since, however, it is quite obvious that there are very few groups in the world today whose members can lay any serious claim to a known common origin, it is not actual descent that is considered essential to the definition of an ethnic group but a belief in a common descent.

There are some aspects of the primordialist formulation with which it is not difficult to agree. Even in modern industrial society, let alone in pre-modern or modernizing societies, most people develop attachments in childhood and youth that have deeply emotive significance, that remain with them through life either consciously, in the actual persistence of such attachments in the routines of daily life, or embedded in the unconscious realms of the adult personality. Such attachments also often provide a basis for the formation of social and political groupings in adult life for those for whom they have a continuing conscious meaning in their daily lives. Even for those persons, particularly in modern societies, who have been removed from their origins or have rejected their childhood identifications, such attachments may remain available in the unconscious to be revived by some appeal that strikes a sympathetic psychic chord.

It is difficult, however, to travel much further than this with the primordialists. First of all, it is clear that some primordial attachments are variable. In multilingual developing societies, many people command more than one language, dialect, or code.[5] Many illiterate rural persons, far from being attached emotionally to their mother tongue, do not even know its proper name. In some situations, members of linguistically diverse ethnic communities have chosen to change their language in order to provide an additional element in common with their group members. In other situations, ethnic group members have deliberately shifted their own language and educated their children in a different language than their mother tongue in order to differentiate themselves further from another ethnic group.[6] Finally, many people, if not most people, never think about their language at all and never attach any emotional significance to it.

Religious identification too is subject to change—and not only by modern cosmopolitan man engaged in enlightened spiritual quests. Shifts in religious practices brought about under the influence of religious reformers are common occurrences in pre-modern, modernizing, and even in post-industrial societies. Sometimes such shifts are clearly designed to promote internal solidarity and external differentiation from other groups.[7]

Even one's place of birth and kinship connections may lose their emotional significance for people or be viewed negatively. A psychoanalyst might argue that these attachments at least pursue men through life and must always remain as potential sources of affective involvement with others. Yet, millions of persons have migrated by choice from their native places in both modern and traditional societies and, while many have retained an emotional attachment to their place of origin, many have chosen to assimilate to their new society and have lost any sense of emotional identification with their homelands. For those who do not migrate, one's place of birth identifies a person, but a sense of identity based on attachment to one's region or homeland usually does not become a politically significant matter for those who remain there unless there is some perceived discrimination against the region and its people in the larger society. Moreover, even the 'fact' of one's place of birth is subject to variation. A person is born in a particular village or town, but one is not born in a 'region', for a region is itself an artificial construct. A person may be born in Savannah, Georgia, and not consider himself a 'Southerner'. It is also possible obviously for 'Southerners' to be born out of their region. Insofar as kinship connections are concerned, the range of genuine kin relationships is usually too small to be of political significance. Fictive kinship relationships may extend the range of some ethnic groups rather broadly, but their fictive character presumes their variability by definition. Consequently, even 'the facts of birth' are either inherently of no political significance or are subject to variation.[8]

As for the argument that it is not place of birth or kinship or mother tongue or native religion that defines ethnicity but a belief in a common descent that draws on one or more of these attachments, it must be conceded that the argument stated in this general form is not without force. Many ethnic communities do explicitly proclaim or implicitly assume that the underlying basis of their unity is shared descent. It is not at all difficult to find a broad spectrum of such communities. Broad as the spectrum may be, however, it will still not suffice to encompass all the culturally-defined collectivities whose members lay claim to special privileges because of some shared cultural features and who are united internally by their attachment to them, unless we define common descent so broadly as to include shared historical, linguistic, or religious experiences. In the latter case, however, we do nothing more than redefine descent to equal shared cultural features.

There are two more serious objections to the primordialist point of view on ethnicity. One is the assumption that sometimes accompanies it that the recognition of distinct primordial groups in a society is sufficient to predict the future development out of them of ethnic communities or nations. This assumption, which is associated principally with the early European ideologists of nationalism, is no longer widely held even by their primordialist descendants, for it is clearly an untenable proposition. A second point of view is more widely held, namely, that ethnic attachments belong to the non-rational part of the human personality and, as such, are potentially destructive of civil society.[9] This notion suffers from two defects. One is that it ignores the possibility that an ethnic identity may be felt or adopted for rational as well as affective reasons to preserve one's existence or to pursue advantage through communal action. The second is the assumption that primordial attachments are more dangerous to civil order than other kinds of potential conflicts, presumably because of their highly emotive character. However, there is no empirical evidence to warrant the view either that primordial conflicts have produced more disruption in civil societies than economic, class conflicts or that the former conflicts are less amenable to compromise than the latter.

While many primordialists will concede that some aspects of culture are changeable and that the boundaries of ethnic groups may be shifted in the course of social and political movements that promote their interest, they stand firm on one point, namely, that ethnic groups properly so-called are groups based on distinctive cultures or origin myths or patterns of exchange with other groups that have core features that persist through time.[10] Even this bedrock position of the primordialists poses problems for the student of comparative ethnic movements. For one thing, while some ethnic groups do draw upon old and rich cultural heritages with a persisting core, many movements create their cultures after-the-fact, as it were. If, on the one hand, there are groups such as the Jewish people whose social and political identities have undergone innumerable transformations while a core culture has been retained and transmitted over the millennia by the rabbinate steeped in the Talmudic tradition and by ordinary believers following their daily 'self-defining routines',[11] there are sufficient examples of other groups whose core cultures are less easy to identify, but that have nevertheless formed a basis for cohesive and sometimes successful ethnic and nationalist movements. The mushroom growth of ethnic political movements in the United States in recent times provides at least a few examples of the latter sort that are more than ephemeral in nature.[12]

A second difficulty with the bedrock primordialist position is that, even where there is a persisting core culture, knowledge of its substance may not be of much use in predicting either the development or the form of ethnic movements on behalf of the cultural groups in question. Certainly a knowledge of the core religious cultures of orthodox Judaism or of traditional Islam in India would have suggested that the least likely possibilities would have been the rise of a Zionist movement or of the movement for the creation of Pakistan, for the traditional keepers of those cultures, the rabbinate and the ulema, have consistently argued that a secular national state is incompatible with either religion. Of course, both the rabbinate and the ulema have been largely responsible for the persistence of Jewish and Islamic communities wherever they have persisted, but they are communities differently defined and bounded than are Israel and Pakistan.

Do these criticisms of the primordialist perspective then mean that any cultural content should be removed entirely from the concept of ethnicity? Is ethnicity to be seen from the extreme instrumentalist point of view as the pursuit of interest and advantage for members of groups whose cultures are infinitely malleable and manipulable by élites? Are 'ethnic conflicts' merely 'one form in which interest conflicts between and within states are pursued',[13] and ethnicity 'a communal type of organization which is manipulated by an interest group in the course of its struggle to develop and maintain its power'?[14] And is culture change part of 'a bargaining process' that can be understood best in terms of a market model by which ethnic group leaders and members agree to give up aspects of their culture or modify their prejudices for the right price?[15] The statements just cited come from a literature that tends to treat cultural factors in ethnic movements as epiphenomenal. Abner Cohen in fact has written about groups that create cultural markers for purposes of internal communication with each other in secret societies and dominant cliques.[16]

The fact that new cultural groups can be created for purposes of economic and political domination, however, does not mean that the primordialist perspective is not relevant to our understanding of ethnic groups with long and rich cultural heritages. In other words, one possible route toward reconciling the perspectives of primordialists and instrumentalists may lie in simply recognizing that cultural groups differ in the strength and richness of their cultural traditions and even more importantly in the strength of traditional institutions and social structure. The persistence over time, for example, of religiously-based communal institutions among Jews and Muslims wherever they are found means that these cultural groups always form potential bases for ethnic movements. However, the mere persistence of the core religious traditions of such groups as these offers no prospect for predicting whether or when ethnic movements will arise among them and whether or not such movements will be effective in mobilizing their members. Such cultural persistence suggests only that it is likely that the groups can be mobilized on the basis of specific appeals and not others and that, when ethnic appeals are made, the pre-existing communal and educational institutions of the groups will, if made available for the purpose, provide an effective means of political mobilization. In short, the values and institutions of a persisting cultural group will suggest what appeals and symbols will be effective and what will not be and may also provide traditional avenues for the mobilization and organization of the group in new directions. Nevertheless, the leaders of ethnic movements invariably select from traditional cultures only those aspects that they think will serve to unite the group and that will be useful in promoting the interests of the group as they define them. When they do so, moreover, they affect the self-definition of the group and its boundaries, often to such an extent that the ethnic community or nationality created out of a pre-existing ethnic group may be a very different social formation from its progenitor. Or, in the case of groups that have had a sense of identity and community even before ethnic mobilization takes place and that contain élites whose traditional right to define the group and its boundaries are well-established, ethnic mobilization led by others than the traditional élites will introduce into the group conflicting definitions of its essence and extent.

Consequently, whether or not the culture of the group is ancient or is newly-fashioned, the study of ethnicity and nationality is in large part the study of politically induced cultural change. More precisely, it is the study of the process by which élites and counter-élites within ethnic groups select aspects of the group's culture, attach new value and meaning to them, and use them as symbols to mobilize the group, to defend its interests, and to compete with other groups. In this process, those élites have an advantage whose leaders can operate most skilfully in relation both to the deeply-felt primordial attachments of group members and the shifting relationships of politics.

The differences of viewpoint between primordialists and instrumentalists have also found expression among South Asia specialists in their efforts to interpret and explain ethnic and nationality movements there. The differences have been most pronounced in discussions of the origins and development of Muslim separatism and the Pakistan movement. From the primordialist point of view, which was also the view of the leaders of Muslim separatism, Hindus and Muslims constituted in pre-modern times distinct civilizations destined to develop into separate nations once political mobilization took place. The differences between the two cultures were so great that it was not conceivable that assimilation of the two could take place and that a single national culture could be created to which both would contribute. The contrary view is that the cultural and religious differences between Hindus and Muslims were not so great as to rule out the creation of either a composite national culture or at least a secular political union in which those aspects of group culture that could not be shared would be relegated to the private sphere. From this point of view, Muslim separatism was not pre-ordained, but resulted from the conscious manipulation of selected symbols of Muslim identity by Muslim élite groups in economic and political competition with each other and with élite groups among Hindus.[17]

This issue has recently been joined again in an exchange between Francis Robinson and me.[18] Although Robinson and I agree on many aspects of the Muslim separatist movement, an apparent difference persists concerning the relative weight to be assigned to the pervasiveness of Islamic values, to the strength of Muslim religious institutions, and to the extent to which a Muslim identity existed in the nineteenth century as constraining factors on the possibilities for Hindu–Muslim cooperation and on the freedom of Muslim élite groups to manipulate symbols of Muslim culture in the political process. Robinson argues that 'the religious differences' between Muslims and Hindus in the nineteenth century, before social mobilization began, 'were fundamental' and that some of those differences, such as on idol worship, on monotheism, and on attitudes toward the cow 'created a basic antipathy' between the two communities 'which helped to set them apart as modern politics and self-governing institutions developed in town, district and province.' The Muslims of Uttar Pradesh (UP), primed by these fundamental religious differences, already conscious of themselves as a separate community, and aware that they were a minority, 'feared that the Hindu majority would not only interfere with their religious practices such as cow-sacrifice, but also . . . would discriminate against them' on such matters 'as education and employment.'[19] In short, Hindus and Muslims in nineteenth-century India were separate religious communities predisposed towards, if not necessarily pre-ordained as, separate national groups. If it was not a foregone conclusion that Hindus and Muslims would go separate ways politically, it was unthinkable that the separate identities of either group could be subordinated or assimilated to the other.

Robinson's argument is not entirely inconsistent with the model developed in my *Language, Religion and Politics in North India* which, although it emphasized the roles played by élite groups in manipulating cultural symbols to create political identities, did not ignore either pre-existing cultural values or intergroup attitudes as factors influencing the ability of élites to manipulate particular symbols. In fact, the model developed in *Language, Religion and Politics* did not take off from an extreme instrumentalist perspective or from the assumption that either élites or the groups whose interests they claim to represent are cultural blank slates. Rather, it began with the following question: Given the existence in a multi-ethnic society of an array of cultural distinctions among peoples and of actual and potential cultural conflicts among them, what factors are critical in determining which of those distinctions, if any, will be used to build political identities? In the model developed in *Language, Religion and Politics*, the factors emphasized were the roles played by particular élite groups, the balance between rates of social mobilization and assimilation between ethnic groups, the building of political organizations to promote group ident-ities and interests, and the influence of government policies. However, it was not assumed that the pre-existing cultures or religious practices of ethnic groups are infinitely malleable by élites.

['Élite Groups, Symbol Manipulation and Ethnic Identity among the Muslims of South Asia', in *Political Identity in South Asia*, ed. David Taylor and Malcolm Yapp (Curzon Press: London, 1979), 35–43: reprinted in Paul R. Brass, *Ethnicity and Nationalism: Theory and Comparison* (New Delhi: Sage, 1991), 69–108.]

BENEDICT ANDERSON

14 Imagined Communities

Before proceeding to a discussion of the specific origins of nationalism, it may be useful to recapitulate the main propositions put forward thus far. Essentially, I have been arguing that the very possibility of imagining the nation only arose historically when, and where, three fundamental cultural conceptions, all of great antiquity, lost their axiomatic grip on men's minds. The first of these was the idea that a particular script-language offered privil-eged access to ontological truth, precisely because it was an inseparable part of that truth. It was this idea that called into being the great transcontinental sodalities of Christendom, the Ummah Islam, and the rest. Second was the belief that society was naturally organized around and under high centres—monarchs who were persons apart from other human beings and who ruled by some form of cosmological (divine) dispensation. Human loyalties were necessarily hierarchical and centripetal because the ruler, like the sacred script, was a node of access to being and inherent in it. Third was a conception of temporality in which cosmology and history were indistinguishable, the orig-ins of the world and of men essentially identical. Combined, these ideas rooted human lives firmly in the very nature of things, giving certain meaning to the everyday fatalities of existence (above all death, loss, and servitude) and offer-ing, in various ways, redemption from them.

The slow, uneven decline of these interlinked certainties, first in Western Europe, later elsewhere, under the impact of economic change, 'discoveries' (social and scientific), and the development of increasingly rapid communica-tions, drove a harsh wedge between cosmology and history. No surprise then that the search was on, so to speak, for a new way of linking fraternity, power and time meaningfully together. Nothing perhaps more precipitated this search, nor made it more fruitful, than print-capitalism, which made it possible for rapidly growing numbers of people to think about themselves, and to relate themselves to others, in profoundly new ways.

If the development of print-as-commodity is the key to the generation of wholly new ideas of simultaneity, still, we are simply at the point where communities of the type 'horizontal-secular, transverse-time' become possible. Why, within that type, did the nation become so popular? The factors involved are obviously complex and various. But a strong case can be made for the primacy of capitalism.

As already noted, at least 20,000,000 books had already been printed by 1500,[1] signalling the onset of Benjamin's 'age of mechanical reproduction.' If manuscript knowledge was scarce and arcane lore, print knowledge lived by reproducibility and dissemination.[2] If, as Febvre and Martin believe, possibly as many as 200,000,000 volumes had been manufactured by 1600, it is no wonder that Francis Bacon believed that print had changed 'the appearance and state of the world.'[3]

One of the earlier forms of capitalist enterprise, book-publishing felt all of capitalism's restless search for markets. The early printers established branches all over Europe: 'in this way a veritable "international" of publishing houses, which ignored national [sic] frontiers, was created.'[4] And since the years 1500–1550 were a period of exceptional European prosperity, publishing shared in the general boom. 'More than at any other time' it was 'a great industry under the control of wealthy capitalists.'[5] Naturally, 'book-sellers were primarily concerned to make a profit and to sell their products, and consequently they sought out first and foremost those works which were of interest to the largest possible number of their contemporaries.'[6]

The initial market was literate Europe, a wide but thin stratum of Latin-readers. Saturation of this market took about 150 years. The determinative fact about Latin—aside from its sacrality—was that it was a language of bilinguals. Relatively few were born to speak it and even fewer, one imagines, dreamed in it. In the sixteenth century the proportion of bilinguals within the total population of Europe was quite small; very likely no larger than the proportion in the world's population today, and—proletarian internationalism notwithstanding—in the centuries to come. Then and now the vast bulk of mankind is monoglot. The logic of capitalism thus meant that once the elite Latin market was saturated, the potentially huge markets represented by the monoglot masses would beckon. To be sure, the Counter-Reformation encouraged a temporary resurgence of Latin-publishing, but by the mid-seventeenth century the movement was in decay, and fervently Catholic libraries replete. Meantime, a Europe-wide shortage of money made printers think more and more of peddling cheap editions in the vernaculars.[7]

The revolutionary vernacularizing thrust of capitalism was given further impetus by three extraneous factors, two of which contributed directly to the rise of national consciousness. The first, and ultimately the least important, was a change in the character of Latin itself. Thanks to the labours of the Humanists in reviving the broad literature of pre-Christian antiquity and spreading it through the print-market, a new appreciation of the sophisticated stylistic achievements of the ancients was apparent among the trans-European intelligentsia. The Latin they now aspired to write became more and more Ciceronian, and, by the same token, increasingly removed from ecclesiastical and everyday life. In this way it acquired an esoteric quality quite different from that of Church Latin in mediaeval times. For the older Latin was not arcane because of its subject matter or style, but simply because it was written at all, i.e. because of its status as *text*. Now it became arcane because of what was written, because of the language-in-itself.

Second was the impact of the Reformation, which, at the same time, owed much of its success to print-capitalism. Before the age of print, Rome easily won every war against heresy in Western Europe because it always had better internal lines of communication than its challengers. But when in 1517 Martin Luther nailed his theses to the chapel-door in Wittenberg, they were printed up in German translation, and 'within 15 days [had been] seen in every part of the country.'[8] In the two decades 1520–1540 three times as many books were published in German as in the period 1500–1520, an astonishing transformation to which Luther was absolutely central. His works represented no less than one third of *all* German-language books sold between 1518 and 1525. Between 1522 and 1546, a total of 430 editions (whole or partial) of his Biblical translations appeared. 'We have here for the first time a truly mass readership and a popular literature within everybody's reach.'[9] In effect, Luther became the first best-selling author *so known*. Or, to put it another way, the first writer who could 'sell' his *new* books on the basis of his name.[10]

Where Luther led, others quickly followed, opening the colossal religious propaganda war that raged across Europe for the next century. In this titanic 'battle for men's minds', Protestantism was always fundamentally on the offensive, precisely because it knew how to make use of the expanding vernacular print-market being created by capitalism, while the Counter-Reformation defended the citadel of Latin. The emblem for this is the Vatican's *Index Librorum Prohibitorum*—to which there was no Protestant counterpart—a novel catalogue made necessary by the sheer volume of printed subversion. Nothing gives a better sense of this siege mentality than François I's panicked 1535 ban on the printing of *any* books in his realm—on pain of death by hanging! The reason for both the ban and its unenforceability was that by then his realm's eastern borders were ringed with Protestant states and cities producing a massive stream of smugglable print. To take Calvin's Geneva alone: between 1533 and 1540 only 42 editions were published there, but the numbers swelled to 527 between 1550 and 1564, by which latter date no less than 40 separate printing-presses were working overtime.[11]

The coalition between Protestantism and print-capitalism, exploiting cheap popular editions, quickly created large new reading publics—not least among merchants and women, who typically knew little or no Latin—and simultaneously mobilized them for politico-religious purposes. Inevitably, it was not merely the Church that was shaken to its core. The same earthquake produced Europe's first important non-dynastic, non-city states in the Dutch Republic and the Commonwealth of the Puritans. (François I's panic was as much political as religious.)

Third was the slow, geographically uneven, spread of particular vernaculars as instruments of administrative centralization by certain well-positioned would-be absolutist monarchs. Here it is useful to remember that the universality of Latin in mediaeval Western Europe never corresponded to a universal political system. The contrast with Imperial China, where the reach of the mandarinal bureaucracy and of painted characters largely coincided, is instructive. In effect, the political fragmentation of Western Europe after the collapse of the Western Empire meant that no sovereign could monopolize Latin and make it his-and-only-his language-of-state, and thus Latin's religious authority never had a true political analogue.

The birth of administrative vernaculars predated both print and the religious upheaval of the sixteenth century, and must therefore be regarded (at least initially) as an independent factor in the erosion of the sacred imagined community. At the same time, nothing suggests that any deep-seated ideological, let alone proto-national, impulses underlay this vernacularization where it occurred. The case of 'England'—on the northwestern periphery of Latin Europe—is here especially enlightening. Prior to the Norman Conquest, the language of the court, literary and administrative, was Anglo-Saxon. For the next century and a half virtually all royal documents were composed in Latin. Between about 1200 and 1350 this state-Latin was superseded by Norman French. In the meantime, a slow fusion between this language of a foreign ruling class and the Anglo-Saxon of the subject population produced Early English. The fusion made it possible for the new language to take its turn, after 1362, as the language of the courts—and for the opening of Parliament. Wycliffe's vernacular *manuscript* Bible followed in 1382.[12] It is essential to bear in mind that this sequence was a series of 'state,' not 'national,' languages; and that the state concerned covered at various times not only today's England and Wales, but also portions of Ireland, Scotland *and France*. Obviously, huge elements of the subject populations knew little or nothing of Latin, Norman French, or Early English.[13] Not till almost a century *after* Early English's political enthronement was London's power swept out of 'France'.

On the Seine, a similar movement took place, if at a slower pace. As Bloch wrily puts it, 'French, that is to say a language which, since it was regarded as merely a corrupt form of Latin, took several centuries to raise itself to literary dignity',[14] only became the official language of the courts of justice in 1539, when François I issued the Edict of Villers-Cotterêts.[15] In other dynastic realms Latin survived much longer—under the Habsburgs well into the nineteenth century. In still others, 'foreign' vernaculars took over: in the eighteenth century the languages of the Romanov court were French and German.[16]

In every instance, the 'choice' of language appears as a gradual, unselfconscious, pragmatic, not to say haphazard development. As such, it was utterly different from the self-conscious language policies pursued by nineteenth-century dynasts confronted with the rise of hostile popular linguistic-nationalisms. [. . .] One clear sign of the difference is that the old administrative languages were *just that*: languages used by and for officialdoms for their own inner convenience. There was no idea of systematically imposing the language on the dynasts' various subject populations.[17] Nonetheless, the elevation of these vernaculars to the status of languages-of-power, where, in one sense, they were competitors with Latin (French in Paris, [Early] English in London), made its own contribution to the decline of the imagined community of Christendom.

At bottom, it is likely that the esotericization of Latin, the Reformation, and the haphazard development of administrative vernaculars are significant, in the present context, primarily in a negative sense—in their contributions to the dethronement of Latin and the erosion of the sacred community of Christendom. It is quite possible to conceive of the emergence of the new imagined national communities without any one, perhaps all, of them being present. What, in a positive sense, made the new communities imaginable was a half-fortuitous, but explosive, interaction between a system of production and productive relations (capitalism), a technology of communications (print), and the fatality of human linguistic diversity.[18]

The element of fatality is essential. For whatever superhuman feats capitalism was capable of, it found in death and languages two tenacious adversaries.[19] Particular languages can die or be wiped out, but there was and is no possibility of man's general linguistic unification. Yet this mutual incomprehensibility was historically of only slight importance until capitalism and print created monoglot mass reading publics.

While it is essential to keep in mind an idea of fatality, in the sense of a *general* condition of irremediable linguistic diversity, it would be a mistake to equate this fatality with that common element in nationalist ideologies which stresses the primordial fatality of *particular* languages and their association with *particular* territorial units. The essential thing is the *interplay* between fatality, technology, and capitalism. In pre-print Europe, and, of course, elsewhere in the world, the diversity of spoken languages, those languages that for their speakers were (and are) the warp and woof of their lives, was immense; so immense, indeed, that had print-capitalism sought to exploit each potential

oral vernacular market, it would have remained a capitalism of petty proportions. But these varied idiolects were capable of being assembled, within
definite limits, into print-languages far fewer in number. The very arbitrariness
of any system of signs for sounds facilitated the assembling process.[20] (At the
same time, the more ideographic the signs, the vaster the potential assembling
zone. One can detect a sort of descending hierarchy here from algebra through
Chinese and English, to the regular syllabaries of French or Indonesian.)
Nothing served to 'assemble' related vernaculars more than capitalism, which,
within the limits imposed by grammars and syntaxes, created mechanically-
reproduced print-languages, capable of dissemination through the market.[21]

These print-languages laid the bases for national consciousnesses in three
distinct ways. First and foremost, they created unified fields of exchange and
communications below Latin and above the spoken vernaculars. Speakers of
the huge variety of Frenches, Englishes, or Spanishes, who might find it
difficult or even impossible to understand one another in conversation, became capable of comprehending one another via print and paper. In the
process, they gradually became aware of the hundreds of thousands, even
millions, of people in their particular language-field, and at the same time that
only those hundreds of thousands, or millions, so belonged. These fellow-
readers, to whom they were connected through print, formed, in their secular,
particular, visible invisibility, the embryo of the nationally-imagined community.

Second, print-capitalism gave a new fixity to language, which in the long run
helped to build that image of antiquity so central to the subjective idea of the
nation. As Febvre and Martin remind us, the printed book kept a permanent
form, capable of virtually infinite reproduction, temporally and spatially. It was
no longer subject to the individualizing and 'unconsciously modernizing'
habits of monastic scribes. Thus, while twelfth-century French differed markedly from that written by Villon in the fifteenth, the rate of change slowed
decisively in the sixteenth. 'By the 17th century languages in Europe had
generally assumed their modern forms.'[22] To put it another way, for now three
centuries these stabilized print-languages have been gathering a darkening
varnish; the words of our seventeenth-century forebears are accessible to us in
a way that his twelfth-century ancestors were not to Villon.

Third, print-capitalism created languages-of-power of a kind different from
the older administrative vernaculars. Certain dialects inevitably were 'closer'
to each print-language and dominated their final forms. Their disadvantaged
cousins, still assimilable to the emerging print-language, lost caste, above all
because they were unsuccessful (or only relatively successful) in insisting on
their own print-form. 'Northwestern German' became Platt Deutsch, a largely
spoken, thus sub-standard German, because it was assimilable to print-German
in a way that Bohemian spoken-Czech was not. High German, the King's
English, and, later, Central Thai, were correspondingly elevated to a new

politico-cultural eminence. (Hence the struggles in late-twentieth-century Europe for certain 'sub-'nationalities to change their subordinate status by breaking firmly into print—and radio.)

It remains only to emphasize that in their origins, the fixing of print-languages and the differentiation of status between them were largely unself-conscious processes resulting from the explosive interaction between capitalism, technology and human linguistic diversity. But as with so much else in the history of nationalism, once 'there,' they could become formal models to be imitated, and, where expedient, consciously exploited in a Machiavellian spirit. Today, the Thai government actively discourages attempts by foreign missionaries to provide its hill-tribe minorities with their own transcription-systems and to develop publications in their own languages: the same government is largely indifferent to what these minorities *speak*. The fate of the Turkic-speaking peoples in the zones incorporated into today's Turkey, Iran, Iraq, and the USSR is especially exemplary. A family of spoken languages, once everywhere assemblable, thus comprehensible, within an Arabic orthography, has lost that unity as a result of conscious manipulations. To heighten Turkish-Turkey's national consciousness at the expense of any wider Islamic identification, Atatürk imposed compulsory romanization.[23] The Soviet authorities followed suit, first with an anti-Islamic, anti-Persian compulsory romanization, then, in Stalin's 1930s, with a Russifying compulsory Cyrillicization.[24]

We can summarize the conclusions to be drawn from the argument [. . .] by saying that the convergence of capitalism and print technology on the fatal diversity of human language created the possibility of a new form of imagined community, which in its basic morphology set the stage for the modern nation. The potential stretch of these communities was inherently limited, and, at the same time, bore none but the most fortuitous relationship to existing political boundaries (which were, on the whole, the highwater marks of dynastic expansionisms).

Yet it is obvious that while today almost all modern self-conceived nations—and also nation-states—have 'national print-languages,' many of them have these languages in common, and in others only a tiny fraction of the population 'uses' the national language in conversation or on paper. The nation-states of Spanish America or those of the 'Anglo-Saxon family' are conspicuous examples of the first outcome; many ex-colonial states, particularly in Africa, of the second. In other words, the concrete formation of contemporary nation-states is by no means isomorphic with the determinate reach of particular print-languages. To account for the discontinuity-in-connectedness between print-languages, national consciousness, and nation-states, it is necessary to turn to the large cluster of new political entities that sprang up in the Western hemisphere between 1776 and 1838, all of which self-consciously defined themselves as nations, and, with the interesting exception of Brazil, as (non-dynastic) republics. For not only were they historically the first such states to emerge on the world stage, and therefore inevitably provided the first real models of what such states should 'look like,' but their numbers and contemporary births offer fruitful ground for comparative enquiry.

[*Imagined Communities* (Verso: London, 1991), 36–46.]

PIERRE VAN DEN BERGHE

15 A Socio-Biological Perspective

The most basic question asked by sociobiology as well as sociology is: why are animals social, that is, why do they cooperate? Why are some species more social than others? The answer was long intuitively known: animals are social to the extent that cooperation is mutually beneficial. What sociobiology does is supply the main genetic mechanism for animal sociality, namely *kin selection* to maximize *inclusive* fitness. Natural selection operates through differential reproduction. Different alleles of the same gene compete with each other, and the ones that are carried by the more reproductively successful individuals have a greater probability of being replicated in the population's next generation. The successful alleles are the ones which, in a given environment, favor the reproductive success or 'fitness' of their carriers.

The great theoretical contribution of sociobiology has been to extend the concept of fitness to that of 'inclusive fitness'.[1] Indeed, an animal can duplicate its genes directly through its own reproduction, or indirectly through the reproduction of relatives with which it shares specific proportions of genes. Animals, therefore, can be expected to behave cooperatively, and thereby enhance each other's fitness to the extent that they are genetically related. This is what is meant by kin selection.[2] Animals, in short, are nepotistic, i.e. they prefer kin over non-kin, and close kin over distant kin. This may happen consciously, as in humans, or, more commonly, unconsciously. Kin selection does not presuppose consciousness in order to be operative.

The propensity to be 'altruistic,' i.e. to contribute to alter's fitness at the expense of ego's fitness, is directly proportional not only to the coefficient of relatedness between ego and alter, but also to the benefit/cost ratio of the altruistic act. To use a human example, a post-menopausal mother could be expected to sacrifice her life more readily for a young adult child about to reproduce than a young mother to forego her life for the benefit of her first foetus. The genetic relationship is the same in both cases (namely, one half), but the fitness cost is low in the first case, high in the second. Altruism, then, is directed mostly at kin, especially close kin, and is, in fact, a misnomer. It represents the ultimate form of genetic selfishness. It is but the blind expression of inclusive fitness maximization. In fact, a simple formula leads one to predict that 'altruism' can be expected if the cost/benefit ratio of the transaction is smaller than the coefficient of relatedness between alter and ego.

There is no reason to doubt that kin selection is a powerful cement of sociality in humans as it is in other animals. Yet, it is also clear that kin selection does not explain all of human sociality. There are, in my view, two additional bases of human sociality: reciprocity and coercion. Rudimentary forms of these are also present in many animals, but human forms of reciprocity and coercion greatly over-shadow in complexity and importance anything we know in other species. Not surprisingly, therefore, even the simplest and smallest human societies, though far less 'perfect' than those of the social insects (termites, ants, bees, wasps), are much more complex than those of any other known species. Reciprocity is cooperation for mutual benefit, and with expectation of return, and it can operate between kin or between non-kin. Coercion is the use of force for one-sided benefit, that is, for purposes of intra-specific parasitism or predation. All human societies continue to be organized on the basis of all three principles of sociality: kin selection, reciprocity, and coercion. However, the larger and the more complex a society becomes, the greater the importance of reciprocity, and, with the emergence of the state, coercion becomes in relation to kin selection.

This is the barest sketch of an argument which [. . .] seeks to reduce individual behavior, social structure and cultural superstructure to the competition for scarce resources between individual organisms, each one acting, consciously or unconsciously, to maximize its gains or minimize its losses. This view of human affairs is sufficiently at variance with much of contemporary social science to arouse passionate rejection as a return to simplistic instinct theory, biological reductionism, speculative evolutionism, social Darwinism, racism, hereditarianism, and so on. [. . .] Suffice it to say that sociobiology is indeed reductionist (as all modern science), evolutionist (as all modern biology), and materialist (as much good social science), but that it is emphatically not a return to social Darwinism, instinct theories or racism, and that it does not belittle the importance of environmental factors, the unique characteristics of *Homo sapiens*, and the significance of human culture. It merely asserts in the most undogmatic fashion that human behavior is the product of a long process of adaptive evolution that involved the complex interplay of genotypical, ecological and cultural factors.

How do these prolegomena relate to race and ethnicity? My central thesis is that both ethnicity and 'race' (in the social sense) are, in fact, extensions of the idiom of kinship, and that, therefore, ethnic and race sentiments are to be understood as an extended and attenuated form of kin selection. Class relations, on the other hand, are in the realm of reciprocity, and are therefore of a fundamentally different nature. In more general form, I am suggesting that there are two broad types of human collectivities: the ones that I shall call Type I tend to be ascriptive, defined by common descent, generally hereditary, and often endogamous, and those of Type II that are joined in the defense of common interests. Type I includes racial, caste and ethnic groups, while Type II encompasses such varied associations as trade unions, political parties, professional bodies, sports clubs, neighborhood groups, parent-teacher associations, and so on. Empirically, of course, a group may have mixed characteristics, as an ethnically-based political party, or a hereditary occupational guild. Nevertheless, in their ideal-typical form, each kind of group has a clearly distinct basis of solidarity: kinship and interest respectively.

Type I groups are generally preferentially or prescriptively endogamous, but internally subdivided into exogamous kin groups: nuclear families, lineages, clans, kindreds. Indeed, until the last few thousand years of human history, Type I groups were synonymous with human societies. They were small in-bred populations of a few hundred individuals, prototypical 'tribes' that regarded themselves as 'the people', sharing common descent, real or putative, and as children of the mythical founder couple or creator god. Members of the tribe, though subdivided into smaller kin groups, saw themselves as a single people, solidary against the outside world, and interlinked by a web of kinship and marriage making the tribe in fact a superfamily. A high rate of inbreeding insured that most spouses were also kinsmen. The cultural inventions of unilineal descent and lineage exogamy permitted the extension of that primordial model of social organization to much larger societies running into the tens of thousands of people, and yet where Type II organizations were almost totally absent (with the exception of age sets).

Ethnic groups, for nearly all of human history, were what geneticists call breeding populations, in-breeding superfamilies, in fact, which not only were much more closely related to each other than to even their closest neighbors, but which, almost without exception, explicitly recognized that fact, and maintained clear territorial and social boundaries with other such ethnic groups. This is, of course, not to deny that migration, conquest, and interbreeding took place with some regularity, and thus that the common ancestry of 'the people' was always partially fictive. But this was also true of smaller kin groups: the *pater* is not necessarily the *progenitor*. That the extended kinship of the ethnic group was sometimes putative rather than real was not the important point. Just as in the smaller kin units, the kinship was real often enough to become the basis of these powerful sentiments we call nationalism, tribalism, racism, and ethnocentrism. The ease and speed with which these sentiments can be mobilized even in modern industrial societies where they have to compete with many Type II groups, the blind ferocity of the conflicts to which these sentiments can lead, the imperviousness of such sentiments to rational arguments are but a few indications of their continued vitality and their primordiality.

What I am suggesting is that ethnocentrism evolved during millions, or at least hundreds of thousands of years as an extension of kin selection. Reciprocity was also involved, especially in the exchange of women in marriage, but as spouses were typically also kinsmen there was no sharp distinction between kin selection and reciprocity. As hominids became increasingly formidable competitors and predators to their own and closely related species, there was a strong selective pressure for the formation of larger and more powerful groups. Group size in hunting and gathering societies was, of course, severely constrained by ecological factors, but, still, there was an obvious selective advantage for kin groups to form those solidary superfamilies we call tribes; this, in turn, as Bigelow[3] so clearly argues, necessarily meant organizing *against* other competing groups, and therefore maintaining and defending ethnic boundaries.

Of Type II groups, little needs to be said here. With the exception of age sets, they tend to be characteristic of larger, more complex, state-organized societies, and therefore to have arisen much later in human evolution, and to be more exclusively cultural. They are, of course, also important, especially in industrial societies, but they are not primordial, they can be more readily formed and disbanded, they are more amenable to cool, rational calculations of interest, and they do not as readily unleash orgies of passion. Nor, of course, have they stamped out Type I groups. Another fundamental difference between Type I and Type II groups is that the former tend to be mutually exclusive in membership and thus to form the basis of most primary relationships, while the latter are segmental, and non-mutually exclusive. Millions of people in individual societies belong to a multiplicity of Type II groups, few of which involve them very deeply or permanently. Some people are ethnically alienated, marginal or mobile or they are the product of mixed marriages, but most people belong to a single ethnic group or sub-group, and remain there for life. Even allowing for all the complications of the real world, and the existence of mixed-type groups, the categorical distinction remains nevertheless quite striking.

Let us return to Type I groups, our special concern here. I have suggested that they evolved as an extension of kin selection, and thus probably have a partial biological basis, in the same sense as human kinship systems are rooted in biology. This contention is, of course, hotly contested by anthropologists such as Sahlins,[4] who counter that human kinship is cultural, not biological. Almost every aspect of human behavior takes a cultural form, from sneezing and defecating to writing poetry and riding a motorcycle. But this is not to say that some of these things do not *also* have a biological basis. I am definitely not arguing that we have a gene for ethnocentrism, or for recognizing kin; rather I am arguing that those societies that institutionalized norms of nepotism and ethnocentrism had a strong selective advantage over those that did not (assuming that any such ever existed), because kin selection has been the basic blueprint for animal sociality. To explain the universality of ethnocentrism and kinship organization in human societies by invoking culture is completely question begging. Culture is merely a *proximate* explanation of why people behave ethnocentrically and nepotistically. As every ethnographer knows, when natives are asked why they behave a certain way, they answer: because it is the custom. The anthropologist then translates: because of his culture; the sociologist says: because he has been socialized into the norms of his society; and the psychologist counters: because of his learning experiences. All of them are right as far as they go, but none of them has explained why all human societies practice kin selection and are ethnocentric.

So far, I have stressed ethnicity rather than race or caste in my treatment of Type I groups. Caste is a very special case, limited, even if one adopts a wide definition of the term, to highly differentiated, stratified societies, and may be considered an extreme case of the grafting of the principle of occupational specialization into what is basically a Type I group. Castes are not unique in being occupationally specialized Type I groups. Ethnic and racial groups also tend to become so.[5] Castes are merely extreme cases of occupational specialization linked with rigid endogamy and hierarchization.

Race is a different matter. First, I should make it clear that, even though I have presented a partially biological argument, I am most emphatically *not* using the word 'race' in the sense of a sub-species of *Homo sapiens*. Instead, I mean by 'race' the social definition which it is variously ascribed in different societies. Social race typically seizes on biologically trivial phenotypes, and, equally typically, corresponds only very imperfectly with genetically isolated populations. It thus has no intrinsic biological significance, as indicated by the fact that only a few of the world's societies use primarily morphological phenotypes to define themselves, and to differentiate outsiders.

At first blush, this would seem to invalidate my argument that ethnic and racial sentiments represent an extension of kin selection. If that is the case, why should most human societies seize primarily on such obviously culturally transmitted traits such as language and dialect, religious beliefs, dress, hair styles, manners, scarifications, and the like as badges of group recognition and membership? If the name of the game is to identify kinsmen in order to enhance one's inclusive fitness, then why are not inherited physical characteristics chosen as recognition signals, rather than acquired cultural traits? Sometimes, of course, morphological phenotypes such as skin color, facial features, stature, hair texture, eye color, and so on are used, not only to define group membership, but also, within the group, as tests of ever-questionable paternity. Generally, however, cultural criteria of membership are far more salient than physical ones, if the latter are used at all. Societies that stress physical phenotypes more than cultural traits are exceptional. Why?

The answer must again be sought in our evolutionary history. Until the last few millennia, that is, until the rise of conquest states, sudden, large-scale, human migration was rare, and human breeding populations were small. There was migration and interbreeding, but on an individual scale, and mostly between neighboring groups. The result was that neighboring populations were typically not sharply discontinuous in their genetic composition. The relative proportions of alleles of the same gene often constituted a gradient as one travelled through several breeding populations. Eye color in Europe would be a good example. The further north one goes, from, say, Sicily to Sweden, the higher the proportion of lightly pigmented eyes. Yet, at no point in the journey is there a noticeable discontinuity. Eye color, therefore, is a poor criterion of national membership in Europe. Indeed, it varies much more *within* national groups, and indeed even within families, than *between* groups.

Now, Europeans do use some morphological phenotypes to distinguish various ethnic groups. They speak loosely of 'Nordic', 'Mediterranean', 'Jewish', and so on, types. In the absence of any other clue, probabilistic guesses are often made on the basis of physical appearance as to a stranger's ethnic origin. Most groups probably have what Hoetink termed a 'somatic norm image,'[6] that is, a mental picture of what a model group member looks like. The point, however, is that morphological phenotypes tend to be used either in the absence of more reliable cultural clues (such as language), or when physical appearance is widely discrepant from the somatic norm image (as, for instance, in Europe with Asians or Africans).

A good test of group membership for the purpose of assessing kin relatedness must meet the basic requirement of discriminating more reliably *between* groups than *within* groups. That is, the criterion chosen must show more *inter*group than *intra*-group variance. Until recently, cultural criteria met that condition far more reliably than physical ones. The problem was for small groups to distinguish themselves from their immediate neighbors, not with unknown populations thousands of kilometers away. Even the most trivial differences of accent, dialect, vocabulary, body adornment, and so on, could be used far more reliably to assess *biological* relatedness or unrelatedness than any physical phenotype.[7] Therefore, whatever test was easiest to apply and correlated best with kin relatedness was used. That the correlation was spurious did not matter. What mattered was that it discriminated accurately.

This theory accounts not only for the general prevalence of cultural diacritica in assessing group membership. It also accounts for the appearance of racism when and where it does occur better than any competing theory. The kin selection argument predicts that physical criteria *will* be salient to the extent that they do a good and easy job of discriminating kin and non-kin. This obviously occurs in the aftermath of large-scale, long-distance migration, whether through conquest, incursions, slavery, indenture, or voluntary immigration. The colonial expansion of Europe beginning some five centuries ago, and all of the massive population transfers it brought in its wake are, of course, the overwhelmingly important genetic event of our species. Predictably, it brought about a great surge in racism, because all of a sudden, it became possible to make a fairly accurate kin selection judgment from a distance of several hundred meters. The Dutchman at the Cape, the Portuguese in Brazil, the Englishman in Kenya did not have to ask questions and pick up subtle clues of accent to detect kin relatedness. By using a simple test of skin pigmentation he could literally shoot and ask questions later at little risk of killing a kinsman. [. . .]

We suggested at the outset that there were three main mechanisms of human sociality: kin selection, reciprocity and coercion. Ethnic and racial groups command our unreasoned loyalty because they are in fact, or at least in theory, superfamilies. But ethnic and race relations are not only relations of cooperation and amity with the in-group; they are equally importantly relations of competition and conflict between groups. While intra-group relations are primarily dictated by kin selection, real or putative, intergroup relations are typically antagonistic. Occasionally, ethnic groups may enter a symbiotic, mutually beneficial relationship based, for instance, on the exploitation of two specialized and noncompetitive niches in the same habitat. Relations between some pastoralist and sedentary groups are of this type. More commonly, there is open competition for, and conflict over scarce resources, and not infrequently the establishment of multi-ethnic states dominated by one ethnic group at the expense of others. Coercion then becomes the basis of interethnic (or inter-racial) relations.

Unlike kin selection and reciprocity which require no justification because they contribute to the fitness of all actors in the system, coercion, which leads to asymmetrical parasitism, often does attempt to legitimate itself. Interestingly, there are but two basic ideologies in support of coercion. One seeks to disguise coercion as kin selection, and here we have the many brands of paternalism and familism that have been used to justify nearly all pre-industrial forms of despotism. The other attempts to present coercion as reciprocity and exchange, it is characteristic of the various 'democratic' ideologies of industrial societies in the last two centuries, from liberalism to socialism. Why this ideological shift from paternalism to *liberté, égalité, fraternité* in justifying tyranny during the last two centuries?

Perhaps this ideological shift reflects in part the increasing incorporation of small nation-states into multi-national states. Paternalism is a peculiarly well suited ideology for the small, ethnically homogeneous nation-state. Not surprisingly, it was independently reinvented in societies as far distant as China, Japan, Inca Peru, Tzarist Russia, Ancient Egypt, Ottoman Turkey, Renaissance Europe and countless African kingdoms. Paternalism works in monoethnic states because the very concept of the nation is an extension of kin selection. For the same reason, it breaks down in multi-ethnic states. It was one thing for the Japanese peasant to look on his emperor as a divine super-father, the living incarnation of Nippon, quite another for the Hindu peasant to regard that polluted beef eater, Queen Victoria, as the living symbol of Mother India. An ideology based on reciprocity, on the other hand, can transcend ethnic boundaries. It is therefore a suitable one for the 90 per cent of the world's states which are multi-ethnic conglomerates, and, furthermore, being ethnically neutral, it exports remarkably well as revolutionary ideology. It is no accident that France launched into the most imperialistic phase of its history immediately after the Revolution.

The ideas sketched here are still tentative. They do not so much supplant other theories of ethnicity and race as supplement them by putting them in the broader context of evolutionary thinking. They do not purport to explain everything about these phenomena; they do not predict detailed historical occurrences, nor account for subtle cultural differences. They do, however, suggest parsimonious hypotheses to account for features of race and ethnicity which had hitherto remained elusive and problematic. Their plausibility to the reader hinges on whether he accepts the most fundamental paradigm for the evolution of different life forms and societal organization on our planet, Darwinian evolutionary theory, and on whether he is willing to apply that enormously successful model to our own species, or prefers to invoke an act of special creation for mankind.

['Race and Ethnicity: A Sociobiological Perspective', *Ethnic and Racial Studies*, 1/4 (1978), 402–7, 409–11.]

JOHN BREUILLY
....
16 The Sources of Nationalist Ideology

A major problem in modern political thought concerns the relationship between state and society. Each seemed on its way to becoming a self-contained sphere. The growth of a free-market economy extending beyond individual states gave rise to ideas about society as a 'private', largely self-regulating set of activities. The growth of bureaucratic absolutism gave rise to the idea of an enlightened state detached from society which it ruled according to rational norms.

This is a very different problem from that concerning the relationship between a government and its subjects. Such a relationship is set wholly 'within' the sphere of politics. One conception of the nation—that is, of the nation as the body of citizens—remains inside that wholly political framework, even if some implicit reference to cultural identity is involved.[1] But the problem of the relationship between society and state concerns the nature of the connection between politics and non-politics. Obviously state and society are not really separate from one another and they are abstractions employed to make sense of complex human affairs. But they seem unavoidable abstractions in the modern world; they have to be given definition and content, and the nature of their relationship with one another has to be established.

One way of doing this is to subordinate one of the categories, state or society, to the other. The most influential accounts, liberal and Marxist, tended to subordinate state to society. The nature of the state and of political conflict was derived from society through concepts such as the social contract or the class struggle. Others, such as Hobbes, sought to deny that society had any independent structure without political order or, like Hegel, regarded the state as the realm of universal values far beyond the petty and sectional concerns of civil society. But, except in certain utopian visions, the sense of an enduring distinction between the two spheres of state and society, and of the problem of their relationship, could never be set aside.

All these various approaches to the problem accepted the distinction and the difficulties it raised, and tried to provide general, rational answers. But from a conservative position the attempt at a general and rational understanding of human affairs itself came under attack. This attack was taken up in a polemical form by Burke in his objections to the pretensions of the French revolutionaries. He believed that their claims to be able to outline an ideal social and political order on the basis of universal reason and then to act politically in order to realise it were based on a false view of what human beings could understand and do. Burke insisted that each society is particular and highly complicated. Human understanding was limited, and, therefore, deliberate interference in the complex web of human affairs which had built up imperceptibly over a long period of time should also be limited. 'The nature of man is intricate; the objects of society are of the greatest possible complexity; and therefore no simple disposition or direction of power can be suitable either to man's nature or the quality of his affairs.'[2]

This set a limit on human reason which went beyond the traditional conservative ideas about man's moral failings. But the advance of 'reason' and the great claims made for rational forces such as the modern state, or the market economy, required an even stronger rebuttal. Burke had simply argued that society was opaque. Far more radical was the argument that each society was unique. From this argument the distinctive features of nationalist ideology were to be derived.

I shall call this idea of uniqueness historicism. A brief review of one German writer, Herder (1744–1803), will supply the principal features of this argument. This is not to suggest that Herder was the first or the only one to advance these ideas, or that he was himself a nationalist. In fact the historicist case had been put earlier and more originally by the Italian writer Vico. Other German thinkers of the late eighteenth century developed historicist ideas. Herder's own political values, such as they were, if anything contradicted his historicist position and cannot be described as nationalist. However, he developed historicist ideas in a particularly striking way and linked them firmly to a particular concept of the nation. Furthermore, his ideas had a direct influence upon those who, during the nineteenth century, began to develop elaborate nationalist ideologies.

Herder grew up in an intellectual environment which was putting increasing emphasis on particularity and variety in human affairs and in which history was developing as a critical discipline. Germany itself was a land of contrast, with many petty states alongside large and powerful ones. But the ideas, and the states, were under pressure, regarded as embodiments of fragmentation and backwardness. Progress and reason suggested an ever greater uniformity and an end to the myriad of small states. Herder reacted strongly against what he regarded as both condescending and threatening, and sought a firm ground from which to defend variety in human affairs.

A good place for seeing what form this defence took is his view of language. His starting point is very simple: only language has made men human.[3] The notion of 'pre-linguistic man' is, for Herder, meaningless. Man is defined by his language capacity. What is more, language can be learnt only in a community. It is synonymous with thought. Every language is different from every other. These points, to which most people today would assent, were not considered beyond debate at the time Herder wrote. Some argued that the origins of human language lay in human invention. Herder rejected this view. But from this position one could go on to make some more far-reaching claims.

If language is thought, and can be learnt only in a community, it follows that each community has its own mode of thought. Furthermore, to go on to argue that languages are unique could lead to the conclusion that each language is not simply a particular way of expressing universal values. Rather, it is the manifestation of unique values and ideas. Understanding of a language comes not by translating it into the terms of 'universal reason' or into another language but by learning it. Language is the property of the community, but it stretches beyond any one generation. It may be modified and adapted according to the needs of the community but it cannot be radically transformed. Moreover, language does not only have continuity through time, but, in its vocabulary, grammar, sounds, etc., has a unity. A language is not an arbitrary collection of utterances. Finally, no language is superior or inferior to any other, as there is no general scale against which all can be measured.

These views are of major significance simply because language is so important in human society. But the arguments can be extended much further if all other human activities are understood as sorts of languages. Dress, architecture, customs, ceremonial, song, law: all these and many other activities can be understood in the same way. Ultimately 'community' is understood as the sum total of these modes of expression. Furthermore, this sum total is itself more than a collection of items and must be grasped as a complex unity. The ambition of the student of any society must be to grasp this unity by learning all the ways of the society in question. Each element in a society only makes sense in terms of the whole, which, in turn, is manifested only through these various elements. Understanding a society is rather like learning a language.

The major form such understanding took was that of history. History has been given a greater or lesser role in the understanding of human affairs from other perspectives, but for historicism history is the only way to understand a society. History is not 'evidence' on which theories could be tested or a charter drawn up from which to justify present decisions. It is not a constraint on the present or a rich profusion of the various forms human nature has assumed. Rather it is the only way to apprehend the spirit of a community; it is the principal way of learning the language of a particular society.

There were various elements within this historical approach. The study of language itself was regarded as particularly important. So also was the study of ordinary people, who were regarded as the core of a society. A concern with folklore which is more than simply antiquarian is largely derived from historicist concerns. Finally, in more modern times an ahistorical approach has been added to these forms of understanding. Certain types of social anthropology insist on the need to understand the whole community, and in its own terms. However, this understanding has little historical dimension. The notion of wholeness tends to be expressed through the idea of every activity having a function within the community.

There are serious problems about the historicist approach. The rejection of universal standards of reason raises problems about the rationality of the terms of analysis that are employed. The need to apprehend the spirit or the 'wholeness' of a society which is central to the historicist position tends to express itself in the form of intuition. It is not relevant to go into these problems or to deal with the major ways in which historicist work has developed. Only in so far as these matters are reflected in the ideology derived from historicism will they be considered.

Translation into Ideology

Strictly speaking it should be impossible for historicism to give rise to political value judgements. At most it could insist that it is wrong to apply one's own judgements to another society. But the intrusion of certain extra ideas into the historicist position could change this.

The most important might be called the idea of authenticity. One can see this idea being introduced in Herder's own writings and used to back up his own rather liberal political values. Herder denied that government could be understood as the product of a social contract or divine agency. Neither has any historical basis. Both seem to involve the notion of a jump from a situation without government to one with government. Both are used, in fact, not as an historical claim but as a way of evaluating government by some universal standard. Herder, instead, insisted that government is a historical development. He argued that society began as a number of families. In this situation no formal system of government was required. But as families joined together to form more extensive societies it became necessary to develop new forms of leadership which took the form of government. The conquest of one society by another also can introduce a separate system of government.

Thus far Herder seems to work from within the historicist position. It is when he evaluates this development that he moves beyond it. Conquest is regarded as the disruption of the natural development of a particular society.

Nature produces families; the most natural state therefore is one people (*Volk*) with a natural character . . .

Nothing seems more obviously opposed to the purpose of government than the unnatural enlargement of states, the wild mixing together of different human species and nations under one sceptre.[4]

Herder particularly objected to large, impersonal 'machine' states such as the Prussia of Frederick the Great, which he saw as the artificial product of war and conquest.

A somewhat similar version of this approach, in more elaborate form, can be found in the work of the Czech historian and nationalist, Palacky. He took over from Herder the idea of the Slavs as a peaceful group of peoples subjected to oppression and exploitation by various robber peoples such as the Magyars and Germans. The Czechs, identified as a language group, began with their free, 'natural' societies; clusters of families with an informal, democratic system of government. Palacky goes on to describe the various conquests. Resistances to these conquests are focused upon as high points in the national history. The Hussite movement is interpreted in this way. The various activities of the Czechs are seen as manifestations of their national spirit. Palacky hoped that his history would help restore a keen sense of national identity which was, in turn, a necessary condition for a reassertion of Czech rights.

This distinction thus drawn between what was natural and unnatural in history is paralleled in the other major areas of historicist concern. Fichte, for example, in the field of language went much further than the aesthetic concern with purifying language. For him language mirrored the national soul, and to purge the language of alien impurities was to defend the national soul against subversion by foreign values. The Germans, he argued, unlike other Teutonic groups, possessed a continuous and 'living' language. But its life required constant protection. Fichte regarded Latin as a dead language, and for him 'dead' took on a powerful, literal meaning. He argued that to take abstract, lifeless Latin terms into German would have a deadening effect. The German language was more concrete. The importation of Latin words would lead Germans to ascribe some of the alien values associated with them to their German 'equivalents'. Gradually the values for which the German words originally stood would be lost. The defence of the living language was simultaneously a defence of the values of the human group using it.[5] In a similar way the racist currents of thought developed in the nineteenth century identified a pure racial group and then sought to protect its purity from outside influences. In both cases defence could also come to take the form of a purge of impure elements in order to return to the pure, 'natural' state of affairs.

In the field of social anthropology similar ends could be reached through the employment of the concept of 'equilibrium'. Changes introduced from outside into a 'tribe' (itself partially a product of historicist intellectual values) could be seen as upsetting the state of equilibrium. Everything in that society could be justified as contributing to the equilibrium. Jomo Kenyatta, having studied in London under the functionalist anthropologist Malinowski, produced an account of the Kikuyu which employed these sorts of ideas.[6] For example, his defence of female circumcision argued that it was arrogant of Europeans to condemn the practice as barbaric. It was not only arrogant, it was mistaken. That condemnation rested on the attempt to apply some universal standard to all social practices. But the practice only had its meaning, its rationality, in the context of a unique community. Within that community this meaning was associated with the way in which the passage from female adolescence to womanhood was marked, and that passage in turn was a major element of the social and sexual structure of Kikuyu society. It was only from within that frame of reference that judgements could be made.

One could multiply examples of this sort many times. The basic assumption is that one can identify a particular human unit—the Czech people, the German language, the Aryan race, the Kikuyu tribe—and establish what is natural within it and use that unit, in its natural state, as the source of value judgements. Deviations from that natural state are, of course, unnatural, and what is unnatural is bad. In this way the historicist concern with understanding society as a unique totality can be transformed into a way of making value judgements about historical change in terms of the way unnatural developments undermine a natural state of affairs.

However, the units identified are necessarily more or less arbitrary ones. Groups and languages can be categorised in many other ways. It is difficult to understand why war and conquest, such frequent occurrences, should be regarded as unnatural. It is difficult to see how the historicist can reconcile himself to not being able to understand the many 'unnatural' societies which exist, and how one understands historical change. Finally, of course, the 'return' to the natural situation can be understood only in a very general and vague way, that is, as a return to the spirit of that past. The Czechs Palacky studied did not and could not have produced Palacky himself or the complex and changing society of Bohemia which gave rise to Czech nationalism. The 'traditional' Kikuyu whom Kenyatta described were heavily Christianised and many of them opposed female circumcision. These arbitrary judgements, justified by the contrast of natural with unnatural, are an essential ingredient of nationalist ideology.

The notion of a return to the spirit of the past was often accompanied by a historical perspective which read the appropriate trends into events. Figures in the past became instruments of the national destiny or obstacles in its path. Thus Heinrich von Treitschke, the German nationalist historian, could defend the actions of the eighteenth-century Prussian state because it was seen as the vehicle of later unification. On the other hand the Habsburg empire, as a multi-national state, and the smaller German states (particularly the allies of Napoleon) were subjected to a much more critical treatment. Associated with this, von Treitschke came to emphasise the role of Protestantism in the German national spirit and to deny the centrality of the Catholic religion in German society. Again, this is arbitrary and inconsistent with a proper historicist approach. So too is the identification of figures from the 'national' past in terms of current political disputes. In the disputes between supporters and opponents of the internal settlement in Zimbabwe there were rival claims to be the true heirs of the participants in the disturbances of 1896–97 in Southern Rhodesia. The movement led by Sithole used populist language; that led by Mugabe used class language; but in both cases the ideological use of history was the same.[7]

The final, and most important, ideological ingredient is the way in which the historicist concept of community is linked to political demands. The demand for a nation-state with many of the features of other nation-states seems hard to reconcile with the justification that a unique nation needs its own special form of independence. Some consistent cultural nationalists have indeed resisted the demand for national self-determination on the grounds that it is an imitation of the West.[8] But this is exceptional. Usually what happens is that nationalist ideology operates with three notions which are mutually incompatible but, if not properly examined, can seem powerfully persuasive.

First, there is the notion of the unique national community. Second, there is the idea of the nation as a society which should have its own state. But in this understanding the basic distinction between state and society is accepted in a way that contradicts the historicist view of community as a whole. Finally the nation is thought of as the body of citizens—that is, a wholly political conception—and self-determination is justified in terms of universal political principles. Nationalist ideology never makes a rational connection between the cultural and the political concept of the nation because no such connection is possible. Instead, by a sort of sleight of hand dependent upon using the same term, 'nation', in different ways, it appears to demonstrate the proposition that each nation should have its nation-state. In this way it can superficially appear to have provided an answer to the problem of the relationship between state and society.

There are numerous variations upon the basic themes I have outlined. The nation can be defined in a great variety of ways, and this can give rise to conflicting claims about who belongs to which nationality. The values of the nation, its true 'spirit', are matters of even greater dispute in which the various claims made have in common only the fact that they can be subjected to no rational tests. The manner in which the contrast between natural and unnatural is drawn also varies widely. These variations will depend on a combination of intellectual tradition, inherent plausibility and political need. Thus the initial impulse behind the categorising of many African societies as tribes can be located in European intellectual traditions. They were adapted to social reality in various ways but retained an inherent plausibility because of the small-scale nature of many African societies. They could be sustained both because their advocates had the power virtually to project their own ideas about social identity on to colonial subjects and because it suited elements in indigenous society to manipulate these categories to their own advantage. Such categories, enshrined in various forms of 'indirect rule', hardened and shaped much political action. In their turn they have shaped territorial nationalist movements—both by forming part of their political material and by forcing nationalists to relate cultural diversity to the claim for territorial rather than 'tribal' independence. The ideology is not, therefore, a gloss upon some pre-existent social reality but a constituent of that reality. A similar argument for the way in which the concept of the 'Oriental' has shaped relations between the West and societies of the Middle and Far East has recently been advanced with great force and subtlety by Edward Said.[9]

Nationalist ideology is neither an expression of national identity (at least, there is no rational way of showing that to be the case) nor the arbitrary invention of nationalists for political purposes. It arises out of the need to make sense of complex social and political arrangements. But that need is itself shaped both by intellectual traditions and the sorts of responses which any intellectual scheme evokes when it is activated in some way or another. At the highest intellectual level anthropologists or scholars of the Orient or political thinkers carefully work through what they regard as the relevant evidence in order to test their ideas. At a practical level administrators, traders, missionaries and others work with particular assumptions about social arrangements and values in order to achieve their own objectives. In so far as they do achieve them they will tend to take these assumptions as true. The same point can be made about nationalists. They also begin with a fund of intellectual assumptions about what society is and how it is organised. They relate these assumptions to their own political projects. In fact they argue that those political projects are determined by their assumptions; that they are the spokesmen for the nation. However, their precise political projects and the manner in which these are carried through are the product of certain political situations rather than the expression of national needs. Nevertheless, the proclamation of such needs as the basis of their politics is an essential ingredient of that politics. Precisely because their assumptions about national identity and need are not purely arbitrary they have a more or less plausible connection with existing social arrangements and needs, with actual beliefs and with often widespread political grievances. But of course the ideology is more than a reflection of those things; rather it incorporates them into a broader vision which transforms their significance. The ideology also provides nationalists with a cause in which not only they themselves but many others genuinely believe, often including opponents who have been brought up with similar intellectual assumptions and values. In so far as nationalist objectives appear relevant to the interests of various political elites and social classes, so far will nationalist ideology be enhanced by the way in which members of these groups can agree that they are part of the nation. In this way nationalist ideology actually brings into being an imitation of its own ideas. In so far as nationalism is successful it appears to be true. That, of course, is its ultimate form of plausibility.

However, I have only considered the intellectual origins of nationalist ideology and its translation into ideological form at a fairly sophisticated level. To work effectively as a popular political ideology it needs simplification, repetition and concreteness. It is because nationalist ideology is particularly adaptive in these ways that it can have great popular appeal. Simplification involves above all the construction of stereotypes. There are stereotypes of the nation in terms of history or racial characteristics or cultural practices as well as stereotypes of enemies. Repetition through speeches, newspaper articles, rallies, songs, etc., is an essential part of the work of a nationalist party. The turning of these simplified and repeated themes into concrete form is achieved primarily through symbolism and ceremonial. [. . .]

Conclusion

[R]eturning to the problem of the relationship of state and society, the nationalist 'solution' to the problem is, on the surface, quite simple. Societies (nations) are unique. Government by alien societies can only do violence to the unique national spirit. Therefore each nation must have its own government. That government is the nation-state. This is not merely an abstract ideal. History can be understood only in terms of the achievements and frustrations of the nation. The demand for statehood is rooted in the national spirit, even if inarticulate and repressed, and the nationalist simply speaks for that spirit.

But the identity of the nation is provided in arbitrary ways. The leap from culture to politics is made by portraying the nation at one moment as a cultural community and at another as a political community whilst insisting that in an ideal state the national community will not be 'split' into cultural and political spheres. The nationalist can exploit this perpetual ambiguity. National independence can be portrayed as the freedom of the citizens who make up the (political) nation or as the freedom of the collectivity which makes up the (cultural) nation. Nationalist ideology is a pseudo-solution to the problem of the relationship between state and society, but its plausibility derives from its roots in genuine intellectual responses to that problem.

The appeal of this pseudo-solution is that it enables the nationalist to take a wide variety of practices and sentiments prevailing among the population of a particular territory and to turn them into political justifications. By *seeming* to abolish the distinctions between culture and politics, society and state, private and public, the nationalist has access to a whole range of sentiments, idioms and practices which would hitherto have been regarded as irrelevant to politics but are now turned into the values underlying political action. It would be wrong to see nationalism as the expression of these values in political form. That view is tantamount to accepting the self-assessment of nationalists. Nationalist ideology works on these values in a new way, and it operates on a great variety of levels. Furthermore, it selects values in ways designed to enhance their political significance. The general point is that this emphasis on cultural distinctiveness and values has particular advantages in a situation where it is possible to mobilise mass support or co-ordinate a wide variety of elites in a bid for territorial independence. It is also of value in an international situation where the claim to state power is regarded as legitimate only if it is couched in the form of national self-determination. Cultural appeals add to that legitimacy and also help provide the basis of support for a nationalist movement which gives its particular claim to state power credibility. The claim to uniqueness is ultimately used to justify the claim to have a state just like any other.

Nationalist ideology has its roots in intellectual responses to the modern problem of the relationship between state and society. This response, above all in the form of historicism, was a serious attempt to deal with the problem and to rebut what it saw as the falsehoods of analysis based on allegedly universal standards of reason. It was turned into ideology by means of notions such as authenticity and teleology. It was also combined in a powerful but illogical way with purely democratic and political values. The net result was to transform certain important ways of understanding human affairs into political ideology which was beyond critical examination. At the same time the historicist concern with history and popular values and practices was turned into various symbolic and ceremonial forms. These had a particularly powerful appeal because of their quality of self-reference and the way they took existing sentiments and actions and transmuted them into political ideology. This appeal in turn was grounded upon the claim to link cultural distinctiveness with the demand for political self-determination. Such claims had to be related to specific interests and only worked in particular sorts of political situations. Furthermore, no particular element within this ideology can be automatically regarded as decisive among supporters. But, with these qualifications, nationalist ideology can still be regarded as a powerful force which was essential in the work of co-ordination, mobilisation and providing legitimacy which was carried out by a nationalist movement.

[*Nationalism and the State* (Manchester University Press: Manchester, 1982), 335–44, 348–51.]

ANTHONY D. SMITH
....

17 **The Crisis of Dual Legitimation**

Why has the rediscovery and repossession of one's communal history, the cultural springboard of ethnic nationalism to this day, become so widespread and necessary a feature of the modern political landscape? The short answer is that historicism is a logical outgrowth of the Enlightenment and of all subsequent enlightenments. The longer answer is that such historical concerns spring from the characteristic divisions among secular intellectuals in search of a viable faith. [. . .]

Central to this transformed position of the secular intellectual was the impact of rationalism and science. The significance of science as an 'effective' mode of cognition lay as much in the social as the intellectual sphere.[1] It was not simply that science was a mode of cognition open to inspection and verification of results and capable of rational exposition and training; its wide range of practical applications in all kinds of circumstances, and the innovative spirit which its successes encouraged, nurtured a self-confidence in purely human faculties that most religious thought and traditional wisdom had denigrated. Faith in human powers of observation and reasoning demanded, moreover, complete freedom from any artificial constraints—social, religious or political—as well as from any intellectual dogma which might deflect or impede rational argument and rigorous experiment.

It was therefore of signal importance to the position of secular intellectuals, both in early modern Europe, and later on in Asia, Africa and the Americas, that rationalism and the scientific temper emerged within the matrix of societies still dominated by religious assumptions and traditions, and usually by ecclesiastical authority. This meant that the quest for scientific truths necessarily took on the nature of a crusade on behalf of freedom of enquiry and the superiority of human reason to divine revelation. It also meant that the educators had to count on opposition, and often repression, by traditional authorities who feared this challenge to their social and political position, as well as to their intellectual monopoly. Powerful, therefore, as the position of the secular intellectual might be, it was also precarious. Though rationalism and science had the potential to destroy the hold of faith on public life, and even disestablish the church, the danger which it constituted for the social fabric evoked immediate and deep antagonisms, which were to set their mark on the ethnic revival.

The very challenge which the educators posed also contributed to their political isolation. Kings, aristocrats and bureaucrats feared the attractions which their ideas might have for wider sections of the population, as much as the radical connotations of the ideas themselves. In some cases, 'enlightened' rulers might coopt a few of the intellectuals and implement aspects of their programmes of reform; but more shrank from such hazardous paths.[2] Nevertheless, even the most reactionary could not remain totally immune to the new ideas or the pervasive influence of the educators. For one thing, few societies enjoyed complete isolation from alien influences; and, in any case, none were free of those social discontents, or political divisions, which allow new ideas to gain access and take root. Nor could rationalism and science be easily divorced from the technological successes which were its fruits in spheres as diverse as armaments and communications or manufacturing industry. Rulers could not easily reject the opportunities for greater effectiveness of control and political action which these technical innovations offered; and, while it was clearly preferable to adopt the techniques without the underlying assumptions, rulers soon found it necessary to compromise with the expertise disseminated by the educators. [. . .]

Let us return for the moment to the collision between rationalism and religious authority. The social context of this conflict was dominated by the emergence of powerful centralised government in a few key political units, usually under absolute monarchs or colonial bureaucracies representing centralised metropolitan states. The fact that the most advanced of these states were historical neighbours and came to constitute a well-defined diplomatic nexus or system of states in the selfsame early modern period which saw the birth of science and rationalism, meant that the new ideas and techniques, and their propagators, had more chances of adoption and dissemination than under feudal or imperial conditions. By its nature, the absolutist territorial state was a competitive unit; the hold of the ruler over his subjects depended upon his ability to succeed in the contest for wealth and power and prestige played out in European and colonial theatres. The Baroque splendours in which the kings lived were designed to impress their counterparts abroad even more than their subjects; but their success in this interstate rivalry in Europe and the colonies depended increasingly upon their ability to incorporate techniques and norms of efficiency into their political apparatus and social fabric. Interstate competition bred, therefore, not only [a] new 'national' sentiment [. . .], but also those drives for scientific and technical modernisation which became so characteristic of western bureaucratic states.[3]

How did this interstate competition affect the position of science and the educators in their conflict with established religious authority? On balance, it helped their cause far more than it impeded it. True, most rulers shied away from coopting the educators into government, and their reform programmes were often timid. In a direct clash, rulers tended to favour the ecclesiastical authorities as part of the established order, which it was unwise to undermine. But, equally, the incorporation of scientific techniques and ideas into the ruler's bureaucratic apparatus—his army, administration and legal system—and the need to encourage secular education among wider circles, in order to produce enough qualified professionals to meet internal and external requirements, consolidated the position of the secular intellectuals and boosted their morale. The rapid growth in the number of such professionals, and the proliferation of educational institutions to train them, served further to entrench the role of the educators. Finally, the spectacular results achieved by the new kind of 'scientific state' with its streamlined and rationalised bureaucracy, confirmed the status of the intellectuals at the cost of religious authority.

At the spiritual level, too, there was a decisive swing towards rationalism and away from revealed authority. The very success of the rationalised bureaucratic state undermined both the negative evaluation of human capacities propounded by traditional religions, and, even more important, the efficacy and legitimacy of divine authority itself.[4] Impressed by the effectiveness of collective action centred on the bureaucratic state, educated men and women began increasingly to doubt the religious assumption of God's omnipotence and His ability or desire to intervene in man's daily life or even in collective crises. At this point, the age-old problem of meaning, the philosophical antinomy of worldly evil and divine omnipotence and perfection, took on a new social and practical relevance.[5] Doubting the efficacy of God's power to intervene in a mechanistic universe, the enlightened also began to question the justice of His dispensation and the legitimacy of His authority. Unable to accept traditional theodicies, and impressed by the evidence of human suffering and injustice, many secular intellectuals embraced radical ideologies which looked to man's collective efforts and political institutions to redress the world's wrongs.[6]

At the centre of this intellectual and emotional revolution lay a crisis of authority. The enlightened replaced the authority of religion and its cosmic dramas with that of the scientific state clothed in the garb of intramundane ideologies of progress. This new construct, the 'scientific state' and its centralised administration, was, after all, enormously impressive. It was also entirely man-made, a human and therefore flexible engine of social change. In the hands of a wise legislator, or well-attuned educators, this motor of modernisation, this solvent of backwardness and tradition-bound structures, could set mankind on the road to that rational harmony of his interests and fulfilment of his talents which had so long eluded him, denied as it was by his dependence upon the deities of conservative and pessimistic faiths. Hence, for many intellectuals, the state came to symbolise the opportunity for a breakthrough towards modernity, and out of the trough of dependence on outside forces beyond their control. And the more the absolutist state had become entrenched in an area or community, the greater the faith that secular intellectuals came to repose in its efficacy.[7]

What this revolution, therefore, entailed was a transposition of the ancient problem of meaning away from the spiritual sphere onto a material and social plane. Injustice and suffering were not divinely ordained instruments of man's spiritual betterment, or inevitable components of earthly imperfection; they were mainly man-made problems with human solutions which men of good faith and intelligence could arrive at and implement for their less fortunate fellow-men. Such a conclusion sapped the vigour of traditional faiths, as it undermined the intellectual edifice of revealed dogma. Above all, it eroded the social and political relevance of religion, and the basis of ecclesiastical authority. Religion became more and more the expression of private convictions, an inspiration or consolation for the inward crises and joys of an individual's life, rather than a matter of public concern or communal action.

Three Routes to Ethnic Historicism

Of course, the actual processes by which faith was sapped and religious authority displaced, in the areas where this occurred, varied greatly in different communities. There was nothing inevitable, either, about the process itself, or about its trajectory. A good many 'modernised' or 'developed' nation-states have powerful ecclesiastical hierarchies, even in communist countries, and a vigorous religious life, private and public.[8] Some intellectuals, and educator-statesmen, have found private ways of reconciling some of the premises of religion with a commitment to social progress through science and rationalist education.[9] Nevertheless, the basic choice between a social structure dominated by religious authority or by 'rational-legal' authority of the scientific state has remained fundamental, at both the intellectual and the social levels. With the advance of secular education and science, more and more people have come to feel the need for some sort of choice or harmonisation between these two polar principles; and this perception of a fundamental choice has had vital social repercussions in the histories of a great number of communities.

Certainly, the discussions of so-called modernist intellectuals were dominated at the outset by such perceptions. Historically and logically, three main positions on the question emerged out of the welter of speculation; and intellectuals have tended to divide along their lines ever since, with a good deal of interchange and even blurring in individual cases between the three options. I [. . .] will [. . .] confine my remarks to showing how each of them has tended to encourage the growth of an historicist outlook, and to discover in the resuscitation of the ethnic community as an historical subject some sort of resolution of their intellectual and emotional dilemmas.[10]

The first route, that of neo-traditionalism, tries to accept the technical achievements and some of the methods of western science and rationalism without any of its underlying assumptions. Socially and politically, it utilises modern methods of mobilising people but for traditionalist ends. A traditionalist is, of course, a self-conscious ideologue; he knows perfectly well that he is manipulating scientific techniques in order to defend traditional values and dogma. He also approaches tradition 'from the outside'; he has seen it through the eye of the unbeliever, if only to reject his error, and of the foreigner, if only to be confirmed the more securely in the sense of what is his own. The neo-traditionalist is, moreover, politically self-conscious: he deliberately chooses secular political means for achieving traditional, religious goals. Thus al-Afghani organised a pan-Islamic crusade, agitating through the press and politically, and mobilising thinking Muslims from Egypt to Pakistan to revive and purify Islam and the Islamic *umma* in the face of western materialism and imperialism.[11] And in India, slightly later, Tilak and Aurobindo were appealing to the masses in an attempt to revive the fortunes of Hinduism at a time when Christianity and westernisation appeared to be eroding traditional faith, and they did so by politicising the tradition and organising the faithful into a modern-style crusade against alien unbelievers.[12]

It is not difficult to see how this kind of modernised religion and politicised tradition lends itself to ethnic historicism and outright nationalism. To use political means to revive one's religious heritage and faith, and to organise the faithful into a political movement, demands a clear conception of the origins, laws of growth and identity of the unit whose solidarity is being sought, in this case, the community of the faithful. It requires, moreover, a sense of the passage of ethnic time and the vicissitudes of the faithful during the course of the centuries. The faithful must be given a history; they must be endowed with a foundation charter; their identity and destiny must be fixed; and their decline from past grandeur and present misfortunes must be explained. The religious congregation must increasingly be turned into an ethnic community, as has happened to the Jews and the Iranian Shi'ites. [. . .]

Neo-traditionalist intellectuals reject, on principle, the rationalist assumptions and critical language which they simultaneously require, if they are to communicate that rejection to their fellow-intellectuals and others. The other two positions, those of the reformists and the assimilationists, accept science and rationalism together with their associated modes of critical reflection, systematic observation and open argument. But, while the assimilationist accepts such rationalism wholeheartedly, his reformist counterpart does so with many reservations. Assimilationists embrace with an almost messianic fervour the rationalist and scientific principles embodied in the modern state, principles in which they not only believe but which also validate their own aspirations for power and prestige. From their ranks have been drawn most of the 'educators', self-styled secular intellectuals bent on regenerating their communities through rationalist education. To these people there was really only one modern, worthwhile civilisation, that of the modern West with its rational discourse and scientific expertise; and they saw their task as that of assimilating themselves and their communities to the norms and lifestyles of that one global civilisation. Assimilationists are, therefore, essentially cosmopolitan in aspiration, even if, in practice, they must always assimilate to a particular cultural variant (English, French, German, American, Russian) of 'modern' scientific civilisation. The point is that, to the assimilationist would-be educator, the 'scientific state' is a universal construct whose effect is the potential solution of the problem of meaning on a global scale. By means of this engine of modernisation, all mankind can pool its resources for the common good, thus rendering the old transcendental and cosmic problems essentially social and practical. Through self-help and collective planning, men can hope to solve problems that are really terrestrial and practical, but which till now had been represented by the traditional theodicies as supramundane, divinely ordained elements of the cosmos. The first task of assimilationists was, therefore, critical and destructive: the breaking down of transcendental mysteries into earthly, practical problems, so that men might be taught the scientific temper and techniques required for self-help programmes of collective regeneration.

But, how then could an assimilationist stance contribute to the rise of ethnic historicism? Is not their critical cosmopolitanism, their future-oriented messianism, incompatible with the cultural foundations of the ethnic revival? It is indeed incompatible. And it required a major reorientation of assimilationist aspirations, before they could lend themselves to an historicist resolution.

That change came for many with the disillusion of their cosmopolitan dreams and messianic ideals. Of course, a few assimilationists managed to slip into the advanced western societies, which they felt embodied their aspirations to be world-citizens. But many more were refused entry. Curiously, the process of rejection began in the western heartlands—in that initial contest between the *philosophes* and the *ancien régime*, which was soon replicated in much of Central and Eastern Europe.[13] Exclusion was even more overt for the messianic intellectuals of the 'Third World'. If they did not come to sense their rejection in the metropolitan lands which they visited, they were left in no doubt of it on their return home. And yet it was not the insults of junior colonial officials that restored the assimilationist intellectual to his community and its history; it was far more the subtle but pervasive sense of distance which European exposure instilled in him, the gulf between his own traditions and the rational-critical discourse of the West.[14]

And so the assimilationist-in-retreat from the scientific state in the West poured all his messianic fervour and ardent hopes back onto the community which he had sought to abandon. Painful though this transformation might be, it was made easier by the fact that the ideology of rational progress, which the assimilationist intellectuals had embraced, furnished them with an evolutionary outlook, which in turn could be harmonised with the history of particular ethnic communities. An ideology of progress entails, after all, a commitment to a linear conception of social development, in which some societies, the 'advanced' ones, are blazing the one and only trail for their 'backward' brethren. A global pioneering ideology implies a theory of stages of advancement and rules of improvement. Given also their revolutionary impulses, assimilationists would be predisposed to an interventionist view of the historical process, one in which the educator could speed up the movement of history. It was therefore not so difficult for a disappointed assimilationist to transfer his progressive and revolutionary ideology from the stage of world history to that of his community within that larger framework. In that way, his disillusion and rejection could be rationalised, even justified, by arguing that progress is slower, more piecemeal and fragmented, and requires a more active intervention in each area; in a word, by being more 'realistic'. Besides, the revolution of reason had not really occurred in the advanced states, even if early enthusiasms had misled many into believing it had; might not their own communities succeed where the advanced western nations had failed? And might not the secular educators fashion a more rational, progressive and scientific state in their own backward areas, than any yet seen in the West?

Such reasonings, at any rate, helped to soften the disillusion of the assimilationists and turn them back to their ethnic homelands. A residual messianic cosmopolitanism still lingered in their hearts; but now it came to inspire their efforts to regenerate their respective ethnic communities and restore their past splendours. The arena of emancipation and revolution was no longer the world at large: it had narrowed itself down to the 'scientific state' of particular ethnic communities, and to the history and destiny of those communities. [. . .]

It is here that the third position, that of reformists, commends itself. For the reformist, despite his commitment to critical rationalism and science, does not completely reject all religious authority or cosmic theodicies. [. . .] [T]he reformist acknowledges the situation of 'dual legitimation', the twin sources of authority in the modern world, that of the divine order and that of the scientific state.[15] To a reformist, God makes history; but so does the man-made 'scientific state'. Revelation and intuition show us the divine plan, even while reason and science allow man to become God's co-worker. Power and value are divided today; man, through the scientific state, commands much value and considerable power, but God, in nature and morality, is the repository of power and value beyond man and his comprehension. In his own terrestrial sphere, man can raise himself; he must not wait till death for emancipation. But, in the sphere beyond, on the cosmic plane, God still rules; and furthermore, He works in man's sphere through man's own efforts. Cautiously optimistic, the reformist believes that God works for man through the scientific state; and man must therefore embrace the collective good which the state furthers, so that he can work with God. And only within a reformed religion can man work with God.

The reformist attempt to reconcile opposites, to harmonise an ancient and profoundly ethical religious tradition with modern, secular rationalism, lies at the root of much liberal and even social-democratic thought. Yet it, too, lends itself to an ethnic historicism. But the process of transformation is more complex. Like the assimilationist, the reformist is asked to determine his own destiny, to raise the collectivity through his own efforts. Self-help, rational choice, collective planning, are therefore as much a part of the mental armoury of reformists as of others. But that is only a predisposing factor. It does not explain the turn into historicism or the return to ethnicity.

Once again, it is a failure that provides the impetus to historicism. Reformists, working to reform their religion so as to adapt it to modern rationalism, necessarily run foul of the ecclesiastical authorities and their neo-traditionalist champions. Only a truly reformed religion, which returns to its original inspiration and sweeps away all meaningless accretions and superstition, along with archaic priestly hierarchies, can reconcile the basic ethical revelation with the demands of reason; and this brings reformers into direct conflict with the ecclesiastical authorities.

In the ensuing conflict, which has often been prolonged and violent, reformists have had only limited success (and that often for quite extraneous political or economic reasons). The inherent difficulties in their position have also been mercilessly exposed. After all, if every feature of traditional religion which fails the 'test of reason', which cannot be reconciled with rationalism, is abolished, what is left of the religion? Why not cross over into an assimilationist secularism? Does not a religious community require continuity and stability in the face of the ever-changing 'spirit of the age' and fluctuating social needs?

One way out of these problems and conflicts is to look to the community itself, its history and culture, for the essential elements of the religion and the criterion of religious reform.[16] In the still-meaningful traditions and beliefs of the community, the reformist discerns the 'essence' of a modern faith. Dead and meaningless rituals and superstitions can now be swept away, on the ground that they no longer play a part in the life of the ethnic community. Furthermore, the reformist looks back to those ages and periods of the community in which religion was pure and the community itself was great. He searches in the past for communal dignity inspired by true faith; and seeks to recreate both through a modernised religious education. In this way, the reformist is led back towards a reconsideration of his ethnic past, in order to salvage the true, the underlying, the pure religion of his people. He becomes more conservative, more defensive, more concerned to preserve a sacred island of ethnic values in a profane world. He historicises the religious tradition, and in the end comes to see the religion as an outgrowth, a creation, of the genius of his community. To save the genuine religion, what is required is not merely a religious reformation, but a spiritual purification which will stem the community's present decline and restore it to its former grandeur. Through spiritual self-help, the dejected ethnic community can be raised up anew. Through a cultural ethnic nationalism, the situation of 'dual legitimation' can be overcome, and the ethnic community can regain its former faith and dignity in a rationalist world.[17]

Each of these three positions—neo-traditionalism, reformism and assimilation—continue to be espoused to this day by intellectuals in many lands; and each in its way continues to lead its devotees, under the pressure of external circumstances, towards an ethnic historicism. For they all concede the twin premises of such historicisms, that entities have origins and purposes in time, and possess identities and boundaries in space, in a world composed of analogous entities. The spiritual situation of intellectuals is, therefore, at once open and circumscribed; they operate within a set of assumptions, yet within that circle can choose between alternative interpretations.[18]

What, then, were the circumstances that precipitated adherents of all three positions toward an historicist resolution? In Europe, a sense of linear time and the quest for origins stemmed, first, from a comparison with the ancients and a growing belief in the possibility of social progress; whereas, outside Europe, this same quest originated from comparisons with former days of communal splendour now brought low by European conquest and cultural influence. Second, within Europe, a new sense of diversity and cultural pluralism arose mainly from interstate rivalries and territorial warfare, followed closely by the discovery of other continents and civilisations and 'exotic' peoples, and the ensuing scramble for colonies; whereas outside Europe, that selfsame sense of diversity emerged more directly from the 'parallel society' created by colonialism, and from the clash of western and indigenous cultures among exposed intellectuals.[19]

Perhaps even more fundamental for the rise of ethnic historicism across the globe has been the growing influence of the educators themselves. The secular intellectuals, as the vanguard of science and critical rationalism, have relentlessly challenged the claims of absolutism, semi-feudal ties and often ecclesiastical authority. Increasingly a transcultural, cosmopolitan community of humanists and scientists, united by books, travel and a common language of discourse, and freed from personal service to aristocratic and chiefly patrons, these secular educators have found a ready market for their ideas among a public hungry for knowledge and innovation. Even neo-traditionalists, who openly repudiate modernity, must operate within this language of critical discourse and address this new educated public.

[*The Ethnic Revival* (Cambridge University Press: Cambridge, 1981), 90, 93–8, 99–104.]

18 Cultural Nationalism and Moral Regeneration

Cultural and Political Nationalism

I propose to demonstrate that [. . .] there are two quite different types of nationalism—cultural and political—that must not be conflated, for they articulate different, even competing conceptions of the nation, form their own distinctive organizations, and have sharply diverging political strategies.

Political nationalists share with cultural nationalists an antipathy to the bureaucratic state, but they tend to look to reason as their ethical source. Their ideal is a civic *polity* of educated citizens united by common laws and mores like the *polis* of classical antiquity. They reject existing political and traditionalist allegiances that block the realization of this ideal, and theirs is a cosmopolitan rationalist conception of the nation that looks forward ultimately to a common humanity transcending cultural differences. But, because the world is divided into a multiplicity of political communities, they are forced to work within a specific territorial homeland in order to secure a state that will embody their aspirations. To mobilize a political constituency on behalf of this goal, political nationalists may be driven to adopt ethnic-historical identities and in the process may become ethnicized and 're-traditionalized'. Their objectives are, however, essentially modernist: to secure a representative state for their community so that it might participate as an equal in the developing cosmopolitan rationalist civilization.

By contrast, the cultural nationalist perceives the state as an accidental, for the essence of a nation is its distinctive civilization, which is the product of its unique history, culture and geographical profile. Unlike the political nationalist, who is fundamentally a rationalist, a cultural nationalist like Herder affirms a cosmology according to which humanity, like nature, is infused with a creative force which endows all things with an individuality.[1] Nations are primordial expressions of this spirit; like families, they are natural solidarities. Nations are then not just political units but *organic* beings, living personalities, whose individuality must be cherished by their members in all their manifestations. Unlike the political nationalist, the cultural nationalist founds the nation not on 'mere' consent or law but on the passions implanted by nature and history.[2]

If for cultural nationalists the nation is an organic entity, it is so, nevertheless, only in a metaphoric sense. It is rather perceived as a complex of individualities, each one of which has equal rights and value to the community. Rejecting the ideal of universal citizenship rights of political nationalism, cultural nationalists demand that the natural divisions within the nation—sexual, occupational, religious and regional—be respected, for the impulse to differentiation is the dynamo of national creativity.[3]

Just as much as the political nationalist, cultural nationalists spurn the otherworldliness of traditional religions in favour of an activist view of man as an autonomous reasoning being.[4] Herder projects the nation as a continuously mobile community over time. Its historic identity and status order must be continuously renovated in terms of the needs of each generation, for no era can provide the model for another.[5] Conflict, therefore, is built into the cultural nationalist conception of the nation, between ageing traditionalists and the educated young. Indeed, evil and decay come to the nation only through an inner degeneration—either from an excess of rationalism that induces a passive dependence on the state or from an ossification of tradition such as was experienced in the Middle Ages.[6]

But if conflict with traditionalism is regarded as necessary by cultural nationalism, its objective is integrative. Unlike political nationalism, which would uproot the traditional status order for a modern legal-rational society, cultural nationalism is a movement of moral regeneration which seeks to re-unite the different aspects of the nation—traditional and modern, agriculture and industry, science and religion—by returning to the creative life-principle of the nation. Since this identity can only be grasped as a living whole—as a differentiated complex of interactive units—that is in continuous evolution, it cannot be codified. It can only be understood genetically and intuitively as a *gestalt*.[7] For this reason, its proponents are not politicians or legislators but are above all historical scholars and artists who form cultural and academic societies, designed to recover this creative force in all its dimensions with verisimilitude and project it to the members of the nation.

The nationalist historians—Palacky of the Czechs, Michelet of the French, Iorga of the Rumanians, Hrushevsky of the Ukrainians—are no mere scholars but rather 'myth-making' intellectuals who combine a 'romantic' search for meaning with a scientific zeal to establish this on authoritative foundations. For only by recovering the history of the nation through all its triumphs and disasters can its members rediscover their authentic purpose. These histories typically form a set of repetitive 'mythic' patterns, containing a migration story, a founding myth, a golden age of cultural splendour, a period of inner decay and a promise of regeneration.[8] Since such histories have only rarely been documented by pre-modern political and religious elites, this quest has resulted in an explosion in the genetic sciences, including archaeology, folklore, philology and topography, in order to resurrect the civilization of 'the people' from the cultural substratum.

But if it is through the historian one learns of the national destiny, the paradigmatic figure of the national community is the artist. For, unlike the great religions, the nationalist cosmology sets up no prophets to be *imitated* nor, indeed, any authoritative class of interpreters. The source of creativity is located not in a timeless supramundane order but in the continually evolving community itself, of which its heroes, religious or secular, can be but *exemplifications* who have to be *emulated* according to the needs of each era.[9] Every true member of the nation, then, is an artist-creator, and the great artists are they who create out of the collective experience of the people, preserved in historical legends, and dramatize their lessons for the present.[10] Kollar, epic poet of the Slavs, Lonnrot, creator of the Finnish epic *Kalevala*, the poet Mickiewicz, author of the *Book of the Polish Nation and of the Polish Pilgrimage*, became fathers of the nation, celebrating heroes who embody the nation's quest for meaning and integration in their martial vigour, seer-like wisdom, love of nature and its collective vitality down the ages. The Karelian region, which the *Kalevala* evoked, became as a sacred area a place of pilgrimage for Finnish nationalists.[11]

Cultural nationalism has everywhere generated a flowering of the historical sciences and the arts as intellectuals have established cultural forums in which to challenge ossified political and cultural elites and to inspire a rising educated generation to campaign to 're-create' the idea of the nation as a living principle in the lives of the people. Cultural nationalism then has a politics, but it is very different from that of the political nationalist in its goals and modes of organization.

The Politics of Cultural Nationalism

Political nationalists have as their objective the achievement of a representative national state that will guarantee to its members uniform citizenship rights. They tend to organize on legal-rational lines, forming centralized apparatuses in order to mobilize different groups against the existing polity and to direct them to this unitary end. For a cultural nationalist such as Herder, however, the state is regarded with suspicion as a product of conquest, and as imbued with an inherent bureaucratic drive that, exemplified in the cosmopolitan imperial state, seeks to impose a mechanical uniformity on living cultures.[12] The glory of a country comes not from its political power but from the culture of its people and the contribution of its thinkers and educators to humanity.

The aim of cultural nationalists is rather the moral regeneration of the historic community, or, in other words, the re-creation of their distinctive national civilization. Since a civilization is a spontaneous social order, it cannot be constructed like a state from above but only resuscitated from the bottom up. Typically cultural nationalists establish informal and decentralized clusters of cultural societies and journals, designed to inspire a spontaneous love of community in its different members by educating them to their common heritage of splendour and suffering. They engage in naming rituals, celebrate national cultural uniqueness and reject foreign practices, in order to identify the community to itself, embed this identity in everyday life and differentiate it against other communities.[13]

It is, of course, true that cultural nationalists are not hostile by definition to independent statehood and, as we shall see, are frequently driven into state politics to defend the cultural autonomy of the nation. But like the Czechoslovak poet, Kollar, they separate the emotional loyalty instinctively given to the cultural from the formal allegiance due to the political nation.[14] An authentic national politics derives not from rationalist constitutions but from a united community shaped by its history, beliefs, customs, industries and habitat.[15]

Unlike political nationalist movements, which may, like the Indian Congress, transform themselves from elite urban-based to mass organizations by promising different groups the redress of grievances in a national state, cultural nationalism remains in 'normal' circumstances a small-scale movement that promotes progress through communal self-help. When given a socio-political programme by crusading journalists, it may, if adopted by a young intelligentsia, develop into a loose network of language societies, dramatic groups, publishing houses, lending libraries, summer schools, agricultural co-operatives and political parties. Even so, it generally remains a minority enthusiasm. The largest of such movements emerging in the Habsburg Empire in the first half of the nineteenth century was Czech with 2,329 members.[16]

In terms of its communitarian goals, cultural nationalism fails. Often unable to extend beyond the educated strata, it is forced to adopt state-oriented strategies by which to institutionalize its ideals in the social order. In this guise, although still an elite movement, revivalism is often of considerable political import. For relatively well-financed revivals, such as the Greek and Magyar movements of the nineteenth century,[17] have provided alternative channels of social mobility for a disaffected intelligentsia, forming them into a counter-culture against the existing polity. At times of political crisis, with the traditional leadership discredited, this intelligentsia, socialized to sacrifice themselves for the nation, has served as a focus of opposition for other aggrieved groups and as a revolutionary strike force against the state.

One of the clearest instances of this political trajectory is provided by early nineteenth-century Czech cultural nationalism. Initially, it was confined to a linguistic and literary revivalism before giving rise to more politicized activities in the 1830s and 1840s. Even then its membership was confined largely to an intelligentsia of teachers, officials, students, lower clergy and some businessmen.[18] It was only the sudden relaxation of censorship on political and journalistic activity as a consequence of the constitutional revolution in Vienna in 1848–9 that gave the nationalist elites the chance to demand cultural autonomy and full civil liberties, in which task they succeeded in mustering the support of the urban middle classes and the peasantry against the Imperial state.[19]

Another example is that of Ukrainian cultural nationalism, which in the later nineteenth century was based around the Shevchenko Scientific Society of

Polish Galicia. Founded in 1873 and named after the dead poet Shevchenko as a symbol of Ukrainian rebirth, this society began with modest objectives: to foster the Ruthenian language and literature of the Ukrainian people and to become a publisher. It quickly developed, however, from an elite academic centre into a broad umbrella organization, directing diverse socio-political movements that were dedicated, first, to nationalize the people, now under the rule of the Poles in Galicia and of the Russians in the Ukraine, and, secondly, to unify them in an independent state. Although based in Galicia, the society received substantial financial and cultural support from the Russian Ukraine.

The major figure of late nineteenth-century Ukrainian nationalism was Hrushevsky, a charismatic populist historian, whose creation of a Ukrainian historical continuity provided the legitimation of Ukrainian communal aspirations against competing Polish and Russian nationalisms. He presided over the society from 1894. Other prominent nationalists were Drakomenov, an important 'progressive' intellectual, and Franko, scholar, poet and socialist intellectual. These three transformed the society first into the major centre for Ukrainian historical and scientific research, and then into a socio-political agent for the regeneration of the Ukrainian people.

Their activities were at first primarily educational—the establishment of a publishing house—but as they attracted the support of a radical populist, minor intelligentsia of peasant origins and then of a small Galician middle class, so an expanding network of educational, professional, economic and paramilitary associations developed. Agricultural co-operatives and credit unions were formed to encourage ethnic pride and self-reliance among the peasantry. Ukrainian revivalism, however, was very much a minority enthusiasm, and, as it encountered fierce opposition from the Poles, it added to its communitarian politics by 1898 a state-directed campaign for a separate Ukrainian university in Lemberg.

The movement gained impetus in Galicia in the new century from measures of democratic reform and from the support of the Habsburg Emperor, anxious to undermine the more powerful Poles. In the Russian Ukraine, the native intelligentsia was predominantly Marxist, but after the failure of the 1905 revolt in Russia it swung increasingly to nationalism, which was able to take advantage of subsequent partial political liberalization. It is true that the active membership of Ukrainian cultural nationalism was still limited in 1914, confined largely to the intelligentsia and the small middle strata of Galicia. But the movement had now formed a cohesive nationalist elite antagonistic to the existing political structures. When, therefore, the Tzarist and Habsburg Empires began to totter during the First World War, this elite was able to seize power and installed Hrushevsky, second only to Shevchenko in the affections of Ukrainian nationalists, as President of the Ukrainian People's Republic in 1918.[20] [. . .]

Cultural Nationalism as a Modernizing Movement

Many scholars would agree [. . .] that cultural nationalism makes a positive contribution to the task of nation building—in other words, to the identification, political organization and unification of the community within a given territory. But even among these, the consensus is that cultural nationalism is a regressive force, a product of intellectuals from backward societies, who, when confronted by more scientifically advanced cultures, compensate for feelings of inferiority by retreating into history to claim descent from a once great civilization. Somehow or other, cultural nationalism, it is argued, is functional for the formation of nations in such backward cultures, but in itself cannot shape their path to socio-political modernization.

This interpretation was first put forward some time ago by the pioneering historian of nationalism, Hans Kohn,[21] but its influence can still be seen in a recent brilliant sociological analysis of nationalism by Ernest Gellner.[22] [. . .] I propose to challenge this orthodoxy. Cultural nationalism, I shall suggest, must be accorded a much more positive role in the modernization process. For it puts forward not a primitivist but an evolutionary vision of the community, and it emerges in conjunction with a trans-national secular culture that perceives the growth of world civilization in polycentric terms. Cultural nationalists act as *moral innovators*, establishing ideological movements at times of social crisis in order to transform the belief-systems of communities, and provide models of socio-political development that guide their modernizing strategies. In the formulation of these objectives, this secular trans-national culture plays an important part.

Kohn argues that there are two forms of nationalism—political, which is 'rational', and cultural, which is 'mystical'—and that the dominance of one over the other is related to the level of socio-political development of a community.[23]

Political nationalism appeared first in the 'West' (by which Kohn means England, France and the Netherlands, Switzerland, the USA and the British dominions), in communities where a sophisticated urban middle-class vernacular culture had gradually developed from the Renaissance onwards and where the effective boundaries of the nation state had or were about to be formed. When nationalism emerged, all that was required was the transformation of the existing state into a people's state. Nationalism here took practical and constitutional forms.

When, however, nationalism arose later in the 'East' (by which Kohn means Central and Eastern Europe and Asia) it was in imitative response to the rationalist culture of the 'West'. Here, no such secular middle class existed. Society was predominantly agrarian with a large peasant mass dominated by a reactionary aristocracy, and frequently with no correspondence between ethnic and political boundaries. Unable to identify with a concrete territorial community, and aware of the social and political backwardness of their culture compared with the 'West', nationalists created a visionary nation based on ancient historical memories and unique cultural attributes, and they asserted, against rationalist citizenship ideals of the 'West', the superior mystical organic bond between peasant, land and community.[24]

This then was a cultural nationalism of historians and artists, which Kohn agrees had an educative effect, creating a national public opinion in favour of an authentic political community based on its 'natural' homelands, and providing thereby a platform for later modernist political nationalist movements. He views cultural nationalism, nevertheless, as a regressive phenomenon incapable of directing the process of modernization.[25]

Gellner presents a similar picture of the paradoxical relationship between cultural nationalism and modernization. It is the creation of intellectuals in backward societies, who, threatened by the advance of an exotic scientific-industrial culture with which they find it difficult to compete, advocate a nostalgic return to the pristine integrated world of the folk and engage in linguistic and cultural reconstruction. Dramatizing the grievances of the indigenous community against an alien bureaucratic order, they often serve as precursors to a nationalist seizure of the state. Their effect, however, is almost the opposite of what they promote. For what they seek is a revived folk community, but what results is rather a modern science-based culture with native idioms.[26]

Kohn and Gellner are surely right to identify cultural nationalism as a *defensive* response by educated elites to the impact of exogenous modernization on existing status orders, which may result, indeed, in a reassertion of traditionalist values in the community, as has occurred in contemporary Islamic countries in the Middle East and Asia. But they are wrong to perceive the celebration of the folk as a retreat into an isolated agrarian simplicity free from all the disorders of civilization.

Almost the opposite is, in fact, the case. Behind this evocation of the folk on the part of intellectuals and the intelligentsia is, first, a dynamic vision of the nation as a high civilization with a unique place in the development of humanity and, secondly, a corresponding drive to recreate this nation which, integrating the traditional and the modern on a higher level, will again rise to the forefront of world progress.

As I argued above, cultural nationalists regard the nation as a spontaneous solidarity that from its foundations is continuously evolving through cycles of achievement and decline. In its golden age it inspires a glorious synthesis of religious and secular cultures and is a seminal contributor to human civilization. Social decay and external cultural and political dependence come from an ossification of its traditions in the hands of its leadership, when it falls prey to cosmopolitan materialist corruptions. Cultural nationalists call on the rising educated generation to break with traditionalism and to restore their country to its former standing in the world, by constructing a modern scientific culture on the ethnic remains of the folk, who, remote from the great metropolitan centres, are the last repository of national traditions. The return to the folk, in short, is not a flight from the world but rather a means to catapult the nation from present backwardness and divisions to the most advanced stage of social development.

Cultural Nationalists as Moral Innovators

Contrary to conventional interpretations, cultural nationalists view conflict as an essential component of social development. Only out of struggle is the nation, always prone to decay, regenerated. Indeed, [. . .] cultural nationalism regularly crystallizes as a movement at times of social discord between traditionalists and modernists generated by the impact of external models of modernization on the established status order, and it promotes the re-integration of the community at a higher level by means of a return to the inspiration of its national past.

As an integrative movement, it repudiates both traditionalism and modernism as degenerations from a national vision that combines the virtues of each: the sense of unique identity given by the former with the idea of the community, embraced by the latter, as an active and equal participator in human progress. Conflict between national members can only occur because of a loss of touch with this national heritage.

Revivalists thus admire the human scale of the traditional community and its rootedness in nature, family, locality and religion, but they reject its other-worldliness and its barriers to the *equal* contribution of all groups (occupational, religious, sexual) to the nation as a corruption of native values. Likewise, they share with rationalist modernizers a commitment to a mobile meritocratic social order and contact with a wider humanity, but they oppose the latter's adherence to external universalist models of modernization, which produce only an anomic cosmopolitanism. History, they argue, shows that social progress comes not from the imposition of alien norms on the community but from the inner reformation of the traditional status order. The recovery of national pride is a prerequisite for successful participation in the wider world.

Cultural nationalists should be seen, therefore, as moral innovators who seek by 'reviving' an ethnic historicist vision of the nation to redirect traditionalists and modernists away from conflict and instead to unite them in the task of constructing an integrated distinctive and autonomous community, capable of competing in the modern world. This they do by introducing into the community a new nationalist ideology in which the accepted meanings of 'tradition' and 'modernity' are transformed. The 'modern' (or, as it is frequently designated, the 'West') is particularized to its adherents as a local manifestation of a universal drive for progress found in all peoples. 'Tradition' has to be undermined in the minds of its believers by demonstrating it to be the product of a mobile society whose glories sprang from an interchange with other cultures. The true matrix for both traditionalist and modernist is, the cultural nationalist proposes, the nation, in whose inner drive for realization all must find their individual and collective meanings.

Cultural nationalism has frequently been noted by scholars as a major force among the intellectuals of backward societies such as late nineteenth-century India and China, faced by the challenge of Western models of modernization.[27] Here society is increasingly polarized between modernizers who, passively oriented to the 'West', despise all that is native, and traditionalists who deny all value to the foreign. Revivalists, such as Swami Vivekananda of the neo-Vedantic movement and Liang Ch'i Ch'ao of the Chinese reform movement, instead defend their community against the external challenge by presenting a polycentric vision of a world of distinct and equal nations, in which their culture has played in the past and will in the future play an active role.

Hence to the traditionalists, Vivekananda proposed as the authentic India, a dynamic Aryan founding civilization that had been in touch with other world centres of learning (Persia and Greece) and that rejected any inherent barriers between the sexes, castes, and between religious and secular branches of knowledge.[28] He attacked the religious taboos on contacts with aliens and the caste laws prescribed by the Brahmin priests as a degeneration from this democratic civilization. To learn from foreign cultures entailed no break with Indian tradition. On the contrary, it was merely a way of recovering skills and knowledge once in Indian possession. Such was his revulsion from the effects of physical and social decay produced by religious quietism, that Vivekananda declared that playing football was a surer way of achieving salvation than reading the Gitas.[29]

To native westernizers, revivalists present the nation as a formative teaching civilization when the 'West' was in darkness. For example, the Chinese scholar Liang Ch'i Ch'ao was wont to argue that the 'West' was once no better than the Chinese were now and that whatever of value to be found in the 'West' had been taken from China. At another time, he suggested from his readings of European history that it was nonsense to take over Western values blindly, for Western progress had emerged out of its unique rhythms of glory and decay.[30] Taking up this theme, the African cultural nationalist Blyden argued that the hegemony of the 'West' was passing. For, according to Western intellectuals themselves, the 'West', having over-developed the material at the expense of the spiritual, was now threatened with an internal crisis. Africans, who had created the formative civilization of the world, were destined for a new mission. For alone they retained their ancient faith in nature, family, community and religion, and by harmonizing this with the new secular sciences, it was the Africans who were set to lift humanity to a new moral and material plane.[31] To be progressive was to be native: the 'West' was an outmoded civilization.

Cultural nationalism then is a political movement. It disavows the passive isolationism of the traditionalists and presents the nation as a progressive culture in active contact with other societies. At the same time it opposes the assimilation of the community to any universal model of development, liberal or socialist. For each nation has its own evolutionary path to follow. Revivalists appeal to the intelligentsia to borrow from other cultures in order to regenerate rather than to efface the national community. Developmental models must be selected and *adapted* in order to realize the natural talents and resources of each culture. Only thus can each nation make its distinctive contribution to humanity.

[*The Dynamics of Cultural Nationalism* (Allen and Unwin: London, 1987), 12–19, 30–6.]

Section III

The Rise of Nations

INTRODUCTION

It is generally accepted that the institutionalization of citizenship differentiates post-eighteenth-century nations from earlier ethnic and territorial communities. But important questions remain. What affinities (if any) do these units have with earlier communities? How far do pre-existing ethnic identities shape the different routes to national formation? And when can we say that nations come into existence?

Hugh Seton-Watson, the historian, distinguishes between the 'old, continuous nations' and new nations. The former, emerging in the course of the Middle Ages, integrated in an evolutionary manner ever-wider sections of the population through state expansion, the growth of trade, communications, and the rise of vernacular literatures. The new nations were formed in the era of nationalism and, as such, were the ideologized products of educated élites who moulded their populations according to the national model of the old nations.

The medieval historian Susan Reynolds, while accepting 'modernist' strictures against 'retrospective nationalism', suggests that we can find analogues of modern nationalism in the medieval *regna*, the kingdoms of common customs, law, and myths of descent found among several peoples of Western Europe. Likewise, John Armstrong, the political scientist, argues that modern nations should be understood not as something unprecedented but as products of a longer cycle of ethnic resurgence and decline over the *longue durée*. Such ethnic identities should not be regarded in the manner of nationalists as fixed essences, but as mutable and fluctuating. To chart the formation of such shifting ethnic identities in early Europe and the Middle East, he adopts the 'boundary approach' of Fredrik Barth, with its focus on symbols and myths which persist even when the content of group identity has changed.

In similar vein, the sociologist Anthony D. Smith argues that one can find two main types of *ethnie* (ethnic communities) in the pre-modern period: the lateral, aristocratic type, which is territorially extensive but lacks social penetration; and the vertical, demotic type, which is more compact, popularly based, and often tied to religious identities. The first type achieves modern nationhood via the bureaucratic state which incorporates the lower social strata, whereas the second achieves national autonomy through a secular intelligentsia which struggles not only against a hostile state but also against the religious custodians of ethnic tradition.

Finally, Walker Connor questions all these interpretations. The ethnographic history of a people often has little relevance to the study of nation formation. Moreover, national consciousness is a mass phenomenon, and the evidence suggests that even in late nineteenth-century Europe identities were local rather than national. In raising the question of when *is* the nation, he also challenges the modernists, since one implication of his argument is that in many cases the achievement of nationhood is doubtful.

19 **Old and New Nations**

It is [. . .] important to distinguish between two categories of nations, which we will call the old and the new. The old are those which had acquired national identity or national consciousness before the formulation of the doctrine of nationalism. The new are those for whom two processes developed simultaneously: the formation of national consciousness and the creation of nationalist movements. Both processes were the work of small educated political elites.

The old nations of Europe in 1789 were the English, Scots, French, Dutch, Castilians and Portuguese in the west; the Danes and Swedes in the north; and the Hungarians, Poles and Russians in the east. Of these, all but three lived in states ruled by persons of their nationality, and therefore needed no national independence movement; though this of course does not mean that these peoples did not suffer from various degrees of political or social oppression, and so, in the opinion of radicals and revolutionaries, 'needed' liberation. The three exceptions were the Scots, who since 1707 had shared a single state with the English and the Welsh, while preserving important institutions of their own; and the Hungarians and Poles, who were simply subjected to foreign rule. The Hungarians had at one time been divided between three states (the Habsburg Monarchy, the Ottoman empire and the principality of Transylvania), but at the end of the eighteenth century were all subject to the Habsburg Monarchy; whereas the Poles had been divided since 1795 between the kingdom of Prussia, the Russian empire and the Habsburg Monarchy. Thus, though Poles and Hungarians had a continuous national consciousness going back for several centuries, the continuity of the Polish and Hungarian sovereign states had been broken.

There were also at this time other communities in which there was, in the educated class, undoubted awareness of a cultural community and a long history, but in which the formation of national consciousness even in the elite was incomplete. Such were the Germans and Italians; perhaps also the Irish, Catalans and Norwegians.

In the rest of Europe there was little sign of national consciousness. In these lands, new nations were formed in the course of the following century, and this process was then extended, by educated elites influenced by European ideas, into the Muslim lands, southern and eastern Asia and sub-Saharan Africa. Nations of European origin also emerged in the colonies of settlement in America, South Africa and Australia.

The distinction between old and new nations seems more relevant than that between 'historical' and 'unhistorical', which came into use in Central Europe in the late nineteenth century. All nations have a history. Some of the communities in which, in 1789, national consciousness did not exist, or was still weak, had had long and brilliant histories—not only the Italians and Germans, but the Greeks and Bohemians and Serbs. However, continuity had been broken by conquest. The basic difference, then, is between old continuous nations and new nations; and it is of some importance for our theme.

The process of formation of national identity and national consciousness among the old nations was slow and obscure. It was a spontaneous process, not willed by any one, though there were great events which in certain cases clearly accelerated it.

In medieval Europe the word *natio* was in legal use, but it did not mean the same thing as the modern 'nation'. Many medieval universities attracted many students from other lands beside their own. These were placed in *nationes*, named after the territories from which the largest number of each originated, but including also persons from other countries.[1]

In Transylvania in the fifteenth century there were three *nationes* recognised by law, who were represented in the Transylvanian Diet: Hungarian, Székély and Saxon.[2] The Hungarian *natio* was confined to persons of noble status, but not to those of Hungarian speech. The Székély and Saxons, in contrast to the Hungarians, had no serfs in their community, and the whole population was to some extent represented.

Though the word *natio* thus varied in meaning, it and its derivatives in modern languages essentially comprised restricted categories. Separate words existed to describe the whole population: *populus, peuple, people, popolo* and *pueblo*. In the lands further east, however, as the ideas of the Enlightenment began to spread, this distinction became blurred. *Volk* in German, and *narod* in the Slav languages, soon came to combine the meanings of *natio* and *populus*, and such adaptations as *Nation* and *natsiya* were little used.[3]

In the case of those which I have called the 'old nations' a process took place of which it is difficult to pinpoint the stages, but of which the result is unmistakable. For example, in 1200 neither a French nor an English nation existed, but in 1600 both were important realities. At the first of these quite arbitrarily chosen dates, the countries now known as France and England were ruled by monarchs and noblemen who spoke the same language, had much the same outlook, and fought wars against each other because of conflicting claims to the territory, or joined each other in fighting the Muslims in the Crusades. Their subjects were mostly serfs, who had no part in public affairs, spoke in both countries a variety of languages, and were bound by duties toward their feudal superiors and the church. At the second date these traditional obligations had not disappeared, but the differences between the peoples of the two countries had enormously increased, while within both countries there was a much stronger and wider sense of community. Englishmen and Frenchmen recognised themselves as such; accepted obligations to the sovereign; and admitted the claim of the sovereign on their loyalty at least in part because the sovereign symbolised the community as a whole, stood for France, or for England. There were of course exceptions to this statement. There were still regions and social strata which had hardly been affected, yet the trend was unquestionable. During the intervening centuries larger sections of the population had been drawn upwards into public life, and the awareness of forming a community had spread downwards into the population. This was largely a matter of economic and social development, of growing trade, specialised manufactures, the rise of cities and the enrichment of merchants. Schools and learning began to flourish (though formal education still only affected a small minority), and the French and English languages became fixed by a growing literature, both religious and secular. This was, to use a modern term, a growth of communication, albeit restricted in scope. In this process geography, economics, language, religion, and the power of the state all played their part. The last was, on balance, the most important, for it was the growth of the monarchical power—of its military, fiscal and bureaucratic controls—which determined the boundaries within which the sense of community should develop.

In the case of the new nations the process is easier to grasp, for it took place over a much shorter period and is well documented. The leaders of national movements since the French Revolution have been by definition articulate persons, and their propaganda among their own populations, designed to implant in them a national consciousness and a desire for political action, though largely conducted by word of mouth, was also put in writing at the time. The growth of new modern means of communication still further accelerated the process in the twentieth century in comparison with the nineteenth. In the case of the new nations of nineteenth and early twentieth century Europe, the main factor in the creation of national consciousness was language. In the formation of the overseas nations of European origin, economic and geographical causes were the most important. In colonial Africa, state boundaries arbitrarily fixed by imperial governments largely determined the units within which the attempt was made to create modern nations. In India and China the attempt to build modern national movements was superimposed on ancient civilisations to which the European categories of nationality had only limited relevance.

A fundamental feature of all these movements is that the nationalist elites were only able to mobilise support from peasants, merchants, artisans or factory workers because many persons in these various classes were discontented with political and social conditions. One may plausibly argue that the foundations of their discontent were economic. Nevertheless the discontent was directed by the nationalist elites into nationalist movements rather than towards economic change. Where this happened, one may say that the masses accepted nationalist rather than social revolutionary leadership. As this book is concerned with nationalist movements, attention will be concentrated inevitably on the activities, political aims and social composition of the nationalist elites rather than on the nature of their followers' economic grievances. Without the discontents there would have been no movements; but without the nationalist elites the movements would not have been nationalist. [. . .]

In the process of formation of national consciousness, and in movements for national independence and unity, there has been in each case a different combination of certain constantly recurring forces: state power, religion, language, social discontents and economic pressures. Where political and social power are concentrated in a group who differ in both religion and language from the majority of the population among whom they dwell, and an educated elite is emerging from that population, then the optimum conditions are given for the rapid growth of a nationalist movement. Where several small elites of different languages are emerging within the same state, or where the population shares either the religion or the language of its rulers but not both, a more complex situation arises, and the tasks of nationalist leaders are more difficult.

[*Nations and States* (Methuen: London, 1977), 6–10.]

<hr>

SUSAN REYNOLDS

20 Regnal Sentiments and Medieval Communities

Most medieval historians would deny that they are nationalists, but that is because, like many historians of the phenomenon of nationalism, they see it as something aggressive, xenophobic, and deplorable, but do not look hard at the ideas which underlie it. Nationalist ideas, however, are more widespread than the unpleasant manifestations of nationalist emotions. The most important is the belief, widely held though seldom recognized and articulated, that 'the world is naturally divided into nations, each of which has its own particular character and destiny'[1] and that nations by their very existence have the right to be self-governing and independent. The nationalist's nation is therefore an essentially corporate body, with essentially political rights. The nation is 'the body which legitimizes the state',[2] whether that state is governed by democratic or authoritarian means, and the nation-state, however governed, is the one sort of state which is by its nature both legitimate and internally cohesive. The fundamental premise of nationalist ideas is that nations are objective realities, existing through history. Some such premise, however unarticulated, seems to be implied in much writings about the history of Europe, including medieval Europe, with its teleological emphasis on the development of modern states—the predestined 'nation-states'. It seems normally to be taken for granted that the nation-states of today are the true nations of history and that only they can ever have inspired loyalties which deserve to be called nationalist. Allowance may be made for units like Scotland or Brittany which are not nation-states but are today claimed to be nations by somebody. None the less, any past unit of government which no one claims to be a nation now is *ipso facto* seen as having been less naturally cohesive in the past. It evidently did not enjoy the manifest destiny to solidarity and survival which is the essential attribute of the true nation.

The trouble about all this for the medieval historian is not that the idea of the permanent and objectively real nation is foreign to the middle ages, as so many historians of nationalism assume, but that it closely resembles the medieval idea of the kingdom as comprising a people with a similarly permanent and objective reality. Not all the kingdoms of the middle ages, however, were destined to become modern states, and if we start from nationalist assumptions we are in danger of prejudging the relative solidarity of those which did and those which did not. A more fundamental distortion arises from the fact that belief in the objective reality of nations inevitably diverts attention from itself: since the nation exists, belief in it is seen not as a political theory but as a mere recognition of fact. The history of nationalism becomes less a part of the history of political thought than of historical geography, while the starting-point of political development becomes the nation, with its national character or national characteristics. This pre-existing nation is then seen as moving through the attainment of 'national consciousness' to find its own rightful boundaries in the nation-state. Perhaps, however, it might be easier to assess the values and solidarities of the past if we considered whether the process may not sometimes have worked the other way round, with units which are perceived as nations as the product of history rather than its primary building-blocks. National character is that which is attributed to any group thought of as a nation: the nation itself is the product of its members' belief that it exists. In medieval terms, it was the fact of being a kingdom (or some lesser, but effective, unit of government) and of sharing a single law and government which promoted a sense of solidarity among its subjects and made them describe themselves as a people—irrespective of any relationship that we can now trace between the medieval 'people' and its kingdom on the one hand and the modern 'nation' and its state on the other.

A first step towards disentangling the political ideas and loyalties of the past from those of the present may be to avoid the confusions which arise from obviously ambiguous terminology. The word 'national' is nearly always misleading. Talk of 'the rise of the national monarchies', for instance, is liable to be either tautological or teleological, or both. The loyalties of people in 'national kingdoms' under 'national monarchies' presumably developed because of the way they thought of themselves then, rather than because their kingdoms developed into nation-states at some later time. It cannot be taken for granted, for instance, that France and England developed directly into nation-states because their monarchies were at all times more 'national' than that of Germany: the point needs to be argued, and it can only be argued by comparing the way people at the time thought of their governments. Calling some monarchies national and others not simply begs the question. The most confusing use of 'national' which still creeps into some medieval histories is that which survives from the nineteenth-century association of nationalism with popular government, and which contrasts 'national' with 'feudal' or 'royal'. 'National armies' were thus armies in which all classes are thought to have served (probably for more patriotic motives than those who served in a 'feudal host') while 'national parliaments' represented everyone in some kind of quasi-democratic way. Language like this casts a blanket of muddled anachronisms over medieval institutions and ideas. Until we can sort out what the medieval idea of a people did and did not have in common with modern nationalism it is better to avoid the words nation and national altogether. The difficulty about avoiding 'national' in medieval contexts is that we lack an adjective derived from 'kingdom'. [. . .] I therefore propose to employ the word 'regnal' whenever I want to describe that which pertains to a kingdom or kingdoms.

Another possible confusion between words and concepts arises from the common translation of the Latin word *gens* as 'race'. This derives from habits formed in the nineteenth century and earlier when 'race' was used widely and loosely—as in 'the English 'race', 'the German (or Germanic) race (or races)', and even 'a royal race of kings'. In the nineteenth century, as in the middle ages, the groups which medieval writers called *gentes*, *nationes*, or *populi* were actually thought of as units of common biological descent (that is, races in the more exact modern sense of the word) as well as of common culture. The history of races was investigated through philology, and 'national character' was explained in terms of biological transmission. Since people believed that descent and culture were closely connected, it was natural that their terminology should reflect the connection. Now, however, the advance of biology, history, archaeology, and linguistics has shown that human society is more complicated than that. The inhabitants of an area are likely to develop a common culture, particularly if they are governed as a unit, and they will then tend to breed with each other more than with outsiders. But the facts of biological descent in the distant past are probably less important for the transmission of culture than is the creation or maintenance of political solidarity in the present: how far they matter is, of course, highly controversial, since the boundary between genetics and culture, nature and nurture, race and nation, is so hard to trace empirically. Nevertheless it seems clear that the boundary exists, that few of the kinds of social and political change which the medieval historian studies can have been caused by genetic change, and that few of the variations in social patterns can have been genetically programmed.

Medieval *gentes* were not 'races' in any sense in which the word can be used without misunderstanding in the late twentieth century. The traditional idea of the 'races of Europe' is not merely morally repugnant in so far as it has been connected with ideas of a hierarchy of races: it is intellectually defective because it implies that cultural and political communities are in reality and in essence also communities of biological descent. Using the word in the older sense therefore invites confusion between what people in the past believed about their common descent and history and what we believe about them. It thereby tends to prevent us from appreciating the force of their beliefs. Incidentally, it also invites us to assume truly racial reasons for medieval hatreds and distrusts: that is, for instance, to assume that Normans were physically distinct from English or English from British. Yet, although medieval people themselves confused culture and descent, the sources do not suggest that physical differences, even where they existed, were as important to them as they are to modern racists. In this context [. . .] race is largely irrelevant, and I propose to translate *gens* not as 'race' (nor yet as 'tribe', which as applied to early medieval peoples carries the same misleading connotations of nineteenth-century ideas), but as 'a people'.

'A people' may also serve as a neutral translation of both *natio* and *populus*. There is no foundation at all for the belief, common among students of modern nationalism, that the word *natio* was seldom used in the middle ages except to describe the *nationes* into which university students were divided. It was used much more widely than that, and often as a synonym for *gens*: any individual writer might, of course, distinguish the two, for instance by giving one a more definitely political connotation than the other, or by using them to distinguish types of social and political unit which seemed to him significantly different. There is, however, no reason to believe that words of this kind were used more precisely and consistently through the centuries than they are today: Isidore of Seville's definitions were no more successful in controlling subsequent usage than are those of the Oxford Dictionary. As a matter of fact Isidore himself drew no clear distinction between the two words. For him, as for others, they do not seem to have any exact or exclusive sense.[3] Moreover, while in some contexts *populus* could mean something more like *plebs*, and be contrasted with *nobiles*, in others it was yet another synonym for *gens*. Like a *gens* or *natio*, a *populus* was thought of as a community of custom, descent, and government—a people.

[*Kingdoms and Communities in Western Europe (900–1300)* (Clarendon Press: Oxford, 1984), 251–6.]

JOHN ARMSTRONG
....

21 **Nations before Nationalism**

Since the late eighteenth century, nationalism has in many respects become the dominant political doctrine. The right of individuals to choose the state to which they belong, that is, to establish territorial political structures corresponding to their consciousness of group identity, has constituted a principal theme of political analysis.[1] My examination, however, stops at the threshold of nationalism, before the period (varying considerably from one part of Europe and the Middle East to another) when consciousness of ethnic identity became a predominant force for constituting independent political structures. A major objective of my work is, indeed, to provide a perspective in which such historically novel demands posed by nationalist movements must confront a lengthy record of human association in which persistent group identity did not ordinarily constitute the overriding legitimization of polity formation.

A time dimension of many centuries (similar to the *longue durée* emphasized by the *Annales* school of French historiography) is essential for disentangling independent ethnic experiences from the effects of diffusion and mimesis. An extended temporal perspective is especially important as a means of perceiving modern nationalism as part of a cycle of ethnic consciousness. Because the epoch of Absolutism that immediately preceded European nationalism involved, at least for elites, an exceptionally strong rejection of ethnic differentiation, nationalism is often seen as utterly unprecedented.[2] A longer look suggests that widespread intense ethnic identification, although expressed in other forms, is recurrent. For example, Absolutist Enlightenment dispersed the revived linguistic consciousness encouraged by Reformation and Counter-Reformation conflicts. One result has been that modern nationalist thought, succeeding to an age of cosmopolitanism, has sought permanent 'essences' of national character instead of recognizing the fundamental but shifting significance of boundaries for human identity.

The importance of focusing on boundaries has been most clearly stated by the Norwegian anthropologist Fredrik Barth.[3] He proposes a social interaction model of ethnic identity that does not posit a fixed 'character' or 'essence' for the group, but examines the perceptions of its members which distinguish them from other groups. Concentration on these attitudinal boundary mechanisms affords three major advantages: (1) Because ethnicity is defined by boundaries, both the cultural and the biological content of the group can alter as long as the boundary mechanisms are maintained. (2) Although Barth points out that his boundaries may have territorial counterparts, he emphasizes that ethnic groups are 'not merely or necessarily based on the occupation of exclusive territories'. (3) Barth's boundary approach facilitates consideration of other ethnic phenomena, exotic from the modern European standpoint, such as the use of languages as alternative codes rather than ethnic identifying symbols or prescriptive communication media.

Anthropological historians have been increasingly obliged to confront the fact, implicit in Barth's approach, that groups tend to define themselves not by reference to their own characteristics but by exclusion, that is, by comparison to 'strangers'. Primitive man, according to this interpretation, was disturbed by the uncanny experience of confronting others who, perforce, remained mute in response to his attempts at communication, whether oral or through symbolic gestures. Terms like 'goyim,' 'barbaroi,' and 'nemtsi' all imply such perception of the human incompleteness of persons who could not communicate with the in-group, which constituted the only 'real men.' Usually, in their original application such terms singled out one or two alien neighbors, and, by reference to such aliens, large ethnic groupings came to recognize their own relatively close relationship. Thus the extensive Germanic groups defined themselves as the people 'between Wend and Walsche,' never using either term to refer to any group that spoke a Germanic tongue. Just as the real referent for Wend shifted, probably, from Finnic reindeer nomads located northeast of the Germanic elements to the Slavs who later occupied the eastern limits of the Germanic sphere, the referent for 'Walsche' (or 'Welsch') changed from Celt alone to Celt, Latinized Celt, and Roman alike, on the southwest confines of the Germanic world.[4] Hence, in a rudimentary way, the Germanic settlement area was delimited in a territorial sense, although its 'boundaries' were very imprecise zones. Similarly, 'Turan,' among the distant Iranian cousins of the Germanic group, apparently originally applied to the Iranians' dark neighbors in what is now Baluchistan. Considerably later, the referent for 'Turan' became the Turkic element intruding into the northeast boundary zone of Iranic settlement.[5]

The French linguist Emile Benveniste is in fundamental agreement with anthropological historians in the conception of the ethnic group as defined by exclusion: 'Every name of an ethnic character, in ancient times, was differentiating and oppositional. There was present in the name which a people assumed the intention, manifest or not, of distinguishing itself from the neighboring peoples, of affirming the superiority derived from a common, intelligible language. Hence the ethnic group often constituted an antithetical duality with the opposed ethnic group.'[6]

Removing the focus of investigation from the internal characteristics of the group to its self-perceived boundaries is, of course, only a start toward an examination of ethnicity in history. [...] At the start it is important to recognize that the conception of the ethnic group or incipient nation as a group defined by exclusion implies that there is no purely definitional way of distinguishing ethnicity from other types of identity. The boundary approach clearly implies that ethnicity is a bundle of shifting interactions rather than a nuclear component of social organization. It is precisely this complex, shifting quality that has repelled many social scientists from analysing ethnic identity over long periods of time. Most who have approached ethnicity have also been attracted by the simplifying assumption that each ethnic group occupies an exclusive territory. Once one abandons the principle of territorial exclusivity, one must recognize that the phenomenon of ethnicity is part of a continuum of social collectivities, including, notably, classes and religious bodies. Over a long period of time each may transmute into one of the others. Consequently, I shall be more concerned with the interaction among class, ethnic, and religious characteristics than with compartmentalizing definitions. Nevertheless, there are certain sociological characteristics that, taken as tendencies rather than as categorically differentiating qualities, serve to distinguish the three kinds of collectivities. [. . .] Where, in practice, ethnicity and religion have coincided, groups exhibit the following characteristics: peculiar linguistic features associated with sacral identity; a high degree of endogamy; symbolic border guards such as peculiar architecture, dress, and manners. The dividing lines between class and ethnicity are sharper but harder to characterize briefly. In the premodern period, functional or occupational differentiation from neighboring social or ethnic groups was a prime distinguishing characteristic both of traditional diasporas and of nomads. Generally, however, a lower class (especially in sedentary agricultural societies) cannot constitute a group as persistently conscious of its identity as an ethnic collectivity.[7] The principal reason is that the incomplete lower-class occupational pyramid does not provide an elite with the communications and bargaining skills needed to legitimize the boundary mechanisms of the class, thereby ensuring its distinct identity within a large polity. Lacking the high-culture capacities a counterelite would provide, an underclass has difficulty resisting manipulation by the elites that guard the myths and symbols common to the society as a whole.

Emergence of such a counterelite is especially difficult in sedentary agricultural societies where dominant elites monopolize communication by symbols and supervise the socialization of all members of the polity by inculcation of myths legitimizing the elite's dominance. Nevertheless, it must be admitted that the inability of peasants, the agricultural underclass, to develop a persistent identity is a matter of degree rather than an absolute. [. . .] Certainly, the presence of very different linguistic patterns among peasants and elites, as contrasted to minor dialect differentiation, made maintenance of a latent but persistently strong identity easier. A major sign of emerging ethnic identification, especially in East Central Europe, has been the appearance of an articulate elite among a mass of peasants hitherto distinguished from other social segments in the polity only by their peculiar folklore and by linguistic patterns restricted to intimate small-group communication.

Once a counterelite peculiar to the incipient ethnic collectivity has developed, it can try to enter into an exchange relationship with the dominant elite of the polity. Indeed, one can posit the potential for such an exchange relationship—although it may be aborted by a *force majeure*—as a major sociological criterion for distinguishing ethnicity from class. In other words, once the occupational pyramid has become complete enough to enable a group to engage in conscious bargaining about its position in the polity rather than incoherent submission to manipulation by the dominant elite, ethnic identification is possible, even where there is no consideration of an autonomous political structure. For groups like diasporas, equipped with unusually sophisticated elites, such an exchange relationship may be crucial for survival. In sum, therefore, there is nothing predetermined about the boundaries that distinguish an ethnic collectivity; but one can point to ways in which these boundaries differ, notably in persistence, from those identifying a class.

The discussion so far has frequently referred to symbols and communication, less often to myth; all three concepts are critical to an analysis of the slow emergence of nations in the premodern period. The primary characteristic of ethnic boundaries is attitudinal. In their origins and in their most fundamental effects, ethnic boundary mechanisms exist in the minds of their subjects rather than as lines on a map or norms in a rule book. Both of these secondary effects are, as symbols, major indicators of boundaries. But failure to grasp the way in which culture is expressed by symbols makes it hard to understand boundary mechanisms that are not expressed in material delineations.[8]

Most often symbolic boundary mechanisms are words. Such words are particularly effective as traffic lights warning a group member when he is approaching a barrier separating his group from another. This intense power of a few symbolic 'border guards' is illustrated by early Yiddish. It was basically an Old High German dialect, but rigorously excluded certain words in the German environment that had specifically Christian connotations. For example, *sëganōn*, 'to bless,' was rejected because it derived from Latin *signare*, 'to make the sign [of the cross],' in favor of retaining the neutral form 'bentshn' from Latin *benedicere*, 'to speak well,' which earlier Jewish communities had incorporated in Southern Laaz, their Romance dialect. Such verbal symbolic devices safeguarded group identity against penetration of Christian concepts. But, as Suzanne Langer points out, significant symbols also include gestures, drawings, musical sounds, and the like.[9] Sometimes a graphic identity symbol, accepted in a routine manner, suddenly acquires intense significance. For centuries the *Reichsapfel*, a globe surmounted by a cross, symbolized the heavenly sphere in the Holy Roman imperial insignia. When Charles V, already king of Spain ruling lands extending around the terrestrial globe, was crowned emperor in 1530, he used the *Reichsapfel* as a symbol of his reinvigorated claims to universal empire. Though there is no specific evidence that Charles V envisaged his overt use of this symbol as a subtle reflection of the ancient Mesopotamian myth that portrayed terrestrial rule as a reflection of heavenly order, the symbolic resonance of the ancient myth may have unconsciously influenced his audience.[10]

Because the cues conveyed by symbols are signals from one ethnic group to others or among members of the same group, symbolic interaction is a type of communication. Perhaps for my purposes it is simplest to regard symbols as the content and communication as the means by which they become effective. Evidently, as in the case of linguistic border guards, symbols are often established as content generations or even centuries before they are communicated as cues to any given members of a group. Consequently, to an extraordinary degree ethnic symbolic communication is communication over the *longue durée*, between the dead and the living. Here, as in other facets of ethnic identity, the persistence of the symbol is more significant than its point of origin in the past. Persistence is closely related to the incorporation of individual symbols, verbal and nonverbal, in a mythic structure.[11]

Over long periods of time, the legitimizing power of individual mythic structures tends to be enhanced by fusion with other myths in a *mythomoteur* defining identity in relation to a specific polity.[12] Identification of these complex structures as mythic does not imply that they are false, any more than references to religious myths call into question their theological validity. Eric Dardel points out that demonstrable historical validity is not the critical aspect of the *mythomoteur*. "The mythic past cannot be dated, it is a part "before time" or, better, outside time. . . . Primordial actions are lost "in the night of time," what happened "once" (nobody knows when) goes on in a floating and many-layered time without temporal location. . . . [The myth narrator or epic poet] draws the audience of the story away, but only to make them set themselves at the desired distance.'[13] A most significant effect of the myth recital is to arouse an intense awareness among the group members of their 'common fate.' From the perspective of myth-symbol theory, common fate is simply the extent to which an episode, whether historical or 'purely mythical,' arouses intense affect by stressing individuals' solidarity against an alien force, that is, by enhancing the salience of boundary perceptions. Consequently, except for the highly differing ways of life discussed in chapters 2 and 4, it is the symbolic rather than the material aspects of common fate that are decisive for identity. Moreover, symbols need not directly reflect the 'objectively' most important elements of the material way of life even when it does constitute a sharply differentiating underlying factor.

Ethnic boundaries fundamentally reflect group attitudes rather than geographical divisions. Myth, symbol, communication, and a cluster of associated attitudinal factors are usually more persistent than purely material factors. When, however, one moves from the purely conceptual to the gritty business of investigating specific ethnic divisions, the utility of tangible indicators becomes evident. Geographic boundaries are not only tangible; they possess other important attributes: they often acquire intense symbolic significance, and the direct impact of political action is frequently earliest and strongest in a geographic context. Another reason for concentrating on boundaries is that a specialized social science discipline, geography, has provided a rich array of secondary sources on the physical boundary. For the purposes of this study, the term 'boundaries' will be reserved for all relevant informal limits resulting from social processes such as linguistic, folkloric, and economic development, whereas 'frontier' will denote borders defined by political action, including the formal action of autonomous ecclesiastical authorities. The distinction between frontier and boundary is highly important in discussing [...] the coincidence of one or more social boundaries, such as language isoglosses with political frontiers. As subtypes of the frontier, zone frontiers, which have been the norm throughout most of history, and the line frontier, increasingly significant in the modern period, should be distinguished.

Reference to geographical boundaries and frontiers affords a cogent introduction to the general problem of methodology. The greatest difficulty in studying cultures dispersed over wide ranges of time and space is phenomenological comparability. A brilliant recent analysis by a Czechoslovak scholar emphasizes the peril, even for students of recent nationalist movements, of assuming that phenomena bearing the same names are truly similar.[14] There is, however, the converse danger: assuming that because movements in cultures remote in time or space from modern Europe employ very different terms, the phenomenon of ethnic identification must be absent. A student of nascent French nationalism expresses this danger succinctly: 'National sentiment, national consciousness flourished at the start of the modern period. Of course, they were not expressed in the terms of nineteenth-century nationalism. The preliminary goals of our research are to find the appropriate terms, the content, and historical significance of national consciousness during the second half of the sixteenth century.'[15]

It is manifestly impossible for a work [...] covering many centuries and cultures to be based on independent deductions from original texts. As Bernard Lewis, a most accomplished Orientalist, has explained, even linguistic knowledge was insufficient for historians dealing with Arabic, Persian, and Turkish sources until they had been published in critical editions accompanied by scholarly elucidations. Up to that time, the danger of misunderstanding the originals was worse than reliance on translations.[16] With my more limited linguistic knowledge, I am wholly dependent, even when I have read critical editions of the 'sources' in their original languages or in scholarly translations, upon the expertise of multitudes of devoted scholars. Dependence upon secondary analyses is enhanced by the esoteric, symbolic terms in which much surviving evidence is couched. Such esoteric communication was especially important for groups whose identity was pervaded by sacral concepts. Yet the fact that the content of sacral symbols remained stable over long periods of time throughout large cultural areas provides an immense advantage for the comparativist. Among Christians, elaborate formal definitions designed to preclude idiosyncratic usage in doctrinal matters were adopted at the Second Council of Nicaea in 787. [...] Such liturgical symbols, strictly regulated in both the Eastern Orthodox and the Latin Catholic churches, came to acquire strong implications for ethnic identity.[17] The persistent constraints that church definitions exerted on ethnic idiosyncrasies in the use of symbols make it possible, as a contemporary historian of Western polity formation explains, to assess subtle shifts in legitimization:

What synodists tried to express in abstract words, or in legal terms, the coronation rite tried to convey in its rubrics, gestures, prayers, and symbols, that is, by liturgical means. Words could have different significations, but liturgical vehicles should (and on the whole did) have only one unambiguous meaning. . . . For these [rites] had not only to be crystal clear and unambiguous, but also and above all readily comprehensible to even the most dull-witted contemporary accustomed to thinking in only the crudest terms.[18]

The assistance provided by the symbolic code, elaborately reconstructed by recent scholarship, is unusually important in the comparativist's direct observation of visual symbols, which in early Christian churches constituted a kind of 'frozen' liturgy. Can the analyst resort to a similar system of visual evidence for Islam, that cultural world so useful for comparison with Christendom? Islamic theology formally eschews the use of symbols. Yet even the lay traveler can discern relationships between one Moslem architectural form, the minaret, and regional ethnic identities. The square Malikite minaret rises above the new as well as the old mosques of Morocco, whereas the mosque of a Cairo suburb retains the intricately decorated polygonal minaret of the Mameluke period, and Turks and Iranians use other forms of minarets to commemorate their own periods of historical greatness.

[*Nations before Nationalism* (University of North Carolina Press: Chapel Hill, NC, 1982), 4–11.]

ANTHONY D. SMITH

22 The Origins of Nations

Bureaucratic 'Incorporation'

The two basic kinds of ethnic core, the lateral and the vertical, also furnish the two main routes by which nations have been created.

Taking the lateral route first, we find that aristocratic *ethnies* have the potential for self-perpetuation, provided they can incorporate other strata of the population. A good many of these lateral *ethnies* cannot do so. Hittites, Philistines, Mycenaeans, even Assyrians, failed to do so, and they and their cultures disappeared with the demise of their states.[1] Other lateral *ethnies* survived by 'changing their character', as [. . .] with Persians, Egyptians and Ottoman Turks, while preserving a sense of common descent and some dim collective memories.

Still others grafted new ethnic and cultural elements on to their common fund of myths, symbols and memories, and spread them out from the core area and down through the social scale. They did so, of course, in varying degrees. The efforts of the Amhara kings, for example, were rather limited in scope; yet they managed to retain their Monophysite Abyssinian identity in their heartlands.[2] That of the Castilians was more successful. They managed to form the core of a Spanish state (and empire) that expelled the Muslim rulers and almost united the Iberian peninsula. Yet, even their success pales before that of their Frankish and Norman counterparts.

In fact, the latter three efforts at 'bureaucratic incorporation' were to prove of seminal historical importance. In all three cases, lower strata and outlying regions were gradually incorporated in the state, which was grounded upon a dominant ethnic core. This was achieved by administrative and fiscal means, and by the mobilization of sections of the populations for inter-state warfare, as in the Anglo-French wars.[3] An upper-class *ethnie*, in other words, managed to evolve a relatively strong and stable administrative apparatus, which could be used to provide cultural regulation and thereby define a new and wider cultural identity.[4] In practice, this meant varying degrees of accommodation between the upper-class culture and those prevalent among the lower strata and peripheral regions; yet it was the upper-class culture that set its stamp on the state and on the evolving national identity.

Perhaps the most clear-cut example is afforded by British developments. As there had been an Anglo-Saxon kingdom based originally on Wessex before the Norman Conquest, the conquered populations could not be treated simply as a servile peasantry. As a result, we find considerable inter-marriage, linguistic borrowing, élite mobility and finally a fusion of linguistic culture, within a common religio-political framework.

In other words, bureaucratic incorporation of subject *ethnies* entailed a considerable measure of cultural fusion and social intermingling between Anglo-Saxon, Danish and Norman elements, especially from the thirteenth century on. By the time of Edward III and the Anglo-French and Scottish wars, linguistic fusion had stabilized into Chaucerian English and a 'British' myth served to weld the disparate ethnic communities together.[5]

I am not arguing that an English nation was fully formed by the late fourteenth century. There was little economic unity as yet, despite growing fiscal and judicial intervention by the royal state. The boundaries of the kingdom, too, both with Scotland and in France, were often in dispute. In no sense can one speak of a public, mass-education system, even for the middle classes. As for legal rights, despite the assumptions behind Magna Carta, they were common to all only in the most minimal senses. For the full development of these civic elements of nationhood, one would have to wait for the Industrial Revolution and its effects.[6]

The ethnic elements of the nation, on the other hand, were well developed. By the fourteenth century or slightly later, a common name and myth of descent, promulgated originally by Geoffrey of Monmouth, were widely current, as were a variety of historical memories.[7] These were fed by the fortunes of wars in Scotland and France. Similarly, a sense of common culture based on language and ecclesiastical organization had emerged. So had a common strong attachment to the homeland of the island kingdom, which in turn bred a sense of solidarity, despite internal class-cleavages. The bases of both the unitary state and a compact nation had been laid, and laid by a lateral Norman-origin *ethnie* that was able to develop its regnal administration to incorporate the Anglo-Saxon population. Yet the full ideology of Englishness had to wait for late-sixteenth- and seventeenth-century developments, when the old British myth gave way to a more potent middle-class 'Saxon' mythology of ancient liberties.[8]

A similar process of bureaucratic incorporation by an upper-class lateral *ethnie* can be discerned in France. Some fusion of upper-stratum Frankish with subject Romano-Gallic culture occurred under the Christianized Merovingians, but a regnal solidarity is really only apparent in northern France at the end of the twelfth century. It was in this era that earlier myths of Trojan descent, applied to the Franks, were resuscitated for all the people of northern France. At the same time, the *pays d'oc*, with its different language, customs and myths of descent, remained for some time outside the orbit of northern bureaucratic incorporation.[9]

Of course, Capetian bureaucratic incorporation from Philip II onwards was able to draw on the glory and myths of the old Frankish kingdom and Charlemagne's heritage. This was partly because the kingdom of the Eastern Franks came to be known as the *regnum Teutonicorum*, with a separate identity. However, it was also due to the special link between French dynasties and the Church, notably the archbishopric of Rheims. The backing of the French clergy, and the ceremony of anointing at coronations, were probably more crucial to the prestige and survival of a French monarchy in northern France before the battle of Bouvines (1214) than the fame of the schools of Paris or even the military tenacity of the early Capetians. There was a sacred quality inhering in the dynastic *mythomoteur* of the Capetians and their territory that went back to the Papal coronation of Charlemagne and Papal legitimation of Pepin's usurpation in AD 754, which the Pope called a 'new kingdom of David'. The religious language is echoed centuries later, when at the end of the thirteenth century Pope Boniface declared: '. . . like the people of Israel . . . the kingdom of France [is] a peculiar people chosen by the Lord to carry out the orders of Heaven'.[10]

Though there is much debate as to the 'feudal' nature of the Capetian monarchy, the undoubted fact is that an originally Frankish ruling-class *ethnie* managed, after many vicissitudes, to establish a relatively efficient and centralized royal administration over north and central France (later southern France). So it became able to furnish those 'civic' elements of compact territory, unified economy, and linguistic and legal standardization that from the seventeenth century onwards spurred the formation of a French nation as we know it. The process, however, was not completed until the end of the nineteenth century. Many regions retained their local character, even after the French Revolution. It required the application of Jacobin nationalism to mass education and conscription under the Third Republic to turn, in Eugene Weber's well-known phrase, 'peasants into Frenchmen'.[11]

An even more radical 'change of character' occasioned by attempted bureaucratic incorporation by a 'lateral' ethnic state is provided by Spain. Here it was the Castilian kingdom that formed the fulcrum of Christian resistance to Muslim power. Later, united with the kingdom of Aragon, it utilized religious community as an instrument of homogenization, expelling those who, like the Jews and Moriscos, could not be made to conform. Here, too, notions of *limpieza de sangre* bolstered the unity of the Spanish crown, which was beset by demands on several sides from those claiming ancient rights and manifesting ancient cultures. Quite apart from the Portuguese secession and the failed Catalan revolt, Basques, Galicians and Andalusians retained their separate identities into the modern era. The result is a less unified national community, and more polyethnic state, than either Britain or France. With the spread of ideological nationalism in the early nineteenth century, these ethnic communities felt justified in embarking on varying degrees of autonomous development, whose reverberations are still felt today. Yet, most members of these communities shared an overarching Spanish political sentiment and culture, over and beyond their often intense commitment to Basque, Catalan or Galician identity and culture.[12]

Historically, the formation of modern nations owes a profound legacy to the development of England, France and Spain. This is usually attributed to their possession of military and economic power at the relevant period, the period of burgeoning nationalism and nations. As the great powers of the period, they inevitably became models of the nation, the apparently successful format of population unit, for everyone else. Yet in the case of England and France, and to a lesser extent Spain, this was not accidental. It was the result of the early development of a particular kind of 'rational' bureaucratic administration, aided by the development of merchant capital, wealthy urban centres and professional military forces and technology. The 'state' formed the matrix of the new population-unit's format, the 'nation'. It aided the type of compact, unified, standardized and culturally homogenized unit and format that the nation exemplifies.

Some would say that the state actually 'created' the nation, that royal administration, taxation and mobilization endowed the subjects within its jurisdiction with a sense of corporate loyalty and identity. Even in the West, this overstates the case. The state was certainly a necessary condition for the formation of the national loyalties we recognize today. However, its operations in turn owed much to earlier assumptions about kingdoms and peoples, and to the presence of core ethnic communities around which these states were built up. The process of ethnic fusion, particularly apparent in England and France, which their lateral *ethnies* encouraged through the channels of bureaucratic incorporation, was only possible because of a relatively homogeneous ethnic core. We are not here talking about actual descent, much less about 'race', but about the *sense* of ancestry and identity that people possess. Hence the importance of myths and memories, symbols and values, embodied in customs and traditions and in artistic styles, legal codes and institutions. In *this* sense of 'ethnicity', which is more about cultural perceptions than physical demography, albeit rooted perceptions and assumptions, England from an early date, and France somewhat later, came to form fairly homogeneous *ethnies*. These *ethnies* in turn facilitated the development of homogenizing states, extending the whole idea of an *ethnie* into realms and on to levels hitherto unknown, to form the relatively novel concept of the nation.

The 'Rediscovery' of the 'Ethnic Past'

In contrast to the route of bureaucratic incorporation by lateral *ethnies*, the process by which demotic *ethnies* may become the bases for nations is only indirectly affected by the state and its administration. This was either because they were subject communities—the usual case—or because, as in Byzantium and Russia, the state represented interests partially outside its core *ethnie*. This subdivision also produces interesting variants on the constitutive political myth, or *mythomoteur*, of vertical *ethnies*.[13]

In all these communities, the fund of cultural myths, symbols, memories and values was transmitted not only from generation to generation, but also throughout the territory occupied by the community or its enclaves, and down the social scale. The chief mechanism of this persistence and diffusion was an organized religion with a sacred text, liturgy, rites and clergy, and sometimes a specialized secret lore and script. It is the social aspects of salvation religions, in particular, that have ensured the persistence and shaped the contours of demotic *ethnies*. Among Orthodox Greeks and Russians, Monophysite Copts and Ethiopians, Gregorian Armenians, Jews, Catholic Irish and Poles, myths and symbols of descent and election, and the ritual and sacred texts in which they were embodied, helped to perpetuate the traditions and social bonds of the community.

At the same time, the very hold of an ethnic religion posed grave problems for the formation of nations from such communities. It transpired that 'religion-shaped' peoples, whose ethnicity owed so much to the symbols and organization of an ancient faith, were often constrained in their efforts to become 'full' nations. Or rather, their intellectuals may find it harder to break out of the conceptual mould of a religio-ethnic community. So many members of such demotic *ethnies* simply assumed that theirs was already, and indeed always had been, a nation. Indeed, according to some definitions they were. They possessed in full measure, after all, the purely ethnic components of the nation. Arabs and Jews, for example, had common names, myths of descent, memories and religious cultures, as well as attachments to an original homeland and a persisting, if sub-divided, sense of ethnic solidarity. Did this not suffice for nationhood? All that seemed to be necessary was to attain independence and a state for the community.[14]

Yet, as these examples demonstrate, matters were not so simple. Quite apart from adverse geo-political factors, social and cultural features internal to the Arab and Jewish communities made the transition from *ethnie* to nation difficult and problematic. The Arabs have been faced, of course, by their geographic extent, which flies in the face of the ideal of a 'compact nation' in its clearly demarcated habitat. They have also had to contend with the varied histories of the sub-divisions of the 'Arab nation', ranging from the Moroccan kingdoms to those of Egypt or Saudi Arabia. There is also the legacy of a divisive modern colonialism, which has often reinforced historical differences and shaped the modern Arab states with their varied economic patterns. Mass, public education has, in turn, like legal rights, been the product of the colonial and post-colonial states and their élites. Above all, however, the involvement of most Arabs and most Arab states with Islam, whose *umma* both underpins and challenges the circle and significance of an 'Arab nation', creates an ambiguous unity and destiny, and overshadows efforts by Arab intelligentsia to rediscover an 'Arab past'.[15]

The Jews were also faced with problems of geographic dispersion, accentuated by their lack of a recognized territory and exile from an ancient homeland. True, in the Pale of Settlement and earlier in Poland, something approaching a public religious education system and common legal rights (albeit restricted) had been encouraged by the *kahal* system and its successors. Yet, though Jews, like Armenians, were compelled to occupy certain niches in the European economy, we can hardly characterize their enclave communities as models of economic unity, let alone a territorial division of labour. Quite apart from these obstacles to national unity, there were also the ambivalent attitudes and self-definitions of Judaism and its rabbinical authorities. Only later, did some rabbis and one wing of Orthodoxy come to support Jewish nationalism and its Zionist project, despite the traditional hopes for messianic restoration to Zion of generations of the Orthodox. The concept of Jewish self-help had become alien to the medieval interpretation of Judaism; and the general notion that the Jews were a 'nation in exile' actually strengthened this passivity.[16]

It was in these circumstances of popular resignation amid communal decline, set against Western national expansion, that a new stratum of secular intelligentsia emerged. Their fundamental role, as they came to see it, was to transform the relationship of a religious tradition to its primary bearers, the demotic *ethnies*. We must, of course, place this development in the larger context of a series of revolutions—socio-economic, political and cultural—which began in the early-modern period in the West. As we saw, the primary motor of these transformations was the formation of a new type of professionalized, bureaucratic state on the basis of a relatively homogeneous core *ethnie*. Attempts by older political formations to take over some of the dimensions of the Western 'rational state' and so streamline their administrations and armies, upset the old accommodations of these empires to their constituent *ethnies*. In the Habsburg, Ottoman and Romanov empires, increasing state intervention, coupled with incipient urbanization and commerce, placed many demotic *ethnies* under renewed pressures. The spread of nationalist ideas from the late-eighteenth century on, carried with it new ideals of compact population-units, popular representation and cultural diversity, which affected the ruling classes of these empires and even more the educated stratum of their subject communities.[17]

For the subject vertical *ethnie*, a secularizing intelligentsia led by educator-intellectuals supplied the motor of transformation, as well as the cultural framework, which among lateral *ethnie* had been largely provided by the incorporating bureaucratic state. It was this intelligentsia that furnished the new communal self-definitions and goals. These redefinitions were not simple 'inventions', or wholesale applications of Western models. Rather, they were derived from a process of 'rediscovery' of the ethnic past. The process tended to reverse the religious self-view: instead of 'the people' acting as a passive but chosen vessel of salvation, subordinate to the divine message, that message and its salvation ethic became the supreme expression and creation of the people's genius as it developed in history.[18]

At the centre of the self-appointed task of the intelligentsia stood the rediscovery and realization of the community. This entailed a moral and political revolution. In the place of a passive and subordinate minority, living precariously on the margins of the dominant ethnic society and its state, a new compact and politically active nation had to be created ('recreated' in nationalist terminology). From now on, the centre stage was to be occupied by the people, henceforth identified with 'the masses', who would replace the aristocratic heroes of old. This was all part of the process of creating a unified, and preferably autarchic, community of legally equal members or 'citizens', who would become the fount of legitimacy and state power. However, for this to occur, the people had to be purified of the dross of centuries—their lethargy, divisions, alien elements, ignorance and so on—and emancipate themselves. That was the primary task of the educator-intellectuals.

The transition, then, from demotic *ethnie* to civic nation carries with it several related processes and movements. These include:

1. a movement from subordinate accommodation and passivity of a peripheral minority to an active, assertive and politicized community with a unified policy;

2. a movement towards a universally recognized 'homeland' for the community, a compact, clearly demarcated territory;

3. economic unification of all members of the territorially demarcated community, with control over its own resources, and movement towards economic autarchy in a competitive world of nations;

4. turning ethnic members into legal citizens by mobilizing them for political ends and conferring on each common civil, social and political rights and obligations;

5. placing the people at the centre of moral and political concern and celebrating the new role of the masses, by re-educating them in national values, myths and memories.

That traditional élites, especially the guardians of sacred texts which had so long defined the demotic *ethnie*, might resist these changes, was to be expected. This meant that the intellectuals had to undercut earlier definitions of the community by re-presenting their novel conceptions through ancient symbols and formats. These were in no sense mere manipulations (though there undoubtedly was individual manipulation, such as Tilak's use of the Kali cult in Bengal); there is no need to unmask what are so patently selective readings of an ethnic past. Yet selection can take place only within strict limits, limits set by the pre-existing myths, symbols, customs and memories of vertical *ethnies*.

['The Origins of Nations', *Ethnic and Racial Studies*, 12/3 (1989), 349–56.]

WALKER CONNOR
....

23   When is a Nation?

A little more than a decade ago Eugen Weber wrote a study with the intriguing title *Peasants into Frenchmen: The Modernization of Rural France, 1870–1914.* The book's convincingly documented thesis was that most rural and small-town dwellers within France did not conceive of themselves as members of a French nation as recently as 1870 and that many still failed to do so as late as World War I. With the partial exception of the regions to the north and east of Paris, the integration of the countryside into the French social and political system was largely fanciful. The typical village was a physical, political, and cultural isolate. The famed road network was in essence a skeleton connecting the major cities to Paris but offering no access roads to the villages. The school system was still inadequate to effect the Jacobin dream of a single and unilingual French nation.[1] To the mass of peasants—and therefore to most inhabitants of France—the meaningful world and identity seldom extended beyond the village. This is how one mid-nineteenth century French observer described life in the countryside: 'Every valley is still a little world that differs from the neighbouring world as Mercury does from Uranus. Every village is a clan, a sort of state with its own patriotism.'[2]

Weber's findings were the more astonishing because conventional scholarship had treated the French nation as one of the very oldest, to many the oldest, of Europe's contemporary nations. Many distinguished historians had written that the French nation had crystallized during the Middle Ages. The French historian Marc Bloch, for example, had asserted: 'that the texts make it plain that so far as France and Germany were concerned this national consciousness was already highly developed about the year 1100'.[3] The Dutch scholar Johann Huizinga considered French and English nationalism 'to be in full flower' by the fourteenth century.[4] To the British scholar Sydney Herbert, 'if the Hundred Years War [1337–1453] between France and England is as far as possible from being a national war in its origins, yet toward its close genuine nationality appears, splendid and triumphant, with Jeanne d'Arc'.[5] Still other historians have perceived the emergence of national consciousness among the French as a post-Medieval development, crediting the Bourbons (1589–1793) with its development, although usually considering the process completed by the reign of Louis XIV (1643–1715). This is how one group of scholars described the situation at the time of his accession.[6]

France, at the middle of the seventeenth century, held the first rank among the powers of Europe . . . For a time France alone in Europe was a consolidated unit of race and institutions, showing the spirit of nationality and employing the agencies and methods of a great modern state.[7]

To stress the obvious, Weber's disclosure that a French identity had still not penetrated the rural masses hundreds—in some cases several hundreds—of years later than scholars had presumed French nationalism to be in full flower, holds potentially immense ramifications for the study of nationalism. Is the French experience unique or has there been a general tendency to assume that national consciousness had rather thoroughly permeated this or that people long before such an assumption was justifiable? Unfortunately, I am unaware of any studies, similar to Weber's, dealing with other national groups. However, there is one source of such data that covers a broad sampling of peoples. Between 1840 and 1915, there occurred a massive migration of peoples from Europe to the United States. For the most part, these migrants were from rural areas, and their education had been either minimal or non-existent. The few intellectuals and those who came from major cities were often aware of their membership in one of the European groupings that are recognized today as nations. Yet the peasants, who were far more typical of the overall population of the countries from which they had migrated, certainly were not. They regularly identified themselves in terms of some other identity or identities. [. . .]

The peasants, who predominated throughout most of Europe, were not until quite recently cognizant of membership in the nations to which nationalist writers and outsiders assigned them. Given that nationalism is a mass, not an élite phenomenon, the contemporary nations of Europe emerged far more recently than has generally been recognized. Indeed, even today Europe is not devoid of peoples whose sense of national consciousness is shrouded in ambiguity. Yugoslavia alone offers three cases: the Montenegrins, Macedonians, and Bosnians. There are Montenegrins, as well as Serbs, who consider Montenegrins part of the Serbian nation. Even more complex is the case of the Macedonians. Bulgaria has traditionally maintained that the Macedonians are Bulgars; Greece has claimed that at least a significant portion of them are Greeks; they have also historically been claimed by the Serbs; since World War II, the Yugoslavian government has insisted that they constitute a separate nation. At least until quite recently, Macedonian opinion has been divided. Majority opinion agreed with Sofia that Macedonians were a branch of the Bulgar nation, while others considered themselves to be either Serb or Greek. There was scant indication of any conviction that Macedonians considered themselves a separate nation. There is little reason to question Belgrade's recent success in encouraging a sense of separate nationhood among the Macedonians, although the 1981 census data, which indicated a total absence of people within Macedonia who claimed either Bulgar or Greek identity, are extremely suspect, particularly given the fact that most Macedonians in the United States continue to feel that they are of Bulgarian stock.[8] As to the Moslems of Bosnia-Hercegovina, they are claimed by both Croats and Serbs, while the government has been promoting a separate Bosnian identity among these people.

Elsewhere in Europe, the Soviets have declared the Moldavians a separate nation and granted them union republic status, despite the contentions of the Romanian government that the Moldavians are Romanian and their language a Romanian dialect. Moreover, despite claims by the Albanian government to the contrary, it is not at all certain that a single Albanian consciousness has truly welded the highland Gegs and more southerly Tosks. Differences in culture, including social organization, are pronounced, although becoming less so. Far more consequential are readily perceptible physical differences between the two peoples, a formidable barrier to the inculcation of the myth of common ancestry that the government so assiduously cultivates.

A reasonably accurate reading of the national consciousness of the masses has therefore often been unobtainable.[9] And in the absence of such information, assertion and counter-assertion have often been passed off for fact. For example, an analysis of recent developments in the Moldavian Soviet Socialist Republic described the Moldavians as a people 'whose members feel ethnically, linguistically, and culturally Romanian'.[10] Perhaps! Yet no evidence is offered to support this unqualified assertion, and the reader must assume on faith that the Soviet now-multigenerational attempt to inculcate a Moldavian national consciousness has not won a single convert. If the Yugoslav government's forty-year programme to convince the Macedonians of a separate national identity has borne fruit, why should we assume that the Soviets' similar and simultaneous programme in Moldavia has been totally barren?

Unsupported assertions played key roles in the creation of the states of Yugoslavia and Czechoslovakia following World War I. Although there were nationalist writers at that time who asserted that the Croatian, Serbian, and Slovene nations had existed as separate identities for generations, the case for a Yugoslavia that would be consistent with Woodrow Wilson's advocacy of the principle of national self-determination was made on the dictum that these three peoples were merely subunits of a Southernslav (Yugoslav) nation. Typical statements found in the programme of groups who were pressuring the victorious powers for a state of the Yugoslavs included:

'The Croats and the Serbs are one nation.'

'Our race, variously known as Serb, Croat and Slovene, is nevertheless, in spite of three different names, but one people—the Jugoslavs.'

'The Croats, Serbs, and Slovenes are one and the same as regards nationality and language, though they were known by different names.'[11] [. . .]

[I]t is doubtful that the rural masses were cognizant of a Croatian or Slovenian identity, much less of still-larger identity as Yugoslav. Similarly, although there were intellectuals at the time who claimed separate nationhood for both the Czech and the Slovak peoples, the 1920 constitution that created Czechoslovakia pronounced the two peoples to be a single 'Czechoslovak nation'. Within two decades the Nazis would take advantage of the hollowness of these fictions by appealing to animosities felt by Croats and Slovenes towards Serbs and by Slovaks towards Czechs. [. . .]

As we noted earlier, national consciousness is a mass, not an élite phenomenon, and the masses' view of group-self has often been indiscernible. Scholars have therefore been over-reliant upon the musings of élites whose generalizations concerning the existence of national consciousness are highly suspect. Indeed, until quite recent times it is doubtful whether ostensibly nationalistic élites even considered the masses to be part of their nation. The Polish and Hungarian gentry, for example, manifested national consciousness and aspirations for generations, while simultaneously imposing a system of serfdom on the masses of their ostensible co-nationals. Perceiving themselves quite correctly as a pariah group, rather than as co-members of a national family, the ostensibly Polish serfs sided against the Polish landlords in 1846, although the latter were fighting for Polish national (read: élite) liberation. A sense of common nationhood is not compatible with a cross-cutting class-cleavage as deep and unremitting as that between slave and landowner.[12] To quote the late Rupert Emerson, the nation is 'the largest community which, when the chips are down, effectively commands men's loyalty, overriding the claims of both lesser communities within it and those which cut across it or potentially enfold it within a still greater society'.[13]

The nation is therefore compatible with those 'lesser' cross-cutting cleavages that an appeal to common nationhood does not or cannot transcend. The institution of serfdom in Eastern Europe prior to the mid-nineteenth century can therefore be treated as *prima facie* evidence of the absence therein of nations, as contrasted with élite group-identities.[14]

In some societies the history of the voting franchise also offers hints of when a nation came into existence. As we are reminded by the history of the rise of national consciousness in, *inter alia*, Japan and Germany, democratic institutions are certainly no prerequisite for nation-formation. However, if a society describes itself as a democracy, then the refusal to permit large sections of the populace to participate in the political process may be viewed as tantamount to declaring that those who are disenfranchised are not members of the nation. If the rights of Englishmen include the right to vote, then what can one say concerning a so-called English nation in which most Englishmen were prohibited from exercising that right? Before 1832, when landlords alone were allowed to vote, it is estimated that only one in sixty adult English males could vote. Following the so-called Reform Bill of that year, one in every thirty male adults would be permitted to do so. In 1867, the franchise was further extended to cover some 80 per cent of all adult males, and in 1918 to cover the remaining 20 per cent of males and all women over thirty years of age. Reflecting on such nineteenth-century limitations on the franchise in Britain and elsewhere,[15] E. H. Carr observed:

Property, sometimes described as 'a stake in the country', was a condition of political rights—and it might be said without much exaggeration—of full membership of the nation . . . The rise of new social strata to full membership of the nation marked the last three decades of the 19th century throughout western and central Europe . . . National policy was henceforth founded on the support of the masses; and the counterpart was the loyalty of the masses to a nation which had become the instrument of their collective interests and ambitions.[16]

The delay—in some cases stretching into centuries—between the appearance of national consciousness among sectors of the élite and its extension to the masses reminds us of the obvious but all-too-often ignored fact that nation-formation is a process, not an occurrence or event.[17] And this, in turn, further thwarts the attempt to answer the question, 'When is a nation?'. Events are easily dated; stages in a process are not. At what point did a sufficient number/percentage of a given people acquire national consciousness so that the group merited the title of nation? There is no formula. We want to know the point in the process at which a sufficient portion of the population has internalized the national identity in order to cause appeals in its name to become an effective force for mobilizing the masses. While this does not require that 100 per cent of the people have acquired such national consciousness, the point at which a quantitative addition in the number sharing a sense of common nationhood has triggered the qualitative transformation into a nation resists arithmetic definition. In most cases we shall probably have to be satisfied with assigning dates after the fact (after an effective illustration of mass mobilization in the name of the nation), although the sophisticated analysis of well-designed polling instruments can be very helpful in probing the breadth of national consciousness.[18] What we can say is that the presence of even substantial numbers of intellectuals proclaiming the existence of a new nation is not sufficient. Nearly a century ago, the Levant produced a bevy of writers proclaiming the reality of the Arab nation; yet even today Arab national consciousness remains anomalously weak.

Although numerous authorities over the decades have addressed the question, 'What is a nation?', far less attention has been paid to the question, 'At what point in its development does a nation come into being?' There is ample evidence that Europe's currently recognized nations emerged only very recently, in many cases centuries later than the dates customarily assigned for their emergence. In the matter of nation-formation, there has been far less difference in the timetables of Western and Eastern Europe than is customarily acknowledged, and the lag time between Europe and the Third World has also been greatly exaggerated. Indeed, in the case of a number of putative nations within Europe, it is problematic whether nationhood has even yet been achieved.

A key problem faced by scholars when dating the emergence of nations is that national consciousness is a mass, not an élite phenomenon, and the masses, until quite recently isolated in rural pockets and being semi- or totally illiterate, were quite mute with regard to their sense of group identity(ies). Scholars have been necessarily largely dependent upon the written word for their evidence, yet it has been élites who have chronicled history. Seldom have their generalities about national consciousness been applicable to the masses, and very often the élites' conception of the nation did not even extend to the masses.

Another vexing problem is that nation-formation is a process, not an occurrence. The point in the process at which a sufficient portion of a people has internalized the national identity in order to cause nationalism to become an effective force for mobilizing the masses does not lend itself to precise calculation. In any event, claims that a particular nation existed prior to the late-nineteenth century should be treated cautiously.

['When is a Nation?', *Ethnic and Racial Studies*, 13/1 (1990), 92–100.]

Section IV

Nationalism in Europe

INTRODUCTION

Serious studies of nationalism began with the exploration of the origins and varieties of the ideology in its European birthplace. The first systematic investigations were those of the historians Carlton Hayes, Louis Snyder, Frederick Hertz, Boyd Shafer, and Hans Kohn before and during the Second World War. Hans Kohn's distinction between 'western' and 'eastern' forms of nationalism has been the focus of much critical attention. In England, France, and America, according to Kohn, a voluntaristic type of nationalism, which regarded the nation as a rational association of common laws in a given territory, was the product of aspirant middle classes; by contrast, in Central and Eastern Europe, and later in Asia, an organic, mystical, and often authoritarian form of nationalism emerged which, in the absence of a middle class, was forged and led by intellectuals.

The French Revolution is often taken to be the first example of European nationalism. The recent detailed study by Liah Greenfeld, however, argues that sixteenth-century England was really the first to identify, and elevate, the whole people as the sovereign nation. Later examples in France, Germany, Russia, and America only added the exclusive and cultural components of the more familiar ethnic nationalisms.

In Eastern Europe, ethnic nationalisms took various forms: aristocratic, bourgeois, popular, and bureaucratic. But Peter Sugar suggests that they shared with other European nationalisms the revolutionary drive to transfer power to 'the people', yet differed, as Kohn had maintained, in translating western political concepts and Herderian cultural-linguistic populism into an East European ethnic idiom which was strongly influenced by religious and state traditions of the area. For Eric Hobsbawm, this divisive ethnic and linguistic nationalism flourished after 1870 because of fear of economic change, massive population movements, and political mobilization. The folkloric rediscovery of 'the people' was closely linked to vernacular languages, but should not be confused with the later political activism which Miroslav Hroch characterizes as 'phase B' of the development of stateless European nationalisms.

Hobsbawm depicts the recent resurgence of ethno-linguistic nationalisms in Europe as defensive protests. For Hechter and Levi, the post-war 'ethnic revival' in the industrial West is the product of 'internal colonialism'. In his major study of this topic, Hechter argued that recent Scottish, Welsh, and Irish nationalisms were examples of the revitalization of ethnicity in the Celtic fringe caused by state expansion, bureaucratic neglect, and the historic exploitation of incorporated peripheries by industrial cores. A later article of his examines the social bases of recent movements for ethnic autonomy, distinguishing between the resulting 'hierarchical cultural division of labour' and the 'segmental' form found in a Scotland that had preserved its key institutions after the Union.

Nationalism is a state of mind. The process of history can be analysed as a succession of changes in communal psychology, in the attitude of man toward all manifestations of individual and social life. Such factors as language, territory, traditions—such sentiments as attachment to the native soil, the *Heimat*, and to one's kin and kind—assume different positions in the scale of values as communal psychology changes. Nationalism is an idea, an idée-force, which fills man's brain and heart with new thoughts and new sentiments, and drives him to translate his consciousness into deeds of organized action. Nationality is therefore not only a group held together and animated by common consciousness; but it is also a group seeking to find its expression in what it regards as the highest form of organized activity, a sovereign state. As long as a nationality is not able to attain this consummation, it satisfies itself with some form of autonomy or pre-state organization, which, however, always tends at a given moment, the moment of 'liberation,' to develop into a sovereign state. Nationalism demands the nation-state; the creation of the nation-state strengthens nationalism. Here, as elsewhere in history, we find a continuous interdependence and interaction.

'Nationality is a state of mind corresponding to a political fact,'[1] or striving to correspond to a political fact. This definition reflects the genesis of nationalism and of modern nationality, which was born in the fusion of a certain state of mind with a given political form. The state of mind, the idea of nationalism, imbued the form with a new content and meaning; the form provided the idea with implements for the organized expression of its manifestations and aspirations. Both the idea and the form of nationalism were developed before the age of nationalism. The idea goes back to the ancient Hebrews and Greeks, and was revived in Europe at the time of the Renaissance and the Reformation. During the period of the Renaissance, the literati rediscovered Greco-Roman patriotism; but this new attitude never penetrated to the masses, and its secularism was soon swept away by the retheologization of Europe through the Reformation and Counter-Reformation. But the Reformation, especially in its Calvinistic form, revived the nationalism of the Old Testament. Under the favourable circumstances which had developed in England, a new national consciousness of the English as the godly people penetrated the whole nation in the revolution of the seventeenth century. Meanwhile in Western Europe a new political power—that of the absolute kings—had developed a new political form, the modern centralized sovereign state; and this became the political form into which, during the French Revolution, the idea of nationalism was infused, filling it with a consciousness in which all citizens could share, and making possible the political and cultural integration of the masses into the nation. With the advent of nationalism, the masses were no longer in the nation, but of the nation. They identified themselves with the nation, civilization with national civilization, their life and survival with the life and survival of the nationality. Nationalism thenceforward dominated the impulses and attitudes of the masses, and at the same time served as the justification for the authority of the state and the legitimation of its use of force, both against its own citizens and against other states.

Sovereignty has a twofold significance. One aspect deals with the relations of the state of its citizens, the other with the relations between states. Similarly, the sentiment of nationalism is double-faced. Intranationally, it leads to a lively sympathy with all fellow members within the nationality; internationally, it finds its expression in indifference to or distrust and hate of fellow men outside the national orbit. In intranational relations, men are guided not only by supposedly permanent common interests, but also by sentiments of sympathy, devotion, and even self-sacrifice. In international relations, they are guided by the supposed lack of permanent common interests among different states, and by sentiments which vary from complete indifference to the most bitter antipathy, and are subject to swift changes within that range. Nationality, which is nothing but a fragment of humanity, tends to set itself up as the whole. Generally this ultimate conclusion is not drawn, because ideas predating the age of nationalism continue to exercise their influence. These ideas form the essence of Western civilization—of Christianity as well as of enlightened rationalism: the faith in the oneness of humanity and the ultimate value of the individual. Only fascism, the uncompromising enemy of Western civilization, has pushed nationalism to its very limit, to a totalitarian nationalism, in which humanity and the individual disappear and nothing remains but the nationality, which has become the one and the whole [. . .]

In the age of nationalism, nations are the great corporate personalities of history; their differences in character and outlook are one of the main factors shaping the course of events. Only in that age, the will of the nations—rather than that of individuals, dynasties, or non-national bodies like churches or classes—assumes decisive importance; therefore an understanding of their history demands a phenomenology of nations and their characters. These characters are not determined prehistorically or biologically, nor are they fixed for all time; they are the product of social and intellectual development, of countless gradations of behavior and reaction, some of which are hardly discernible in the flux of the past, from which the historian selects what seem to him to be the essential and characteristic elements in a pattern of almost confusing complexity. While the formation of national characters has gone on through many centuries, the crystallization has taken place in the age of nationalism. In the Western world, in England and in France, in the Netherlands and in Switzerland, in the United States and in the British dominions, the rise of nationalism was a predominantly political occurrence; it was preceded by the formation of the future national state, or, as in the case of the United States, coincided with it. Outside the Western world, in Central and Eastern Europe and in Asia, nationalism arose not only later, but also generally at a more backward stage of social and political development: the frontiers of an existing state and of a rising nationality rarely coincided; nationalism, there, grew in protest against and in conflict with the existing state pattern—not primarily to transform it into a people's state, but to redraw the political boundaries in conformity with ethnographic demands.

Because of the backward state of political and social development, this rising nationalism outside the Western world found its first expression in the cultural field. It was at the beginning the dream and hope of scholars and poets, unsupported by public opinion—which did not exist, and which the scholars and poets tried to create—a venture in education and propaganda rather than in policy-shaping and government. At the same time all rising nationalism and the whole modern social and intellectual development outside Western Europe were influenced by the West, which for a long time remained the teacher and the model. Yet this very dependence on the West often wounded the pride of the native educated class, as soon as it began to develop its own nationalism, and ended in an opposition to the 'alien' example and its liberal and rational outlook.

Each new nationalism, having received its original impulse from the cultural contact with some older nationalism, looked for its justification and its differentiation to the heritage of its own past, and extolled the primitive and ancient depth and peculiarities of its traditions in contrast to Western rationalism and to universal standards. Nationalism in the West arose in an effort to build a nation in the political reality and the struggles of the present without too much sentimental regard for the past; nationalists in Central and Eastern Europe created often, out of the myths of the past and the dreams of the future, an ideal fatherland, closely linked with the past, devoid of any immediate connection with the present and expected to become sometime a political reality. Thus they were at liberty to adorn it with traits for the realization of which they had no immediate responsibility, but which influenced the nascent nation's wishful image of itself and of its 'mission.' While Western nationalism was, in its origin, connected with the concepts of individual liberty and rational cosmopolitanism current in the eighteenth century, the later nationalism in Central and Eastern Europe and in Asia easily tended towards a contrary development. Dependent upon, and opposed to, influences from without, this new nationalism, not rooted in a political and social reality, lacked self-assurance; its inferiority complex was often compensated by over-emphasis and overconfidence, their own nationalism appearing to nationalists in Germany, Russia, or India as something infinitely deeper than the nationalism of the West, and therefore richer in problems and potentialities. The quest for the meaning of German, Russian, or Indian nationalism, the musing about the 'soul' or the 'mission' of the nation, an endless discussion of its relation to the West, all that became characteristic of this new form of nationalism.

Nationalism in the West was based upon a nationality which was the product of social and political factors; nationalism in Germany did not find its justification in a rational societal conception, it found it in the 'natural' fact of a community, held together, not by the will of its members nor by any obligations of contract, but by traditional ties of kinship and status. German nationalism substituted for the legal and rational concept of 'citizenship' the infinitely vaguer concept of 'folk,' which, first discovered by the German humanists, was later fully developed by Herder and the German romanticists. It lent itself more easily to the embroideries of imagination and the excitations of emotion. Its roots seemed to reach into the dark soil of primitive times and to have grown through thousands of hidden channels of unconscious development, not in the bright light of rational political ends, but in the mysterious womb of the people, deemed to be so much nearer to the forces of nature. This difference in the concepts of nation and nationalism was a historical consequence of the difference in effect produced by Renaissance and Reformation between Germany and Western Europe.

In the West, Renaissance and Reformation created a new society in which the middle classes and secular learning gained a growing preponderance, and the universal and imperial Roman concept of the medieval world was abandoned not only in fact, but also in theory. But in Central and Eastern Europe this medieval idea of world empire lingered and even gathered new strength from antiquarian research—the unreal though fascinating strength of a phantom world. The Renaissance and the Reformation had not deeply changed the political and social order in Germany as they had in the West; they were purely scholarly and theological events. Farther east they did not penetrate at all—Russia and the Near East remained untouched—and thus the old cleavage between the Western and the Eastern Empire deepened.

[*The Idea of Nationalism* (Macmillan: New York, 1945), 18–20, 329–31.]

LIAH GREENFELD

25   Types of European Nationalism

National identity in its distinctive modern sense is [. . .] an identity which derives from membership in a 'people,' the fundamental characteristic of which is that it is defined as a 'nation.' Every member of the 'people' thus interpreted partakes in its superior, elite quality, and it is in consequence that a stratified national population is perceived as essentially homogeneous, and the lines of status and class as superficial. This principle lies at the basis of all nationalisms and justifies viewing them as expressions of the same general phenomenon. Apart from it, different nationalisms share little. The national populations—diversely termed 'peoples,' 'nations,' and 'nationalities'—are defined in many ways, and the criteria of membership in them vary. The multiformity which results is the source of the conceptually evasive, protean nature of nationalism and the cause of the perennial frustration of its students, vainly trying to define it with the help of one or another 'objective' factor, all of which are rendered relevant to the problem only if the national principle happens to be applied to them. The definition of nationalism proposed here ['. . . nationalism locates the source of individual identity within a "people", which is seen as the bearer of sovereignty, the central object of loyalty, and the basis of collective solidarity.'[1]] recognizes it as an 'emergent phenomenon,' that is, a phenomenon whose nature—as well as the possibilities of its development and the possibilities of the development of the elements of which it is composed—is determined not by the character of its elements, but by a certain organizing principle which makes these elements into a unity and imparts to them a special significance.[2]

There are important exceptions to every relationship in terms of which nationalism has ever been interpreted—whether with common territory or common language, statehood or shared traditions, history or race. None of these relationships has proved inevitable. But from the definition proposed above, it follows not only that such exceptions are to be expected, but that nationalism does not have to be related to *any* of these factors, though as a rule it is related to at least some of them. In other words, *nationalism is not necessarily a form of particularism*. It is a political ideology (or a class of political ideologies deriving from the same basic principle), and as such it does not have to be identified with any particular community.[3] A nation coextensive with humanity is in no way a contradiction in terms. The United States of the World, which will perhaps exist in the future, with sovereignty vested in the population, and the various segments of the latter regarded as equal, would be a nation in the strict sense of the word within the framework of nationalism. The United States of America represents an approximation to precisely this state of affairs.

As it is, however, nationalism is the most common and salient form of particularism in the modern world. Moreover, if compared with the forms of particularism it has replaced, it is a particularly effective (or, depending on one's viewpoint, pernicious) form of particularism, because, as every individual derives his or her identity from membership in the community, the sense of commitment to it and its collective goals is much more widespread. In a world divided into particular communities, national identity tends to be associated and confounded with a community's sense of uniqueness and the qualities contributing to it. These qualities (social, political, cultural in the narrow sense, or ethnic)[4] therefore acquire a great significance in the formation of every specific nationalism. The association between the nationality of a community and its uniqueness represents the next and last transformation in the meaning of the 'nation' and may be deduced from the zigzag pattern of semantic (and by implication social) change.

The word 'nation' which, in its conciliar and at the time prevalent meaning of an elite, was applied to the population of a specific country (England) became cognitively associated with the existing (political, territorial, and ethnic) connotations of a population and a country. While the interpretation of the latter in terms of the concept 'nation' modified their significance, the concept 'nation' was also transformed and—as it carried over the connotations of a population and a country, which were consistent with it—came to mean 'a sovereign people.' This new meaning replaced that of 'an elite' initially only in England. [. . .] Elsewhere the older meaning long remained dominant, but it was, eventually, supplanted.

The word 'nation,' meaning *sovereign* people,' was now applied to other populations and countries which, like the first nation, naturally had some political, territorial, and/or ethnic qualities to distinguish them, and became associated with such geo-political and ethnic baggage. As a result of this association, 'nation' changed its meaning once again, coming to signify *'a unique* sovereign people.' (These changes are shown in Figure 1.) The last transformation may be considered responsible for the conceptual confusion reigning in the theories of nationalism. The new concept of the nation in most cases eclipsed the one immediately preceding it, as the latter eclipsed those from which it descended, but, significantly, this did not happen everywhere. Because of the persistence and, as we shall see, in certain places development and extension of structural conditions responsible for the evolution of the original, non-particularistic idea of the nation, the two concepts now coexist.

The term 'nation' applied to both conceals important differences. The emergence of the more recent concept signified a profound transformation in the nature of nationalism, and the two concepts under one name reflect two radically different forms of the phenomenon (which means both two radically different forms of national identity and consciousness, and two radically different types of national collectivities—nations). [. . .]

The original modern idea of the nation emerged in sixteenth-century England, which was the first nation in the world (and the only one, with the possible exception of Holland, for about two hundred years). The individualistic civic nationalism which developed there was inherited by its colonies in America, and later became characteristic of the United States.

Particularistic nationalism, reflecting the dissociation of the meaning of the 'nation' as a 'people' extolled as the bearer of sovereignty, the central object of collective loyalty, and the basis of political solidarity, from that of an 'elite,' and its fusion with geo-political and/or ethnic characteristics of particular popula-

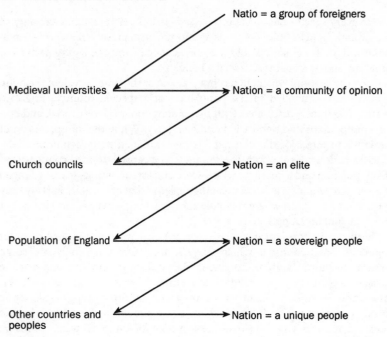

FIG. 1.

tions, did not emerge until the eighteenth century. This happened on the continent of Europe, whence it started to spread all over the world. Collectivistic nationalism appeared first, and almost simultaneously, in France and Russia, then, close to the end of the eighteenth century and in the beginning of the nineteenth, in German principalities. While France, from many points of view, represented an ambivalent case (its nationalism was collectivistic and yet civic), Russia and Germany developed clear examples of ethnic nationalism.

When nationalism started to spread in the eighteenth century, the emergence of new national identities was no longer a result of original creation, but rather of the importation of an already existing idea. The dominance of England in eighteenth-century Europe, and then the dominance of the West in the world, made nationality the canon. As the sphere of influence of the core Western societies (which defined themselves as nations) expanded, societies belonging or seeking entry to the supra-societal system of which the West was the center had in fact no choice but to become nations.[5] The development of national identities thus was essentially an international process, whose sources in every case but the first lay outside the evolving nation.

At the same time, for several reasons, every nationalism was an indigenous development. The availability of the concept alone could not have motivated anyone to adopt a foreign model, however successful, and be the reason for the change of identity and the transformation which such fundamental change implied. For such a transformation to occur, influential actors must have been willing, or forced, to undergo it. The adoption of national identity must have been, in one way or another, in the interest of the groups which imported it.[6] Specifically, it must have been preceded by the dissatisfaction of these groups with the identity they had previously. A change of identity presupposed a crisis of identity.

Such was in fact the case. The dissatisfaction with the traditional identity reflected a fundamental inconsistency between the definition of social order it expressed and the experience of the involved actors. This could result from the upward or downward mobility of whole strata, from the conflation of social roles (which might imply contradictory expectations from the same individuals), or from the appearance of new roles which did not fit existing categories. Whatever the cause of the identity crisis, its structural manifestation was in every case the same—'anomie.'[7] This might be, but was not necessarily, the condition of the society at large; it did, however, directly affect the relevant agents (that is, those who participated in the creation or importation of national identity). Since the agents were different in different cases, the anomie was expressed and experienced differently. Very often it took the form of status-inconsistency, which, depending on its nature, could be accompanied by a profound sense of insecurity and anxiety.

The specific nature of the change and its effects on the agents in each case profoundly influenced the character of nationalism in it. The underlying ideas of nationality were shaped and modified in accordance with the situational constraints of the actors, and with the aspirations, frustrations, and interests which these constraints generated. This often involved reinterpreting them in terms of indigenous traditions which might have existed alongside the dominant system of ideas in which the now rejected traditional identity was embedded, as well as in terms of the elements of this system of ideas itself which were not rejected. Such reinterpretation implied incorporation of pre-national modes of thought within the nascent national consciousness, which were then carried on in it and reinforced.

The effects of these structural and cultural influences frequently combined with that of a certain psychological factor which both necessitated a reinterpretation of the imported ideas and determined the direction of such reinterpretation. Every society importing the foreign idea of the nation inevitably focused on the source of importation—an object of imitation by definition—and reacted to it. Because the model was superior to the imitator in the latter's own perception (its being a model implied that), and the contact itself more often than not served to emphasize the latter's inferiority, the reaction commonly assumed the form of *ressentiment*. A term coined by Nietzsche and later defined and developed by Max Scheler,[8] *ressentiment* refers to a psychological state resulting from suppressed feelings of envy and hatred (existential envy) and the impossibility of satisfying these feelings. The sociological basis for *ressentiment*—or the structural conditions that are necessary for the development of this psychological state—is twofold. The first condition (the structural basis of envy itself) is the fundamental comparability between the subject and the object of envy, or rather the belief on the part of the subject in the fundamental equality between them, which makes them in principle interchangeable. The second condition is the actual inequality (perceived as not fundamental) of such dimensions that it rules out practical achievement of the theoretically existing equality. The presence of these conditions renders a situation *ressentiment*-prone irrespective of the temperaments and psychological makeup of the individuals who compose the relevant population. The effect produced by *ressentiment* is similar to that of 'anomie' and to what Furet, discussing Tocqueville's argument regarding the emphasis on equality in pre-revolutionary France, calls 'the Tocqueville effect.'[9] In all these cases the creative impulse comes from the psychologically unbearable inconsistency between several aspects of reality.

The creative power of *ressentiment*—and its sociological importance—consists in that it may eventually lead to the 'transvaluation of values,' that is, to the transformation of the value scale in a way which denigrates the originally supreme values, replacing them with notions which are unimportant, external, or indeed bear in the original scale the negative sign. The term 'transvaluation of values' may be somewhat misleading, because what usually takes place is not a direct reversal of the original hierarchy. Adopting values directly antithetical to those of another is borrowing with the opposite sign. A society with a well-developed institutional structure and a rich legacy of cultural traditions is not likely to borrow lock, stock, and barrel from anywhere. However, since the creative process resulting from *ressentiment* is by definition a reaction to the values of others and not to one's own condition regardless of others, the new system of values that emerges is necessarily influenced by the one to which it is a reaction. It is due to this that philosophies of *ressentiment* are characterized by the quality of 'transparency': it is always possible to see behind them the values they disclaim. *Ressentiment* felt by the groups that imported the idea of the nation and articulated the national consciousness of their respective societies usually resulted in the selection out of their own indigenous traditions of elements hostile to the original national principle and in their deliberate cultivation. In certain cases—notably in Russia—where indigenous cultural resources were absent or clearly insufficient, *ressentiment* was the single most important factor in determining the specific terms in which national identity was defined. Wherever it existed, it fostered particularistic pride and xenophobia, providing emotional nourishment for the nascent national sentiment and sustaining it whenever it faltered.[10]

It is possible, then, to distinguish analytically three phases in the formation of specific nationalisms: structural, cultural, and psychological, each defined by

the factor dominant in it. The adoption of a new, national identity is precipitated by a regrouping within or change in the position of influential social
groups. This structural change results in the inadequacy of the traditional
definition, or identity, of the involved groups—a crisis of identity, structurally
expressed as 'anomie'—which creates among them an incentive to search for
and, given the availability, adopt a new identity. The crisis of identity as such
does not explain why the identity which is adopted is *national*, but only why
there is a predisposition to opt for some new identity. The fact that the identity
is *national* is explained, first of all, by the availability at the time of a certain type
of ideas, in the first case a result of invention, and in the rest of an importation.
(It is this dependence on the idea of the nation, ultimately irreducible to
situational givens and solely attributable to the unpredictable ways of human
creativity, that makes national identity a matter of historical contingency
rather than necessity.) In addition, *national* identity is adopted because of its
ability to solve the crisis. The variation in the nature of the crises to which all
specific nationalism owe their inception explains some of the variation in the
nature of different nationalisms.

The adjustment of the idea of the nation to the situational constraints of the
relevant agents involves its conceptualization in terms of indigenous traditions. This conceptualization further distinguishes every national identity.

Finally, where the emergence of national identity is accompanied by *ressentiment*, the latter leads to the emphasis on the elements of indigenous traditions—or the construction of a new system of values—hostile to the principles
of the original nationalism. The matrix of the national identity and consciousness in such cases evolves out of this transvaluation of values, the results of
which, together with the modifications of the original principles reflecting the
structural and cultural specificity of each setting, are responsible for the
unique, distinct character of any one nationalism.

[*Nationalism: Five Roads to Modernity* (Harvard University Press; Cambridge, Mass.,
1992), 7–9, 14–17.]

PETER SUGAR

26 **Nationalism in Eastern Europe**

Just as in western Europe and Germany, nationalism in eastern Europe was a
revolutionary force aiming at transferring sovereignty from the rulers to the
people (irrespective of who 'the people' were). Eastern European nationalism
shared with all others the basically anticlerical, constitutional, and egalitarian
orientation that gave it its revolutionary character. In spite of these similarities
eastern European nationalism differed substantially from that of Germany and
western Europe. [. . .] Keeping in mind the features that eastern European

nationalism shared with the West, as well as those which differentiated it, we can divide it [. . .] into four main groups. For convenience's sake we will call them bourgeois, aristocratic, popular, and bureaucratic eastern European nationalisms. Manifestations of almost all varieties can be detected in every region of eastern Europe. Yet at least in the early periods of nationalism, one of them dominated, and put its imprint on subsequent developments.

Of these four varieties, bourgeois nationalism most resembled that of the West. The aristocratic version, basically a contradiction in terms, produced the least constructive results. Popular nationalism vaguely resembles Jacksonian democracy, while the bureaucratic variety has much in common with the nationalism of the newly emerging countries of Africa and Asia in our days. Bourgeois nationalism triumphed only among the Czechs. Poland and Hungary are the best examples of the second, or aristocratic; Serbia and Bulgaria of the third; Turkey, Greece, and Romania of the fourth. There are good explanations for this development. [. . .]

In the Czech provinces of the Habsburg Empire the aristocracy was powerful but foreign. Unable to share the aspirations of a population to which they did not belong, the nobles in these lands could not take effective advantage of their power. When their interest coincided with that of the rest of the population, as in the case of the struggle for more local and less centralized government, aristocrats and commoners collaborated. But this occasional partnership was insufficient to assure a leading role to the aristocracy in the shaping of Czech nationalism. At the same time these provinces, which had been closely associated with Germany and western Europe all through their history, shared the intellectual and economic progress of the West and were, therefore, able to approach nationalism in an almost western manner. This tendency was not only reinforced but to a large extent determined by the economic development of Bohemia and Silesia in the eighteenth century. Moravia, more backward in this respect, always tended to be more conservative than were the other two provinces whom it followed only because alone it could achieve nothing. In the two industrially most advanced provinces, a real third estate and within it a strong and viable bourgeoisie had developed and was ready to assume leadership by the time nationalism began to be a force. The various interests of the middle class were already strong enough by the time of the death of Maria Theresa to bridge, at least temporarily, the gap between Czech and German and to hold their own against both aristocracy and the lower classes. When, in the second half of the nineteenth century, Germans and Czechs ceased to cooperate, and most of the nobles and class-conscious workers were placed into the 'enemy camp' as far as the Czechs were concerned, their nationalism became even more western or bourgeois in its outlook. From the beginning, in its advocacy of constitutional monarchy, parliamentarianism, federalism, paternalistic democracy, and economic emphasis, Czech nationalism closely resembled that of the classical liberals in the

West. But there were also significant differences between Czech and western bourgeois nationalism, placing the Czech variant, according to our definition, in the eastern European family of nationalism.

As the Czechs had no state of their own, they were forced to include linguistic equality among the goals they tried to achieve within the framework of the Habsburg Empire. This lack of a state also made it imperative for Czechs to champion outdated rights and institutions (*Staatsrecht*, and so on) to justify their other demands. Consequently their outlook became less realistic and more historical-traditional than the bourgeois nationalism of western Europe. They looked to the West, sharing its traditions and development, but geography and political realities forced their nationalism into an eastern mold.

In Poland and Hungary, the situation was quite different from that in the Czech lands, although both countries had had close relations with the West for centuries. First of all, hostility to practically everything German was not as late in developing in these countries as it was among the Czechs, but was of long standing. Second, both countries lacked a real middle class, and a large percentage of those who could be called bourgeois were Germans. Finally, the aristocracies that controlled both the agrarian economy and the local and central legislatures were the most numerous in Europe. Within the ranks of the nobility there were great divisions—magnates and gentry were separated not only by the relative importance of their titles, but also by wealth, political influence, and levels of education. The interests of aristocracy and bourgeois often clashed, but facing rulers and commoners they managed to present a united front. Together they had an economic, political, and ecclesiastic power monopoly buttressed and protected by social status that produced enough strength to challenge even royal power. Charles VI (Charles III in Hungary) and Maria Theresa were forced and able to manage and manipulate the Hungarian nobility fairly successfully; Joseph II, the Saxon kings, and Stanislas Augustus in Poland were less successful. All of them, even Joseph II, realized sooner or later that they could not rule without the cooperation of the nobility.

The nobles looked at nationalism as a new, additional argument that could be used by them in their battle against their rulers, foreign or native, and it made relatively little difference to them under what flag they fought this battle. As long as they were able to equate *natio* with the 'political nation,' the *una eademque nobilitas* (to use the phrase of the Hungarians), and by doing this expand the circle of their supporters without giving up any or only secondary privileges, they were ready to become nationalists and to use their arguments. Nationalism was, as far as they were concerned, only a new proof of the correctness of their belief that the only legitimate source of power was the nation that they identified with their class. When pressed or in need of help, the nobles were willing to share some of their privileges with certain people, but they never admitted that others were entitled to what they enjoyed. They reserved for themselves the right to decide when, and who should be admitted, and to what degree, into membership in the political nation. They considered participation in the political life of their countries not a right but a privilege based on historic-feudal documents and tradition. Consequently their nationalism, although honestly patriotic and often revolutionary, remained exclusive, tradition bound, and estate conscious. This tendency was only reinforced by the policies of their adversaries, the emperors of Austria and Russia and the kings of Prussia.

Although commoners rose to positions of prominence in the nineteenth century in partitioned Poland and Hungary, the prestige of the nobility remained strong enough to induce those members of the middle class who achieved economic or political eminence to adopt the values and the way of life of the aristocracy. The nationalism of Poland and Hungary remained aristocratic until the end of the second World War. The spirit animating it did not change even if the personalities promoting it were non-nobles. This is why we cannot agree with the arguments presented by Endre Arató.[1] In regard to Hungary alone, he differentiates between the manifestations of aristocratic and bourgeois nationalism and his views of aristocratic nationalism do not differ substantially from that presented in these pages. Arató recognizes that aristocratic nationalism was dominant in Hungary in the developing years of modern nationalism, but he claims that it was superseded by bourgeois nationalism in the two decades following 1830. The main difference between the two, in Arató's opinion, was that while aristocratic nationalism was mainly political in a narrow class sense, bourgeois nationalism placed the main emphasis on economic reform and in general paralleled the dominant trends of western nationalism in its demands. While Arató is correct in pointing to certain desiderata voiced by the leaders of the Lower House of the Hungarian Parliament in the 1840s, he forgets to mention the importance of economic issues in the unsuccessful negotiations that took place during the previous decades between the aristocratic nationalists and Vienna. Julius Moskolezy's study[2] shows quite clearly the importance of economic considerations in the program of those whom Arató considers aristocratic nationalists. Even if we admit that in the 1840s economic issues were stressed more than they had been previously, we must remember that

men like Kossuth tried to connect the claims of supremacy of the estate-conscious nobility with the demands of newly emerging nationalism. They opposed the crown as champions of the nation state concept, but denied to their non-Magyar fellow citizens the right to develop their nationalities in the name of the old Hungarian estate-state.[3]

In this quotation we find not only the reason for the tragic civil war that raged in Hungary in 1848–49 when national unity was so badly needed, but an additional explanation of why and how Hungarian nationalism retained its aristocratic character. It might have been the large number of minorities living within the boundaries of what the Magyars and Poles considered to be their countries that made them believe that they had to protect historical rights. The result is still the same.

The Romanian boyars were in the same advantageous position that the Hungarian and Polish nobles enjoyed. In spite of men of the stamp of Constantin Golescu, they stuck to their reactionary views consistently, in 1821, 1831–32, and 1848, until any solution under their leadership became impossible. The liberal group that emerged and was defeated in 1848 was too small and too powerless after that date to assert itself in the difficult political situation that prevailed in Moldavia and Wallachia prior to the Crimean War. Finally the various views expounded by the different nationalistic groups in the Principalities found little or no echo among the Romanians living in Transylvania, the Bukovina, or Bessarabia. The only point on which all Romanians agreed was the desire for national unity. The only form of nationalism that could count on the support of all Romanians was irredentist. This form of nationalism could offer hope for final success after 1859 when a united Romania made it an official state policy, and by so doing, the government became the leader of the national movement. Irredentist nationalism became the slogan with which the bureaucracy justified its actions and omissions and its condemnation of all opposition as unpatriotic. Nationalism became identified not only with nation and state, but also with the policy of the government.

Bureaucratic nationalism also developed in Greece and Turkey. While the Greek movement started among the merchants and other middle-class elements, this group lacked leadership, was dispersed all over Europe, and was unable to shape events during Greece's war of independence. The civil war that paralleled this event also proved that no other element of the population was able to impose its views on the rest. Greek factionalism remained a serious problem, making united action difficult even after Greece had gained her independence following the intervention of the Great Powers. Under these circumstances only the government and the bureaucracy could make their voices heard effectively everywhere in the country. The foreign dynasties and their military and civil servants, both foreign and domestic, were anything but popular and were in need of an issue that could unite the factions of the population and reconcile it with the government. Irredentist nationalism offered the solution for these needs and developed into the main domestic and foreign propaganda weapon that was entirely in the hands of the government. For reasons somewhat different from those in Romania, the same type of nationalism developed in Greece also. When one thinks of the Venizelist invasion of Asia Minor after the first World War and the Cyprus controversy in our days, it becomes quite evident how little the nature of Greek nationalism has changed since its inception.

Turkey presents the clearest case of bureaucratic nationalism. In this country the possibilities for the development of various kinds of nationalism were the most limited in all of eastern Europe. There was neither an aristocracy nor a middle class in the Ottoman Empire, and the clergy could not espouse nationalism, an ideal that clashed with Muslim theology and political theory. The intellectual and political life of the Turks in the Ottoman Empire was limited almost entirely to the military and civil servants, including students of the schools that trained people for jobs in the bureaucracy. Ideas of change and reform were limited to this circle and always had the improvement of the state's administrative organs and international position as its goals. Nationalism developed slowly under these circumstances. At first it was not an independent philosophy or movement, but simply an additional tool in the hand of those who tried to reorganize the bureaucratic machinery and strengthen the state. The first Turk who separated nationalism from bureaucratic reform and treated it as an issue by itself was Ziya Gökalp (1875–76–1924) whose first writings appeared in 1911, but his ideas failed to influence the Turkish masses, although they shaped the thinking of many of his politically minded contemporaries, including Mustafa Kemal. It was the latter who tried to make nationalists of the Turks, but even he insisted on a special kind of nationalism that suited his plans and his vision of his country's future. His government promulgated the official nationalism of the Kemalist movement and opposed all its other manifestations. Not until the second half of the 1930s do we find significant nationalistic manifestations in Turkey that are free from bureaucratic sponsorship.

Popular nationalism, which could also be called populist or egalitarian nationalism, emerged in Serbia and Bulgaria. In these lands the long years of Ottoman rule had a leveling effect. The nobility had disappeared except in Bosnia and Macedonia where conversion to Islam had saved the estates of certain families. Not too numerous, these Muslim Slavs did not appear to differ from the feudatory and later hereditary Turkish landlords until the linguistic issue became important in the eyes of the Serb and Bulgarian nationalists. But because the lands that these people inhabited were not incorporated into Serbia or Bulgaria until the twentieth century, when nationalism was firmly enough established to be able to handle the seeming contradiction presented by the speech and faith of these people, their existence had little influence on the nationalism of Serbs and Bulgarians during its formative period. During these years the growing Slav merchant class was still too small to offer leadership. When it did, as in Bulgaria in the middle decades of the nineteenth century, it was both idealistic and realistic enough to develop an egalitarian policy. The views of the great peasant masses were, as those of this class usually are, basically democratic and directed mainly against landlordism. The facts that the landlords were mostly foreigners and that the traditional institutions and language of the peasantry had survived centuries of foreign rule thanks to the millet system furnished the ingredients for the development of popular nationalism.

This type of nationalism was developed by the native lower clergy and the Serbs and Bulgarians, mainly merchants, who lived outside the borders of the Ottoman Empire. The clergy's grievances and goals were similar to those of the peasantry, from which most of them sprang. In their case, *diocese* took the place of land and *foreign bishops* that of the foreign landlords. The Serbs of the Vojvodina and the Military Border, the Bulgars in Istanbul, Russia, Wallachia, and later Serbia furnished the required sophistication and the theoretical nationalist justification that shaped the native ingredients into popular nationalism. Under the existing social and economic conditions this was the only form of nationalism that could go beyond theory in Serbia and Bulgaria. As in the aristocratic nationalism of Hungary and Poland, the popular nationalism of Serbia and Bulgaria was subsequently diluted by princes, bureaucrats, and the advocates of the middle class, but it never lost its basic approach and character. Bulgaria was called 'the peasant state' with good reason.[4] It takes little imagination to find one of the reasons for the grave difficulties Yugoslavia had to face between the two great wars of this century in the conflicting approaches to nationalism that the major nationalities of this country favored. Serbia's basic popular approach was weakened and became partly aristocratic when Beograd (Belgrade) tried to dominate Zagreb and Ljubljana. Neither approach suited the Croats whose approach was a mixture of the aristocratic and bureaucratic, nor the Slovenes, whose nationalism was bourgeois. Three different approaches to nationalism produced three different views of the state that their union had created. The tendency of the broad approach represented by the pan-movements, in this case Yugoslavism, was replaced and reversed when the varying nationalisms of three disparate people had to be reconciled within one state structure. Nationalism, which originally justified the demands for independence and union, revealed itself as a force that found its goal in itself.

['External and Domestic Roots of Eastern European Nationalism', in Peter F. Sugar and Ivo J. Lederer (eds.), *Nationalism in Eastern Europe* (University of Washington Press: Seattle, 1969), 46–54.]

ERIC HOBSBAWM

27 The Rise of Ethno-Linguistic Nationalisms

Once a certain degree of European development has been reached, the linguistic and cultural communities of peoples, having silently matured throughout the centuries, emerge from the world of passive existence as peoples (*passiver Volkheit*). They become conscious of themselves as a force with a historical destiny.

They demand control over the state, as the highest available instrument of power, and strive for their political self-determination. The birthday of the political idea of the nation and the birth-year of this new consciousness, is 1789, the year of the French Revolution.[1]

Two hundred years after the French Revolution no serious historian and, it is hoped, no one who has read up to this point in the present book, will regard statements like the one quoted above as other than exercises in programmatic mythology. Yet the quotation seems a representative statement of that 'principle of nationality' which convulsed the international politics of Europe after 1830, creating a number of new states which corresponded, so far as practicable, with one half of Mazzini's call 'Every nation a state', though less so with the other half, 'only one state for the entire nation'.[2] It is representative, in particular, in five ways: in stressing linguistic and cultural community, which was a nineteenth-century innovation, in stressing the nationalism that aspired to form or capture states rather than the 'nations' of already existing states, in its historicism and sense of historic mission, in claiming the paternity of 1789, and not least in its terminological ambiguity and rhetoric.

Yet while the quotation at first sight reads like something that might have been written by Mazzini himself, in fact it was written seventy years after the 1830 revolutions, and by a Marxian socialist of Moravian origin in a book about the specific problems of the Habsburg empire. In short, while it might be confused with the 'principle of nationality' which transformed the political map of Europe between 1830 and the 1870s, in fact it belongs to a later, and different, phase of nationalist development in European history.

The nationalism of 1880–1914 differed in three major respects from the Mazzinian phase of nationalism. First, it abandoned the 'threshold principle' which was central to nationalism in the Liberal era. Henceforth *any* body of people considering themselves a 'nation' claimed the right to self-determination which, in the last analysis, meant the right to a separate sovereign independent state for their territory. Second, and in consequence of this multiplication of potential 'unhistorical' nations, ethnicity and language became the central, increasingly the decisive or even the only criteria of potential nationhood. Yet there was a third change which affected not so much the non-state national movements, which now became increasingly numerous and ambitious, but national sentiments within the established nation-states: a sharp shift to the political right of nation and flag, for which the term 'nationalism' was actually invented in the last decade(s) of the nineteenth century. Renner's quotation represents the first two, but (coming from the left) very distinctly not the third of these changes.

There are three reasons why it has not often been recognized how late the ethnic-linguistic criterion for defining a nation actually became dominant.

First, the two most prominent non-state national movements of the first half of the nineteenth century were essentially based on communities of the educated, united across political and geographical borders by the use of an established language of high culture and its literature. For Germans and Italians, their national language was not merely an administrative convenience or a means of unifying state-wide communication, as French had been in France since the ordinance of Villers-Cotterets in 1539, or even a revolutionary device for bringing the truths of liberty, science and progress to all, ensuring the permanence of citizen equality and preventing the revival of *ancien régime* hierarchy, as it was for the Jacobins. It was more even than the vehicle of a distinguished literature and of universal intellectual expression. It was the *only* thing that made them Germans or Italians, and consequently carried a far heavier charge of national identity than, say, English did for those who wrote and read that language. However, while for the German and Italian liberal middle classes language thus provided a central argument for the creation of a unified national state—in the first half of the nineteenth century this was not yet the case anywhere else. The political claims to independence of Poland or Belgium were not language-based, nor indeed were the rebellions of various Balkan peoples against the Ottoman Empire, which produced some independent states. Nor was the Irish movement in Britain. Alternatively, where linguistic movements already had a significant political base, as in the Czech lands, national self-determination (as opposed to cultural recognition) was not yet an issue, and the establishment of a separate state was not seriously thought of.

However, since the later eighteenth century (and largely under German intellectual influence) Europe had been swept by the romantic passion for the pure, simple and uncorrupted peasantry, and for this folkloric rediscovery of 'the people', the vernacular languages it spoke were crucial. Yet while this populist cultural renaissance provided the foundation for many a subsequent nationalist movement, and has therefore been justifiably counted as the first phase ('phase A') of their development, Hroch himself[3] makes it clear that in no sense was it yet a political movement of the people concerned, nor did it imply any political aspiration or programme. Indeed, more often than not the discovery of popular tradition and its transformation into the 'national tradition' of some peasant people forgotten by history, was the work of enthusiasts from the (foreign) ruling class or elite, such as the Baltic Germans or the Finnish Swedes. The Finnish Literature Society (founded 1831) was established by Swedes, its records were kept in Swedish, and all the writings of the chief ideologue of Finnish cultural nationalism, Snellman, appear to have been in Swedish. While nobody could possibly deny the widespread European cultural and linguistic revival movements in the period from the 1780s to the 1840s, it is a mistake to confuse Hroch's phase A with his phase B, when a body of activists devoted to the political agitation in favour of the 'national idea' has come into existence, and still less his 'phase C', when mass support for 'the national idea' can be counted on. As the case of the British Isles shows, there is, incidentally, no necessary connection between cultural revival movements of this kind and subsequent national agitations or movements of political nationalism, and, conversely, such nationalist movements may originally have little or nothing to do with cultural revivalism. The Folklore Society (1878) and the folksong revival in England were no more nationalist than the Gypsy Lore Society.

The third reason concerns ethnic rather than linguistic identification. It lies in the absence—until quite late in the century—of influential theories or pseudo-theories identifying nations with genetic descent. We shall return to this point below.

The growing significance of 'the national question' in the forty years preceding 1914 is not measured simply by its intensification within the old multinational empires of Austro-Hungary and Turkey. It was now a significant issue in the domestic politics of virtually all European states. Thus even in the United Kingdom it was no longer confined to the Irish problem, even though Irish nationalism, under that name, also grew—the number of newspapers describing themselves as 'national' or 'nationalist' rose from I in 1871 through 13 in 1881 to 33 in 1891—and became politically explosive in British politics. However, it is often overlooked that this was also the period when the first official recognition of Welsh national interests as such was made (the Welsh Sunday Closing Act of 1881 has been described as 'the first distinctively Welsh Act of Parliament')[4] and when Scotland acquired both a modest Home Rule movement, a Scottish Office in government and, via the so-called 'Goschen Formula', a guaranteed national share of the public expenditure of the United Kingdom. Domestic nationalism could also—as in France, Italy and Germany—take the form of the rise of those right-wing movements for which the term 'nationalism' was in fact coined in this period, or, more generally, of the political xenophobia which found its most deplorable, but not its only, expression in anti-Semitism. That so relatively tranquil a state as Sweden should in this era have been shaken by the national secession of Norway (1907) (which was not proposed by anyone until the 1890s) is at least as significant as the paralysis of Habsburg politics by rival nationalist agitations.

Moreover, it is during this period that we find nationalist movements multiplying in regions where they had been previously unknown, or among peoples hitherto only of interest to folklorists, and even for the first time, notionally, in the non-western world. How far the new anti-imperialist movements can be regarded as nationalist is far from clear, though the influence of western nationalist ideology on their spokesmen and activists is undeniable—as in the case of the Irish influence on Indian nationalism. However, even if we confine ourselves to Europe and its environs, we find plenty of movements in 1914 that had existed hardly or not at all in 1870: among the Armenians, Georgians,

Lithuanians and other Baltic peoples and the Jews (both in Zionist and non-Zionist versions), among the Macedonians and Albanians in the Balkans, the Ruthenians and the Croats in the Habsburg empire—Croat nationalism must not be confused with the earlier Croat support for Yugoslav or 'Illyrian' nationalism—among the Basques and Catalans, the Welsh, and in Belgium a distinctly radicalized Flemish movement, as well as hitherto unexpected touches of local nationalism in places like Sardinia. We may even detect the first hints of Arab nationalism in the Ottoman empire.

As already suggested most of these movements now stressed the linguistic and/or ethnic element. That this was often new can be readily demonstrated. Before the foundation of the Gaelic League (1893), which initially had no political aims, the Irish language was not an issue in the Irish national movement. It figured neither in O'Connell's Repeal agitation—though the Liberator was a Gaelic-speaking Kerryman—nor in the Fenian programme. Even serious attempts to create a uniform Irish language out of the usual complex of dialects were not made until after 1900. Finnish nationalism was about the defence of the Grand Duchy's autonomy under the Tsars, and the Finnish Liberals who emerged after 1848 took the view that they represented a single bi-lingual nation. Finnish nationalism did not become essentially linguistic until, roughly, the 1860s (when an Imperial Rescript improved the public position of the Finnish language against the Swedish), but until the 1880s the language struggle remained largely an internal class struggle between the lower class Finns (represented by the 'Fennomen' who stood for a single nation with Finnish as its language) and the upper-class Swedish minority, represented by the 'Svecomen' who argued that the country contained two nations and therefore two languages). Only after 1880, as Tsarism shifted into its own russifying nationalist mode, did the struggle for autonomy and for language and culture come to coincide.

Again, Catalanism as a (conservative) cultural-linguistic movement can hardly be traced back further than the 1850s, the festival of the Jocs Florals (analogous to the Welsh Eisteddfodau) being revived not before 1859. The language itself was not authoritatively standardized until the twentieth century, and Catalan regionalism was not concerned with the linguistic question until the middle or later 1880s. The development of Basque nationalism, it has been suggested, lagged some thirty years behind that of the Catalan movement, although the ideological shift of Basque autonomism from the defence or restoration of ancient feudal privileges to a linguistic-racial argument was sudden: in 1894, less than twenty years after the end of the Second Carlist War, Sabino Arana founded his Basque National Party (PNV), incidentally inventing the Basque name for the country ('Euskadi') which had hitherto not existed.

At the other end of Europe the national movements of the Baltic peoples had hardly left their first (cultural) phases by the last third of the century, and in the remote Balkans, where the Macedonian question raised its bloodstained head after 1870, the idea that the various nationalities living on this territory should be distinguished by their *language*, was the last of many to strike the states of Serbia, Greece, Bulgaria and the Sublime Porte which contended for it. The inhabitants of Macedonia had been distinguished by their religion, or else claims to this or that part of it had been based on history ranging from the medieval to the ancient, or else on ethnographic arguments about common customs and ritual practices. Macedonia did not become a battlefield for Slav philologists until the twentieth century, when the Greeks, who could not compete on this terrain, compensated by stressing an imaginary ethnicity.

At the same time—roughly, in the second half of the century—ethnic nationalism received enormous reinforcements, in practice from the increasingly massive geographical migrations of peoples, and in theory by the transformation of that central concept of nineteenth-century social science, 'race'. On the one hand the old-established division of mankind into a few 'races' distinguished by skin colour was now elaborated into a set of 'racial' distinctions separating peoples of approximately the same pale skin, such as 'Aryans' and 'Semites', or, among the 'Aryans', Nordics, Alpines and Mediterraneans. On the other hand Darwinian evolutionism, supplemented later by what came to be known as genetics, provided racism with what looked like a powerful set of 'scientific' reasons for keeping out or even, as it turned out, expelling and murdering strangers. All this was comparatively late. Anti-Semitism did not acquire a 'racial' (as distinct from a religio-cultural) character until about 1880, the major prophets of German and French racism (Vacher de Lapouge, Houston Stewart Chamberlain) belong to the 1890s, and 'Nordics' do not enter the racist or any discourse until about 1900.

The links between racism and nationalism are obvious. 'Race' and language were easily confused as in the case of 'Aryans' and 'Semites', to the indignation of scrupulous scholars like Max Muller who pointed out that 'race', a genetic concept, could not be inferred from language, which was not inherited. Moreover, there is an evident analogy between the insistence of racists on the importance of racial purity and the horrors of miscegenation, and the insistence of so many—one is tempted to say of most—forms of linguistic nationalism on the need to purify the national language from foreign elements. In the nineteenth century the English were quite exceptional in boasting of their mongrel origins (Britons, Anglo-Saxons, Scandinavians, Normans, Scots, Irish, etc.) and glorying in the philological mixture of their language. However, what brought 'race' and 'nation' even closer was the practice of using both as virtual synonyms, generalizing equally wildly about 'racial'/'national' character, as was then the fashion. Thus before the Anglo-French Entente Cordiale of 1904, a French writer observed, agreement between the two countries had been dismissed as impossible because of the 'hereditary enmity' between the two races.[5] Linguistic and ethnic nationalism thus reinforced each other.

It is hardly surprising that nationalism gained ground so rapidly from the 1870s to 1914. It was a function of both social and political changes, not to mention an international situation that provided plenty of pegs on which to hang manifestos of hostility to foreigners. Socially three developments gave considerably increased scope for the development of novel forms of invent- ing 'imagined' or even actual communities as nationalities: the resistance of traditional groups threatened by the onrush of modernity, the novel and quite non-traditional classes and strata now rapidly growing in the urbaniz- ing societies of developed countries, and the unprecedented migrations which distributed a multiple diaspora of peoples across the globe, each strangers to both natives and other migrant groups, none, as yet, with the habits and conventions of coexistence. The sheer weight and pace of change in this period would be enough to explain why under such circumstances occasions for friction between groups multiplied, even if we were to over- look the tremors of the 'Great Depression' which so often, in these years, shook the lives of the poor and the economically modest or insecure. All that was required for the entry of nationalism into politics was that groups of men and women who saw themselves, in whatever manner, as Ruritan- ians, or were so seen by others, should become ready to listen to the argument that their discontents were in some way caused by the inferior treatment (often undeniable) of Ruritanians by, or compared with, other nationalities, or by a non-Ruritanian state or ruling class. At all events by 1914 observers were apt to be surprised at European populations which still seemed completely unreceptive to any appeal on the grounds of nationality, though this did not necessarily imply adherence to a nationalist programme. US citizens of immigrant origins did not demand any linguistic or other concessions to their nationality by the Federal Government, but neverthe- less every Democratic city politician knew perfectly well that appeals to the Irish as Irish, to Poles as Poles, paid off.

As we have seen, the major political changes which turned a potential receptivity to national appeals into actual reception, were the democratiza- tion of politics in a growing number of states, and the creation of the modern administrative, citizen-mobilizing and citizen-influencing state. And yet, the rise of mass politics helps us to reformulate the question of popular support for nationalism rather than to answer it. What we need to discover is what precisely national slogans meant in politics, and whether they meant the same to different social constituencies, how they changed, and under what circumstances they combined or were incompatible with other slogans that might mobilize the citizenry, how they prevailed over them or failed to do so.

The identification of nation with language helps us to answer such ques- tions, since linguistic nationalism essentially requires control of a state or at least the winning of official recognition for the language. This is plainly not equally important for all strata or groups within a state or nationality, or to every state or nationality. At all events problems of power, status, politics and ideology and not of communication or even culture, lie at the heart of the nationalism of language. If communication or culture had been the crucial issue, the Jewish nationalist (Zionist) movement would not have opted for a modern Hebrew which nobody as yet spoke, and in a pronunciation unlike that used in European synagogues. It rejected Yiddish, spoken by 95% of the Ashkenazic Jews from the European East and their emigrants to the west—i.e. by a substantial majority of all the world's Jews. By 1935, it has been said, given the large, varied and distinguished literature developed for its ten million speakers, Yiddish was 'one of the leading "literate" languages of the time'. Nor would the Irish national movement have launched itself after 1900 into the doomed campaign to reconvert the Irish to a language most of them no longer understood, and which those who set about teaching it to their countrymen had only themselves begun to learn very incompletely.

Conversely, as the example of Yiddish shows, and that golden age of dialect literatures, the nineteenth century, confirms, the existence of a widely spoken or even written idiom did not necessarily generate language-based nationalism. Such languages or literatures could see themselves and be seen quite consciously as supplementing rather than competing with some hegemonic language of general culture and communication.

[*Nations and Nationalism since 1780* (Cambridge University Press: Cambridge, 1990), 101–11.]

MICHAEL HECHTER AND MARGARET LEVI

28 Ethno-Regional Movements in the West

By definition, ethnoregional movements rest upon regional claims to ethnic distinctiveness. This is what distinguishes ethnoregionalism from other kinds of regionalism couched solely in terms of material demands. Ethnic distinctiveness results from the imputation of meaning and honor to linguistic, religious, or phenotypical markers. Though the nature of any ethnic identity is to some extent dictated by the kind of marker with which it is associated, the fact is that such identities can be established on the basis of a wide variety of these markers.[1] Further, the meaning of the same marker can vary in different social settings. Thus the distinction between Protestants and Catholics in Ireland is clearly an ethnic one, but in France it carries with it no parallel connotation. There is more hostility and mistrust between Flemings and Walloons in Belgium than there is between German and French-speakers in Switzerland. Last, it is noteworthy that in an area of Celtic nationalism in the British Isles there should be so much of a Welsh problem, yet so little of a Cornish one. That the solution to this last problem cannot be due to linguistic factors is clear from examination of the Irish and Scottish cases, where ethnic identification persists despite the nearly universal adoption of the English language.

The explanation of all of these puzzles must lie in the realm of history: the history of relations between Protestants and Catholics must be very different in Ireland than in France. But this is as vacuous a solution as it is unexceptionable. In what fundamental respects do the histories of these groups differ?

In order to answer this question it is necessary to have a theory of ethnic group formation. There are an infinite number of differences between the histories of any two peoples. Thus, serious exploration of the causes of differing patterns of intergroup relations must be guided by a theory that directs special attention to a small number of significant factors, allowing the vast number of remaining ones to be ignored because they are held to be causally insignificant.

Elsewhere, Hechter[2] attempted to sketch out a simple theory of this kind. In *Internal Colonialism* it was argued that ethnic solidarity among any objectively-defined set of individuals is principally due to the existence of a *hierarchical* cultural division of labor that promotes reactive group formation. This kind of a cultural division of labor is typically found in regions that have developed as internal colonies. While the majority of the ethnoregional movements in western Europe appear to have emerged in just such regions[3] several important examples—among them the movements in Scotland,[4] Catalonia, and the Spanish Basque regions—do not easily fit this model. In more recent work[5] a second, and equally important *segmental* dimension of the cultural division of labor was identified; this leads to interactive group formation. It will be seen that this second dimension has special significance for these apparently anomalous cases of western European ethnoregionalism. Reactive group formation is largely a function of the group's relations with other groups in its environment, while interactive group formation is at least potentially capable of being determined by the group itself.

The first (hierarchical) mechanism contributing to the formation of the ethnic groups is the extent to which group membership determines individual life-chances. The greater this is, the greater the psychic significance of ethnicity for the individual—and, by extension, for the group as a whole. Alternatively, when one's life-chances are seen to be independent of inclusion in a particular ethnic group, the subjective significance of membership in that group will tend to recede or to disappear altogether. In societies where individuals are assigned to occupations solely on ascriptive criteria, ethnic identity will be equally strong among all groups. But this is far from the situation in the capitalist democracies of western Europe. In these societies ethnic identity will tend to be strongest among those groups placed at the *bottom* of the stratification system. This is because the structure of life-chances in predominantly proletarian ethnic groups is considerably more restricted than it is in predominantly bourgeois groups. Group formation hence takes place on a reactive basis.

The second (segmental) mechanism contributing to the formation of ethnic solidarity is the extent to which members interact wholly within the boundaries of their own group. The most critical locus of this interaction is the work site, and the best single indicator of it is the degree to which group members monopolize certain niches in the occupational structure. Occupational specializations of this kind contribute to group solidarity by establishing settings for personal contact that strengthen ties between individuals of the same ethnicity, and by providing these individuals with a set of common material interests that serve to reinforce informal social ties. Moreover, monopolization is a resource of the group that provides incentives for the reproduction of the group across the generations.

Together, these two mechanisms help explain why certain regions in the old states of western Europe continue to maintain an ethnic identity distinct from that of their respective cores despite a century or more of industrialization. In one type of region, individuals adhering to the peripheral culture (for example, those with a distinctive language or religion) are principally found in low ranking positions in the regional class structure. In the other, individuals adhering to the peripheral culture have succeeded in monopolizing valued niches in the occupational structure, and, perhaps, key institutional spheres, as well. Both kinds of situations are predicated upon the existence of a distinctive culture in peripheral regions. But how has peripheral cultural distinctiveness managed to survive in western Europe?

This is far from an idle question, for one of the principal tasks of the modern state has been to promote cultural universalism within its boundaries as a means of extending its legitimacy. When and where it was possible, the western European core regions attempted to impose a single language, religion, and—in the broadest possible sense—culture upon all of their subjects. But this ideal could not always be realized. In some territories, the peripheral culture remained beyond the reach of the centralizing state; in others, the peripheral culture was protected by the existence of distinctive regional institutions.[6] The first circumstance promotes reactive, the second interactive group formation.

The prospects for reactive group formation are maximized in the relatively backward 'nations without history',[7] the internal colonies, of western Europe. Peripheries such as Ireland, Wales, Brittany, Corsica, Galicia, and Friesland were annexed outright by their respective cores. Although annexation did tend to strip these peripheries of their most important culturally distinctive governmental institutions, some aspects of peripheral culture could, under specific conditions, persist none the less. The fact that a group of individuals bearing culture X is conquered by a larger group bearing culture Y has no necessary consequence for resulting patterns of intergroup assimilation. What is important are the patterns of contact between these groups in the peripheral setting.

To the extent that there is very little contact between the groups, there will be no incentive for one to assimilate to the culture of the other (and acculturation will be ruled out by definition). This occurred frequently in geographically remote agrarian regions of western Europe where production was principally carried out in family smallholdings and where the centralizing state did not intrude. Peripheral culture could persist without difficulty in these isolated regions until it became threatened by exogenous forces. In the absence of extensive in-migration (such as occurred in Wales upon the exploitation of enormous reserves of coal beginning around 1850) the first important outside threat—universal public education in the language of the core—did not generally arise until the late nineteenth century. Thereafter, print and electronic media appeared on the horizon. Each of these incursions spelled danger for the survival of peripheral culture. However, state-wide education also provided a stimulus to reactive collective action designed to protect the traditional culture and local institutions from the predations of the central state. The growing importance of the world-wide norm of national self-determination that had emerged from mid nineteenth-century Europe was an additional, if limited, countervailing force. Under the impetus of this norm, intellectuals in the peripheries began to instigate literary and political movements designed to uphold and maintain the peripheral cultures.

In some cases, peripheral cultures could also persist in the face of extensive contact with core culture. An increase in intergroup interaction will not lead to culture change if this interaction is carried out across class lines, and, indeed, it can increase the potential for mobilization by the 'subordinated' cultural group.[8] Thus if most of the contacts between Xs and Ys are simultaneously contacts between proletarians and bourgeoisie, very little culture shift should be expected to occur on this account alone.[9] And this is precisely what happens in regions that have become internal colonies.

If the prospects for reactive group formation are maximized in regions having undergone internal colonial development, the prospects for interactive ethnic group formation are maximized in regions with considerable institutional autonomy. Institutional survivals are usually found in states where the core was unable to completely subdue the periphery by military means. Two factors in particular seem responsible for these peripheral institutional survivals. If the periphery had a state apparatus of its own prior to its incorporation, annexation was much more costly. In this case the relative strength of the periphery is responsible for the institutional survivals. But the strength of the core varied, as well. Weak cores had difficulty annexing strong peripheries. Even some relatively strong cores did not resort to annexation when a large proportion of their revenues was generated by overseas trade that could easily be monitored in a small number of seaports.[10] For all of these different reasons, the periphery could be incorporated by diplomatic means, through a Treaty of Union, granting its rights to some of its own institutions. [. . .] Scotland provides an excellent example. The Act of Union between Scotland and England (1707) provided for the legitimacy of distinctively Scottish legal, educational, and ecclesiastical institutions. All three of these central institutions differ significantly from their English counterparts.

Once a periphery has attained a degree of institutional autonomy—by whatever means—the groundwork for interactive group formation has been laid. For one of the things these distinctive institutions do is to create important occupational niches for incumbents who adhere to the peripheral culture. These incumbents often owe their very jobs to the existence of the culture. For example, there is little doubt that Scottish lawyers face considerable professional competition, but it is important to note that this will never be competition from *English* lawyers because the two types of law are incommensurable. In this way Scotland's institutional autonomy is responsible for sustaining an important segment of the 'old' Scottish bourgeoisie. This provides a substantial material incentive for the reproduction of Scottish culture through history. It also serves to anchor the social base of Scottish ethnicity firmly within the bourgeoisie. But the existence of these institutions insures that nearly all strata in the population come into regular contact with the peripheral culture, and thus are likely to identify with it. Hence the social base of ethnoregionalism in such territories will be relatively broad.

Of course peripheral institutional autonomy is not the only cause of the emergence of ethnic specializations in valued occupations. Neither Catalonia nor the Basque country in Spain have had the same kind of continuous institutional autonomy with which Scotland has been blessed. Despite this, Catalans and Basques have succeeded in monopolizing certain bourgeois occupations within their regions. The reason for this undoubtedly lies in the peculiar character of Spanish national development. Spain is a rare example of a western European state whose core, Castile, is less economically developed than some of its culturally-distinct peripheries.

It must be emphasized that the persistence of ethnoregionalism in any capitalist society is always a phenomenon requiring explanation. This is because free markets for labor, capital, and commodities should discourage the spatial concentration of any ethnically distinctive group and facilitate its eventual assimilation. The failure of assimilation in certain western European peripheral regions attests to the existence of hierarchical or segmental cultural divisions of labor. These systems of ethnic stratification provide the structural bases for the establishment and reproduction of distinctive ethnic identities over time. However, while the mechanisms of ethnic group formation can be understood with the aid of a general model of this type, the origins of the cultural division of labor in a specific region must be sought in the particular historical circumstances of that area; thus they cannot be accounted for by any universal theory.

The social structural factors discussed above only partially explain variations in the *intensity*, or the strength and durability of ethnoregional movements. One of the major conclusions of the recent literature on social movements is that, given the appropriate socio-economic conditions, a group will engage in collective action only if it has the organizational capacity to do so.[11] This in turn depends on the tolerance of dissident cultural and political organization by the central state; an infrastructure of pre-existent voluntary associations; and the resources necessary to sustain organized activity. However, most of the variables identified as determinants of social movements remain unmeasured—and possibly unmeasurable.[12] What follows is an attempt to elaborate these variables for the special case of ethnoregionalism. Of necessity the status of our explanation of the intensity and, later, of the timing of ethnoregionalism is considerably more tentative than our conclusions concerning its social base.

Ethnoregionalism is likely to exist to the extent that the central state tolerates cultural and political diversity. This tolerance is reflected in the administration, legislation, and electoral system of the country as a whole.

To illustrate: the French state has historically been much less tolerant of cultural diversity than the British. Despite the fact that Whitehall exercises considerable supervision over education (and other social services) in Britain, schools vary widely in terms of curriculum as well as languages of instruction. Although English is the official language, Welsh has been taught in the elementary schools since 1888.[13] Moreover, in the nineteenth century the Nonconformists gained a major foothold in Wales, and as a result the Church of England was disestablished there. On the other hand, the French state has long made clear its emphasis on religious and cultural standardization.[14] Catholicism is by far the dominant religion, and French is the only official language for teaching and governmental business. Until quite recently Breton was unavailable in the schools, which have a highly uniform curriculum. Indeed, historically the French state has erected numerous legal and administrative barriers to the maintenance of the Breton language and culture.[15]

The basis of this distinction between Britain and France is found in the administrative arrangements of the two countries. Since the sixteenth century, France has had an extremely hierarchical administrative system, a system reinforced and strengthened by Napoleon. The centerpiece was the *intendant* and is now the prefect. This is an appointed office, held by a civil servant. Because of the close link between the center and periphery, mediated by the prefect, the French claim to have perfected 'administrative decentralization'. However, this relationship is one of inequality. Through *tutelle* (tutelage) the local administration is very much subordinated to and controlled by the central one.[16]

In principle Britain has been way behind France in terms of delegating administrative responsibility to organs below that of the national ministry.[17] None the less, for centuries there have been administrative offices within the national bureaucracy that both recognize and presumably represent the distinct concerns, of particular regions, especially Wales, Scotland, and Northern Ireland. Indeed, 'The territorial distribution of authority in the United Kindom . . . has led many observers of British political practice to conclude that the unitary system of British government is in fact federal'.[18]

The difference between Britain and France on the question of cultural diversity is also reflected in the legislation affecting the peripheral regions. Since the late nineteenth century (and even earlier), the British parliament has passed numerous laws not only directed at Wales specifically but granting it special privileges in regards to education, housing, and other governmental functions. The French National Assembly in its legislation is less likely to differentiate Brittany or any other region, and until quite recently its laws have been aimed at promoting similarities—rather than recognizing distinctiveness—among the peripheral areas of the country.

It should therefore be expected that the less standardization of culture and language required by a particular state, the greater the infrastructure of cultural associations in the ethnoregion, *ceteris paribus*.

An ethnoregional movement ultimately rests on communal association based in the traditional culture. Language societies, cultural festivals, and dissident religious sects provide the necessary internal organizations of the region that is the prerequisite for a social movement. They are the institutional base from which ethnoregionalism springs.[19] The preservation of rituals from the past promotes a sense of community not only for people whose social structural roles make them feel marginal within society as a whole,[20] but also for those who wish to change the allocation of societal resources. This sense of community can consequently become the basis for collective action of a political sort.

This suggests that ethnoregional movements are most likely to form in those areas where the cultural institutions are most prevalent.

An organizational infrastructure does not rest solely on communal associations, however. Under certain conditions, functional or class associations can also be transformed into a base for ethnoregionalism. Such associations are likely to arise when the national market penetrates the area and if the central state permits their existence.[21] What potentially distinguishes mineworker unions in South Wales and agricultural syndicates in *Basse Bretagne* from similar functional associations elsewhere is the fact that their membership is largely composed of a distinct ethnic group. Even so, miners are likely to ally with miners and farmers with farmers in state-wide unions and, ultimately, state-wide political parties unless ethnic discrimination makes that impossible. In that case, such trade unions and syndicates may identify with the ethnoregional movement.

The infrastructure of voluntary associations sets the limits for the potential numerical strength of an ethnoregional movement, but its durability depends on the development of a political organization with the resources to mobilize, guide, and sustain the latent membership. The first condition for the existence of such an organization is its legality within the state. It is very difficult to maintain a political organization of any kind in the face of concerted governmental repression.[22]

Political organization can take many forms. It can engage in violence, protest, and/or the collection of votes. It is likely, although unproven, that the electoral arrangements of the state partially determine which form it will take. Obviously, where multipartism is permitted, the organization of an ethnoregional party becomes viable. Some electroal mechanisms, most notably proportional representation, inevitably lead to multipartism.[23] However, in states possessing such mechanisms the development of ethnoregional parties is hardly a surprise: the system was designed to encourage such parties in order to institutionalize potential conflict emanating from the ethnoregions. As Rokkan argues. 'The introduction of proportional representation was essentially part of a strategy of national integration—an alternative to monopolization of influence or civil war'.[24]

Other electoral mechanisms, such as the single-member district and party government, discourage third parties. Countries with such mechanisms are likely to have two major parties, both of which are centrist and conciliatory of the diverse interests they must of necessity represent. Even so, such countries can also give rise to ethnoregional parties. Indeed, the central decision-making inherent in the disciplined parliamentary parties of the Canadian and, by extension, British sort tend 'to encourage regional and cultural protest parties'.[25]

What this suggests, of course, is that the social base and organizational infrastructure are more important determinants of the growth of an ethnoregional party than the national electoral system, given the legality of such a party. However, the electoral system can facilitate or hinder this form of political organization. Moreover, countries that actively encourage multipartism are more likely to have stable ethnoregional parties than those that do not.

The durability of an ethnoregional organization further rests on its demonstrated ability to deliver on its promises. Any organization attempting to deliver collective goods must offer selective incentives, particular benefits an individual derives from membership that are not otherwise available.[26] The most important incentives are generally material. For a political organization this means jobs, housing, welfare, or other governmental services for constituents. Whether or not an organization can procure such benefits depends on the responsiveness of the legislators and administrators to its demands, which in turn depends on their vulnerability to the strategy—violence, protest, or bloc voting—utilized by the organization.[27] However, a political organization cannot always choose the strategy that would be most effective. The locus of governmental policy making, for example who determines and collects taxes, makes a difference for how change can be brought about in the state.[28] Electoral arrangements have implications for coalition strategies. And how many people potentially can be mobilized by the organization affects party influence.

In other words, an ethnoregional organization, like any other political organization, needs to procure material benefits for its constituents in order to maintain itself. This requires power that comes as a result of central state vulnerability to the strategy chosen by the organization. Such vulnerability is a reflection of administrative and electoral arrangements, the size of the organization's latent membership, and, in addition, exogenous forces to be discussed in the next section.

But incentives need not only be material. They may also include social and ideological satisfactions. In this regard ethnoregional organizations have distinct advantages over their counterparts arising in regions that are not culturally distinct. One incentive is the culture itself: the organization reaffirms its existence and provides opportunities to identify oneself as a member of a cherished ethnic group. The claim of historical nationhood and the consequent demand for special recognition serve as additional justifications for the organization's existence. Finally, the culture produces its own leaders, and leaders are essential for transforming the membership of all types of voluntary associations into voters for and activists in political parties and organizations, particularly in the absence of material incentives.[29] Why such entrepreneurs should focus their energy on ethnoregional instead of state-wide organizations or private enterprise is a direct consequence of the cultural division of labor in which they find themselves. Territories having talented and ambitious individuals who experience blocked mobility are more likely than others to produce leaders concerned with changing the status quo.[30]

This brings us almost complete circle. In our admittedly tentative model, the most important determinant of the intensity of the ethnoregional movement is the existence of the culture on which the ethnoregion is based. Central state tolerance of cultural diversity makes possible not only the continued existence of the culture but also of the organizational infrastructure required by a social movement. The extensiveness of this infrastructure combines with national electoral and administrative arrangements to determine the form and durability of the ethnoregional organization. In other words, the central state acts on the culture in such a way as to encourage or discourage ethnoregionalism.

Last is the problem of *timing*. The timing of ethnoregional movements is a function of changes in the social base, the organizational capacity, and, the specific programs and policies of the state.[31] The relative importance of these three kinds of changes can only be unravelled in future studies. But it is a safe bet that changes in state policy explain much about the ebb and flow of ethnoregional movements. The reason for this is simple: state programs provide both resources around which to make demands and targets of attack.[32] Certainly, since 1945, there has been an increased involvement of all the western European states in their peripheral regions. On Keynesian principles, it has increasingly become the role of government to intervene in the economy in order to control the business cycle and to prevent high unemployment. This has led to enormous growth in public sector employment as well as concern with the economic underdevelopment of the regions. Indeed, state expenditures and state employment have been increasingly used to reduce the economic disadvantages and the levels of unemployment of the peripheral regions. As the state becomes more central in economic decision-making, it increasingly replaces private sector employers as the focus for discontent.[33] This is likely to be true in the regions as well, and the growth of ethnoregional organization is one indicator that it is. Indeed, as the state becomes the target of attack and discontent, the likelihood that it will make additional concessions to the periphery increases which, in turn, provides the organizational resources and incentives that further aid in the creation of ethnoregionalism.

Finally, since it appears that outbreaks of separatism are clustered in particular historical periods, this suggests there must also be an international dimension to the problem. It may be worth speculating about this dimension. It is possible to locate two periods of heightened ethnoregional activity in western Europe, 1905 to 1921, and 1965 to the present day. (Even this crude generalization is belied in part by the Spanish case, where both Catalans and Basques were reasonably active before [and during] the Civil War.) As a rule, the world-wide interwar depression was not conducive to ethnoregionalist political mobilization. Perhaps this is because a contraction of available resources allows the ideology and politics of class to come into its own. During the Cold War period, from 1945 to 1963, the peripheries remained quiescent. When détente between the United States and the Soviet Union become institutionalized, the question of international security receded in importance. Meanwhile major changes in the world economy mirrored these international political developments. Basically, the world economy became very much more open. These changes in the international system are evidently associated with an increase in ethnoregional political mobilization.

Decolonization went hand in hand with a general lowering of international barriers to trade—especially protectionism. Regional customs unions like the European Economic Community are a reflection of this change. All told the issue of a large home market became less important for a national economy than was the case in an era of protectionism. The possibility of separation could begin to make economic sense in the peripheries, whereas in the past it had seemed a ticket to oblivion. It could also make military sense. The advent of nuclear technology in warfare meant that national security arrangements had to be arranged under an American or Soviet umbrella. This internationalization of defense also had the effect of encouraging separatism. If the North

Atlantic Treaty Organization is responsible for the defense of large states such as France and West Germany, it could also be used to defend smaller states like Scotland or Catalonia.

Thus major structural changes in the world system have reduced in no small way the cost of ethnoregionalism in discontented peripheral areas. What had previously been seen as a series of unthinkable obstacles to the realization of sovereignty in peripheral regions now have become routinely discussed matters in political and academic circles. Whether or not an independent Scotland can be viable is a legitimate question—even a fashionable one—for research, and the conclusions of competent investigators have by no means settled the issue.

If these shifts in the international system have reduced the costs of ethnoregionalism in the discontented peripheries, what can be said about its benefits? From the strictly economic point of view it cannot be denied that political incorporation has seldom ended the relative economic disadvantages of the peripheral regions. For this reason regional elites have begun to make the argument that sovereignty can lead to material advantages. The basis of this claim does not rest on the region's gaining control over valuable resources that might spur on an otherwise lackluster economy. Rather, the argument ultimately rests upon the economic gains of efficient management. It is held that a decision-maker in Edinburgh can better determine what is needed in Fifeshire than a decision-maker in London. Local rule eliminates much unproductive bureaucracy. Smaller decision-making units are more capable of adapting to changes in the environment than large ones, and may be more efficient to boot. The demand for decentralized authority has become a desired goal for many different kinds of social units and interest groups in advanced societies: school districts are a good example in the United States.

But the final benefit perceived by the ethnoregionalists is essentially moral. They can and do appeal to the norm that all peoples should have self-determination. In the absence of this norm they would have little chance of success.

It is necessary to conclude this brief overview with a note of caution. For reasons spelled out previously, the conclusions of the first and second sections of this paper should be regarded as tentative at best. While we are confident that a complete explanation of ethnoregionalism involves, at a minimum, the kinds of variables described in these sections, we can make no claim that this is an exhaustive list of its determinants. And the causal relations sketched out in these sections remain untested. It does seem obvious that a full analysis of ethnoregionalism must include processes operating at widely different levels of aggregation—starting at microscopic settings for interaction, then moving to the level of the state, and finally to the international system as a whole. Clearly, the cultural division of labor is a necessary condition for the development of ethnoregionalism, but it is also an insufficient one. At this point the relative importance of determinants at the levels of the state and the international system cannot easily be assessed. This remains a critical agenda for further work in the explanation of ethnoregionalism, and of social movements in general. But, as the complexity of these issues is formidable, such work must proceed with care and due attention to issues of theory and method.

['The Comparative Analysis of Ethnoregional Movements', *Ethnic and Racial Studies*, 2/3 (1979), 262–74.]

Section V

....

Nationalism outside Europe

....

INTRODUCTION

The earliest nations and national states may be European, but nationalism is a truly global movement and cultural system. In fact, nationalist movements emerged at roughly the same time in the New World as in the Old. This was due, as Benedict Anderson argues, to a combination of communications and colonial administration, or 'pilgrim creole functionaries and provincial creole printmen'. This was especially true of the creole-led uprisings in Latin America in 1810, but they had been preceded by the neo-classical nationalism (in Roman dress) of the American revolutionaries, reminding us that territory and communications can take the place of language and religion in separating peoples and endowing them with myths and symbols of unique identity.

In Asia religion remained a dominant social bond. Indian nationalisms were steeped in Hindu and Muslim traditions, and in their responses to disruptive European ideas and colonial institutions Indian intellectuals fashioned ideologies of religious activism to mobilize the masses against British rule. Elie Kedourie claims that, in adopting the 'cult of the dark gods', the marginalized men of Africa and Asia adapted a European Christian tradition of millennialism to their own ethnic ends. Similarly, Partha Chatterjee shows the modernity and constructed nature of the Northern Aryan and Hindu version of Indian nationalism, noting how it excludes Muslim and other minority traditions, as well as the other regions of India. Mary Matossian depicts the archaism and ambivalence of Asian intellectuals in general, the result of the tensions generated by 'delayed industrialization' and of their sense of backwardness in relation to an economically advanced West. But these élites operate within the parameters of their distinctive ethnic and religious traditions, especially where a strong sense of community is engendered by such religions as Islam in India, as Francis Robinson demonstrates in reply to Paul Brass's more 'instrumental' approach.

In Africa, too, the social and political impact of the West helped to politicize ethnic divisions and create the conditions for ethnic and territorial nationalisms; here, Crawford Young describes the ways in which the colonial state has shaped African categories and communities. Benjamin Neuberger's exploration of the political thought of African statesmen and intellectuals complements Young's analysis, particularly in the contrasts which are drawn between 'state and nation' in Africa and Europe.

The nationalism of the new states of Africa and Asia has important economic dimensions. Economic policies, often shaped by nationalist ideologies, have emphasized the importance of what Harry Johnson terms 'psychic income', or status and cultural rewards, above the purely material benefits of policies of nationalization of personnel and manufacturing industrialization. The drive for autarchy has been one of nationalism's main goals, but it operates in a world of very unequal international division of labour, bringing sharp dilemmas for the new states, of the kind familiar from *dependencia* theories.

BENEDICT ANDERSON
....

29   Creole Pioneers of Nationalism

The striking fact is that 'each of the new South American republics had been an administrative unit from the sixteenth to the eighteenth century.'[1] In this respect they foreshadowed the new states of Africa and parts of Asia in the mid twentieth century, and form a sharp contrast to the new European states of the late nineteenth and early twentieth centuries. The original shaping of the American administrative units was to some extent arbitrary and fortuitous, marking the spatial limits of particular military conquests. But, over time, they developed a firmer reality under the influence of geographic, political and economic factors. The very vastness of the Spanish American empire, the enormous variety of its soils and climates, and, above all, the immense difficulty of communications in a pre-industrial age, tended to give these units a self-contained character. (In the colonial era the sea journey from Buenos Aires to Acapulco took four months, and the return trip even longer; the overland trek from Buenos Aires to Santiago normally lasted two months, and that to Cartagena nine.) In addition, Madrid's commercial policies had the effect of turning administrative units into separate economic zones. 'All competition with the mother country was forbidden the Americans, and even the individual parts of the continent could not trade with each other. American goods en route from one side of America to the other had to travel circuitously through Spanish ports, and Spanish navigation had a monopoly on trade with the colonies.'[2] These experiences help to explain why 'one of the basic principles of the American revolution' was that of 'uti possidetis by which each nation was to preserve the territorial status quo of 1810, the year when the movement for independence had been inaugurated.'[3] Their influence also doubtless contributed to the break-up of Bolívar's short-lived Gran Colombía and of the United Provinces of the Rio de la Plata into their older constituents (which today are known as Venezuela–Colombia–Ecuador and Argentina–Uruguay–Paraguay–Bolivia). Nonetheless, in themselves, market-zones, 'natural'-geographic or politico-administrative, do not create attachments. Who will willingly die for Comecon or the EEC?

To see how administrative units could, over time, come to be conceived as fatherlands, not merely in the Americas but in other parts of the world, one has to look at the ways in which administrative organizations create meaning. The anthropologist Victor Turner has written illuminatingly about the 'journey', between times, statuses and places, as a meaning-creating experience.[4] All such journeys require interpretation (for example, the journey from birth to death has given rise to various religious conceptions.) For our purposes here, the modal journey is the pilgrimage. It is not simply that in the minds of Christians,

Muslims or Hindus the cities of Rome, Mecca, or Benares were the centres of sacred geographies, but that their centrality was experienced and 'realized' (in the stagecraft sense) by the constant flow of pilgrims moving towards them from remote and *otherwise unrelated* localities. Indeed, in some sense the outer limits of the old religious communities of the imagination were determined by which pilgrimages people made. [. . .] The strange physical juxtaposition of Malays, Persians, Indians, Berbers and Turks in Mecca is something incomprehensible without an idea of their community in some form. The Berber encountering the Malay before the Kaaba must, as it were, ask himself: 'Why is this man doing what I am doing, uttering the same words that I am uttering, even though we can not talk to one another?' There is only one answer, once one has learnt it: 'Because *we* . . . are Muslims.' There was, to be sure, always a double aspect to the choreography of the great religious pilgrimages: a vast horde of illiterate vernacular-speakers provided the dense, physical reality of the ceremonial passage; while a small segment of literate bilingual adepts drawn from each vernacular community performed the unifying rites, interpreting to their respective followings the meaning of their collective motion. In a pre-print age, the reality of the imagined religious community depended profoundly on countless, ceaseless travels. Nothing more impresses one about Western Christendom in its heyday than the uncoerced flow of faithful seekers from all over Europe, through the celebrated 'regional centres' of monastic learning, to Rome. These great Latin-speaking institutions drew together what today we would perhaps regard as Irishmen, Danes, Portuguese, Germans, and so forth, in communities whose sacred meaning was every day deciphered from their members' otherwise inexplicable juxtaposition in the refectory.

Though the religious pilgrimages are probably the most touching and grandiose journeys of the imagination, they had, and have, more modest and limited secular counterparts. For our present purposes, the most important were the differing passages created by the rise of absolutizing monarchies, and, eventually, Europe-centred world-imperial states. The inner thrust of absolutism was to create a unified apparatus of power, controlled directly by, and loyal to, the ruler *over against* a decentralized, particularistic feudal nobility. Unification meant internal interchangeability of men and documents. Human interchangeability was fostered by the recruitment—naturally to varying extents—of *homines novi*, who, just for that reason, had no independent power of their own, and so could serve as emanations of their masters' wills. Absolutist functionaries thus undertook journeys which were basically different from those of feudal nobles. The difference can be represented schematically as follows: In the modal feudal journey, the heir of Noble A, on his father's death, moves up one step to take that father's place. This ascension requires a round-trip, to the centre for investiture, and then back home to the ancestral demesne. For the new functionary, however, things are more complex. Talent, not death, charts his course. He sees before him a summit rather than a centre. He travels up its corniches in a series of looping arcs which, he hopes, will become smaller and tighter as he nears the top. Sent out to township A at rank V, he may return to the capital at rank W; proceed to province B at rank X; continue to vice-royalty C at rank Y; and end his pilgrimage in the capital at rank Z. On this journey there is no assured resting-place; every pause is provisional. The last thing the functionary wants is to return home; for he *has* no home with any intrinsic value. And this: on his upward-spiralling road he encounters as eager fellow-pilgrims his functionary colleagues, from places and families he has scarcely heard of and surely hopes never to have to see. But in experiencing them as travelling-companions, a consciousness of connected-ness ('Why are *we* . . . *here* . . . *together?*') emerges, above all when all share a single language-of-state. Then, if official A from province B administers prov-ince C, while official D from province C administers province B—a situation that absolutism begins to make likely—that experience of interchangeability requires its own explanation: the ideology of absolutism, which the new men themselves, as much as the sovereign, elaborate.

Documentary interchangeability, which reinforced human interchange-ability, was fostered by the development of a standardized language-of-state. As the stately succession of Anglo-Saxon, Latin, Norman, and Early English in London from the eleventh through the fourteenth centuries demonstrates, *any* written language could, in principle, serve this function—provided it was given monopoly rights. (One could, however, argue that where vernaculars, rather than Latin, happened to hold the monopoly, a further centralizing function was achieved, by restricting the drift of one sovereign's officials to his rivals' machines: so to speak ensuring that Madrid's pilgrim-functionaries were not interchangeable with those of Paris.)

In principle, the extra-European expansion of the great kingdoms of early modern Europe should have simply extended the above model in the develop-ment of grand, transcontinental bureaucracies. But, in fact, this did not hap-pen. The instrumental rationality of the absolutist apparatus—above all its tendency to recruit and promote on the basis of talent rather than of birth—operated only fitfully beyond the eastern shores of the Atlantic.

The pattern is plain in the Americas. For example, of the 170 viceroys in Spanish America prior to 1813, only 4 were creoles. These figures are all the more startling if we note that in 1800 less than 5% of the 3,200,000 creole 'whites' in the Western Empire (imposed on about 13,700,000 indigenes) were Spain-born Spaniards. On the eve of the revolution in Mexico, there was only one creole bishop, although creoles in the viceroyalty outnumbered *peninsu-lares* by 70 to 1. And, needless to say, it was nearly unheard-of for a creole to rise to a position of official importance in Spain. Moreover, the pilgrimages of creole functionaries were not merely vertically barred. If peninsular officials could travel the road from Zaragoza to Cartagena, Madrid, Lima, and again Madrid, the 'Mexican' or 'Chilean' creole typically served only in the territories of colonial Mexico or Chile: his lateral movement was as cramped as his vertical ascent. In this way, the apex of his looping climb, the highest administrative centre to which he could be assigned, was the capital of the imperial administrative unit in which he found himself. Yet on this cramped pilgrimage he found travelling-companions, who came to sense that their fellowship was based not only on that pilgrimage's particular stretch, but on the shared fatality of trans-Atlantic birth. Even if he was born within one week of his father's migration, the accident of birth in the Americas consigned him to subordination—even though in terms of language, religion, ancestry, or manners he was largely indistinguishable from the Spain-born Spaniard. There was nothing to be done about it: he was *irremediably* a creole. Yet how irrational his exclusion must have seemed! Nonetheless, hidden inside the irrationality was this logic: born in the Americas, he could not be a true Spaniard; *ergo*, born in Spain, the *peninsular* could not be a true American.

What made the exclusion appear rational in the metropole? Doubtless the confluence of a time-honoured Machiavellism with the growth of conceptions of biological and ecological contamination that accompanied the planetary spread of Europeans and European power from the sixteenth century onwards. From the sovereign's angle of vision, the American creoles, with their ever-growing numbers and increasing local rootedness with each succeeding generation, presented a historically unique political problem. For the first time the metropoles had to deal with—for that era—vast numbers of 'fellow-Europeans' (over three million in the Spanish Americas by 1800) far outside Europe. If the indigenes were conquerable by arms and disease, and controllable by the mysteries of Christianity and a completely alien culture (as well as, for those days, an advanced political organization), the same was not true of the creoles, who had virtually the same relationship to arms, disease, Christianity and European culture as the metropolitans. In other words, in principle, they had readily at hand the political, cultural and military means for successfully asserting themselves. They constituted simultaneously a colonial community and an upper class. They were to be economically subjected and exploited, but they were also essential to the stability of the empire. One can see, in this light, a certain parallelism between the position of the creole magnates and of feudal barons, crucial to the sovereign's power, but also a menace to it. Thus the *peninsulares* dispatched as viceroys and bishops served the same functions as did the *homines novi* of the proto-absolutist bureaucracies. Even if the viceroy was a grandee in his Andalusian home, here, 5,000 miles away, juxtaposed to the creoles, he was effectively a *homo novus* fully dependent on his metropolitan master. The tense balance between peninsular official and creole magnate was in this way an expression of the old policy of *divide et impera* in a new setting.

In addition, the growth of creole communities, mainly in the Americas, but also in parts of Asia and Africa, led inevitably to the appearance of Eurasians,

Eurafricans, as well as Euramericans, not as occasional curiosities but as visible social groups. Their emergence permitted a style of thinking to flourish which foreshadows modern racism. Portugal, earliest of Europe's planetary conquerors, provides an apt illustration of this point. In the last decade of the fifteenth century Dom Manuel I could still 'solve' his 'Jewish question' by mass, forcible *conversion*—possibly the last European ruler to find this solution both satisfactory and 'natural'. Less than a century later, however, one finds Alexandre Valignano, the great reorganizer of the Jesuit mission in Asia between 1574 and 1606, vehemently opposing the admission of Indians and Eurindians to the priesthood in these terms.

All these dusky races are very stupid and vicious, and of the basest spirits . . . As for the *mestiços* and *castiços*, we should receive either very few or none at all; especially with regard to the *mestiços*, since the more native blood they have, the more they resemble the Indians and the less they are esteemed by the Portuguese.[5]

(Yet Valignano actively encouraged the admission of Japanese, Koreans, Chinese, and 'Indochinese' to the priestly function—perhaps because in those zones mestizos had yet to appear in any numbers?) Similarly, the Portuguese Franciscans in Goa violently opposed admission of creoles to the order, alleging that 'even if born of pure white parents [they] have been suckled by Indian ayahs in their infancy and thus had their blood contaminated for life.'[6] Boxer shows that 'racial' bars and exclusions increased markedly during the seventeenth and eighteenth centuries by comparison with earlier practice. To this malignant tendency the revival of large-scale slavery (for the first time in Europe since antiquity), which was pioneered by Portugal after 1510, made its own massive contribution. Already in the 1550s, 10% of Lisbon's population were slaves; by 1800 there were close to a million slaves among the 2,500,000 or so inhabitants of Portugal's Brazil.[7]

Indirectly, the Enlightenment also influenced the crystallization of a fatal distinction between metropolitans and creoles. In the course of his twenty-two years in power (1755–1777), the enlightened autocrat Pombal not only expelled the Jesuits from Portuguese domains, but made it a criminal offence to call 'coloured' subjects by offensive names, such as 'nigger' or 'mestiço' [sic]. But he justified this decree by citing ancient Roman conceptions of imperial citizenship, not the doctrines of the *philosophes*. More typically, the writings of Rousseau and Herder, which argued that climate and 'ecology' had a constitutive impact on culture and character, exerted wide influence. It was only too easy from there to make the convenient, vulgar deduction that creoles, born in a savage hemisphere, were by nature different from, and inferior to, the metropolitans—and thus unfit for higher office.

Our attention thus far has been focussed on the worlds of functionaries in the Americas—strategically important, but still small worlds. Moreover, they were worlds which, with their conflicts between *peninsulares* and creoles, predated the appearance of American national consciousness at the end of the eighteenth century. Cramped viceregal pilgrimages had no decisive consequences until their territorial stretch could be imagined as nations, in other words until the arrival of print-capitalism.

Print itself spread early to New Spain, but for two centuries it remained under the tight control of crown and church. Till the end of the seventeenth century, presses existed only in Mexico City and Lima, and their output was almost exclusively ecclesiastical. In Protestant North America printing scarcely existed at all in that century. In the course of the eighteenth, however, a virtual revolution took place. Between 1691 and 1820, no less than 2,120 'newspapers' were published, of which 461 lasted more than ten years.

The figure of Benjamin Franklin is indelibly associated with creole nationalism in the northern Americas. But the importance of his trade may be less apparent. Once again, Febvre and Martin are enlightening. They remind us that 'printing did not really develop in [North] America during the eighteenth century until printers discovered a new source of income—the newspaper.'[8] Printers starting new presses always included a newspaper in their productions, to which they were usually the main, even the sole, contributor. Thus the printer-journalist was initially an essentially North American phenomenon. Since the main problem facing the printer-journalist was reaching readers, there developed an alliance with the post-master so intimate that often each became the other. Hence, the printer's office emerged as the key to North American communications and community intellectual life. In Spanish America, albeit more slowly and intermittently, similar processes produced, in the second half of the eighteenth century, the first local presses.

What were the characteristics of the first American newspapers, North or South? They began essentially as appendages of the market. Early gazettes contained—aside from news about the metropole—commercial news (when ships would arrive and depart, what prices were current for what commodities in what ports), as well as colonial political appointments, marriages of the wealthy, and so forth. In other words, what brought together, on the same page, *this* marriage with *that* ship, *this* price with *that* bishop, was the very structure of the colonial administration and market-system itself. In this way, the newspaper of Caracas quite naturally, and even apolitically, created an imagined community among a specific assemblage of fellow-readers, to whom *these* ships, brides, bishops and prices belonged. In time, of course, it was only to be expected that political elements would enter in.

One fertile trait of such newspapers was always their provinciality. A colonial creole might read a Madrid newspaper if he got the chance (but it would say nothing about his world), but many a peninsular official, living down the same street, would, if he could help it, *not* read the Caracas production. An asymmetry infinitely replicable in other colonial situations. Another such trait was plurality. The Spanish-American journals that developed towards the end of the eighteenth century were written in full awareness of provincials in worlds parallel to their own. The newspaper-readers of Mexico City, Buenos Aires, and Bogota, even if they did not read each other's newspapers, were nonetheless quite conscious of their existence. Hence a well-known doubleness in early Spanish-American nationalism, its alternating grand stretch and particularistic localism. The fact that early Mexican nationalists wrote of themselves as *nosotros los Americanos* and of their country as *nuestra América*, has been interpreted as revealing the vanity of the local creoles who, because Mexico was far the most valuable of Spain's American possessions, saw themselves as the centre of the New World. But, in fact, people all over Spanish America thought of themselves as 'Americans,' since this term denoted precisely the shared fatality of extra-Spanish birth.

At the same time, we have seen that the very conception of the newspaper implies the refraction of even 'world events' into a specific imagined world of vernacular readers; and also how important to that imagined community is an idea of steady, solid simultaneity through time. Such a simultaneity the immense stretch of the Spanish American Empire, and the isolation of its component parts, made difficult to imagine. Mexican creoles might learn months later of developments in Buenos Aires, but it would be through Mexican newspapers, not those of the Rio de la Plata; and the events would appear as 'similar to' rather than 'part of' events in Mexico.

In this sense, the 'failure' of the Spanish-American experience to generate a permanent Spanish-America-wide nationalism reflects both the general level of development of capitalism and technology in the late eighteenth century and the 'local' backwardness of Spanish capitalism and technology in relation to the administrative stretch of the empire. (The world-historical era in which each nationalism is born probably has a significant impact on its scope. Is Indian nationalism not inseparable from colonial administrative-market unification, after the Mutiny, by the most formidable and advanced of the imperial powers?)

The Protestant, English-speaking creoles to the north were much more favourably situated for realizing the idea of 'America' and indeed eventually succeeded in appropriating the everyday title of 'Americans'. The original Thirteen Colonies comprised an area smaller than Venezuela, and one third the size of Argentina. Bunched geographically together, their market-centres in Boston, New York, and Philadelphia were readily accessible to one another, and their populations were relatively tightly linked by print as well as commerce. The 'United States' could gradually multiply in numbers over the next 183 years, as old and new populations moved westwards out of the old east coast core. Yet even in the case of the USA there are elements of comparative 'failure' or shrinkage—non-absorption of English-speaking Canada, Texas's decade of independent sovereignty (1835–46). Had a sizeable English-speaking community existed in California in the eighteenth century, is it not likely that an independent state would have arisen there to play Argentina to the Thirteen Colonies' Peru? Even in the USA, the affective bonds of nationalism were elastic enough, combined with the rapid expansion of the western frontier and the contradictions generated between the economies of North and South, to precipitate a war of secession *almost a century after the Declaration of Independence*; and this war today sharply reminds us of those that tore Venezuela and Ecuador off from Gran Colombía, and Uruguay and Paraguay from the United Provinces of the Rio de la Plata.

By way of provisional conclusion, it may be appropriate to re-emphasize the limited and specific thrust of the argument. [. . .] It is intended less to explain the socio-economic bases of anti-metropolitan resistance in the Western hemisphere between say, 1760 and 1830, than why the resistance was conceived in plural, 'national' forms—rather than in others. The economic interests at stake are well-known and obviously of fundamental importance. Liberalism and the Enlightenment clearly had a powerful impact, above all in providing an arsenal of ideological criticisms of imperial and *anciens régimes*. What I am proposing is that neither economic interest, Liberalism, nor Enlightenment could, or did, create *in themselves* the *kind*, or shape, of imagined community to be defended from these regimes' depredations; to put it another way, none provided the framework of a new consciousness—the scarcely-seen periphery of its vision—as opposed to centre-field objects of its admiration or disgust. In accomplishing *this* specific task, pilgrim creole functionaries and provincial creole printmen played the decisive historic role.

[*Imagined Communities*, rev. edn. (Verso: London, 1991), 52–65.]

30   Dark Gods and their Rites

The nationalist interpretation of the Bhagavad-Gita, arbitrary and ill-founded as it was, made it into a subversive book stocked by terrorist societies together with revolvers and sulfuric acid. Tilak[1] was, of course, not the only one to jazz up The Song of the Lord in this manner. A very good and apposite example of this process may be found in the writings of Bipin Chandra Pal (1858–1932). Pal goes so far as to make of the Gita a 'messianic' document promising salvation by divine prodigies—a notion entirely alien to Indian thought. The masses, he says, had always believed in Krishna: 'What they wanted was a practical application of that faith, not as a mere religious or spiritual force, but as a social, and, perhaps, even as a political, inspiration. Krishna stood too far away from the present. As God, he is no doubt present in spirit always and everywhere. What they craved for was his manifestation in the flesh . . . A fresh cry now went up from the heart of his chosen people for a fresh advent of the Saviour.' We may safely assert that the fresh cry of which Pal speaks did not go up from the masses. Rather—and this is what makes the passage just quoted highly interesting—it was the utterance of the minority of Western-educated Indians who imbibed current European political thought, heavily impregnated as it is with political messianism. Pal shows himself quite aware of the mechanism by which a traditional religion and its venerable sacraments and familiar hymns can be used to mobilize the masses for political ends: 'The authors of the French Revolution,' he points out, 'made grotesque attempts to replace the old sacraments of Catholicism by new ones, representing the new civic order which they were trying to set up in the land. In India, among the Hindus, civic religion is growing through an easy and natural process, out of the old symbolism and ritualism of the people. Hinduism has, indeed, like all ethnic systems, this advantage over credal religions, that its symbols and rituals, its sacraments and mysteries, are all partly religious and partly civic, partly social and partly spiritual. In fact, in Hinduism, the social and the spiritual are strangely blended together. Consequently, the new national spirit has found apt vehicles for expressing itself in the current religious rites and formulas of the people.' Pal himself gives a very good instance of this politicization of originally religious notions. The word *Swaraj* is today commonly taken to mean political self-government and is inseparably associated with the struggle of the Congress Party to overthrow British rule. This word was originally a term of Hindu philosophy and meant the state of self-rule or self-control in which a man abstains from action and escapes from the painful and evil cycle of perpetual reincarnation. *Swaraj*, Pal tells us, 'was borrowed by politics from the highest philosophical and religious literature of the people. . . . The term is used in the Vedânta to indicate the highest spiritual state, wherein the individual, having realized his identity with the Universal, is not merely freed from all bondage, but is established in perfect harmony with all else in the world.' 'The concept,' he adds, 'involves not merely national freedom; but universal federation also'! By the time Gandhi finished with it, *swaraj* was mired in all the impure passions of cupidity and domination and had simply come to mean that not a man called Akbar, or a man called Curzon, but a man called Nehru should rule India.

Pal illustrates also in another way the use of religion for political purposes. In a speech of 1907 he aptly described the British administration as based upon *maya* or illusion, and elsewhere he says that British rule over Indians was not due to their physical or intellectual or moral superiority but to 'pure hypnotism'. This interesting suggestion is clearly derived from classical Indian thought, for which the world and all phenomena are mere illusion from which the wise man seeks release. This notion that all human actions and feelings are an illusion Pal exploits by suggesting that the proper technique by which to break the spell of the British magic is to weave a more potent counterspell:

'The nationalist school exposed the hollowness of all these [British] pretensions. It commenced to make, what are called counterpasses in hypnotism, and at once awoke the people to a sense of their own strength, an appreciation of their own culture, and has created a new conviction that they, too, like the other races of the world, have a distinct mission and destiny.' A noble and profound idea is thus drained of its significance and made into a trivial—albeit powerful—instrument of political warfare.

One of the 'counterpasses' which Pal and other Indian nationalists employed was the revival of the cult of Kali, 'the grim goddess,' as he described her, 'dark and naked, bearing a garland of human heads around her neck—heads from which blood is dripping—and dancing on the prostrate form of Shiva or the Good.' It was before Kali, the goddess of destruction, that terrorist societies made their initiates take this vow: 'I will not be bound by the tie of affection for father, mother, brother, sister, hearth and home . . . If I fail to keep this vow, may the curse of Brahmins, of father and mother, and of the great patriots of every country speedily reduce me to ashes.' How the cult of Kali and the modalities of this cult were exploited for political ends may again be illustrated by a speech of Pal's at a political rally in which he recommended the worship of Rahbha Kali which is white not black and to which a sacrifice of white, not black, goats was acceptable. If at every new moon 108 white goats were sacrificed, this, Pal said, would be a good thing. The theme was taken up by another speaker whose words made clearer the allusion to the white goats: for this speaker advised his audience to go abroad and learn the manufacturing of bombs and other destructive weapons and then to come back to their country and sacrifice at every new moon 108 whites.

Pal and the other nationalist leaders were educated men, which, in the circumstances, meant that they were touched by European notions and could no longer have an innocent and unselfconscious faith in Kali. How can we explain these fervent appeals to dark goddesses, garlands of human heads, and dripping blood? This was, we suspect, conscious and deliberate manipulation of what must have been, in their eyes, primitive superstition. But Pal and his fellow Indians were not the only nationalist leaders in Asia and Africa to appeal to these superstitions. Jomo Kenyatta, for instance, who studied anthropology with Professor B. Malinowski in London, in his well-known *Facing Mount Kenya*[2] glorified cliterodectomy as practiced among the Kikuyu. The passage is remarkable and deserves quotation: 'When this preparation is finished, a woman specialist, known as *moruithia*, who has studied this form of surgery from childhood, dashes out of the wood, dressed in a very peculiar way, with her face painted with white and black ochre. This disguise tends to make her look rather terrifying, with her rhythmic movements accompanied by the rattles tied to her legs. She takes out from her pocket . . . the operating Gikuyu razor . . . and in quick movements, and with the dexterity of a Harley Street surgeon, proceeds to operate upon the girls. With a stroke she cuts off the tip of the clitoris. . . . As no other part of the girl's sexual organ is interfered with, this completes the girl's operation.' Kenyatta goes on to attack missionary and official doctors who denounce cliterodectomy as a barbaric custom and a menace to women in childbirth: they are 'irresponsible,' 'more to be pitied than condemned,' and 'their objectivity is blurred in trying to unravel the mystery of the *irua* [i.e. circumcision].' This mystagogy Professor Malinowski in his introduction to the book called 'a personal statement of the new outlook of a progressive African,' an African 'who presents the facts objectively, and to a large extent without any passion or feeling.' The latter statement may leave us skeptical, but we cannot help in this case as in that of Bipin Chandra Pal feeling quite puzzled. How can an educated Hindu promote the worship of Kali with her necklace of human heads, why does a 'progressive African' and a member, to boot, of Professor Malinowski's discussion class at the London School of Economics celebrate the mystery of cliterodectomy? [. . .]

Of the dark gods and their rites, we said that they represented a revulsion against Europe. But is this a satisfactory way of describing the matter? [. . .] The invocation of Kali and the praise of cliterodectomy was the work of men deeply touched by European ideas, men who, in words Malinowski used in introducing the work of his pupil Kenyatta, 'have suffered the injury of higher education.' The appeal to the past, the idea that every nation is defined by its past and therefore must have a past to be defined by, underlies the doctrine of nationalism, and this strand of the European intellectual tradition was, as we have shown, taken up by Asians and Africans. Here we may speak of an adaptation or even imitation of European ideas and not of revulsion against Europe. And on second thoughts it may seem to us that the bloodthirsty appeal to Kali and the deliberate obscurantism apparent in a defense of cliterodectomy are likewise an imitation and adoption of another feature of the European intellectual tradition, a feature which has always existed, albeit generally hidden and latent, but which has become more manifest and influential in the last few centuries. It is perfectly true that the stresses and strains brought about by contact with and subordination to Europe predisposed Asians and Africans to the acceptance of this strand in the European tradition but the fact remains that this particular strand was dominant in Europe itself at the time of its greatest expansion overseas.

Nationalism, we have said, rests on the assumption that a nation must have a past. It also rests on another assumption, no less fundamental, namely, that a nation must have a future. This assumption is a variant of the idea of progress which has been the dominant strand in modern European culture. Faith in progress has assumed many forms and variants, but essentially it is a belief that history will not let us down, that no catastrophe is final, no disaster irremediable. This is the prevailing note in modern culture. [. . .]

If, then, we should ask whether the worship of Kali or similar phenomena represent a revulsion against Europe, our answer would have to be negative. These disconcerting reactions by educated and sophisticated men—and it is only the sophisticated who harbor and propagate such notions—represent not so much a revulsion against the European tradition as the adoption and adaptation of certain of its features—features which became prominent in Europe itself at the very moment when it was coming in close and dominating contact with Asia and Africa. Bakunin's aim, 'to regroup this world of brigands into an invincible and omni-destructive force,' is in a line of succession from Robespierre's conjunction of virtue and terror and has for its counterpart B. C. Pal's glorification of Kali, the goddess of destruction with the garland of human heads round her neck. We may say in short that the mainspring of nationalism in Asia and Africa is the same secular millennialism which had its rise and development in Europe and in which society is subjected to the will of a handful of visionaries who, to achieve their vision, must destroy all barriers between private and public.

['Introduction' to Elie Kedourie (ed.), *Nationalism in Asia and Africa* (Weidenfeld and Nicolson: London, 1971), 73–7, 92–3, 106.]

PARTHA CHATTERJEE
....

31 National History and its Exclusions

The idea that 'Indian nationalism' is synonymous with 'Hindu nationalism' is not the vestige of some premodern religious conception. It is an entirely modern, rationalist, and historicist idea. Like other modern ideologies, it allows for a central role of the state in the modernization of society and strongly defends the state's unity and sovereignty. Its appeal is not religious but political. In this sense, the framework of its reasoning is entirely secular. A little examination will show that compared to Mrityunjay's historiography, which revolved around the forces of the divine and sacred, Tarinicharan's is a wholly secular historiography.

In fact, the notion of 'Hindu-ness' in this historical conception cannot be, and does not need to be, defined by any religious criteria at all. There are no specific beliefs or practices that characterize this 'Hindu,' and the many doctrinal and sectarian differences among Hindus are irrelevant to its concept. Indeed, even such anti-Vedic and anti-Brahmanical religions as Buddhism and Jainism count here as Hindu. Similarly, people outside the Brahmanical religion and outside caste society are also claimed as part of the Hindu jāti. But clearly excluded from this jāti are religions like Christianity and Islam.

What then is the criterion for inclusion or exclusion? It is one of historical origin. Buddhism or Jainism are Hindu because they originate in India, out of debates and critiques that are internal to Hinduism. Islam or Christianity come from outside and are therefore foreign. And 'India' here is the generic entity, with fixed territorial definitions, that acts as the permanent arena for the history of the jāti.

What, we may ask, is the place of those inhabitants of India who are excluded from this nation? There are several answers suggested in this historiography. One, which assumes the centrality of the modern state in the life of the nation, is frankly majoritarian. The majority 'community' is Hindu; the others are minorities. State policy must therefore reflect this preponderance, and the minorities must accept the leadership and protection of the majority. This view, which today is being propagated with such vehemence in postcolonial India by Hindu-extremist politics, actually originated more than a hundred years ago, at the same time Indian nationalism was born.

Consider the utopian history of Bhudeb Mukhopadhyay, written in 1876.[1] The army of Ahmad Shah Abdali is engaged in battle with the Maratha forces in the fields of Panipat. A messenger from the Maratha commander comes to Ahmad Shah and says that although the Muslims had always mistreated the Hindus, the Hindus were prepared to forgive. 'You may return home unhindered with all your troops. If any Musalman living in India wishes to go with you, he may do so, but he may not return within five years.'

This is, of course, 'the history of India as revealed in a dream': Ahmad Shah therefore says:

'Go to the Maharashtrian commander and tell him that . . . I will never attack India again.'

Hearing this, the messenger saluted [Ahmad Shah] and said, '. . . I have been instructed to deliver another message. All Musalman nawabs, subahdars, zamindars, jagirdars, etc. of this country who choose not to accompany you may return immediately to their own estates and residences. The Maharashtrian commander has declared, "All previous offenses of these people have been condoned." '

There is then held a grand council of all the kings of India in which the following proposal is made:

Although India is the true motherland only of those who belong to the Hindu jāti and although only they have been born from her womb, the Muslims are not unrelated to her any longer. She has held them at her breast and reared them. The Muslims are therefore her adopted children.

Can there be no bonds of fraternity between two children of the same mother, one a natural child and the other adopted? There certainly can; the laws of every religion admit this. There has now been born a bond of brotherhood between Hindus and Muslims living in India . . .

Now all will have to unite in taking care of our Mother. But without a head, no union can function. Who among us will be our leader? By divine grace, there is no room left for debate in this matter. This throne which has been prepared for Raja Ramchandra . . . will never be destroyed. There, behold the wise Badshah Shah Alam coming forward to hand over of his own accord his crown, and with it the responsibility of ruling over his empire, to Raja Ramchandra.

Thus, the Mughal emperor hands over his throne to the Maratha ruler Ramchandra. 'As soon as the assembly was dissolved and everyone rose from their seats, no one was able to see Shah Alam again. Seated on the throne of Delhi was Raja Ramchandra of the dynasty of Shivaji, on his head the crown given to him by Shah Alam.'

It may be mentioned that in this imaginary council a constitution is then promulgated more or less along the lines of the German Reich, with strongly protectionist economic policies that succeed, in this anticolonial utopia, in keeping the European economic powers firmly in check.

The second answer, which also made the distinction between majority and minority 'communities,' is associated with what is called the politics of 'secularism' in India. This view holds that in order to prevent the oppression of minorities by the majority, the state must enact legal measures to protect the rights and the separate identities of the minorities. The difficulty is that the formal institutions of the state, based on an undifferentiated concept of citizenship, cannot allow for the separate representation of minorities. Consequently, the question of who represents minorities necessarily remains problematic, and constantly threatens the tenuous identity of nation and state.

There was a third answer in this early nationalist historiography. This denied the centrality of the state in the life of the nation and instead pointed to the many institutions and practices in the everyday lives of the people through which they had evolved a way of living with their differences. The writings of Rabindranath Tagore in his post-Swadeshi phase are particularly significant in this respect. The argument here is that the true history of India lay not in the battles of kings and the rise and fall of empires but in this everyday world of popular life whose innate flexibility, untouched by conflicts in the domain of the state, allowed for the coexistence of all religious beliefs.

The principal difficulty with this view, which has many affinities with the later politics of Gandhism, is its inherent vulnerability to the overwhelming sway of the modern state. Its only defense against the historicist conception of the nation is to claim for the everyday life of the people an essential and transhistorical truth. But such a defense remains vulnerable even within the grounds laid by its own premises, as is shown rather interestingly in Rabindranath's hesitation in this matter. Reviewing Abdul Karim's history of Muslim rule in India, Rabindranath remarks on the reluctance of Hindus to aspire to an achievement of power and glory which would lead them to intervene in the lives of other people and on their inability to cope with those who do.[2] The political history of Islam and, more recently, the history of European conquests in the rest of the world show, he says, that people who have world-conquering ambitions hide under the edifice of civilized life a secret dungeon of ferocious beastliness and unbridled greed. Compared to this, it often seems preferable to lie in peace in a stagnant pool, free from the restlessness of adventure and ambition.

But the fortifications put up by the *śāstra* have failed to protect India and conflicts with other peoples have become inevitable. We are now obliged to defend our interests against the greed of others and our lives against the violence of others. It would seem to be advisable then to feed a few pieces of flesh to the beast which lies within us and to have it stand guard outside our doors. At the very least, that would arouse the respect of people who are powerful.[3]

None of these answers, however, can admit that the Indian nation as a whole might have a claim on the historical legacy of Islam. The idea of the singularity of national history has inevitably led to a single source of Indian tradition, namely, ancient Hindu civilization. Islam here is either the history of foreign conquest or a domesticated element of everyday popular life. The classical heritage of Islam remains external to Indian history.

The curious fact is, of course, that this historicist conception of Hindu nationalism has had few qualms in claiming for itself the modern heritage of Europe. It is as rightful participants in that globalized domain of the modern state that today's contestants in postcolonial India fight each other in the name of history.

There was a fourth answer, so unclear and fragmented that it is better to call it only the possibility of an answer. It raises doubts about the singularity of a history of India and also renders uncertain the question of classical origins. This history does not necessarily assume the sovereignty of a single state; it is more confederal in its political assumptions.

Surprisingly, there is a hint of this answer in Bankim's own writings.[4] 'Just because the ruler is of a different jāti does not mean that a country is under subjection.' Indeed, it was Bengal under the independent sultans that Bankim regarded as the birthplace of the renaissance in Bengali culture.

History tells us that a principal consequence of subjection is that the intellectual creativity of a subject jāti is extinguished. Yet the intellect of the Bengali shone more brightly during the reign of the Pathans. . . . Never before and never after has the face of Bengal lit up more brightly than in these two hundred years.[5]

How did we come upon this *renaissance*? Where did this sudden enlightenment in the intellectual life of the jāti come from? . . . How was this light extinguished?[6]

It was Emperor Akbar, upon whom we shower praises, who became Bengal's nemesis. He was the first to make Bengal a truly subject country . . . The Mughal is our enemy, the Pathan our ally.[7]

There is a great disjuncture here between the history of India and the history of Bengal. The putative center of a generically sovereign state, coextensive with the nation, also becomes uncertainly located. Bankim notes that the

Aryans appeared in Bengal at a much later date; does this weaken the claims of the Bengali upon the classical heritage of the Aryans?

Many will think that the claims of Bengal and Bengalis have now become less formidable, and that we have been slandered as a jāti of recent origin. We who flaunt our ancient origins before the modern English have now been reduced to a modern jāti. But it is hard to see why there should be anything dishonorable in all this. We still remain descendants of the ancient Arya jāti: no matter when we may have come to Bengal, our ancestors are still the glorious Aryans.[8]

But, on the other hand, the question is raised: who of the Bengalis are Aryans? What is the origin of the Bengali jāti? Bankim looked for answers to these questions in a long essay, 'The Origins of the Bengalis.' The 'scientific' evidence he accumulated in support of his arguments will now seem extremely dubious, and this is now one of his least remembered essays. But its conclusion was not very comfortable for the writing of a singular history of the Indian nation.

The English are one jāti, the Bengalis are many jāti. In fact, among those whom we now call Bengali can be found four kinds of Bengalis: one, Aryan; two, non-Aryan Hindu; three, Hindu of mixed Aryan and non-Aryan origin; and four, Bengali Musalman. The four live separately from one another. At the bottom of Bengali society are the Bengali non-Aryans, mixed Aryans and Bengali Muslims; the top is almost exclusively Aryan. It is for this reason that, looked [at] from the outside, the Bengali jāti seems a pure Aryan jāti and the history of Bengal is written as the history of an Aryan jāti.[9]

Elements of this alternative history can be found not only in Bankim but in other writers as well. Rajkrishna Mukhopadhyay, whose book provided the occasion for Bankim's first comments on the history of Bengal, observed that unlike in other parts of India, Islam did not spread in Bengal by the sword.[10] Krishnachandra Ray compares the British period with that of Sultani or Nawabi rule and notes that in the latter 'there was no hindrance to the employment in high office of people of this country.'[11] And the process of 'nationalization' of the last nawab of Bengal, which reached its culmination in Akshaykumar Maitreya's Sirājuddaulā (1898), has already been noted.

The question is whether these two alternative forms of 'national' history— one, a history of the bhāratavarṣīya, assuming a classical Aryan past and centred in northern India, and the other of Bengalis of many jāti, derived from uncertain origins—contained in the divergences in their trajectories and rhythms the possibility of a different imagining of nationhood. It is difficult now to explore this possibility in positive terms, because the second alternative in the pair has been submerged in the last hundred years by the tidal wave of historical memory about Arya-Hindu-Bhāratavarṣa. But the few examples considered here show that it would be impossible, according to this line of thinking, to club Pathan and Mughal rule together and call it the Muslim period, or to begin the story of the spread of Islam in Bengal with 'Muhammad instructed his followers to take up the sword and destroy the infidels.'

It might be speculated that if there were many such alternative histories for the different regions of India, then the center of Indian history would not need to remain confined to Aryavarta or, more specifically, to 'the throne of Delhi.' Indeed, the very centrality of Indian history would then become largely uncertain. The question would no longer be one of 'national' and 'regional' histories: the very relation between parts and the whole would be open for negotiation. If there is any unity in these alternative histories, it is not national but confederal.

[*The Nation and its Fragments* (Princeton University Press: Princeton, NJ, 1993), 110–15.]

FRANCIS ROBINSON

32 Islam and Nationalism

There would appear to be a tendency amongst Muslims to organize in politics on the basis of their faith. Where Muslims predominate, organizations take the form of Islamic political parties such as the Muslim Brotherhood of Egypt or the Jama'at-i-Islami of Pakistan, whose aim has been to ensure that state and society run as far as possible along what they consider to be Islamic lines. Where Muslims form a minority, there frequently springs up a demand that Muslims should be organized as a separate political community, either as a separate nation-state or as a state within a state. [. . .]

One example of Muslim separatism, that of the Muslims of the United Provinces who were at the heart of the drive to create Pakistan, has received more scholarly attention than most examples. In his book *Language, Religion and Politics in North India*, Paul Brass has explained the phenomenon thus: there was little in the objective differences between Hindus and Muslims, and not much more in their revivalist movements to make their separation inevitable. What was crucial was the process of 'symbol selection'; and the fact that Muslim elites chose divisive rather than composite symbols. 'Muslim leaders in north India in the late nineteenth century', Brass writes, 'did not recognize a common destiny with the Hindus, because they saw themselves in danger of losing their privileges as a dominant community . . .' So they chose to emphasize 'a special sense of history incompatible with Hindu aspirations and a myth of Muslim decline into backwardness'.[1] According to Brass, if Muslims organize on the basis of their faith in politics, it is because Muslim elites perceive it to be the most effective way of keeping or gaining political power. [. . .]

The ideas associated with creating and sustaining 'the best nation raised up for men' contained in the Islamic tradition (that Muslims form part of a community; that the laws of the community are God-given; that it is the duty of the ruler to put them into effect; that he must have the power to do so; that all Muslims are brothers; and that they are distinct from and superior to non-Muslims) have continually influenced many north Indian Muslims to-wards trying to realize the ideal religio-political community. Moreover, as a minority in the midst of idolators, abiding concerns were both to draw sharp distinctions between the idolators and themselves and to ensure that Islam lived hand in hand with power. Understandably, these were concerns which grew in force with the decline of Mughal power and the emergence of the modern state in non-Muslim hands. Their action is evident amongst the ulema whose very raison d'être was to strive to create the Sharia community, and for whom ideas must frequently have operated as a motivating force. Even when the influence of these ideas drove members of the Indian ulema in opposite political directions in the twentieth century, there is no doubting their separat-ist force. If those of the ulema who supported the League saw the creation of an Islamic state as the only way of protecting the Sharia when the British left, those of the ulema who supported the Congress envisaged a Muslim future in India which was not much less separate and in which the sense of Muslim identity would always be made to compete strongly with that of Indian nationality. Turning to the secular, or secularizing elite, the influence of these ideas, though less direct and harder to assess, is still strong. Even without powerful religious sanction, which is not to say that many who were not members of the ulema were not deeply committed Muslims, they still under-laid men's assumptions about the world and helped to form what were emo-tionally the most satisfying ends.

If this understanding of the formative influence of the ideal of the Islamic community on Muslim political behaviour is correct, it must be seen to work more widely than just amongst the United Provinces Muslims, and so it does. Take, for instance, the Moplahs of south India who have shown for eight centuries that it is possible to survive as a Muslim community under non-Muslim rule. They have asserted with a practice of suicidal jihad the distinction between the Muslim community and the Hindus and Christians who lived around them;[2] in recent years they have demonstrated a powerful sense of asabiyya with Muslims elsewhere on the subcontinent; while the essentially separatist tendencies in their outlook are revealed in their strong preference to act politically through an exclusively Muslim party whose demand for the creation of a Moplah-dominated district of Mallapuram was granted in 1969.[3] This achievement, we are told, 'met an important psychological need';[4] within the limits of what was possible some of the Moplahs of Kerala had at last succeeded in combining Islam with power. We know enough about the Moplahs to sense with some confidence the way in which their vision of the world has been shaped by Islam, and how this has influenced their politics. We do not as yet know enough to assert the same of the Deccani Muslims who support the Majlis-e-Ittehadul-Muslimeen with its demand to establish a separ-ate Muslim state in Andhra Pradesh,[5] or of the Labbais of Tamil Nadu who identified strongly with the movement for Pakistan,[6] or of the Maharashtrian

Muslims who in recent years have joined the Muslim League in increasing numbers.[7] But it seems likely that the ideal of the Islamic community shaped and shapes their apprehension of what is legitimate, desirable and satisfactory political action.

Considering Muslim minorities in Asia more generally, a similar relationship between ideas associated with creating and sustaining the Muslim community and political separatism is evident. In the Philippines close connections have been drawn between the resurgence of Islam since World War Two, with a consequent deepening of religious consciousness and the growth of more orthodox religious practice, and the movement of Muslim Filipinos to set up a separate Muslim state.[8] In China, for centuries, large numbers of Muslims have resisted absorption into the dominant culture. Muslims have preserved their sense of superiority and distinctiveness; they have built strong communal organizations; and throughout they have enhanced their consciousness of the *umma* 'by cultivating in the Muslim the centrality of Arabia, Islam, the Islamic Empire, and Islamic traditions and values'.[9] Not surprisingly, they have not been able to identify with the unitarian Confucian and Communist states, and have followed a politically separate path as far as possible. 'China is not the fatherland of the Hui nationality', they declared during the Hundred Flowers relaxation of 1956, 'Arabic is the language of the Hui people . . . All the Hui people of the world belong to one family.'[10]

If the Islamic ideal of the religio-political community has such influence amongst Muslim minorities, it would appear also to have influence in states where the population is largely or entirely Muslim. Indeed, there is hardly a Muslim state in the world which does not have a party whose professed aim is to impose its vision of the Islamic ideal on contemporary politics and society. And whatever the motives of the leaders and followers of the Muslim Brotherhood of Egypt, the Jama'at-i-Islami of Pakistan, or the Fadayan-i Islam of Iran, there can be no doubt that their vision is formed, and limited, by the Islamic tradition. Nowhere has this process been more minutely observed in recent years than in Kessler's study of the rise of the Pan-Malaysian Islamic party to power in the Kelantan province of eastern Malaysia. Here an anthropologist with an historian's perspective shows how in the 1950s and 1960s Islamic social theory continuously impinged upon and shaped political developments.[11] The experience of Muslim-majority societies confirms our understanding of the pervasive influence of the Islamic ideal, the one difference being that whereas in minority communities a primary problem is uniting power to Islam, in majority communities it is uniting Islam to power.

The fundamental connection between Islam and political separatism suggests further modifications to Brass's theory of nation-formation. To those factors that are already agreed to be significant:[12] the ability of UP Muslims to draw on cultural and historical symbols with an appeal to a large part of the community; the existence of powerful elites willing to promote a communal identity; the fact that objective differences between Hindus and Muslims were not great enough of themselves to fuel a separatist movement; the determination of Muslims to defend Muslim interests; the importance of competition from an increasingly assertive Hindu revivalism and the significance of the imperial system of political control, we must add the religio-political ideas of Islam, in particular those that stress the importance of the existence of a Muslim community. We see these ideas not only limiting the range of legitimate actions for the elite, which is the process implied in (though not specifically expanded in) Brass's article for [*Political Identity in South Asia*], but also forming their own apprehensions of what was possible and of what they ought to be trying to achieve. Brass had made a bold attempt to delineate the realm in which the laws of competition for power are absolute. But the example of Muslim separatism would suggest that the area in which we can see politics as autonomous must be cut down yet further than he has been prepared to admit.

This conclusion has broader theoretical implications. Brass hints at its significance for political science in the discussion at the beginning of his article when he points to the fundamental conceptual differences that exist among scholars over the processes by which nations are formed. Some, the 'primordialists', argue that every man carries with him through life attachments (to birthplace, kin, religion, language etc.) that are the 'givens' of the human condition, that are rooted in the non-rational foundations of the personality, and that provide the basis for an easy affinity with other people from the same background. Others, the 'instrumentalists', argue, as Brass seemed to do in *Language, Religion and Politics*, that ethnicity is to be seen 'as the pursuit of interest and advantage for members of groups whose cultures are infinitely malleable and manipulable by elites'.[13] These are extreme positions; the answer, as Brass himself now suggests, lies somewhere between the two. He veers towards the 'instrumentalists'' position in which the autonomy of politics is considerable. Nation formation, he says, is 'the process by which elites and counter-elites within ethnic groups select aspects of the group's culture, attach new value and meaning to them, and use them as symbols to mobilize the group, to defend its interests, and to compete with other groups'.[14] These elites are fancy-free and constrained only by the cultures of the groups they wish to lead. We propose that Islamic ideas had a moulding and on occasion a motivating role to play amongst the elites of the UP, that they seem to have played a similar role amongst the elites in other Muslim societies, and that the continuing power of these ideas suggests that the balance of the argument should shift more towards the position of the primordialists.

['Islam and Muslim Separatism', in D. Taylor and M. Yapp (eds.), *Political Identity in South Asia* (Curzon Press: London, 1979), 78, 79, 104–7.]

33 Ideologies of Delayed Development

The impact of the modern industrial West is the initial challenge in the industrially backward country. The various ways in which the West has disrupted traditional societies are beyond the scope of this analysis. The point to note here is that irreversible processes are set in motion. The contemporary scene is littered with fallen idols, desecrated by unsanctioned violence, an uncomfortable place in which to live. Thus, all ideologies of delayed industrialization are essentially revolutionary—in Mannheim's usage, utopian.[1] They direct activity toward changing a social order which is already changing. Even the superficially conservative ideologies turn out to be pseudo-conservative in the sense that they advocate a change in the status quo. Pseudo-conservative or radical, these ideologies advocate the manipulation of the disagreeable Present. In this sense, *Les extremes se touchent*.

The first problem of the 'assaulted' intellectual is to assume a satisfactory posture vis-à-vis the West. The position taken is frequently ambiguous, embracing the polar extremes of xenophobia and xenophilia. The intellectual may resent the West, but since he is already at least partly Westernized, to reject the West completely would be to deny part of himself.

The intellectual is appalled by discrepancies between the standard of living and 'culture' of his own country, and those of modern Western nations. He feels that something must be done, and done fast. He is a man on the defensive, searching for new defensive weapons. As Gamal Abdul Nasser wrote to a friend in 1935:

Allah said, 'Oppose them with whatever forces you can muster!' But what are these forces we are supposed to have in readiness for them?[2]

Another characteristic of the 'assaulted' intellectual is his uneasy attitude toward himself and his own kind—the intelligentsia and middle classes. Often he scorns his kind (and by implication, himself) as 'pseudo,' 'mongrel,' neither truly native nor truly Western. In order to find self-respect, he goes in search of his 'true self'; he tries to 'discover India'; he revisits the West. For example, Gandhi wrote in 1908:

You, English, who have come to India are not good specimens of the English nation, nor can we, almost half-Anglicized Indians, be considered as good specimens of the real Indian nation.[3]

Speaking of the lack of good Indonesian literature, Sjahrir wrote in 1934:

In reality, our cultural level is still too low for a real renaissance. There is no thought, no form, no sound, and what is worse, there is not yet enough earnestness and integrity among us. There is still only unsavory counterfeit, which is published with great fuss, but which still has little merit.[4]

Nehru, while in prison in 1944, recalled:

The present for me, and for many others like me, was an odd mixture of medievalism, appalling poverty and misery and a somewhat superficial modernism of the middle classes. I was not an admirer of my own class or kind, and yet inevitably I looked to it for leadership in the struggle for India's salvation; that middle class felt caged and circumscribed and wanted to grow and develop itself.[5]

Nehru leans toward xenophilia, but his close associate Gandhi took an emphatic xenophobic posture. He asserted that Indians, to be successful in dealing with the British, must 'consciously believe that Indian civilization is the best and that the European is a nine days' wonder.' Of course, Indian civilization has some defects, he admits, such as child marriage and religious prostitution. But, 'the tendency of Indian civilization is to elevate the moral being, that of the Western civilization is to propagate immorality.'[6]

The 'assaulted' intellectual works hard to make invidious comparisons between his own nation and the West. He may simply claim that his people are superior, as did Gandhi: 'We consider our civilization to be far superior to yours.'[7] Or he may hold that his ancestors had already rejected Western culture as inferior. But these assertions can elicit conviction only among a few and for a short while. More often the intellectual says, 'We are equal to Westerners,' or 'You are *no better* than I am.' Around this theme lies a wealth of propositions: (1) 'In the past you were no better (or worse) than we are now.' (2) 'We once had your good qualities, but we were corrupted by alien oppressors.' (3) 'We have high spiritual qualities despite our poverty, but you are soulless materialists.' (4) 'Everything worthwhile in your tradition is present or incipient in ours.' The slogan, 'trade, not aid,' when used metaphorically, is another variation on this theme. The nationalist claims to seek a blend of the 'best' in East and West. But why must both East and West inspire the new culture? Behind this there is perhaps the implicit wish to see the 'East' a genuine partner, an equal, of the West.

The foregoing postures vis-à-vis the West may be comforting to the intellectual, but they will not stimulate action unless certain imperatives are 'deduced' from them. For example, 'We must purge our national culture of alien corruptions and realize our true character which has been lying dormant within us.' But doses of self-criticism are equally important incentives to action, because they make it impossible to relax in complacency. In 1931, Joseph Stalin, leader of one of the most spectacular cultural transformations in human history, told Soviet industrial managers,

One feature of the history of old Russia was the continual beatings she suffered for falling behind, for her backwardness. She was beaten by the Mongol khans. She was beaten by the Turkish beys. She was beaten by the Swedish feudal lords. She was beaten by the Polish and Lithuanian gentry. She was beaten by the Japanese barons. All beat her—for her backwardness: for military backwardness, for cultural backwardness, for political backwardness, for industrial backwardness, for agricultural backwardness. She was beaten because to do so was profitable and could be done with impunity . . .

That is why we must no longer lag behind . . . We are fifty or a hundred years behind the advanced countries. We must make good this distance in ten years. Either we do it, or they crush us.[8]

Another man who administered blunt criticism was Mustafa Kemal Ataturk, who told the Turkish Grand National Assembly in 1920,

We have accepted the principle that we do not, and will not, give up our national independence. Although we always respect this basic condition, when we take into consideration the level of prosperity of the country, the wealth of the nation, and the general mental level, and when we compare it with the progress of the world in general, we must admit that we are not a little, but very backward.[9]

Ataturk praised the Turkish nation, however, for high moral qualities and great past achievements. Although he was probably a xenophile by conviction, he succeeded to a remarkable degree in overcoming the xenophobia of his people by means of his ideological rhetoric. When it was suggested that to borrow from the West 'all that Turkey needs' might conflict with the national ideal, Ataturk retorted that the national principle itself had become *internationally* accepted; and also,

Countries are many, but civilization is one and for the progress of a nation it is necessary to participate in this one civilization.[10]

Ataturk justified the importation of specific alien inventions, such as terms from non-Turkish languages, with the assertion that the so-called import was actually indigenous: according to the Sun Language Theory, Turkish was the mother of all the languages of the world, so that 'borrowed' words were actually prodigal sons come home. This technique of encouraging an import by calling it indigenous was complemented by the technique of eradicating the indigenous by calling it imported. For example, Ataturk pointed out that the fez was a headgear imported from Europe a hundred years before.

When the intellectual in an industrially backward country surveys modern Western civilization, he is confronted with five hundred years of scientific, artistic, social, economic, political, and religious developments. He sees a flood of heterogeneous Western cultural elements, from jazz to steel mills, pouring into his country. Then, fearing that he will be 'swamped' by the deluge, and lose his own identity, he tries to control cultural imports. In order to do this, he must find a standard to determine exactly what should be borrowed. The standard used by the nationalist is that the element to be imported should be in 'conformity' with his own national culture and should serve to strengthen his nation. This formula is very elastic, and can be used to justify the borrowing or rejection of practically anything. But the Marxist-Leninist holds that the element to be imported should be one that is 'progressive' in terms of the

Marxist-Leninist pattern of social evolution. According to this pattern, the 'bourgeois' West is decaying; it is the 'toilers' of both East and West who ride the wave of the future. Imperialism is the highest and the last stage of capitalism. However, Western industrialism and science are the great hope for the non-Western peoples; and the Soviet Union is represented as a model of rapid industrialization and scientific development. If the industrially backward nation borrows from the West only what is most 'progressive,' it can skip a part, or a stage, of the long and difficult social development of the West. Then, as the West decays, the former backward nations will surpass the best that the West has ever achieved.

The tension between archaism and futurism is another ambiguity in ideologies of delayed industrialization. It is closely related to the xenophobia–xenophilia tension, because the West is 'the new' and the native culture is 'the old' at the onset of contact.

Archaism is an attempt to resurrect a supposed 'golden age,' or some part of it. This 'golden age' is usually not in the disagreeable recent past, but in a more remote period, and it can only be recovered by historical research and interpretation. For example, Mussolini gloried in imperial Rome and the medieval 'corporate state'; the Slavophiles glorified the peasant *mir* and the indigenous Christian Orthodox practices in Russia; the Shintoists revived an ancient mythology that deified the Emperor; Sun Yat-sen and Chiang Kai-shek exhorted the Chinese to revive Confucian ethics; Gandhi urged that India return to the age of 'Rama Raj'; and Ataturk exulted in the barbaric virtues of the Osmanli nomads. According to Gandhi,

It was not that we did not know how to invent machinery, but our forefathers knew that, if we set our hearts after such things, we would become slaves and lose our moral fibre. They, therefore, after due deliberation, decided that we should only do what we could with our hands and feet. They further reasoned that large cities were a snare and a useless encumbrance and that people would not be happy in them, that there would be gangs of thieves and robbers, prostitution and vice flourishing in them, and that poor men would be robbed by rich men. They were, therefore, satisfied with small villages.[11]

According to Mussolini,

Rome is our point of departure and of reference; it is our symbol, or if you like, it is our Myth. We dream of a Roman Italy, that is to say wise and strong, disciplined and imperial. Much of that which was the immortal spirit of Rome resurges in Fascism.[12]

According to Sun Yat-sen,

So, coming to the root of the matter, if we want to restore our race's standing, besides uniting all into a great national body, we must first recover our ancient morality—then, and only then can we plan how to attain again to the national position we once held.[13]

But Nehru condemns archaism:

We have to come to grips with the present, this life, this world, this nature which surrounds us with its infinite variety. Some Hindus talk of going back to the Vedas; some Moslems dream of an Islamic theocracy. Idle fancies, for there is no going back, there is no turning back even if this was thought desirable. There is only one-way traffic in Time.[14]

Archaism may slip into a futuristic ideology, such as Marxism, and create an ambiguity. Adam Ulam has suggested that Marxism has its greatest appeal for semi-proletarianized or uprooted peasants who are nostalgic for the 'good old days' when their actions were governed by nature, the village elders, the family patriarch, and the religious authorities—instead of the less congenial factory boss and the State. To the uprooted peasant Marxism offers a comforting strain of archaism: that is, it envisions a utopia in which state and factory, as coercive institutions, have 'withered away.'[15]

Whenever a resurrection of the past is contemplated, the question arises, 'What part of the past?' or 'Which age was our golden age, and why?' Sometimes the age selected is an imperial age, when the people in question enjoyed their greatest authority over others. Sometimes a period of 'pristine simplicity' is admired. But new imperial conquests are incompatible with the weak political and economic position of industrially backward countries, and a return to the 'simple life' is incompatible with industrialization. In such cases archaism is not a solution to the problem at hand, but an escape from it.

However, there are more constructive uses of the past. The intellectual may discover that in the remote past his people possessed the very virtues which are supposed to make a modern nation great. For example, the Kemalists glorify their ancestors as brave, tolerant, realistic, generous, peaceful, and respectful of women; in short, 'spiritual' exemplars of the well-bred Western European gentleman. These 'genuine' Turks were temporarily 'corrupted' by Arab-Persian-Byzantine culture, but they are now due to take their rightful place among 'civilized' nations. The manifest content of such an ideological position may be archaistic, but its latent content is futuristic.

The Communists also use the past in this way. But they have characteristic standards for determining what elements of the past are desirable. The Chinese Communists have cultivated peasant literature and art because they are 'progressive,' being products of a 'progressive' class; whereas gentry culture is rejected as 'feudal.' In the Soviet Union the pre-revolutionary leaders most cherished by the Communist regime are those it considers 'progressive' for their time (such as Peter the Great), whereas 'reactionaries' (such as Dostoyevsky, until recently) have been under a cloud.

Nationalists, when selecting elements from their past, ask, 'What will tend to strengthen the nation?' But tradition has lost its natural charm, and traditionalism is something the nationalist must 'work at.' He uses the shared traditions of his people as raw material with which to build national morale; but tradition is a means, existing only for the sake of national strength, and not as an axiomatic, self-justified good.[33] For example, Sun Yat-sen said in 1924:

Our position now is extremely perilous; if we do not earnestly promote nationalism and weld together our four hundred millions into a strong nation, we face a tragedy—the loss of our country and the destruction of our race. To ward off this danger, we must espouse Nationalism and employ the national spirit to save the country.[16]

There are other uses of the past besides escapism, the sanctioning of innovations, the glorification of 'progressive' individuals and groups, and national self-strengthening. The past may be used to eradicate what the intellectual feels to be undesirable in the present and for the future. By publicizing the results of historical research, showing that a supposedly indigenous cultural element (like the fez) is of foreign origin, he may thereby stigmatize it. He may use other grounds to stigmatize the Ottoman and Chinese literary languages; they are the languages of reactionary and oppressive ruling classes who have cared only for their own welfare, rather than the welfare of the people.

The concern of both nationalists and Communists for vernacular languages and peasant arts is closely related to a third problem of the 'assaulted' intellectual; his relationship with the uneducated masses. Some intellectuals have a sentimental, patronizing, or contemptuous attitude toward the masses. Sun Yat-sen said,

The Ming veterans spread the idea of nationalism through the lower classes; but, on account of their childish understanding, the lower classes did not know how to take advantage of the ideas, but were, on the contrary, made tools of by others.[17]

Mohammed Naguib of Egypt wrote in 1955:

Given the deplorable conditions in Egyptian villages, however, the distinction between compulsion and cooperation is irrelevant. The average *fellah* has fallen too low to be able to help himself without a great deal of compulsory assistance from the government.[18]

Other intellectuals, like Nehru, wonder if the peasants are the 'true' Indians, while they (the intellectuals) are only 'pseudos.' The Russian Narodniki went 'back to the people' to learn from them and to teach them; and so have Turkish intellectuals in our own century. Undeniably, many intellectuals have felt sincere compassion for the sufferings of the peasants and sincere respect for the folk arts. But it is unlikely that the attitude of an intellectual toward the uneducated masses in an industrially backward country (or in any country) is free from ambiguity: he looks up to 'the people' and down on 'the masses.'

However he may feel about the majority of his compatriots, the intellectual must face the practical problems of industrialization and modernization. The intellectual knows that a government which really *represents* the thinking of the uneducated masses will not attack these problems boldly and comprehensively. The peasant may long for riches, but he is not eager to give up his traditional ways. To attain its ends, the intelligentsia must arouse the masses to strenuous effort, or, as Alexander Gerschenkron puts it, give them an emotional 'New Deal.'[19]

The intelligentsia must provide just the right amount of criticism, and just the right amount of comfort necessary to make the masses follow its lead into the 'battle' of industrialization. That is why ideologies of delayed industrialization condemn the peasant for his backwardness, and then praise him for being a *real* representative of the indigenous culture. Such ideologies may stand for class equality and simultaneously exhort the masses to follow orders and to accept unequal rewards, both as individuals and as occupational groups. This does not mean that 'assaulted' intellectuals are necessarily cynical and manipulative; they may be sincerely attached to contradictory premises.

In most cases, when an ideology of delayed industrialization emerges, the traditional rulers (king, sultan, tsar, etc.) have been overthrown, or are on the verge of being overthrown. But when traditional rulers remain in power, as in Japan, they are supported by new social groups and assume new social functions. They must now mobilize the masses to meet the challenge of the modern industrial West. Whether there has been a massive social revolution or a 'circulation of elites,' the cultural revolution is inevitable.

Rupert Emerson has suggested that if reform and revolution in industrially backward countries are led by Westernized intellectuals drawn from various social strata rather than by traditional elites, the prevalent ideology tends to include a stronger egalitarian element. The intelligentsia, having no solid power base of its own, is especially in need of mass support. This is particularly true, he believes, in areas which have been longest under Western domination, such as India, where the traditional native elite lost most of its power and indoctrination in Western political values went deep. But in countries like Japan, where the traditional elite took command of social and economic reform, the prevalent ideology tends to put a premium on hierarchical values: loyalty, obedience, respect.[20] This theory may be useful in explaining differences between developments in India and Japan, but its applicability elsewhere is dubious. It is important here to distinguish between symbolic values, which may be egalitarian, and their accompanying operational values, which may be hierarchical. It is also important to define 'equality': is it legal, economic, spiritual, or does it refer to the possession of a common culture?

The tension between egalitarian and hierarchical values is sometimes resolved theoretically by the doctrine of 'tutelage.' According to this doctrine democracy must be introduced into a country in two stages. In the first stage, a single, 'all-people's' party of the most 'enlightened' and 'progressive' elements of the nation takes over the government and acts as a faculty for educating the masses in democratic ways. At some time in the indefinite future the masses will be ready for direct self-government and the 'all-people's' party will 'wither away.' This doctrine, with various modifications, has appeared in Turkey, India, and China; but when the doctrine has been applied, it has led to a variety of unexpected results.

In order to understand an ideology it is important to determine what problems its initiators are trying to solve. In the case of intellectuals in industrially backward countries, the three main problems are: (1) What is to be borrowed from the West? (2) What is to be retained from the nation's past? (3) What characteristics, habits, and products of the masses are to be encouraged? It is remarkable that intellectuals in widely separate parts of the world have reacted similarly to these problems.

['Ideologies of "Delayed Industrialization": Some Tensions and Ambiguities', in J. H. Kautsky (ed.), *Political Change in Underdeveloped Countries* (Wiley: New York, 1962), 254–64.]

CRAWFORD YOUNG

34 The Colonial Construction of African Nations

Overall, th[e] radical reorganization of African political space into various forms of the territorial colonial state had a profound impact upon cultural self-definitions in the societies concerned. Policies pursued in the edification of the colonial state dramatically altered the existing cultural geography, though this was not necessarily their conscious purpose. While the effects were myriad, we will concentrate here upon three dimensions which appear particularly important: the ideology and practice of classification; the impact of the administrative framework; and the unequal provision of opportunities for social promotion.

The state, confronted with a diverse set of colonial subjects, set about the task of classifying them. The fruitful possibilities of sustaining divisions were not absent from the taxonomic calculus, but these were not the only reasons. The science of colonial domination required a process of sorting and labelling; early colonial archives are filled with the results of the laborious inquests into local societies earnestly conducted by the first generation of field administrators. Few of these departed from the cognitive map Southall has urged upon us, in which collective identities are 'interlocking, overlapping, multiple.'[1] Rather the standard presumption was of discrete, bounded groups, whose distribution could be captured on an ethnic map.

Further, colonial state-builders rarely grasped the crucial fact that political and cultural affinities had no necessary overlap. Colson states this point with particular force: 'In fact, political and ethnic boundaries rarely coincided in pre-colonial Africa. Human ambitions were too pressing to allow people to remain static over long periods. States expanded when they were sufficiently powerful to do so. Communities competed with one another to attract settlers and thereby gain supporters.'[2]

In the extreme case, the colonial state veritably breathed life into quite novel categories of identity. This occurred most frequently in areas under British rule; as Apthorpe argues, 'certainly in Anglophone Africa, what happened was the colonial regimes administratively *created* tribes as we think of them today.'[3] The British concept of the colonial state, outside the settler zones, presumed the colonial infrastructure to be an administrative overlayer coordinating a congeries of 'native states.' The habit of classification was strongly influenced by the Indian context, which had persuaded the British of the importance of distinctions of language, religion, and community; a number of the first genera-tion of British pro-consuls in Africa, such as Lugard, had begun their colonial careers in India. The French and Portuguese generally devoted less time and energy to the classificatory exercise because of their more centralized and unitary state ideologies. Belgium fell between the two; while the public doc-trine of the Belgian state was modelled upon the French, the saliency of the Walloon–Flemish cleavage in Belgian national life, and the large impact of nationalist Flemish missionaries in shaping the cultural policy of the state, drew the Belgian colonial state into the exercise of group designation more actively than their French and Portuguese counterparts.

This is not, of course, to suggest that the colonial state, where its attachment to classification was strong, was engaged in a conscious process of fabrication of ethnic groups. Nor, even where the taxonomic demiurge was most promin-ent, did all identities find their origin in this way. But even historically well-established collective representations underwent modification. A glance at the Uganda situation will help elucidate this point.

The British encountered two major kingdoms, with cultural charters that evidently sustained an active sense of social membership. The ethnic cate-gories 'Ganda' and 'Nyoro' have an antiquity that stretches well back into the pre-colonial past. However, the boundaries and meaning attached to each of these collectivities were significantly altered. The Kingdom of Buganda, which chose partnership with the British, had its domain doubled, and came to incorporate a number of groups that, a century ago, were not self-classified as Ganda, and not part of the Kingdom. During the era of British rule, Ganda identity acquired much more extensive ideological elaboration at its core, and successfully assimilated most of its expanded perimeter—save only those areas annexed from the Kingdom of Bunyoro, where the incorporative process was checked by the well-entrenched Nyoro affiliation.

The Bunyoro area also experienced important changes. In this instance, the Kingdom resisted British overrule, partly because of the British alliance with the rival Buganda state. The needs of colonial security were thus best met by minimizing its scale, most notably by encouraging the secession of an insurgent principality of Toro. Though the Toro area had unmistakably formed part of the Nyoro cultural complex in the nineteenth century, politically as well as linguistically, the colonial state classified it as a separate entity. Not only was it created as a separate administrative entity, but also its regional variant of the Bunyoro language was treated as a distinct speech code. By the end of the colonial era, the sense of Toro distinctiveness was well established, even though the historical proximity to Bunyoro was recognized.

The Ankole pattern was a third form of categorization. In this area, there had been a small principality bearing that name, containing two quite distinctive groups, who shared a language but occupied distinctive ecological niches: Hima (cattle-herders) and Iru (cultivators). The colonial state chose to extend the authority of this state over several other principalities, using a common administrative designation (Ankole) and ethnonym (Banyankole) to apply to the whole. While the cultural ideologies which grew around these reclassifications were more fractured than in the Buganda case, the valuable inquest into identity in Ankole by Segall and Doornbos clearly establishes the penetration of the social consciousness by the enlarged 'Ankole' identity.[4]

In other parts of Uganda, ethnonyms were applied to congeries of groupings in which the British recognized close similarities of language, genealogical charters, and sometimes regional rites. Such groups as the Teso, Acholi, Gisu, and Kiga took form in this way. Patterns of language standardization played an important part, as did administrative regroupings. Such authoritative agencies as schools helped transmit these reformulated and extended identities to the young. So also did other social learning experiences, such as enhanced consciousness of other communities, who did appear more different than other members of the 'collective we' which arose out of this state-originated classification.

Rwanda and Burundi are also examples of critical transformations of metaphors of commonality under colonial rule. 'Tutsi' and 'Hutu' were not colonial innovations. However, the Germans and especially the Belgians, in molding these historical states into the indirect rule model, made of these concepts much more systematic and extensive classifications of the subject populace. This stands out with particular clarity in the Rwanda case where, at the onset of colonial rule, only in the central core of the Rwandan kingdom had 'Tutsi' and 'Hutu' acquired comprehensive social meaning as labels associated with dominance and subordination, respectively. In the outer perimeter of this expanding state, where looser tributary relations applied, the evidence of oral tradition shows that 'Tutsihood' and 'Hutuhood' were much more diffuse concepts. The colonial state absorbed the ideology of domination of the central Rwandan state, codified and rationalized it, and extended it throughout the domain. The consequences of this are illustrated in the intriguing difference today between 'Kiga' in southwest Uganda and those now labelled 'Hutu' across the border in Rwanda; a century ago there was no meaningful linguistic, cultural, or identity difference. Drawing of the colonial border left the contemporary Kiga outside the orbit of the colonial indirect rule state of Rwanda, and eventually left them with a different sense of ethnic community.

Identity building according to the prescription of the colonial state does not necessarily work. The failure of the French effort in interwar Morocco to propagate a Berber collective identity is a useful example. Certain French colonial circles were persuaded to foster Berberhood, on the grounds that the various (and quite numerous) groups that spoke related non-Arabic languages might eventually be willing candidates for absorption of French culture if, as a first step, their linkages with Arab and Islamic institutions were severed. The high water mark of the 'Berber policy' was the 1930 Berber *dahir* (edict), which an unwilling Sultan was compelled to promulgate, removing Berber populations from the jurisdiction of Islamic law. In reality, the Berber policy served above all to stimulate the growth of Moroccan and Arab-focused nationalism; as Gellner puts it, 'The Berber sees himself as a member of this or that tribe, within an Islamically-conceived and permeated world—and not as a member of a linguistically defined ethnic group, in a world in which Islam is but one thing among others.'[5]

The ethnic classification policy has been most systematically—indeed, ruthlessly—pursued by South Africa, especially since *apartheid* became state ideology in 1948. Here we find the state following curiously contradictory policies. On the one hand, in its social and economic policies, the underlying principle of discrimination is race. The civil society with which the state is identified is limited to whites (including such 'honorary whites' as the Japanese). Anomalous practices were eliminated, whereby limited numbers of Africans and Coloreds had, in Cape and Natal provinces, acquired the membership in civil society symbolized by the franchise under British rule. Although the two major ethnic communities of European extraction, Afrikaners and English, were highly self-conscious and often antagonistic collectivities, state ideology stressed their common share in civil society. With respect to Africans, massive efforts were deployed to valorize African ethnic classifications, where the ethnonyms and especially their territorial referents are generally of relatively recent derivation.

The impact of the Christian missions also deserves mention in considering the impact of classifications. While not directly a part of the state domain, for the early and middle stages of the colonial era the missions were virtual auxiliaries of the state. They had generally viewed the colonial framework as indispensable to guarantee them security and favorable operating conditions; in return, they offered moral fealty and propagated the concept of the 'civilizing mission' of the mission power, from whose citizenry they were predominantly recruited. Except in the Islamic zones, cultural policy was consigned to a large extent by the state to the evangelical agencies. Because cultural policy included such critical spheres as education and language, we may consider the Christian missions as an informal extension of the state domain, exercising delegated sovereignty.

The effective operating and choice-making unit, for the missions, was not the territory, but the congregation: the mission order in the Catholic instance, or, for the Protestants, the mission society related to a particular sect. Within a given colonial territory, on both the Catholic and Protestant sides of the great religious divide, there was a territorial partition by congregation. While subect to some overall state regulation, especially from the 1920s, the mission congregations had a broad autonomy of choice in both their educational philosophies and language strategies, both of which were to have important impact upon the configurations of cultural pluralism subsequently.

In organizing their labors, mission congregations faced immediate decisions on language. Unlike the state administrators, they did not really have the options of working only in the metropolitan language, as the nature of their task compelled much more intimate contact. Missionaries thus set themselves to the task of identifying, classifying, and reducing to writing selected African languages. On the basis of the most slender knowledge, resource-maximizing choices were necessary, to identify a language which ideally could serve throughout the territorial domain of the congregation. The very act of producing grammars and dictionaries, printing manuals and catechismic materials (and, for Protestants, Bibles), and using this new mission-standard form as the base for the embryonic primary schools and evangelical instruction introduced a radically new element into the dynamics of linguistic change in Africa.

By way of illustration of the potential impact of these policies, we may note some intriguing contrasts in linguistic development in Zaire. In terms of the size of the cultural group, and its proximity to the initial poles of European penetration, the cultural observer a century ago might have forecast that Kikongo was destined for linguistic pre-eminence. Yet today it is on the defensive, and probably receding as a major language. Crucial to this outcome was the peculiar way in which the Kongo linguistic zone was partitioned between mission congregations: on the Catholic side, Walloon Scheutists in Mayombe, Redemptorists in the Matadi area, Flemish Jesuits centered in Kisantu, while on the Protestant side Swedes operated north of the river, American Baptists towards the West, and the English Baptist Mission Society in the eastern areas. Each of these mission societies developed its own standard version, based upon local dialectical forms. The resulting institutionalized fragmentation of the language has been a major barrier to its diffusion as a lingua franca. In the case of Lingala, Flemish Scheutists played the predominant role in standardizing the written form; in addition, the key city of Kinshasa lay primarily within the Scheutist domain, and thus its schools generally utilized Lingala, a fact of critical importance in the postwar years when the city population rapidly expanded and school availability increased.

We should also note the critical role of the alien colonial state in generalizing self-conscious racial categories. The sharp distinction was drawn in all colonial legal codes between Europeans, accorded a privileged juridical status akin to that of metropolitan public law, and 'subjects,' or 'natives.' The state generally equipped itself with an arsenal of peremptory legislation giving its agents summary powers to uphold its hegemony. Issues of personal status and local conflicts not affecting the security of the colonial state, or its major activities, could be left to 'customary law,' under colonial supervision. But the state needed the authority to secure a flow of labor, and to punish challenges to its authority. In this respect, Africans were generally conceived of as a single implicitly racial category of subjects. The racial consciousness dimension of African nationalism clearly arises in response to the categorization.

The nature of the administrative subdivisions created by the colonial state likewise was to have a major impact upon ethnic identifications. This occurred both in terms of the territorial jurisdictions defined for 'native administration,' and for the regional entities which constituted the operating levels of exercise of colonial hegemony over the African periphery. While, at the margins, these were in a constant process of rectification and adjustment in function of the cultural logic and bureaucratic imperatives of the moment, there was an underlying continuity to many of the units thus established, which served as central reference points in the lives of the subject populace. Especially for the 'indirect rulers,' 'tradition' was invoked as a warrant for the circumscriptions thus created. Historical sanction could certainly be found for many of the choices made, even though a fluid and dynamic process was congealed and frozen by the new and external logic of the colonial state, whose bureaucratic rationality required territorially discrete jurisdictions.

Further, groups began to perceive that their status in the eyes of the alien state depended in part upon approximation of a norm of centralized indigenous authority equated, from an evolutionary perspective, with the stage of political development. Societies equipped with a centralized, hierarchical, bureaucratized political superstructure were, in European eyes, at a higher stage of development than those lacking the grace-giving institution of kingship. The rulers of such entities as Buganda, Barotseland, and the Northern Nigerian emirates were accorded a kind of deference and esteem by the British which was denied to lesser African authorities, as were the Kings of Rwanda and Burundi by the Belgians. In British Nigeria, this status hierarchy was given formal administrative recognition by officially ranking chiefs as first, second, or third class. Deference to a ruler was seen as radiating beyond the royal enclosure to the entire group thus recognized. Thus, movements arose in the days before independence to wrench higher esteem from the status-regulating colonial state by demanding creation of a paramount ruler where none had existed historically (Chagga, Tiv, Idoma, among others), or claiming a higher classification for an existing chief. This kind of movement reached its most extreme point in Uganda in the 1950s, in the chorus of demands for creation of 'constitutional heads' (monarchs) for the kingless districts. These claims were a means for achieving status parity with Buganda, whose ruler was chauffeured in a Rolls-Royce a millimeter longer than that of the British Governor.

The colonial state also had a pervasive impact on patterns of subsequent cultural identity and conflict through the unequal development of its territorial space. The role of differential access to modernization is well known, and does not require lengthy exposition. The locus of major urban centers, the routes chosen for major axes of communication—road and rail—the siting of major centers of cash employment, the distribution of post-primary educational facilities, the production zones for the export crops encouraged or imposed by the colonial administration: all these factors facilitated the ascension into higher social roles of relatively large numbers of some ethnic communities, while marginalizing others.

['Ethnicity and the Colonial and Post-Colonial State in Africa', in Paul Brass (ed.)
Ethnic Groups and the State (Croom Helm: London, 1985), 73–81.]

BENYAMIN NEUBERGER

35 State and Nation in African Thought

Most writers and experts on nationalism accept the notion that state and nation are in some way linked and that the definition of the one impinges on the definition of the other. As there are many theories on the character of the state and of the nation, there are also widely different theories as to the nature of the link between state and nation. While one scholar may argue that the 'state need not be a nation. A nation must be a state,'[1] another sociologist of nationhood may arrive at an opposite conclusion and interpret the current trend in the world as moving toward a situation where 'each state is also a nation' and not toward the vision of 'each nation is also a state,' which was the goal of liberal and humanitarian nationalism in the nineteenth century.[2] Yet a different view is represented by Elie Kedourie, who supports a non-etatist concept of nationhood and a nonnational concept of the state. According to Kedourie, states need not become nations, and many of the most stable states and empires of the past have never been nations.[3] Kedourie's doctrine of separation of state and nation is rejected by Rupert Emerson on empirical rather than normative grounds. Emerson does not accept the possibility of separating state and nation in our age, because nations either establish states, take over states, or grow with states.[4] Emerson's position is shared by C. J. Friedrich, who concedes that 'nationalities have been the destroyers of states as often as they have been associated with the construction of states.' State destruction is inextricably linked with state building, for any state destruction also means some new state building. Friedrich's conclusion is unmistakenly clear: 'Both nation and state are incomplete when they are not linked.'⁵ To us, Emerson's and Friedrich's analysis seems closer to reality. Now that humanity has eaten the fruit of nationalism, Kedourie's separation of state from nation seems impossible to defend. Nations demand the existence of states as living nation-states, aspired to nation-states, or remembered nation-states. And every modern state needs the legitimacy of nationalism, a nationalism based on an existing nation or on the aspiration to build a nation. In the past century we have witnessed the etatization of nationalism and the nationalization of state patriotism.

For Africa's leaders the connection between state and nation, or in the particular African context, between state and projected nation, is a self-evident truism. Thus for Sékou Touré, 'L'Etat, il est l'ensemble des structures organiques de la Nation',⁶ while for Léopold Senghor, 'The state is the expression of the nation, it is primarily a means to achieve the nation.' Senghor also warns that 'political history teaches us that the lack of state organization is a weakness that brings on the fatal disintegration of the nation.'⁷ Most African leaders agree with this thesis. Those African leaders who believe in the existence of separate nations which will not be able to integrate into the projected nation within the colonial boundaries will usually become supporters and leaders of secessionism. Thus they affirm and confirm that they too see in the coincidence of state and nation in a nation-state the normative standard to which the African state system should and will adjust. The African view on the nature of the relation between state and nation is thus in accord with classical nationalist thought in nineteenth-century Europe. Both in European and African nationalism, the nation-state that combines one state with one nation is regarded as optimal and ideal. The European and African varieties of nationalism differ only in how one is to achieve the common ideal of the nation-state. While in nineteenth-century Europe the personalities and identities of the nations were crystallized, this is not the case in present-day Africa. In Europe, nationalists called upon the state system to change and adapt in order to achieve the final coincidence of states and nations. In Africa almost all leaders—with the exception of the secessionists—aim to achieve the same overlapping of states and nations by the building of nations within existing states.

A notable exception are the Nigerian leaders who have the vision of a multinational state somewhat resembling the Soviet Union. As with the Soviet Union, the size of the country, the complexity of the ethnic map, and the existence of large ethnic-cultural clusters that are hardly assimilable may have played a central role in Nigerian political thought. But even the proponents of a multinational Nigeria must have sensed that in the long run one state will not preserve many nations. Thus, although Azikiwe, Awolowo, and Gowon talk about the Igbo, Yoruba, Kanuri, Hausa, and other groups as existing 'nations,' they sometimes cannot avoid envisaging a projected Nigerian nation. Obafemi Awolowo,[8] the most consistent advocate of multinational federalism in Nigeria, concedes that the one Nigerian state is bound by its very existence to create emotional loyalty and attachment. If that is so, what Awolowo is really saying is that the multinational state will in due time transform itself into a uninational state, a nation-state. The same ambiguity and ambivalence is also discernible in Soviet political thought on the issue of multinationality within one state. Simultaneously with the organization of the Soviet Union as a multinational state according to the Leninist principle of nationalities, there was proclaimed the goal of superseding multinationality by the spread of one language and one proletarian culture, which would be national only 'in form' and by the creation of a 'new Soviet man.' The analogy for the projected Nigerian nation is in this case a projected Soviet nation, while the Igbo, Hausa, Yoruba, or Kanuri are the equivalents of the Russians, Ukrainians, Armenians, or Letts. Both the Soviet and Nigerian leaders know, either consciously or unconsciously, that the inseparable linkage between state and nation since the French revolution can only mean that multinational states will either proceed toward the evolution of one nation in a nation-state or that the breakup of the multinational state will become inevitable. The evolution of a national identity and loyalty in Switzerland and even in Belgium and Canada and, at the same time, the breakup of the Ottoman and Habsburg Empires that failed to implant a sense of Ottoman or Habsburg nationhood, demonstrate this point all too well.

In Europe, states established nations and nations established states. Meinecke's *Kulturnation* of Central and Eastern Europe, where nations established states, and the *Staatsnation* of Western Europe, where states developed nations, are models of different paths to modern nation-states. In France and Britain, the state created the nation by separation from other states, by communication and economic integration, by administrative penetration and educational-cultural homogenization, and by linguistic assimilation and the enforcement of one law and thus transformed the multi-ethnic and nonnational kingdoms into nation-states. The African situation of states without nations has its parallels and analogies in European history. The nation-building process initiated by the state, within the state, and for the state was described by David Hume many years before the colonization and decolonization of Africa. To him, 'Where a very extensive government has been established for many centuries it spreads a national character over the whole empire and communicates to every part a similitude of manners.'[9] René Johannet emphasized in the particular case of France and Britain the role of the dynasty, for 'the cause of the statue is not the marble but the artist'. In France and Britain monarchs who were not nationalists had built nations. The nation-state was the result of their policies without this ever having been their objective.

Linguistic homogenization was promoted for reasons of administrative efficiency; it had no roots in nationalist motivation and ideology.

African statesmen and nation builders are in a very different situation, for they operate in an age in which nationalism has become a major ideology. Africa's leaders consciously aim to build nations on the foundation of the existing states. While for the absolute monarchs of Europe, the nation-state was a product or by-product of policy, for African leaders it is a target of policy. Thus the African leaders' objective is a *Staatsnation*, but their outlook is more comparable to the founders of the European *Kulturnation*. Even in Europe we have similar cases which do not fit Meinecke's *Staatsnation-Kulturnation* dichotomy. Massimo d'Azeglio's words, 'We have made Italy, now we have to make Italians' are words of a nationalist without a nation, a nationalist ruling a state-nation rather than a nation-state. Thus even in his respect the African situation is far from being unique and without analogies in the history of European nationalism.

My analysis shows that there are three and not two differing paths on the way to the modern nation-state. One way to create the nation-state is for a nation led by nationalist leaders to break away from states that are larger than the envisaged nation-state. A second possibility for the growth of a nation-state is to have states led by nonnationalist leaders who almost accidentally build nations without aiming to directly. The third way to achieve the nation-state is to have states led by nationalist leaders whose objective it is to give the external shell of the state an internal national content. The second path to the nation-state was open in the prenationalist age; it is now closed and thus only the first and third possibilities remain open for African leaders who operate in an age which has witnessed the universal spread of nationalism.

African secessionist leaders follow the East European pattern of attempting to build states out of nations. Nevertheless, there are differences between Polish, Czech, Croatian, and Romanian nationalism in the pre-independence period and Biafran, Eritrean, or Southern Sudanese nationalism in the Africa of the 1960s. The first difference is that the stateless European nations almost without exception based the legitimacy of their nationalism, their solidarity, and their demands on the assertion that a nation-state of theirs had existed in the remote past. Thus the old Bohemian Kingdom was portrayed as a state of the Czech people, the Kingdom of Poland was regarded as a Polish nation-state, and ancient Greece was shown to be a precursor of the Greek nation-state to be reborn. Biafrans and Southern Sudanese cannot and do not claim that an Igbo or Southern Sudanese nation-state has existed in the past. Although most African secessionist movements are not based on memories of historic states, and European separatism definitely is, the exceptions to this rule detract somewhat from its significance. Thus Romanians fought for a state that never existed in the past, while Katangese, Baganda, and Eritrean separatists attempted to legitimize secessionism by referring to historic states. Another difference between Poles and Biafrans, Croats, and Southern Sudanese is the degree of the 'nationness', in the amount of ethnic solidarity, cultural homogeneity, and the dominance of national as opposed to parochial loyalty and feeling. While the Biafrans and Southern Sudanese were 'nations' to a greater degree—at least during their intense struggle for independence—than Nigerians and Sudanese, they were at the same time more 'projected nations' than existing nations, in comparison to the Poles and Croats before World War I. Ethnic loyalty and solidarity with fellow Dinka, Shilluk, Igbo, Efik, Baluba, and Moslem Eritreans was much stronger than Polish, Czech, or Greek subnationalist regionalism or parochialism, and the opposite is true for nationalism. A special case are the Somali, who rule a quasi-'European' nation-state and follow a policy of tenacious irredentism. I. M. Lewis very well defined their nation-state building process as being 'from nation to state,'[10] and thus they too follow the *Kulturnation* model of Eastern Europe.

All other major African leaders are, like Massimo d'Azeglio, already part and parcel of the nationalist era. They desire to accelerate a process which lasted for hundreds of years in Britain and France because it was not propelled but merely evolved. They clearly and consciously follow the Western European way and aim to achieve a nation-state 'from state to nation.' Zambia's President Kaunda said that 'our aim has been to create genuine nations from the sprawling artifacts the colonialists carved out.'[11] Cameroun's President Ahidjo sees the institutions of the state as a means to achieve nationhood. For him, 'L'intégration nationale c'est l'adaptation des citoyens aux différentes structures d'Etat.'[12] The same is true for Senghor, who writes, 'The state is . . . primarily a means to achieve the nation.'[13] A similar view is expressed by Touré, who indirectly compares Africa with the European nation-building process by stressing that 'en Afrique c'est l'Etat qui construit la nation',[14] because 'the state exists before the nation is shaped.'[15] Yakubo Gowon also compares African and European nation building. He sees the process but not the pace as essentially the same in Africa and Western Europe: 'A newly independent African state struggles against great odds of history, geography, ethnography and evil effects of imperialism to build a nation in less than a fiftieth of the time it took European states to build theirs.[16]

The analysis of the interrelationship of state and nation in African political thought and practice reveals that essentially we are witnessing similar historical processes and philosophical attitudes which characterized modern European history. This refutes the case for European and African uniqueness and evidences the existence of universal rules and trends that lead to the building of states, nations, and nation-states.

['State and Nation in African Thought', *Journal of African Studies*, 4/2 (1977), 199–205.]

As an ideology or state of political feeling, nationalism can be conceived of [. . .] as attaching utility or value to having certain jobs held or certain property owned by members of the national group rather than by non-members of the national group. (The difference between the two concepts, though this is a difference largely of degree rather than of kind, is that the utility accrues to members of the national group whether or not they themselves hold the jobs or the property in question; the consequences of this difference are elaborated subsequently.) In this context, it is most useful to employ a broad definition of property ownership, one including in property not merely the ownership of physical or financial assets but also rights to certain kinds of jobs, since job opportunities are property in the sense of yielding a stream of income to the holder. Nationalism can accordingly be conceived of as a state of social psychology or political sentiment that attaches value to having property in this broad sense owned by members of the national group.

The question that immediately arises is, To what kinds of property does this utility of nationality become attached? Clearly, in some sense it is the 'important' or prestigious or socially relevant kinds of property that acquire this added value. One such, obviously, is the result of cultural and artistic activities—the national literature, music, and drama. Another is positions of authority in the governmental apparatus and in the social structure. Still another comprises particular types of economic activity and economic roles that carry superior status (and usually superior income also).

A related question is, What determines which specific items of property acquire added value from nationalism? There seem to be two major ways in which nationalistic utility can be acquired. One is internal, through observation within the country of foreign operations there; the property yielding income and status to the foreigner becomes the property valued by the nationalists. This mechanism of generating nationalistic utility is particularly important in ex-colonial countries or countries where foreign investment and alleged 'economic imperialism' have been significant, where nationalism seeks particularly to replace the officialdom of the colonial power and the executives and shareholders of the foreign enterprises with nationals. The other mechanism is external, through contact with and observation of other nations, which provides knowledge of what forms of property are highly regarded in such societies.

Both of these mechanisms involve the determination of the nationalistic values of specific forms of property by imitation or emulation of other countries, either of their actual practices or of the 'image' of themselves they project abroad. The importance of international emulation in determining nationalistic objectives is evident in a variety of areas. Examples in [various] fields readily spring to mind, such as the importance frequently attached to the winning of Olympic medals by a country's athletes, or the tendency of the allocation of resources for scientific research in the more advanced countries to be dominated by the spectacular accomplishments of other countries.

The next step in the analysis is to recognize that the benefits from the gratification of nationalist sentiment are of two sorts, particular and general, or tangible and intangible. The particular benefits are the incomes and prestige that accrue to those nationals who acquire the property rights or the offices and employment opportunities in which nationalism invests. The general benefits consist of the psychic satisfaction derived by the community at large from gratification of the taste for nationalism. It is important to notice here the concentration of the tangible benefits on the subgroup of nationals that is eligible to hold the property or to fill the positions, as distinguished from the dispersion of the intangible benefits, which presumably accrue to the whole national society in so far as its members share the taste for nationalism. It is the intangible benefits that give national ownership of property the character of a collective consumption good—one for which consumption by one individual does not preclude consumption by another—and for the economist raises the difficult problem of how to determine the optimal quantity to supply.

The tangible benefits are directly or indirectly economic, and are of considerable value to the individuals who may receive them; thus the bias of the democratic process toward producer interests becomes relevant. These individuals have an economic incentive to pursue these prospective benefits through the cultivation of nationalism. Further, given the mechanisms by which nationalistic utility become attached to specific items of property, these items will tend to be such as to yield tangible benefits primarily to the educated, the entrepreneurially qualified classes, some at least of the wealthy, and other elite groups, so that there is an inherent class slant to the economic interest in pursuing nationalism.

There is, moreover, a natural consilience of the strictly economic interests in nationalism and the cultural interests in nationalism. Both the intellectuals engaged in cultural activities and the owners and managers of communications media have an interest in nationalism, particularly when it can be combined with a linguistic difference, but even when it cannot, because nationalism creates a monopolistic barrier to competition from other countries' purveyors of the same sorts of cultural products. Thus cultural nationalism complements economic nationalism, both involving tangible benefits in the form of protection of the market for the services of individuals. This consideration suggests also that the strength of economic and cultural interests in nationalism will vary with the threat of competition and the need for protection of the market. One would expect to find nationalist sentiment strongest where the individuals concerned are most vulnerable to competition from foreign culture or from foreign economic activities; conversely, one would expect to find that the nations that are leading culturally and economically will tend to be internationalist and cosmopolitan in outlook, because this would tend to extend the market area for their cultural and economic products. These expectations accord broadly with experience.

We now turn from nationalism as a political ideology to nationalism as an economic program. As such, nationalism seeks to extend the property owned by nationals so as to gratify the taste for nationalism. There are a variety of methods available for accomplishing this objective.

One obvious method is confiscation, that is, the forced transfer of property from foreign owners to nationals. Here it is important to notice a certain ambiguity in the concept of confiscation, extremely useful to nationalists, which arises because what appears to be confiscation may not really be confiscation in the fundamental economic sense of the term. For example, nationalizing the civil service, or nationalizing the administrative and executive jobs in a particular enterprise, may appear to transfer property of value from the foreigners to the nationals. But in so far as the foreigners were receiving a fair price for their skilled qualifications, and nationalization involves replacing them with nationals of inferior skills at the same salaries, the effect is primarily to transfer income within the national group, toward the individuals favored with promotion at the expense of the general community which must bear the costs of poorer administration, inferior economic efficiency, or deterioration of the quality of the service that results.

The result of nationalizing jobs is not, of course, necessarily merely a transfer of income among nationals. If previously there has been genuine discrimination against nationals, for example, where the civil servants have been of a foreign nationality even though their jobs could be performed as efficiently or more efficiently by nationals available at lower salaries, there will be a genuine transfer of income from foreigners to nationals, since discrimination against nationals in employment gives foreigners a source of monopoly gain at the expense of nationals. It is always difficult to determine, however, whether the employment of non-nationals represents discrimination against nationals or reflects their inferior quality; under competitive conditions there is a presumption in favor of the latter assumption. The possibility of discrimination apart, nationalizing jobs is a matter of transferring income among members of the national group, with side-effects in reducing aggregate real income by reducing the efficiency of performance. Genuine confiscation, which transfers valuable property from foreigners to nationals, is therefore largely confined to property in the narrow sense, that is, to the tangible wealth—cash, securities, real property, and enterprises—owned in the country by foreigners.

The alternative to confiscation is investment of resources or purchase, that is, the use of wealth or savings that otherwise would be available for other purposes to purchase material property or job opportunities for nationals. This may be effected directly through public investment, or indirectly through various policies influencing private investment. The public investment method includes both the nationalization of existing foreign enterprises with fair compensation and the use of development funds or public revenue to create new enterprises. The method of influencing private investment involves using tariffs and related policies to stimulate industries of the kind desired; these policies also entail public investment, in the sense that the use of the tariff, for example, involves imposing a tax on the consumer in the form of higher prices, the revenue from which goes to subsidize the creation of the protected enterprises by the private entrepreneurs who then receive the higher prices. [. . .]

The major implications of the theory of nationalist economic policy presented in this article may now be briefly summarized.

One implication is that nationalism will tend to direct economic development policy along certain specific lines; these lines might represent economic optimality, and would do so if the conditions posited by some familiar economic arguments were present. Failing empirical validation of those arguments, however, the consequence will be a reduction of material production below the economy's potential.

In the first place, nationalist economic policy will tend to foster activities selected for their symbolic value in terms of concepts of 'national identity' and the economic content of nationhood; in particular, emphasis will be placed on manufacturing, and, within manufacturing, on certain industries possessing special value symbolic of industrial competence (such as the steel and automotive industries). Secondly, nationalist economic policy will foster activities offering prestigious jobs for the middle class and/or the educated class; the nature of such activities varies with the stage of development, very underdeveloped countries favoring bureaucratic jobs offering steady incomes for routine work, more advanced countries favoring managerial and professional jobs suitable for the products of the educational system, fairly mature countries favoring jobs in higher education and research. Thirdly, nationalism will tend to favor both extensive state control over and extensive public ownership of economic enterprises: state control provides employment for the educated directly, in the central control system, while both the control system and public ownership give the government social control over the allocation of jobs to nationals.

A second implication is that nationalism will tend to direct economic policy toward the production of psychic income in the form of nationalistic satisfaction, at the expense of material income. If attention is confined to material income alone, a third implication is that nationalism will tend to redistribute material income from the lower class toward the middle class, and particularly toward the educated middle class; in this respect, nationalism reinforces the trend of modern society toward the establishment of a class structure based on educational attainment.

This last implication relates to material income only, and does not necessarily imply that the lower classes are worse off because of nationalism when both real and psychic income are reckoned into the account. It is quite possible that the psychic enjoyment that the mass of the population derives from the collective consumption aspects of nationalism suffices to compensate them for the loss of material income imposed on them by nationalistic economic policies, so that nationalistic policies arrive at a quite acceptable result from the standpoint of maximizing satisfaction. It may even be that nationalistic policies are the cheapest and most effective way to raise real income in less developed countries; in some cases, one suspects, the prospects for genuine economic growth are so bleak that nationalism is the only possible means available for raising real income.

It would seem, however, that the lower classes are unlikely to be net gainers from economic nationalism, due to the effects of ignorance and the costs of acquiring information in concentrating political power in the hands of pressure groups, and the general tendency for producer interests to dominate over consumer interests that results from the natural response of voters to the high cost and negligible value of acquiring political information. The tendency for the mass of the population to suffer losses from economic nationalism is probably reinforced in the new nations by the prevalence of systems of one-party government, in which the party is based largely on urban support and frequently exercises a virtual monopoly over the country's communications system.

Even though nationalism may involve a substantial redistribution of real income toward the middle class at the expense of the mass of the population, this redistribution may perform a necessary function in the early stages of forming a nation, in the sense that the existence of a substantial middle class may be a prerequisite of a stable society and democratic government. In other words, an investment in the creation of a middle class, financed by resources extracted from the mass of the population by nationalistic policies, may be the essential preliminary to the construction of a viable national state. This problem, however, belongs in the spheres of history, sociology, and political science rather than economics.

['A Theoretical Model of Economic Nationalism in New and Developing States', *Political Science Quarterly*, 80 (1965), 176–80, 182–5.]

Section VI

Nationalism and the International System

INTRODUCTION

Nationalism has had, and continues to have, an enormous impact on the state system and global security. That impact is traced in the classic statements of Edward Carr and Alfred Cobban. Carr distinguishes three phases of nationalism—dynastic, mass-democratic, and socialized nationalism—from the early modern era to the mid-twentieth century; his sceptical realism in the immediate aftermath of the Second World War's drastic simplification of the ethno-political map is rooted in his concern with the conditions of a stable global order in an epoch of great economic development. The transformations wrought by the French Revolution in the international order are well brought out by Cobban; these were not only economic and political, but involved fundamental conceptual changes, by which sovereignty was transferred to culturally defined units of population, and became an expression of the 'will of the people'.

Why these changes became apparent first in Europe is explored by Charles Tilly. He lists a number of preconditions for the transition from a universal Christendom to a system of national states, including Europe's protected geopolitical position, the relationship between lords and serfs, the wealth of its urban centres, its cultural unity, and the links between warfare and the state, a theme explored further in the extract from Michael Howard's book. Tilly suggests, too, a useful distinction between the long-drawn-out formation of national states, mainly in the West, and the more deliberate engineering of national states as a result of wars and treaties. Such processes, however, were always incomplete, and recently even the West has been troubled by the demands of unsatisfied 'peripheral' and minority ethnies, as we are reminded by Arendt Lijphart's penetrating critique of modernization and other theories.

Ethnic nationalism has been an even more powerful force in Africa and Asia, and has threatened the viability of many of the new states. The reasons for this are explored by Donald Horowitz as part of his wide-ranging analysis of ethnic conflict in Africa and Asia. Through a typology of secessionism based on the levels of economic and educational progress and backwardness in groups and regions, he demonstrates that backward groups in poor regions are much more likely to try to break away from existing states than more advanced groups in regions with more resources. We must, of course, distinguish between the conditions of bids for ethnic secession and the factors which ensure their success. The international community, as Mayall argues, has generally been hostile to any redrawing of the map which is not part of the decolonization process, especially where ethnic bids have no regional patronage; with the exceptions of Singapore and Bangladesh, there were no successful secessionist movements between 1944 (Iceland) and 1991. Since 1991 at least eighteen new states have come into existence, fourteen of them out of the former Soviet Union; some of the reasons for this are analysed in the informative survey by John Armstrong of the course and prospects of each of the ex-Soviet republics.

37 Three Phases of Nationalism

The first period begins with the gradual dissolution of the mediaeval unity of empire and church and the establishment of the national state and the national church. In the new national unit it was normally the secular arm which, relying on the principle *cuius regio, eius religio*, emerged predominant; but there was nothing anomalous in a bishop or prince of the church exercising territorial sovereignty. The essential characteristic of the period was the identification of the nation with the person of the sovereign. [. . .]

The second period, which issued from the turmoil of the Napoleonic Wars and ended in 1914, is generally accounted the most orderly and enviable of modern international relations. Its success depended on a remarkable series of compromises which made it in some respects the natural heir, in others the antithesis, of the earlier period. Looked at in one way, it succeeded in delicately balancing the forces of 'nationalism' and 'internationalism'; for it established an international order or framework strong enough to permit of a striking extension and intensification of national feeling without disruption on any wide scale of regular and peaceful international relations. Put in another way, it might be said that, while in the previous period political and economic power had marched hand in hand to build up the national political unit and to substitute a single national economy for a conglomeration of local economies, in the 19th century a compromise was struck between political and economic power so that each could develop on its own lines. Politically, therefore, national forces were more and more successful throughout the 19th century in asserting the claim of the nation to statehood, whether through a coalescence or through a break-up of existing units. Economically, on the other hand, international forces carried a stage further the process inaugurated in the previous period by transforming a multiplicity of national economies into a single world economy. From yet a third angle the system might be seen as a compromise between the popular and democratic appeal of political nationalism and the esoteric and autocratic management of the international economic mechanism. The collapse of these compromises, and the revelation of the weaknesses and unrealities that lay behind them, marked the concluding stages of the second period. The failure since 1914 to establish any new compromise capable of reconciling the forces of nationalism and internationalism is the essence of the contemporary crisis.

The founder of modern nationalism as it began to take shape in the 19th century was Rousseau, who, rejecting the embodiment of the nation in the personal sovereign or the ruling class, boldly identified 'nation' and 'people'; and this identification became a fundamental principle both of the French and of the American revolutions. It is true that the 'people' in this terminology did not mean those who came to be known to a later epoch as the 'workers' or the 'common people'. [. . .] Nevertheless this middle-class nationalism had in it from the first a democratic and potentially popular flavour which was wholly foreign to the 18th century. [. . .] The nation in its new and popular connotation had come to stay. International relations were henceforth to be governed not by the personal interests, ambitions and emotions of the monarch, but by the collective interests, ambitions and emotions of the nation.

The 'democratization' of nationalism imparted to it a new and disturbing emotional fervour. With the disappearance of the absolute monarch the personification of the nation became a necessary convenience in international relations and international law. But it was far more than a convenient abstraction. The idea of the personality and character of the nation acquired a profound psychological significance. Writers like Mazzini thought and argued about nations exactly as if they were sublimated individuals. Even to-day people are still capable, especially in English-speaking countries, of feeling a keen emotional excitement over the rights or wrongs of 'Patagonia' or 'Ruritania' without the slightest knowledge or understanding of the highly complex entities behind these abstractions. [. . .]

The third period brings yet another change in the character of the nation. The catastrophic growth of nationalism and bankruptcy of internationalism which were the symptoms of the period can be traced back to their origins in the years after 1870 but reach their full overt development only after 1914. This does not mean that individuals became in this period more outrageously nationalist in sentiment or more unwilling to cooperate with their fellow-men of other nations. It means that nationalism began to operate in a new political and economic environment. The phenomenon cannot be understood without examination of the three main underlying causes which provoked it: the bringing of new social strata within the effective membership of the nation, the visible reunion of economic with political power, and the increase in the number of nations.

The rise of new social strata to full membership of the nation marked the last three decades of the 19th century throughout western and central Europe. Its landmarks were the development of industry and industrial skills; the rapid expansion in numbers and importance of urban populations; the growth of workers' organizations and of the political consciousness of the workers; the introduction of universal compulsory education; and the extension of the franchise. These changes, while they seemed logical steps in a process inaugurated long before, quickly began to affect the content of national policy in a revolutionary way. The 'democratization' of the nation in the earlier part of the century had resulted in the establishment of popular control over the functions of maintaining law and order, guaranteeing the rights of property and, in general, 'holding the ring' for the operations of an economic society managed and directed from another centre under rules of its own. The 'socialization' of the nation which set in towards the end of the century brought about a far more radical change. Hitherto, as Peterloo and the fate of the Chartists had shown, the masses had had little power to protect themselves against the immense hardships and sufferings which *laissez-faire* industrialism imposed on them. Henceforth the political power of the masses was directed to improving their own social and economic lot. The primary aim of national policy was no longer merely to maintain order and conduct what was narrowly defined as public business, but to minister to the welfare of members of the nation and to enable them to earn their living. The democratization of the nation in the second period had meant the assertion of the political claims of the dominant middle class. The socialization of the nation for the first time brings the economic claims of the masses into the forefront of the picture. The defence of wages and employment becomes a concern of national policy and must be asserted, if necessary, against the national policies of other countries; and this in turn gives the worker an intimate practical interest in the policy and power of his nation. The socialization of the nation has as its natural corollary the nationalization of socialism.

[*Nationalism and After* (Macmillan: London, 1945), 2, 6–7, 8–9, 17–19.]

ALFRED COBBAN
....

38 **The Rise of the Nation-State System**

The rise of the idea of sovereignty was not altogether favourable to the continued growth of nation states [. . .]. It emphasised the rights of government, and so intensified the process of unification in nation states which were already set in that path; but it also militated against the development of the process where different political entities prevailed, as in the petty states of Germany and Italy, or the great dynastic empire of the Habsburgs. The process of formation of nation states therefore experienced a setback at the end of the Middle Ages, from which it did not recover until the nineteenth century. During the early modern period also the word nation changed its significance: it lost its linguistic and acquired an almost exclusively political meaning. The possession of a separate government came to be the criterion of nationhood, though the smaller independent states were not commonly termed nations. Vattel, in the very first sentence of his treatise on international law, assumes that state and nation are synonymous. By the eighteenth century, in fact, most of the cultural and linguistic significance had been emptied out of the word nation. It merely meant the state considered from the point of view of the ruled rather than the ruler. The Dictionary of the *Academie Française* as late as

1878 was still giving as its primary definition of the nation, 'the totality of persons born or naturalised in a country and living under a single government.'

Already, however, by the end of the Middle Ages, a number of nation states existed, in which political unity was combined with a greater or less degree of cultural unity. The history of Europe is unique in that nowhere else, and at no other time, has such a considerable group of nation states survived in geographical contiguity and close association with one another over a period of many centuries. Nowhere else, moreover, until we come to the contemporary extra-European development of nationalism under Western inspiration, do we find a civilisation passing out of medieval conditions and yet continuing to be organised largely on a national basis. It is therefore justifiable to regard the development of a widespread civilisation, in which nation states have not passed away before the attack of the imperial principle, as a peculiar characteristic of the Western world. During the modern period in Europe, it is true, there has been a tendency towards the amalgamation of the medieval nations into larger political units. The persistence, despite this tendency, of the political divisions of Europe is to be explained in the first place by the absence of any power capable of uniting the whole Continent under its military dominion. Lacking such a unifying force, the peoples of Europe, instead of being assimilated to one another, grew more distinct. The unifying forces of Latin Christendom became weaker after the Reformation and the shifting of the focus of European society from the Mediterranean to the Atlantic coastline; while a further source of political cleavage was to be found in the division into Latin, German and Slav, three large groups none of which was strong enough to conquer or absorb the others.

The consequence was that European politics were kept in a perpetually unstable equilibrium on the system of balance of power. Such a result is inevitable wherever a number of independent states, none of them strong enough to establish a permanent dominion over the rest, are in continuous contact with one another. The relations of the city-states of ancient Greece presented a similar situation and a similar consequence. If any state grew powerful enough to threaten the balance, sooner or later it drew on itself the enmity of a more powerful coalition. The island state of Great Britain played an essential part in the maintenance of this balance. Too small and too separate to aim at continental empire, it was at the same time protected from conquest by its naval power. In every century since the decline of the Middle Ages British power has intervened to prevent the establishment or consolidation of a European hegemony by a dominant military power. The advantages and disadvantages of this system of balance, and of the survival in Europe of so many independent states, are both obviously great, but it is not for us to discuss them here.

Out of this division of Europe into a large number of independent states there gradually evolved the idea of a right of independence on the part of these states. Grotius and his successors in the development of international law upheld this principle, which found its most striking expression, towards the end of the eighteenth century, in the reaction against the partitions of Poland. A new factor appeared in the protests against the extinction of the Polish state, as it had in those provoked, a little earlier, by the sale of Corsica by the Genoese to the French. 'Thus,' said Burke of the latter, 'was a nation disposed of without its consent, like the trees on an estate.'[1] 'It is making fools of people,' wrote Rousseau, 'to tell them seriously that one can at one's pleasure transfer peoples from master to master, like herds of cattle, without consulting their interests or their wishes.'[2] We can see in such quotations the beginning of a new association between the ideas of the political state and the national community, in consequence of which the idea of the nation state at last appears in its modern form. But to understand its new significance we must turn to what was a necessary preliminary to the new stage in its history, the assertion of the right of democratic self-government.

The long history of representative institutions, which, like the nations themselves, are a product of the Middle Ages, may seem to contradict the attribution of a recent origin to democracy. But medieval representative institutions were extinguished in many countries, and declined in importance in practically all, when the New Monarchy of the sixteenth century appeared, and with it the later medieval or renaissance conception of sovereignty. Although in one or two states, such as England, the history of representative institutions forms an unbroken chain from the Middle Ages to the present day, their revival and extension throughout Europe were not a direct consequence of these survivals, but of the attempt at the end of the eighteenth century to create a democratic government of a new type in France. The French Revolution must not be thought of as no more than a struggle to establish in France principles of government that already existed, although perhaps in an imperfect form, in those countries where medieval representative institutions survived. It was a revolution of a far wider compass than this would imply, a revolution not only in the institutions, but in the political ideas of the Western world. By proclaiming the principle of popular sovereignty, the French revolutionaries fundamentally altered the prevailing conception of the state, and opened a fresh chapter in the history of the nation state. It was through the combination of the revolutionary idea of democratic sovereignty with the new importance attached to national differences that the nation state ceased to be a simple historical fact and became the subject of a theory.

The nation states of the Middle Ages, as I have said, had been the creation of the political power of the monarchies, though it was also held that the people were an active participant in the political power of the state. This attitude of mind, which was inherited by the Contractual school of thought, came to be generally accepted in the seventeenth and eighteenth centuries. It was maintained, in the words of Locke, that, 'Wherever any number of men so unite into one society as to quit every one his executive power of the Law of Nature, and to resign it to the public, there and there only is a political or civil society.' The belief that their agreement to establish a common legislature and government was the factor which made a collection of individuals into a state was still the prevailing view on the eve of the French Revolution, when Sieyes defined the nation as 'a body of associates living under one common law and represented by the same legislature.' There was one fundamental change, however. The great achievement of revolutionary political thought, for good or evil, was the conception of government as a manifestation of the democratic will, and the identification of the state as sovereign with the people. This was the meaning of Sieyes when he said that the *tiers état*, the people, was nothing and ought to be everything; and it was what the revolutionaries meant when they declared, 'Sovereignty is one, indivisible, inalienable and imprescriptible: it belongs to the nation.'

During the last century and a half, beginning with the revolt of the American colonies, there has been a renewed wave of nation state making, but in place of a feudal monarchy the unifying power has been the will of the people, or at least of the politically conscious classes, though a part has also been played in this movement by military powers such as Piedmont and Prussia. It is to be noted that both in the medieval and the modern periods of the formation of nation states, the process has been a political one, initial differences of language, race or culture being of comparatively minor account. The Americas provide many modern examples of this fact. Belgium and South Africa belong to the same class of political nations, of which the classic example is Switzerland.

The modern conception of the nation state did not remain purely political, however. A new meaning, as I have said, had been acquired by the nation during the second half of the eighteenth century, a development parallel with, although distinct from, the rise of the democratic idea of the state. It was an important element in the early romantic movement, and is particularly associated with the medieval revival. Among the manifestations of a new attitude towards the nation are: the writing of the first national hymn of Norway and the first history of Norway inspired by the idea of Norwegian independence, both in 1772; the development of national ideas in the Austrian Netherlands and the revival of the term *Belges*; the writing of a Finnish national poem; the demand for Parliamentary independence in Ireland; the appearance of the American nation. Many other examples might be found of the increased significance of the idea of nationality in this period, which was also that in which Herder, the best-known and the most influential of the prophets of the new idea of the nation, was writing. There is no need to summarise here the well-known history of the nationalist movement, though it is to be noted that histories of nationalism which find its origin in the French Revolution and the Napoleonic Wars omit its initial phase. The point to be emphasised is that whereas before the French Revolution there had been no necessary connection between the state as a political unit and the nation as a cultural one, the combination of these two elements in a single conception was the significant fact in the phase that now opened in the history of the nation state.

Although nation states had existed for centuries, before the nineteenth century no specific relationship had been posited between culture or language and the political state. Some states were more or less culturally united, others were composed of culturally disparate elements. The matter was not one that was regarded as of fundamental importance. It did not occur to anyone to criticise the Habsburg Empire on the ground that its peoples spoke different languages, had different cultures, and apart from their allegiance to a common dynasty were even separate political communities. For the *ancien régime* one state was as good as another. In the definition of the state communal ties, and all aspects of social life that were not narrowly and directly governmental, played no part. The state was a juristic and territorial concept. It was the land, and its ruler the lord of the land. The new idea of the nation changed all this. In October, 1789 the *roi de France et de Navarre* became *roi des Français*, and during the next half-century the nation state entered on a new stage in its history. Hitherto it had been a historical fact: now it became a theory. It was embodied in the theory of nationalism, which posited as an ideal the identification of cultural and political communities in a universal system of nation states.

As an agency of destruction the theory of nationalism proved one of the most potent that even modern society has known. Empires or states that were not homogeneous in culture and language were undermined from within, or assaulted from without; nation after nation broke away from its traditional allegiances. But there was less success in the task of rebuilding a stable system of states on the ruins of older political structures.

An admirable example of the consequences of the attempt to fuse together the political and cultural ideas of the nation is provided by Hungary, which was at the end of the nineteenth century the solitary survivor in Central Europe of the medieval nation states of the type of England and France. Her tragedy was that, as a result of Turkish and Habsburg domination, she had never been able to push the process of nation-making to completion throughout her territories, and her unassimilated peoples were consequently caught up in the cultural nationalist movement of the nineteenth century. In place of the slow but successful assimilation that had gone on in previous centuries, a desperate policy of compulsory Magyarisation was now adopted, which only accelerated the onset of disaster. The fatal conflict of two different ideas of the nation comes to the surface in the Hungarian Law of Nationalities of 1868, which declares, 'All citizens of Hungary . . . form a single nation—the indivisible unitary Magyar nation—to which all citizens of the country, irres-pective of nationality, belong.'³ At a time when the other peoples of Central Europe were struggling to convert their cultural nationalities into politically independent states, Hungary was still attempting to force her way in the opposite direction, from political to cultural unity.

During the nineteenth century the belief in the ideal identification of cultu-ral or linguistic nation and political state obtained widespread acceptance, though among the voices raised in protest against the new nationalist gospel were those of Proudhon, Le Play, Bakunin, Lecky and Acton. The conception of the nation state which was embodied in nineteenth-century nationalism attained its highest point in 1919 and the following years, but it was a mistake to suppose that this was the end of its history. Already there was ample justification for asking whether the idea of the nation state that prevailed would be a permanent factor in political ideology. We must at least observe that the assumption of a necessary coincidence between the political and cultural divisions of mankind, far from enshrining the wisdom of the ages, is a modern invention. If it looks back to anything it is to tribal barbarism; but in the Middle Ages, when actually the modern nations were being made, such a faith as nationalism would have been appropriate only to the heretic and the traitor.

At different times different institutions have embodied the political ideals of man. We need not here pass judgement on the historic process which has at one time fixed men's hearts on the city or the nation, at another on a civilisa-tion or an empire. The truth is that while loyalty to the community in which for the time being are enshrined the highest aspirations of social organisation is a perennial quality in human nature, the object of that loyalty has varied widely from age to age. There is little to suggest that the combination of cultural and political unity in the idea of the nation state is the last, or that it is the highest, of those mortal gods to which men have sometimes paid undue adoration. This does not mean that we are free to choose one or another, as the fancy takes us. We are children of our age, and must obey its dictates, but we should be careful not to read the history of five thousand years in terms of the last one hundred and fifty. Nations and states grew up and flourished in the medieval world long before such a faith as nationalism was thought of. The state system of Europe has changed century by century, and there are no signs that its evolution has come to an end. The least we can say in conclusion to this brief outline of its history is that we should be prepared to examine with as open a mind as our day and generation permits the still dominant idea of the culturally and politically united nation state.

[*The Nation State and National Self-Determination*, rev. edn. (Collins: London, 1969), 30–8.]

Suppose [. . .] that the analyses of European experience in this book have gotten European state-making right. (I apologize for any strain to the reader's imagination.) How would the *substance* of what we say affect existing theories of 'political development?' If the world had remained the same kind of place from 1500 to now, some of the inferences would be fairly easy to make. We would return to the general conditions which appear to have favored the survival of particular political units in Europe, and their transformation into national states. To repeat [. . .], they were: (1) the availability of extractible resources; (2) a relatively protected position in time and space; (3) a continuous supply of political entrepreneurs; (4) success in war; (5) homogeneity (initial or created) of the subject population; (6) strong coalitions of the central power with major segments of the landed elite. We would then add some features of the European state-making process [. . .]: (7) the high cost of state-building; (8) the intimate connection between the conduct of war, the building of armies, the extension and regularization of taxes and the growth of the state apparatus; (9) the large role of alternating coalitions between the central power and the major social classes within the subject population in determining the broad forms of government; and (10) the further effect of homogenization—or its absence—on the structure and effectiveness of government.

If these were, indeed, the main generalizations one could make about the formation of national states, they would leave untouched many portions the behaviour analysts of 'political development' have sought to explain; our formulations hardly bear on such questions as how citizens become well-informed, efficacious, concerned, and so on. Nevertheless, they would touch available theories in some vulnerable points. They portray the main processes which bring the national state to a dominant position as coercive and extractive.

Our conclusion in that regard is not the usual observation of hard-nosed government advisers: 'some minimum of order' is necessary so the regime can get on with its work of social transformation. Instead, our study of the European experience suggests that most of the transformations European states accomplished until late in their histories were by-products of the consolidation of central control; that the forms of government themselves resulted largely from the way the coercion and extraction were carried on; that most members of the populations over which the managers of states were trying to extend their control resisted the state-making efforts (often with sword and pitchfork); and that the major forms of political participation which westerners now complacently refer to as 'modern' are for the most part unintended outcomes of the efforts of European state-makers to build their armies, keep taxes coming in, form effective coalitions against their rivals, hold their nominal subordinates and allies in line, and fend off the threat of rebellion on the part of ordinary people.

If, again, we were dealing today with the same kind of world that fostered the formation of national states in Europe, we would have to challenge the conventional portrait of a 'modernizing' elite pitted against 'traditional' authorities and a passive, unmobilized and/or traditional mass. [. . .]

If the European experience were our only guide, we would have to rule the image quite wrong. For the most part, that experience does not show us modernizing elites articulating the demand and needs of the masses, and fighting off traditional holders of power in order to meet those needs and demands. Far from it. We discover a world in which small groups of power-hungry men fought off numerous rivals and great popular resistance in the pursuit of their own ends, and inadvertently promoted the formation of national states and widespread popular involvement in them. [. . .]

There is, however, one feature of the European state-making experience that will help us build a bridge from past to present. That is the existence in Europe itself of two large processes of state formation, and the general shift from one toward the other. The first is the extension of the power and range of a more or less autonomous political unit by conquest, alliance, bargaining, chicanery, argument, and administrative encroachment, until the territory, population, goods, and activities claimed by the particular center extended either to the areas claimed by other strong centers or to a point where the costs of communication and control exceeded the returns from the periphery. Those expansive processes dominated the state-making experience in Brandenburg-Prussia, France, England, Spain, and so on. Yet we cannot ignore a second large process, consisting of the more or less deliberate *creation* of new states by existing states. The carving of Yugoslavia and Czechoslovakia out of the trunk of the Austro-Hungarian Empire is a relatively pure case, Napoleon's formation of the Batavian Republic, the Cisalpine Republic, and other temporary states a more special (but not uncommon) variety of the process, and the final consolidation of Germany and Italy, combinations of the center-to-periphery and external-creation processes. Even in the creation of new states by autonomist rebellions like those of Portugal and The Netherlands in 1640, the acquiescence or collaboration of existing states became increasingly crucial. From 1648 onward, the ends of wars provided the principal occasions on which the creation of new states occurred.

Let me not claim too much. The formation of Zaïre in the 1960s out of what had been for a while the Belgian Congo was not 'just like' the creation of a united Italy in the 1860s out of what had been a string of states dominated by Austria. The most important point of contact between the two processes is their involvement in the general movement toward a worldwide state system. Schematically, it goes like this: (1) the formation of a few early national states amid a great variety of other political structures in Europe; (2) the mapping of most of Europe into distinct national states through wars, alliances, and a great variety of other maneuvers; (3) the extension of political and economic domination from that European base to much of the rest of the world, notably through the creation of client states and colonies; (4) the formation—through rebellion and through international agreement—of formally autonomous states corresponding approximately to the clients and colonies; (5) the extension of this state system to the entire world.

If we still dared call these blocks of events 'phases' after the difficulties that term has already caused, we would have to place Italy in phase 2, Zaïre in phase 4 of the historical movement. Phases 2 and 3 overlapped considerably in time; indeed, if we consider such cases as the geographic expansion of Russia or the dismemberment of the Ottoman Empire, the distinction between the two begins to dissolve. The extension to the entire world is still going on; Antarctica, for example, remains in political limbo. Yet the distinction of that extension from phase 4, the formation of formally autonomous states, is mainly a matter of convenience. The main rhythm, then, has three beats: (1) the formation and consolidation of the first great national states in commercial and military competition with each other, accompanied by their economic penetration of the remainder of Europe and of important parts of the world outside of Europe: roughly 1500 to 1700; (2) the regrouping of the remainder of Europe into a system of states, accompanied by the extension of European political control into most of the non-European world, save those portions already dominated by substantial political organizations (e.g. China and Japan): roughly 1650 to 1850; (3) the extension of the state system to the rest of the world, both through the acquisition of formal independence by colonies and clients, and through the incorporation of existing powers like China and Japan into the system: roughly 1800 to 1950. If this scheme is correct, the study of European state-making has at least one point of relevance to the politics of the contemporary world: Europeans played the major part in creating the contemporary international state-system, and presumably left the imprints of their peculiar political institutions on it. It is probably even true (although not for the reasons usually adduced) that a state which has adopted western forms or organization will have an easier time in the international system; after all, the system grew up in conjunction with those forms.

At the same time as the state system absorbs the entire world, the individual state may be losing part of its significance. I ended with speculations about the devolution of power away from the nation-state both upward and downward: toward the regional grouping and the compact of superstates above, toward the subnational region, ethnic population, or racial group below. Perhaps the two movements are complementary, with the segments of the population which were demobilized as the state became supreme renewing their bids for autonomy as they see the state increasingly constrained by powers outside it.

Perhaps the European national state grew up at a scale roughly matched to the markets, capital, communications, and productive organization of the seventeenth or eighteenth centuries, but increasingly irrelevant to the scale and manner of interdependence prevailing in the twentieth century. Perhaps control of a contiguous territory was peculiarly advantageous to the land- and water-bound technologies of the European state-making eras, but an obstacle to full exploitation of technologies of flight, electric power and electronic information-handling.

For all these perhapses, we must wait and see. But remember the definition of a state as an organization, controlling the principal means of coercion within a given territory, which is differentiated from other organizations operating in the same territory, autonomous, centralized and formally coordinated. If there is something to the trends we have described, they threaten almost every single one of these defining features of the state: the monopoly of coercion, the exclusiveness of control within the territory, the autonomy, the centralization, the formal coordination; even the differentiation from other organizations begins to fall away in such compacts as the European Common Market. One last perhaps, then: perhaps, as is so often the case, we only begin to understand this momentous historical process—the formation of national states—when it begins to lose its universal significance. Perhaps, unknowing, we are writing obituaries for the state.

['Western State-Making and Theories of Political Transformation', in Charles Tilly (ed.), *The Formation of National States in Western Europe* (Princeton University Press: Princeton, NJ, 1975), 632–8.]

MICHAEL HOWARD
....
40 **War and Nations**

Mazzini and other nationalists in the early part of the nineteenth century [believed] that the assertion and fulfilment of the principle of national self-determination would eventually bring about perpetual peace. But they accepted that the peace to which they looked forward so confidently was only the light at the end of a tunnel of violent and inevitable struggle—much as their successors, the social revolutionaries, believed that the just social order to which they aspired could be achieved only by violent and, if need be, bloody revolution.

From the very beginning the principle of nationalism was almost indissolubly linked, both in theory and practice, with the idea of war. For Hegel, for Fichte and Arndt, those Prussian thinkers whose ideas were to be archetypical for so much nineteenth-century nationalism, war was the necessary dialectic in the evolution of nations. As one deputy at the Frankfurt Assembly of 1848 put it, 'Mere existence does not entitle a people to political independence; only the force to assert itself as a state among others'.[1] In nation-building as in revolution, force was the midwife of the historical process.

The terrible thing is that, historically speaking, these thinkers were right. It is hard to think of any nation-state, with the possible exception of Norway, that came into existence before the middle of the twentieth century which was not created, and had its boundaries defined, by wars, by internal violence, or by a combination of the two. These wars, in many cases, had been fought not between peoples but between princes asserting juridical claims to what they regarded as their personal property; but they were none the less decisive in the creation of these coherent political units out of which 'nations' were to evolve. Indeed such dynastic wars could in themselves create national self-consciousness, as the Hundred Years War did certainly for the English and to some extent the French.

The true national content of such early struggles is hard to evaluate. Later generations have enveloped them in so impenetrable a fog of historical myth that such figures as Henry V and Joan of Arc sometimes seem as legendary as King Arthur and his knights of the Round Table. For as nations came to define themselves and trace their origins, the history of their conflicts with one another became a central part of this process of definition, and the concept of the 'nation' became inseparably associated with the wars it had fought. British nationalistic history is the history of its battles—Bannockburn, Creçy, Agincourt, the Armada, Waterloo; wars fought for the most part by a monarchy, but a monarchy which through the sheer process of fighting (and more important, winning) them, became a focus for national sentiment. For France the wars and victories of the old monarchy were to be almost obliterated by the victories more directly associated with the French *people*; Marengo, Austerlitz, Jena, Wagram, battles won by conscript armies commanded by officers who had risen from the ranks. For Germany the foundations laid by the Wars of Liberation in 1813–15 were to be crowned by the military achievements of Sadowa, Gravelotte and Sedan—wars won not by princes but by great popular armies. For the United States the nation was moulded by the War of Independence and united by the result of the Civil War, whose climactic battle of Gettysburg has entered deep into the national myth. Such battles were decisive acts made possible only by the mobilisation of national resources and the exercise of the national will. They epitomised national solidarity and self-sacrifice. But yet more important were the political consequences that flowed from them, the part they played in creating a power structure in which some nations survived and flourished as independent entities and others disappeared, some for centuries, some for good.

It is a chastening exercise to recall the states that have disappeared as the result of unsuccessful wars—or have never succeeded in coming into being. There were the crusader kingdoms of the Middle East. Rather nearer home for me, and nearer our own time, there was the Duchy of Burgundy, which contested the hegemony of Western Europe with the Kingdom of France in the middle of the fifteenth century and under more skilful leadership might have obtained it. In Eastern Europe there is, or was, the great principality of Lithuania. Further south the ethnic blocs of the Ukraine and Armenia struggled for centuries and in vain for political self-expression. The Kurds struggle still. In the Mediterranean a different turn of history might have produced for us a wealthy and independent Kingdom of Catalonia. In Africa we have in our own time witnessed the establishment and disappearance of the state of Biafra. And most interesting of all, and most significant in its consequences for the history of the world, in North America there briefly appeared in the middle years of the last century, with every appearance of permanence and economic advantage, the Confederate States of America. One could draw an interesting map of the world depicting these defunct or still-born states, or indicating how the frontiers of existing states would differ if they had lost some of the wars that they won. The harsh fact is that the state structure of the international system as it exists today is not the result of peaceful, teleological growth, the evolution of nations whose seeds have germinated in the womb of time and have come to a natural fruition. It is the result of conflicts that might, in very many cases, have been resolved differently. [. . .]

Up till our own century, then, war has been a principal determinant in the shaping of nation-states. That there have been other determinants goes without saying; the growth of wealth, the emergence of a regional élite alienated from the existing authorities, the incidence of economic oppression, the collapse of traditional centres of power; these are only some of the most obvious. But whether these contributory causes will effectively result in the formation of a new political unit, sovereign within its own territories, will almost invariably be determined by the use, or the effective threat, of armed force. It is true—and indeed it is one of the few blessings of our disturbed century—that within the past thirty years well over fifty new sovereign states have achieved independence without the use of violence; but that independence was the indirect result of the defeat, or the exhaustion, of their former imperial masters in the Second World War, enhanced by the successful example of those peoples, in South-East Asia and elsewhere, who had successfully fought for their independence. [. . .] [I]t became clear to the rulers of European empires that the day when they could maintain suzerainty over distant dependencies with a minimal use of military force had long since disappeared. Now the cost of maintaining imperial rule outweighed any possible benefits. For Britain, the traditional problem of 'Imperial Defence' ceased to be one of maintaining order in subjected territories, and became one, no less difficult and not particularly welcome, of protecting those dependencies, whether as close at hand as Ulster or as distant as the Caribbean or the Falkland Islands, which for reasons of their own wanted to *remain* British.

Interestingly enough the new nations that have achieved independence without having to fight for it are no less militant in their outlook than those who did. Indeed in the successor states of sub-Saharan Africa where the transition to freedom took place under the most peaceful circumstances imaginable—Ghana, Nigeria, Uganda—the military rapidly achieved a political dominance that owed nothing to any contribution they might have made to any struggle for independence. In fact in states where such a struggle really had taken place, however, such as Yugoslavia, Algeria and Vietnam, it is not evident that the military enjoy either social prestige or political power. The effort that peacefully-born successor-states devote to their armed forces, to say nothing of the strident tone of their discourse in international affairs, suggests that they feel almost a sense of guilt that they should have escaped the usual bloody *rites de passage*.

Such wars for freedom, or for national self-determination, are now the only armed conflicts generally held to be legitimate, or 'just'; apart, that is, from simple wars for self-defence. In the nineteenth century Europeans on both sides of the Atlantic considered that they had a self-evident right to settle in territories they found agreeable and to subjugate any native inhabitants as might offer resistance. This claim based on cultural superiority was to be used in our own time by the Third Reich, to justify their wars in Eastern Europe and their grotesque attempts to 'colonise' Poland and the Ukraine—history repeating itself, not as farce but as nightmare. That was the last imperial war. No one has yet shown any inclination to imitate it.

In fighting to preserve their old Empires, or perhaps to carve out new ones, states have justified themselves in different ways. The French justified fighting to maintain their presence in Algeria by claiming it as part of the metropole. The British justified their operations in Kenya and Malaya by claiming that these were intended to pave the way to peaceful self-rule; as indeed they most successfully did. The Russians justified their entry into Afghanistan, as into other places before that, by the professed need to suppress those subversive elements which were preventing the true voice of the people from being heard. The United States likewise justified its intervention in Vietnam by citing the need to establish political conditions of order that would make it possible for the true wishes of the people to be consulted. The popular will has everywhere displaced dynastic right as the accepted criterion of legitimate government, and at least lip service has to be paid to it. Those states which continue to exercise control over territories in open defiance of the wishes of the population find themselves the objects of universal condemnation.

[*The Lessons of History* (Oxford University Press: Oxford, 1991), 39–43.]

41 Ethnic Conflict in the West

1. *The transaction-integration balance.* The main thrust of the theories of modernization is that assimilation and integration are promoted by social mobilization—especially [. . .] in the first stage of political and economic development and especially if the processes of mobilization are not too rapid. However, these theories also concede that under certain circumstances the relationship may be reversed. When social communication, trade, and various other kinds of transactions increase at a rapid rate, assimilation may not only lag behind but may actually decrease. For instance, in Deutsch's first and most famous work on nationalism, he already hints not only that assimilation is slow and must be 'counted in decades and generations,' but also that the comparatively faster growth of communications may have a negative effect on it: 'linguistically and culturally . . . members of each group are outsiders for the other. Yet technological and economic processes are forcing them together, into acute recognition of their differences and their common, mutual experience of strangeness, and *more conspicuous differentiation and conflict may result.*'[1] Deutsch specifies two likely outcomes here: a reversal not only of the assimilation among groups, but even of their capacity to coexist peacefully.

This important theme is elaborated in Deutsch's subsequent publication, which is concerned with the conditions of integration, defined as 'the attainment of a sense of community, accompanied by formal or informal institutions or practices, sufficiently strong and widespread to assure peaceful change.' Deutsch argues that 'the number of opportunities for violent conflict will increase with the volume and range of mutual transactions,' because the various kinds of transactions throw 'a burden upon the institutions for peaceful adjustment or change.' Consequently, the prevention of conflict depends on the ability of integration to keep pace with the growth of transactions. How difficult it is to maintain this balance is indicated by Deutsch's description of it as a *race* between the two processes: 'the race between the growing rate of transaction among populations in particular areas and the growth of integrative institutions and practices among them.'[2]

If modernization leads to rapidly increasing social transactions and contacts among diverse groups, strain and conflict are more likely to ensue than greater mutual understanding. This explanation undoubtedly applies to much of the ethnic conflict that has taken place in Third World countries since their political and economic takeoff a few decades ago, but is it also valid for the First World? The difficulty is that, according to the analogy with the Third World, ethnic conflict in Western countries should have reached its high point in the wake of the Industrial Revolution more than a century ago instead of during the past decade. Connor attempts to resolve this problem by asserting that modernization in the West only led to intensive intrastate transactions and communications at a rather gradual pace, and that these quantitative increases did not add up to a qualitative breakthrough until after World War II. This was 'the point at which a significant number of people perceived that the cumulative impact of the quantitative increases in the intensity of intergroup contacts ... constituted a threat to their ethnicity,' and it 'represented, in political terms, a qualitative transformation.'[3]

2. *The 'horizontalization' of vertical ethnic groups.* Whether or not Connor's claim is valid is an empirical question, but to the extent that the rapid multiplication and intensification of contacts do create interethnic tensions, these tensions are likely to be aggravated by the awareness of significant inequalities among the ethnic groups. Imbalances tend to foster feelings of superiority in the more-favored groups and of resentment and frustration among the less-favored groups. [. . .]

3. *The expanding scope of state intervention.* The rapid growth in the scope and volume of state activities in the years since World War II has added to the problem of the perceived inequalities among ethnic groups. First of all, because hardly any public policy has a strictly equal impact on different groups and regions, the increase of state activities has also increased the possibility that unequal treatment will occur by chance. Second, if a governmental action is explicitly designed to counteract the uneven impact of the processes of modernization and if its purpose is, therefore, to equalize regional and group differences, it may paradoxically still be perceived as unequal and unfair treatment. The poorer regions and groups will feel relatively deprived to begin with, and may well regard remedial action by the government as inadequate— a tendency that is reinforced by the egalitarian expectations raised by the growth of state intervention. At the same time, their more prosperous counterparts will feel relatively deprived of governmental support and hence will also feel they are the victims of unfair discrimination. Especially in recent years, these problems have been aggravated by the general decline in the quality and effectiveness of governmental performance.

Another paradox is that the perception of inequalities, beyond calling forth claims for the redress of these inequalities, may also trigger ethnic demands for autonomy or secession—which are not very likely to bring greater equality! Inequalities tend to be greater among than within sovereign states, and in federal than in unitary states.

4. *The decreasing displacement of ethnic conflict.* The previous arguments relied on a comparison of the relative *positions* of ethnic and socioeconomic cleavages. A closely related argument focuses on the comparison of the relative *salience* of ethnic and other cleavages. The point of departure is again that ethnic cleavages are primarily vertical, that socioeconomic cleavages can be depicted as horizontal, and that these cleavages, therefore, do not coincide. Other politically relevant cleavages, in particular the religious ones, generally

do not coincide with ethnic cleavages either, although they tend to cut across each other at a more acute angle than the ethnic and socioeconomic cleavages. The previous argument was that ethnic conflict becomes more likely when the ethnic cleavage deviates from its vertical position. The present argument is that the probability of conflict along the ethnic cleavage increases when the horizontal socioeconomic cleavage and other relevant cleavages that do not coincide with the ethnic dividing line lose their salience. [. . .]

In this context, the end-of-ideology theory becomes relevant again. [I]t was wrong to expect a decline of ethnic conflict analogous to the decline of the ideological conflict between the political left and right. We can now turn the argument around completely: it was as a *result* of the decreasing salience of ideological conflict along the horizontal left–right cleavage—and, to a lesser but still significant extent, the declining importance of religious differences— that ethnic conflicts have reemerged in recent years. The ethnic cleavages have long been less salient but more persistent than these competing cleavages. This explanation means that the wrong question was asked: it should not be Why has ethnic conflict suddenly reappeared? but Why has it been dormant for so long? The answer is that it was temporarily displaced by more salient conflicts.

5. *The new wave of democratization.* The theory of the end of ideology is important for an additional reason. If [. . .] the end of ideology is itself an ideology and does not constitute the end of the ideological dialectic, it suggests the question What do the new antitheses that challenge the ideology of conservative socialism consist of? One of these appears to be the ideology of participatory democracy, which rejects the kind of democratic regime that conservative socialism implies. Haas asserts that the new Europe is charac- terized by 'a pragmatic synthesis of capitalism and socialism in the form of democratic planning,' and he aptly describes its decision-making mechanism as follows: 'It features the continuous participation of all major voluntary groups in European society through elaborate systems of committees and councils. The technical bureaucracies of trade unions, industrial associations, bankers and farmers sit down with the technocrats from the ministries of finance, labor and economics—or with central government planning offices—to shape the future.'[4] This is the type of government that Robert A. Dahl has labeled the 'new democratic Leviathan,' as a reaction to which he predicted the emer- gence of 'radical efforts (the shape of which we cannot foresee) to reconstruct the Leviathan to a more nearly human scale.'[5]

The shape that the opposition to the new Leviathan has assumed, so far, borrows to a large extent from traditional democratic theory and does not represent a qualitative break with the past. What is important for the purposes of this essay is that all of the manifestations of the new wave of democratiza- tion encourage ethnic demands. First of all, it has entailed greater activity and a new stridency on the part of a variety of groups, including ethnic ones, that do not belong to the decision-making establishment. Second, these groups tend to be more concerned about minority rights than majority rule—in line with the priorities of ethnic groups. Third, their prescriptions for reconstructing the new Leviathan 'to a more nearly human scale' are the rather traditional ones of decentralization, autonomy, regionalization, and grass-roots democracy. These general tendencies have given a powerful boost to specific ethnic demands. Finally, as Huntington has pointed out, the 'expansion of participation could make postindustrial society extraordinarily difficult to govern.'[6] Therefore, to the extent that widespread and relatively unstructured political participation increases governmental inefficiency and immobilism, demands for ethnic autonomy will be spurred even further.

The relationship between democratization and ethnic demands proposed here differs from the usual one. Ethnic pluralism is usually the independent variable and democracy the dependent variable, and the question is whether or not a society divided ethnically or otherwise can sustain a democratic regime. The converse relationship links democracy as the independent variable with ethnic pluralism as the dependent variable, or more specifically, democratization with ethnic conflict. In Third World countries, the process of democratization and the encouragement of mass participation have undoubtedly strengthened ethnic feelings and demands. During the first wave of democratization in Western countries in the late nineteenth and early twentieth centuries, the stimulation of ethnicity was much less pronounced. This may also explain the impetus belatedly given to it by the second wave of democratization.

['Political Theories and the Explanation of Ethnic Conflict in the Western World', in Milton Esman (ed.), *Ethnic Conflict in the Western World* (Cornell University Press: Ithaca, NY, 1977), 55–62.]

DONALD HOROWITZ

42 The Logic of Secessions

Despite its frequency, secession is a variable phenomenon. Some movements emerge early in the life of a new state, seemingly with little provocation. Others develop only after a prolonged period of frustration and conflict. Some movements simmer for years, even decades, and in the end may come to nothing, whereas others burst quickly into warfare. But many movements never even reach a slow simmer, much less a quick boil.

To discern patterns of secession, it is necessary to recognize that this is a special species of ethnic conflict, but a species nonetheless. Though modified by their territorial character, secessionist conflicts partake of many features that ethnic conflict in general exhibits. Calculations of group interest play their part, although some ethnic groups opt for secession when it does not appear to be in their interest to do so. In decisions to secede, group interest is alloyed with enmity and offset by apprehension. The roots of those decisions are to be found in the texture of group relations.

One fairly firm rule of thumb can be laid down at once. Whether and when a secessionist movement will emerge is determined mainly by domestic politics, by the relations of groups and regions within the state. Whether a secessionist movement will achieve its aims, however, is determined largely by international politics, by the balance of interests and forces that extend beyond the state. Occasionally, considerations of means available to support secessionist movements, including external assistance, may modify secessionist sentiment—though separatists are often surprisingly heedless of such prudential constraints. Occasionally, too, external relations reinforce separatist proclivities, as for example when Kurds and Southern Sudanese took exception to pan-Arabist activities in Baghdad and Khartoum. Secession lies squarely at the juncture of internal and international politics, but for the most part the emergence of separatism can be explained in terms of domestic ethnic politics.

To this broad rule of thumb, there is a major exception. A group that might otherwise be disposed to separatism will not be so disposed if its secession is likely to lead, not to independence, but to incorporation in a neighboring state, membership in which is viewed as even less desirable than membership in the existing state. The cases in which this is likely to occur involve irredentism, where an international boundary divides members of a single ethnic group. The Baluch and Pathans of Pakistan, for example, are likely to limit their separatist activity to the extent that it makes them vulnerable to incorporation in Afghanistan or, in the Baluch case, Iran. The Ewe of Ghana are not likely to do anything that would risk merger into Togo. Similar considerations, however, will not restrain the Malays of Southern Thailand, many of whom might indeed prefer to join Malaysia. This does not indicate under what conditions irredentism will occur; it merely highlights what is, in at least a few important cases, a limitation on domestically generated collective inclinations.

At this point, a definitional issue intrudes, one well illustrated by the limited goals of some of the groups just mentioned. Should the terms *separatism* and *secession* be confined to movements aiming explicitly at an independent state or extended to movements seeking any territorially defined political change intended to accord an ethnic group autonomous control over the region in which it resides? Conceived in the latter way, separatism would include ethnic demands for the creation of separate states within existing states or for a broad measure of regional autonomy, short of independence.

There is some ground for thinking that groups demanding complete independence may have the strongest sense of grievance. The contrast between Catalan and Basque claims in Spain is revealing on this score, Catalan ethnic sentiment runs as deep as Basque sentiment does, and it probably has broader support. But Basque political organizations have more frequently turned to violence and more frequently demanded independence, whereas Catalan organizations have aimed at autonomy within Spain. Franco's severe repression of the Basques, many of whom had supported the Republicans, probably helps explain the unyielding character of some Basque organizations. (So, too, may the fact that Basques also reside on the French side of the border, making independence a more attractive goal.) In the Basque case, at least, there seems to be a clear and direct linkage between ethnic antipathy and declared political objectives.

In many other cases, however, this linkage is more tenuous. The Kurds in Iraq consistently denied that their objective was independence. Even as they fought and died in the 1960s and 1970s, they eschewed anything beyond regional autonomy. The reason, presumably, was tactical: had they declared independence as their goal, the Iraqi Kurds would have engendered hostility from neighboring regimes in Syria, Iran, and Turkey, all of which have Kurdish minorities. In the 1974 warfare in Iraq, Iran supplied arms, food, and cross-border facilities for the Kurdish fighters, and this support particularly insured that the movement demanded only autonomy.

Demands can also shift from autonomy to independence and back again, depending on the state of negotiations between central governments and separatists. The Moro National Liberation Front in the Philippines moved from autonomy demands to demands for separate statehood after the Philippine government adopted a decentralization plan the MNLF found wanting. The Mizo National Front in India followed the same path, agreeing to a solution within the framework of Indian federalism in 1976 but, after a ceasefire broke down three years later, returning to warfare to achieve independence. Other movements, such as the Southern Sudanese, equivocated on their demands, using ambiguous terms like 'self-determination' to cover internal differences. The Chad National Liberation Front, presumed to be fighting a war for the secession of the North, long refused to declare its objectives, and eventually most of the country, including the capital, was in rebel hands. Tactics play a large role in the statement of objectives.

The often tactical nature of demands, their elasticity, even fickleness, the willingness of independence movements to settle for much less than statehood, and the occasional interest of secessionists in capturing the whole state if that proves possible—all of these argue for an inclusive conception of separatism and secession, terms I shall therefore use interchangeably. Such a conception should embrace movements seeking a separate region within an existing state, as well as those seeking a separate and independent state.

'Inevitably,' wrote Immanuel Wallerstein at the time of the Katanga secession, 'some regions will be richer (less poor) than others, and if the ethnic claim to power combines with relative wealth, the case for secession is strong. . . . [E]very African nation, large or small, federal or unitary, has its Katanga.'[1] Wallerstein was right to link the ethnic claim with the character of the region from which the ethnic group springs. These are the two conditions that matter most. But he limited the potential for secession unduly when he confined it to relatively wealthy regions. In point of fact, there are several paths to secession, and rich regions are not the leading secessionists. They are far outnumbered by regions poor in resources and productivity. Despite strong feelings of alienation—or worse—neither Ashanti in Ghana nor the Western Region of Nigeria nor Buganda in Uganda, all prosperous regions, made a serious effort to secede. By contrast, wars have been fought by peoples in the poor regions of, among many others, the Southern Sudan, the Southern Philippines, and Northern Chad. Why this is so we shall soon see.

Table [1] provides a simple matrix of potential secessionists. It includes groups that have and have not attempted to secede. The variables are straightforward. They are based on the positions of ethnic groups and regions relative to others in the state.

Separatist ethnic groups are characterized as 'backward' or 'advanced' for shorthand purposes, in accordance with our earlier discussion of group juxtapositions. An advanced group is one that has benefited from opportunities in education and non-agricultural employment. Typically, it is represented above the mean in number of secondary and university graduates, in bureaucratic, commercial, and professional employment, and in per capita income. [. . .] [C]ertain stereotypes are commonly associated with these attributes. Advanced groups are generally regarded by themselves and others as highly motivated, diligent, intelligent, and dynamic. Backward groups, less favorably situated on the average in terms of educational attainment, high-

TABLE 1. *Potential secessionists, by group and regional position*

	Backward Groups	Advanced Groups
Backward regional economies	Southern Sudanese	Ibo in Nigeria
	Karens, Shans, others in Burma	Tamils in Sri Lanka
	Muslims in the Philippines	Baluba (Kasai) in Zaire
	Muslims in Chad	Lozi in Zambia*
	Kurds in Iraq	Kabyle Berbers in Algeria*
	Nagas and Mizos in India	
	Muslims in Thailand	
	Bengalis in Pakistan	
	Northerners in Ghana*	
Advanced regional economies	Lunda in Zaire	Sikhs in Indian Punjab
	Bakonjo in Uganda	Basques in Spain
	Batéké in Gabon*	Yoruba in Nigeria*
		Baganda in Uganda*

* Denotes groups that have not had a strong secessionist movement.

salaried employment, and per capita income, tend to be stereotyped as indolent, ignorant, and not disposed to achievement. Just as group position and the putative qualities associated with it are potent factors in ethnic conflict generally, so do they condition collective orientations to the possibility of secession.

Separatist regions are characterized as backward or advanced by the relative economic position of the region, as measured by regional income per capita excluding remittances from other regions (which would likely be terminated or reduced in the event of secession). I say 'measured by,' but in fact data on regional income per capita are only sporadically available, and rarely available on a reliable basis for Asian and African countries. While this excludes the possibility of analysis based on precise degrees of regional backwardness, advancement, or disparity between the two in given countries, identification of backward and advanced regions is not difficult. The same is true, of course, regarding group position.

This characterization of both regions and groups ignores some common complexities. The table assumes the existence of geographically concentrated ethnic groups that may or may not become separatist. However, many groups that possess a geographically identifiable homeland are no longer geographically concentrated. Large numbers of group members may live outside the home region, a circumstance likely to have some impact on the emergence of separatism. Conversely, a secessionist region often contains more than one major ethnic group, and the groups may differ in their position relative to groups outside the region. Likewise, the measurement of regional position by per capita income may obscure important elements of intraregional difference. Eritrea, for example, has had industrially developed cities but an exceedingly poor countryside: which is the politically relevant reality? Then, too, although I shall speak of a backward region and an advanced region, as if any state had only two regions, rarely is a state so clearly bifurcated. I shall deal with some of these complexities at later points, but for the moment it is best to proceed with a simpler framework.

The interplay of relative group position and relative regional position determines the emergence of separatism. In stressing this interplay, I mean to reject direct causal relationships between regional economic disparity and ethnic secession. If degree of regional economic disparity alone determined the emergence of separatism, it would be reasonable to expect the preponderance of such movements in those states occupying the middle-income levels, for in such states regional economic disparities seem to be greatest. But no such tendencies can be identified. Secession is attempted in low-income states like Ethiopia and Chad, as well as in the Philippines and Nigeria, countries with incomes four to six times higher; and, needless to say, it is an issue in a number of economically developed countries, too. Relative regional position is a causal element in the emergence of secession, not because it predicts separatism in any straightforward way, but because it conditions the claims ethnic groups make and their response to the rejection of those claims.

The four categories of potential secessionists depicted in the table differ from each other in several major respects. The demands the groups advance before separatist sentiment crystallizes, the events that move the groups to secession, the calculations that attend the decision to separate, and the timing of the decision all vary according to whether the group is considered backward or advanced and whether it resides in a backward or advanced region. Table [1] does not provide an exhaustive enumeration of movements, of which there have been dozens, if not hundreds, in the post-colonial period. Furthermore, the table includes some non-secessionist groups for comparison. Even so, the table suggests the prevalence of backward regions among secessionists. In part, this may be a function of the coincidence of regional backwardness with geographic distance from the center. Economic backwardness is more common on the periphery. In states where the span of governmental control is limited, peripheral areas might more readily contemplate secession. Yet the logic of secession comprehends much more than just the difficulty of the center in exerting control. Distance is but a minor factor in the overall prevalence of backward regions among secessionists. Indeed, there is more than one rationale for the secession of a backward region. There are four different paths to ethnic secession, which correspond to the four different cells of the table. [. . .]

Table [2] summarizes much of the discussion so far. It makes clear just how much can be deduced from group and regional position. Backward groups tend to measure disadvantage in terms of deviation from some concept of proportionality in relation to population. Advanced groups gauge deprivation by discrimination, utilizing a standard of proportionality in relation to merit. Advanced regions tend to complain of revenue–expenditure imbalances. Backward regions may also complain of inadequate expenditure if they receive from the center less than their per capita share, albeit more than their contribution to revenue. Backward regions that are the home of advanced groups, however, tend not to complain of revenue imbalances, probably because they receive remittances from outside the region and certainly because they eschew claims based on numbers. Here, too, there is more than one criterion of proportionality.

The four categories of political claims are, as the table shows, a combined function of group and regional characteristics. These claims do not, however, invariably ripen into secession. The columns headed 'Precipitants' and 'Calculations' indicate when dispositions to secede are likely to emerge. Precipitants tend to be events that have the effect of rejecting unequivocally claims put forward by ethnic groups. In the case of backward groups, [. . .] precipitants foreshadow political domination. In the case of advanced groups, precipitants tend to reduce the advantages of remaining in the undivided state. In short, precipitants may act either to raise the costs or to reduce the benefits of

TABLE 2. *The disposition to secede*

Group and region	Political claims	Precipitants	Calculations	Timing, relative frequency
Backward group in backward region	Proportionality in civil service, occasionally also in revenues	Denial of proportionality in civil service; symbolic issues like language and religion; influx of advanced civil servants	Secede despite economic costs	Early, frequent
Advanced group in backward region	Nondiscrimination; no revenue issue	Severe discrimination; repeated violence; migration back to home region	Secede only if economic costs are low	Late, somewhat frequent
Advanced group in advanced region	Nondiscrimination; spend revenue where generated	Severe discrimination; violence and migration back to home region if population exporter	Secede only if economic costs are low	Late, rare
Backward group in advanced region	Proportionality in civil service; spend revenue where generated	Denial of proportionality; political claims made by immigrant strangers in the region	Secede regardless of economic benefits or costs	Early, rare

remaining in the state—provided, of course, that benefits and costs are understood to embrace nonmaterial as well as material values.

Indeed, the table makes clear that separatism results from varying mixes of sheer economic interest and group apprehension. Economic interest may act either as an accelerator or a brake on separatism. Yet, among the most frequent and precocious secessionists—backward groups in backward regions—economic loss or gain plays the smallest role, ethnic anxiety the largest.

The precipitating events and the calculations that follow them are not inexorable. Claims need not be denied. Advanced civil servants need not be posted to backward regions. Advanced groups from population-exporting regions can be protected from discrimination and violence; they need not migrate home. Much depends on the reception accorded group claims. The conditions that promote a disposition to secede, though derived from group and regional position, are subject to intervention and deflection. The list of potential candidates for secession is much longer than the list of actual secessionists. Some Basques in Spain want independence; but Nigerian Yoruba, who might have chosen to secede, chose not to; and Baganda, who threatened secession, did not follow through. The Ibo fought a war of secession; but the Lozi, not treated like the Ibo, did not secede; and the Tamils of Sri Lanka might still go either way. Backward groups are frequent secessionists, but the Northerners in Ghana, every bit as backward as Northerners in Nigeria—and far less powerful—have not even mooted secession. Likewise, the backward Batéké in Southeast Gabon, a region rich in uranium and manganese, have evidenced no serious inclination toward a Katanga-like secession. Every category of regional group has its negative cases.

Moreover, as I have suggested all along, there are varying thresholds of secession and therefore differential frequency of secession among the various categories of groups. Clearly, backward groups in backward regions are easily persuaded that it is in their interest to leave. So are backward groups in advanced regions, but there are many fewer such groups in a position to secede. Despite their generally greater reluctance to secede, there are differences among advanced groups. Advanced groups from advanced regions often receive extraregional benefits that are not confined to remittances from migrant sons and therefore not terminated precipitously if back-migration should occur. They are less likely to secede. As the last column in the table shows, the four paths to secession are not equally well-trodden.

The much greater frequency of secessionist movements in backward regions has a number of important implications. Many regions that choose secession are likely to be economically least capable of sustaining themselves. This applies particularly to the secession of backward groups in backward regions. They may also be short on administrative capacity and personnel. However, the position of advanced groups in backward regions is at least equivocal. They will have no shortage of administrative talent, once their migrant sons return to the region. But this surfeit of talent may quickly become a drain on the budget. The experience of Biafra and Benin's difficulties in reabsorbing civil servants it had exported to other West African states both attest to this.

No doubt many countries once proclaimed 'unviable' have survived. It is all too easy to exaggerate the economic problems a secessionist region will face. Yet there is no gainsaying the fact that a great many regions that do manage to secede can be expected to have post-secession economic difficulties.

The distinction between early and late seceders—which, as the table makes clear, is largely coterminous with the distinction between backward and advanced groups—also has important consequences. In general, late secessions are more cohesive, better organized, and more often conducted under the auspices of a political party than are early secessions. Early secessions in countries like Chad, the Sudan, and Burma consisted of more than one movement. The secessionist regions were heterogeneous, and the secessions occurred so soon after independence that no political party had a chance to capture the support of the entire region. Because it was not centrally organized, the warfare was sporadic, and—except in the Sudan—there was no single organization in a position to make peace. In Chad, for example, an amnesty was accepted by members of one ethnic group fighting in one region but ignored by other groups fighting elsewhere. In all the cases, the fighting lingered on for many years; in Burma, it still does. In the late secessions of Biafra and Bangladesh, by contrast, the movements were under much tighter control. The fighting was more intense, widespread, and simultaneous in all areas; and victory for one side or the other was quicker and more decisive.

In the case of groups likely to become late seceders, if seceders at all, there is more time to work on policies averting secession and, because of their reluctance to secede, more latitude regarding the actual substance of policies that might prove sufficient to avert secession. There is also, however, more time for both sides to prepare for the battle when it comes: to cement foreign alliances, procure sophisticated weapons, and organize the secessionist region and the rump region for war. This extra time, preparation, and organization are likely to insure that the resolution of the fighting, when it eventually occurs, will be clear-cut.

[*Ethnic Groups in Conflict* (University of California Press: Berkeley, Calif., 1985), 230–6, 258–62.]

JAMES MAYALL

43 Irredentist and Secessionist Challenges

The Conventional Interpretation

The contemporary interpretation of national self-determination is highly conventional: in effect its application has been tied in time and space to the withdrawal of the European powers from their overseas possessions. This formulation has been enthusiastically accepted by the African and Asian successor states. Thus in 1961 Jawaharlal Nehru finally overcame his scruples about political violence and sanctioned the forceful incorporation of Goa into India without reference to Goan opinion.[1] And in 1967, after the inhabitants of Gibraltar had voted overwhelmingly to maintain the *status quo*—in a 97 per cent poll there were only 44 dissenters—the United Nations Committee on Colonialism ruled that British rule was a violation of the Charter because the inhabitants were not indigenous.[2] [. . .]

The most that can be said for the conventional (i.e. anti-colonial) interpretation of national self-determination is that it is a sensible compromise. Given the indeterminacy of the idea of the collective self on the one hand, and the impossibility within the contemporary stock of political ideas of arriving at an alternative justification of political authority on the other, it represents some kind of deal, albeit a somewhat shabby one, between the entrenched forces of liberal rationalism and those of historical essentialism. Like all compromises, sensible though they may seem to the practical men who negotiate them, the conventional interpretation of national self-determination remains vulnerable to attack from those who believe that the compromisers have misunderstood either the essential nature of their historical claim or its essential rationality. Although there are many points where the two aspects overlap, it may be helpful, if only for presentational purposes, to identify the main essentialist challenge to the international order with irridentism and the main rationalist challenge with secession.

Irridentism

The doctrine of irridentism is derived from the Italian, *irridenta*, meaning those territories, Trente, Dalmatia, Trieste, Fiume which although culturally Italian remained under Austrian or Swiss rule and thus *unredeemed* after the unification of Italy itself. In modern political usage the term has come to mean any territorial claim made by one sovereign national state to lands within another. These claims are generally supported by historical and/or ethnic arguments: that is, the irridentist state insists that part of its rightful homeland has been unjustly taken from it, or that a part of the nation itself has been falsely separated from the organic national community.

Although, in all cases, irridentist claims are made by one state on the territory (the real estate so to speak) of another, irridentist clams vary, nonetheless, in the extent to which they combine the elements of territoriality for its own sake and genuine national sentiment. A current if extreme example was provided by the Argentine claim to the Malvinas or Falkland Islands which has been deliberately kept in the forefront of the Argentine national consciousness by the process of official national propaganda and censorship. All Argentinian maps show the islands as belonging to the Argentine. Argentinian history books describe them as an integral part of the nation, despite the fact that there has been virtually no Argentinian population on the islands for 150 years and not much before that.[3]

An example of irridentism, where a claim to territory was combined with arguments about the allegiance of the population, is provided by the Moroccan claim to Mauritania in the early 1960s. As with the Argentine's claim to the Falklands/Malvinas, the Moroccan claim was historical. In this case the claim was based on the overlordship or suzerainty which the Moroccan sultans had exercised over the peoples of Mauritania before the establishment of the French Empire in West Africa and the French protectorate over Morocco itself.[4] What gave the claim its salience in the politics of contemporary Morocco was the fact that the vision of a greater Morocco was shared by the ruling dynasty and by the Istiqlal, the nationalist part which in most other respects was in opposition to the regime. In this case irridentism opened up a prospect of a bipartisan foreign policy.

Two politically more ambiguous examples of modern irridentism are provided by the Spanish claim to Gibraltar on historical and geo-political grounds, and the Republic of Ireland's commitment to a united Ireland. Given the historical consciousness of the Spanish and Irish people (whether it is true or false is not here in question) and consequently their latent national consciousness (i.e. it is always available for political mobilisation) it seems unlikely that any Spanish or Irish government would be able to abandon their claims altogether. At the same time, in neither country is the irridentist question a major national issue, and indeed it is very often an embarrassment to the authorities.[5]

The Spanish claim is embarrassing because, given the expressed wishes of the population of Gibraltar on the one hand, and the Spanish government's accession into the EEC and its desire to integrate itself into the Western Alliance on the other, the claim, and the friction it engenders, inevitably seem anachronistic. By contrast, the Irish commitment to unity is embarrassing because the Irish government is heir to the partition agreement which established the Republic as an independent state. The Irish government knows that if it were to honour its commitment to unification, it would, even on the most optimistic assumptions, have to underwrite a different social order in the north, including secular education and welfare services of a kind which are not available in the Republic. On probably more realistic assumptions, it would find itself saddled with a civil war in the north which could well spread to the south and threaten its legitimacy. As yet no solution to the Irish question is in sight, and all recent Irish governments have consequently preferred the *status quo*.

These examples of modern irridentism, in which claims to land and appeals to popular sentiment are conjoined, suggest a general feature of irridentist claims. Since they are mostly claims by what may loosely be called the national core, which already has its own independent government, to peripheral lands (with or without the allegiance of their populations), they are available to governments as a mobilisation instrument, a means of securing popular support at times when, for whatever reason, such support seems particularly desirable.

Of course there are risks involved in cynically playing the irridentist card. If, as the Argentinian Junta discovered, a government is capable of arousing national dreams but cannot deliver what it promises, it may not be forgiven. Its successor will be left with the unpalatable task of containing the irridentist passion without disowning the claim. But while playing the irridentist card is likely to have unforeseen consequences, it remains broadly true that pressing an irridentist claim, where one is available, is an option which governments can choose to exercise. It is a way of tapping the well-springs of popular support even if, having switched the tap on at will, it cannot always be turned off.

The PLO, an organization without a territory or a state, is a spectacular exception to this rule. So long as it had no realistic chance of securing an independent state of Palestine, its irridentism was unequivocal, covering the entire state of modern Israel. Yasser Arafat's public acknowledgement of Israel's right to exist, made before the United Nations General Assembly in December 1988, has created a new political context. If the PLO is to have any chance of capitalising on this new situation, it will have to dilute the claim by deliberate use of ambiguity. In other words, it will have to behave more like an established irridentist government, for whom pressing its claim is a policy option rather than an ideological imperative. Whether the leadership of the organization will be allowed, by its own internal critics and its opponents in Israel, to act in this way remains to be seen.

The case which most clearly demonstrates the rule is also an exception to it. In 1960 the Republic of Somalia came into being as a result of a union of the British and Italian Trust territories. From its inception the new state had an irridentist constitution: the national flag was a five-pointed star, each point symbolising a centre of Somali population, only two of which were contained within the Republic. The other three centres were in Djibouti on the Red Sea, in the North-Eastern province of Kenya and in the Ogaden region of Ethiopia. Under their constitution Somali governments were committed to work for reunification.[6]

What makes Somali irridentism exceptional is first the fact that, uniquely in Africa, national sentiment is a mass rather than an elite phenomenon, and secondly that the Somali clan which has dominated the government in Mogadishu for most of the period since independence has extensive kinship links with the population living in the Ogaden. The combination of these two factors has kept unification as the dominant theme of Somali politics from the beginning, and has consequently isolated Somalia from its neighbours. Somali irridentism led to a defence treaty between Ethiopia and Kenya which survived both the 1974 revolution in Ethiopia and the United States negotiation of facilities for its Rapid Deployment Forces with Somalia and Kenya, and attempts to align the two regimes against 'Marxist' Ethiopia.[7]

Nevertheless, between 1969, when Siad Barre ousted the civilian government in a military *coup d'état*, and 1977, when he finally expelled his Russian allies and attempted unsuccessfully to take the Ogaden by force, his government endeavoured to conform to the general pattern. There is no evidence to suggest that the Russians, with whom the Somalis negotiated a friendship treaty involving extensive military and civilian aid in return for naval facilities for the Soviet forces, ever encouraged the government to press their territorial claim. And indeed for much of this period Barre's policy was publicly aimed at bringing about substantial change in the character of Somali society. His attempt at a revolution from above involved him in deliberately attempting to relocate many Northern nomads in the South as settled agriculturalists. It also involved censoring popular music on Somali radio: the oral tradition of Somali poetry, translated into a modern musical idiom adapted for the transistor age, was a vehicle for an alternative and irridentist form of political mobilisation.

It was only after the Ethiopian revolution had led to the general collapse of central authority and a revival of separatist sentiment throughout the country (not just in the Ogaden) that a combination of external opportunity—the Russian support for the revolution made a reversal of alliances seem plausible—and popular disaffection with his economic policies, led Siad Barre to embark on his disastrous policy of supporting the West Somali Liberation Front (WSLF) with regular and irregular military forces from within Somalia itself. The change in the Somali constitution after the country's defeat in 1978 was an attempt once again to bring popular irridentist sentiment firmly under the control of the central government.

Secession

The second challenge to the orthodox interpretation of self-determination as a once and for all event, secession, is, in a sense, a mirror image of the irridentist challenge. Successful secession is very rare; the creation of the state of Bangladesh in 1971 is the only pure example since 1945. However, the term is also used to describe unsuccessful separatist rebellions against the state. Indeed it is frequently used to describe any attempt by a national minority to exercise its right to self-determination by breaking away either to join another state or more often to establish an independent state of its own, or at least an autonomous region within an existing state. Such attempts are sometimes outright bids for independence, as when Biafra tried to secede from the Nigerian Federation between 1967 and 1970, or in the continuing Eritrean struggle against its incorporation in Ethiopia. On other occasions, as in Southern Sudan, Baluchistan or among the Sikhs of the Punjab, they are contests in which the options of national autonomy within the state or independence are both kept deliberately open.

But if tactical calculations of this kind are an integral part of secessionist as of irridentist politics, there is one vital difference—the attempt to secede, unlike the attempt to advance some irridentist claim, is never a *mere* move within the existing system of inter-state power rivalries. Secession depends on group sentiment and loyalty—not just on a disputed title to land or a doctrine of prescriptive right. In the final analysis, it is a form of mass politics organised from below rather than imposed from above through propaganda and the apparatus of the state. In this sense, it constitutes the nationalist challenge to the society of states taken to its logical conclusion and therefore in its purest form.

A tentative conclusion may be drawn from this observation: other things being equal, it seems likely that irridentist claims (except where they are supported by powerful secessionist sentiment) will be defeated if and when they are submitted to legal arbitration. The conclusion is tentative because international lawyers themselves will not lay down general principles in the absence of an authoritative judicial ruling on the matter; which in this case is lacking. The fact that the British, Spanish and Argentinian governments have all refused to seek the opinion of the International Court of Justice on the status of Gibraltar and of the Falklands/Malvinas islands suggests that they still have doubts as to which way the ruling would go. Such evidence as does exist suggests strongly that, were an irridentist claim to be submitted to the Court on the basis of historical title only and without reference to the wishes of the inhabitants of the disputed territory, it would be regarded as an anachronistic hangover from the period of prescriptive right.

This conclusion can be inferred as much from claims which have not been submitted to arbitration as from those which have. Although the British have not been prepared to submit their sovereignty over Gibraltar or the Falklands to arbitration one would expect Spain and Argentina (the irridentist states in these disputes) to have sought a judicial ruling if they were sure of the outcome; but both governments have consistently refused to do so.

The same conclusion can be drawn by reviewing the fate of the only competitor to the doctrine of state sovereignty to have survived into the contemporary world, namely the doctrine of suzerainty. Compare for example the case of Tibet[8] with that of Morocco. When the Chinese communists invaded Tibet and the Dalai Lama fled to India in 1951, neither the Indian nor the British government were prepared to support Tibetan claims to national self-determination, and to sponsor Tibet's membership of the United Nations. The reason was that although the British had established a *de facto* protectorate over Tibet, as part of their policy of securing their Indian Empire against Tsarist expansion, neither they, nor the successor Indian government, had ever challenged Chinese claims to suzerainty. Throughout Chinese history strong governments in Peking had exacted tribute from Lhasa and weak ones, by their neglect, allowed the country to assume an isolated independence. There is little doubt that an extremely important factor in their decision to acquiesce in Chinese occupation was that neither the Indian nor the British governments had the ability or inclination to intervene militarily on the side of the Tibetans. But the acknowledged weakness of their own legal position *vis-à-vis* Tibet undoubtedly reinforced their lack of political will.

Morocco's claims to territory beyond its own borders (originally to the whole of Mauritania, more recently to Western Sahara) also rests on a doctrine of prescriptive suzerainty rather than on an appeal to the principle of popular sovereignty, even though these claims have always been popular with the Moroccan population. Originally, the Moroccan sultanate was not a territorial state in the modern sense and the ruler's authority, which was religious as well as secular, extended as far as his armies could march in pursuit of tribute, an event which, as in the case of China's relations with Tibet, occurred only at irregular intervals. However, Moroccan claims have twice been tested in international organizations—first with regard to Mauritania and secondly, to the Western Sahara.

In 1960, Morocco was briefly able to secure the support of the Arab League for its Mauritanian claims, and with the help of the Soviet Union, to keep Mauritania out of the United Nations. By the autumn of 1961 this support had crumbled and although the dispute rumbled on for some time, King Hassan formally abandoned the claim in 1969 and the next year concluded a Treaty of Solidarity with the Mauritanian government.[9] In 1974, acting through the United Nations, Morocco again sought to establish the validity of a territorial claim, this time by requesting an Advisory Opinion from the World Court on the Western Sahara. The Court's judgement accepted that historically there were 'loyalties of allegiance' between Morocco and some tribes living in the territory, but also held that these could not be used to pre-empt or withhold the right of a local population to self-determination.[10]

If this conclusion holds, territorial irridentism may not constitute a permanent or standing threat to the international order. Claims to title of this kind belong to the same intellectual and diplomatic world as arguments about the legitimate ceding of territory to another state as part of a dynastic marriage settlement, or as in the case of Quebec, as a result of defeat in war. Secession, by contrast, does constitute a standing challenge to an international order based on the sovereign state. It does so because, on the one hand, it belongs to the modern 'rationalist' world in which the right to self-determination is held to be a fundamental human right, while, on the other, aggressive war, and therefore the possibility of acquiring title by conquest, is proscribed under the United Nations Charter. The only way out of this impasse is to resort to the conventional interpretation of national self-determination as reflected in the existing state order. This is so obviously a fiction that it must in turn constitute a provocative invitation to secessionist nationalists.

The Preconditions for National Success

The short, but largely accurate answer to the [. . .] question [. . .]—namely, under what circumstances is the nationalist challenge most likely to succeed— is that territorial revision is very rare and so presumably therefore are the circumstances which are conducive to it.

On one account there are in the world about 8,000 identifiably separate cultures; yet there are only 159 independent states.[11] Clearly the odds on a successful nationalist assault on the existing state order are very long. Why should this be so? The obvious answer is again straightforward. The three great waves of modern state creation—in Latin America in the nineteenth century, in Europe after 1919, and in Asia, Africa, the Caribbean and the Pacific after 1945—have all been associated with the collapse of empires. There are no more empires to collapse and therefore very limited poss- ibilities for further state creation by this route. I refer here, of course, to formal imperial structures, not the informal systems of economic and polit- ical influence such as those headed by the United States and the Soviet Union. These hegemonic systems no doubt limit, in varying degrees, the actual independence of their subordinate members, but since they do not obliterate their legal status, any nationalist revolt against the prevailing order, as in Hungary, Czechoslovakia and Poland on the one side, or in Cuba and more recently Central America on the other, is a revolt *within* the existing territorial dispensation not against it.

The conclusion is strengthened by the fact that, for different reasons, the two superpowers share the general bias within the society of states against territorial change. The United States is currently opposed to revolutionary change which is almost invariably viewed by Americans as a victory for communism, despite the justification of secession contained in the Declaration of Independence. The Soviet Union has always regarded support for the principle of national self-determination as a tactic to be pursued when it would advance the cause of the revolution rather than as an end in itself, despite the right of secession which is enshrined in the Soviet constitution. And, as the time approaches when non- Russians will outnumber Russians in the Soviet population, it is a fair guess that, even as a tactic, they are likely to be reluctant to support secessionists in case they reopen the national question within the Soviet Union itself. It is, therefore, not merely legal and political opinion within the state system which has at- tempted to freeze the territorial map; this outcome also corresponds to the interests and policies of the two major powers. Since secessionists must take on the state, they have little choice but to seek external assistance; and on the evidence advanced so far little hope of obtaining it.

It is not true to claim, however, that there has been no territorial change since 1945 other than that brought about by the withdrawal of European imperial power; nor that secessionists have been totally unsuccessful in appealing for outside help, even from the superpowers. This is an area in which the dangers of false analogies are more than usually apparent—except in the underworld of gun-running, there is no international solidarity amongst secessionists and it is difficult therefore to apply the analysis of one case to that of another. Nonetheless the record suggests that there are three sets of circumstances under which the negative conclusion that secession is doomed to failure should be relaxed, or at least qualified.

REGIONAL PATRONAGE

If the two superpowers have been reluctant to support secession, the strategic stalemate between them has on one occasion provided the opportunity for a regional power to come to the assistance of a nationalist movement. To show how restricted such opportunities are in practice one need only compare the pattern of external assistance to the Bengali struggle against West Pakistan, which led to the creation of the state of Bangladesh in 1971, with Somalia's unsuccessful efforts to solicit support for the struggle of the Ogaden Somali against Ethiopia. In the former case, American diplomatic support for Pakistan was cancelled out by Soviet support for India; and although the American sixth fleet manoeuvred in the Bay of Bengal, and the Indian Prime Minister, Mrs Gandhi, signed a friendship treaty with the Soviet Union before she took any independent action herself, India was able to intervene, and to inflict a humiliating defeat on the Pakistani forces, without seriously risking the escalation of the conflict. India, of course, had interests of its own in coming to the support of the East Pakistan Bengalis: the civil war was inflicting an intolerable and politically dangerous refugee burden on Bengal, notoriously one of India's most volatile states; at the same time the dismemberment of Pakistan would put India's hegemony in the sub-continent beyond question. For a year or so the new state was kept out of the United Nations, but by 1974 the *fait accompli* had been accepted and Bangladesh was recognised, even by Pakistan itself.[12]

By contrast, in the Horn of Africa, while the two superpowers were similarly in stalemate, there was no local power with sufficient interest in the conflict to defy the norms of international society. Successive Somali governments recognised that they could only secure their pan-Somali goals with external support. But neither the Soviet Union, with which Somalia was allied between 1969–1977, nor the United States after the Russians had been expelled from Mogadishu were willing to challenge Ethiopia's territorial integrity. To have done so would not only have risked a direct confrontation between the two superpowers, but would also have alienated the rest of Africa whose governments were determined to maintain the existing territorial settlement. It is not possible to say which of these two 'scenarios' is more typical of the contemporary international scene, but the fact that Bangladesh is the only completely new state created by secession since 1945 should perhaps provide a warning against generalisation from this single example.

SUPERPOWER COMPETITION

Although the American and Soviet governments have refused to commit themselves openly in support of nationalist movements whose aim is to secede from an existing state, their ideological rivalry has often led them to encourage ethnic separatism covertly and manipulatively. In such cases their motive is presumably to weaken the other side or secure a short-run tactical advantage in their own power political struggle. As we have already noted, Soviet support for the principle of national self-determination has always been primarily tactical, so it was a matter of little surprise that they supported the Eritrean struggle before the Ethiopian revolution and withdrew their support afterwards. Similarly, at the height of the Sino-Soviet dispute, which was also a period of close relations between China and Pakistan, the Soviet Union allegedly supported the Baluchi nationalists in their insurgency, but took care to stop well short of encouraging them to press their cause to the point of secession from Pakistan.[13]

The Americans have also frequently encouraged separatist movements as a way of obtaining leverage in their global diplomacy. One of the clearest examples is provided by the support which the Shah of Iran and the Americans together provided to the Kurdish rebellion in Iraq.

In 1975, a leaked United States Congressional intelligence report made it abundantly clear that an independent Kurdistan was not on the agenda. Instead the United States 'preferred . . . that the insurgents simply continue a level of hostilities sufficient to sap the resources of our allies' [Iran] neighbouring country [Iraq]. This policy was not imparted to our clients [the Kurds] who were encouraged to continue fighting.'[14]

Although the issue is not one of separatism, it seems clear that American support for Jonas Savimbi's UNITA in Angola is similarly dictated by considerations of extraneous political expediency. In this case the motive appears to be American hostility to the MPLA government whose victory in the Angolan civil war depended on Soviet and Cuban assistance, and their desire to pressure the Angolan government into cooperating with the United States and South Africa to secure an international settlement of the Namibian dispute. Presumably, from the nationalist point of view, such unprincipled support is better than nothing, particularly as it allows them to continue the struggle. Since international politics are notoriously unpredictable, for some nationalists who have no illusions about the realist political game, accepting such help may in the end prove worthwhile. However, if the Kurds, whose peoples are divided between Iran, Iraq, Turkey and the Soviet Union, are taken as the model, this seems most unlikely.

CONSTITUTIONAL SEPARATION

We must finally consider the possibility of secessionist demands being peacefully accommodated, of states putting themselves into partial liquidation in much the same way as the European powers scuttled their African empires after 1960. This final qualification to the conclusion that the territorial map has been frozen into its present shape once and for all is the most conjectural of all.

If we discount the breakup of Malaysia, which was itself a creation of British decolonisation policy, and of such paper unions as the United Arab Republic (Egypt and Syria) and the Union of African states (Ghana, Guinea and Mali), none of which resulted in any real integration, the only relatively peaceful modern secessions were Norway from Sweden in 1905 and the Irish Free State from the United Kingdom in 1921. What if anything, of a general nature, can be said of the Swedish and British decisions to acquiesce in nationalist demands for constitutional separation?

Neither was unacrimonious, particularly the secession of Ireland which, given the turbulent history of British occupation, should arguably not be described as peaceful separation at all. On the other hand neither the British nor the Swedish governments were in the end prepared to preserve the unity of the state if that meant forcefully suppressing constitutional demands for separation and plunging their countries into civil war.

Behind their reluctance to preserve the unity of the state at all costs there were, it seems, two kinds of structural restraint. First, in all four countries there was an historical sense of identity, which preceded the nationalist era—and was generally acknowledged. In the case of Sweden and Norway the union only dated from 1815 and was stated to be between two equal kingdoms.[15] In the case of Ireland, partly as a result of the machinations of the Protestant Ascendency, the English had never succeeded in co-opting the local Irish elite into the British system as they had done in Scotland and Wales.[16]

Secondly, at the time of these secessions, the contending parties were all led by liberal nationalists. It is true that the Republican issue introduced an additional complication to the British conflict with Ireland, but in the end, although it served to fuel the post-independence civil war in Ireland, its importance was symbolic rather than ideological in any deep political sense. The Norwegian and Irish nationalists shared the same political values and belief in the parliamentary system as the Swedes and the British; and this finally eroded their enthusiasm for maintaining unity by occupation.

Since the 1960s, the countries of the industrial west have witnessed something of an ethnic revival.[17] Where this neo-nationalist sentiment has been used as the basis of an armed insurgency against the state, and as a justification for urban terrorism (as with the Basque movement ETA or the Provisional IRA), it has been resisted with considerable determination and often ruthlessness. Where it has been used to mobilise a constituency within the framework of constitutional politics (as in Scotland and Wales in the 1960s and 1970s), there have generally been attempts by the state to accommodate regional demands for greater autonomy, always stopping well short of any discussion of independence. However, what would happen if having been granted a measure of autonomy, ethnic regions were to demand their right of self-determination and constitutional separation?

It looked for a time in the 1970s as though Quebec might provide a test case for the industrial countries on this question. The tide of Quebecois separatism seems to have ebbed, but if the demand for an independent Quebec was to re-emerge, and to be demonstrably supported by a substantial majority of the province's citizens, it seems unlikely that its separation would be resisted by force of arms, even though logically there would be no difference between the challenge posed by Quebec to the integrity of the Canadian state and that posed by Biafra to Nigeria or Bangladesh to Pakistan.

My conjecture is that while separation will undoubtedly be resisted, if the demand persists, it may be easier to accommodate in industrial societies than in other kinds of society where all opposition tends to be defined as treason. The plausibility of this conjecture rests on an assumption that a shared political culture, in which a belief in individual civil and political rights is deeply entrenched, will act ultimately as a constraint on the use of state power to suppress those rights. It is supported also by the vertical integration of the modern international system [. . .].

The integration of the modern world economy under the impact of liberal capitalism, has in many ways contributed to the modern nation-state, while the alleged inequity of the international division of labour has often fuelled nationalist reactions. At the same time, for those who are deeply involved in the world economy, it has undoubtedly raised the costs of dismembering the state. Modern enterprises generally prefer economic to political risk taking and are in a myriad of ways dependent on the state to provide them with a stable environment in which to operate.

[*Nationalism and International Society* (Cambridge University Press: Cambridge, 1990), 55–69.]

JOHN ARMSTRONG

44   Towards a Post-Communist World

Ukraine

Soviet observers realized that without Ukraine the USSR or its successor would cease to be a superpower. Moreover, as the days following the abortive coup demonstrated, the much smaller Belarus is likely to follow Ukraine's lead.[1] The internal situation of Ukraine is, however, more complicated than that of any other union republic. Although the Christian–Muslim fault line lightly touches the Ukrainian republic, the Orthodox–Catholic division is critical. This dividing line cuts across the West Ukrainian area of 10 million people, but some districts (notably Transcarpathia) are mixed. For West Ukraine, which is the bastion of the independence movement, ethno-religious factors have been fundamental. All nationally conscious Ukrainians (as well as liberal Russians) deplore Russian Orthodox Church collaboration, after 1944, with the communist regime in violently suppressing the Ukrainian Catholic Church. The Orthodox argument that it was merely redressing a wrong that is four centuries old—the transfer of numerous West Ukrainian Orthodox congregations to Roman allegiance—rings hollow when confronted by the reality of past KGB repression and manifest West Ukrainian fervor for Byzantine-rite Catholicism today. A more serious problem for the future is friction between Greek Catholics, who have regained their ecclesiastical structure and many church buildings, and the restored Ukrainian Autocephalous Orthodox Church (likewise opposed to the Moscow Patriarchate) that competes with it in some West Ukrainian regions.

During 1988–91, West Ukrainian enthusiasm for independence was partly offset by popular sentiments in the ethnically mixed southeastern region. This region was the power base from which many Communist party and KGB officials trained in Brezhnev's Dnepropetrovsk apparatus originated. In 1972, Petro Shelest, the Ukrainian republic first secretary, was removed for fostering a distinctive Ukrainian culture; his replacement was V. V. Shcherbyts'kyi, a hard-line member of the Dnepropetrovsk clique. He harshly repressed literary dissent, and remained a key factor in central control of Ukraine until 1989. Months later (in March 1990), the party leaders who succeeded Shcherbyts'kyi were able to obtain a large parliamentary majority in a fairly honest election; in March 1991, a 70-percent majority endorsed the Union Treaty.

The nuances of the referendum in Ukraine were significant, however. The Ukrainian parliament had added a second question to gauge the population's views on Ukrainian sovereignty. Sovereignty was affirmed in all but one province—the Crimea—by majorities often greater than those supporting the Union Treaty. In itself, it is hard to grasp what acceptance of the elastic term 'sovereignty' implied; but voting for it was a learning experience on the road to independence. West Ukrainian provinces rejected both the Union Treaty and sovereignty by overwhelming majorities, voting instead for a third option—outright independence.

More important, perhaps, than formal votes were the actions of Ukrainian miners. In the ethnically mixed Donbass, coal miners followed the lead of the Kuzbass (Western Siberia) miners by striking during the late summer of 1989. The Donbass miners sharply rejected calls by Ukrainian nationalist emissaries to turn the strike into a pro-independence movement. More recently, though, both Kuzbass and Donbass miners, disappointed by the results of strikes over purely economic questions, have moved toward advancing political programs. For some Ukrainian mine crews, these included an endorsement of sovereignty and insistence on withholding Ukrainian products from the center.

The miners' lukewarm reaction was a major factor pushing the Ukrainian popular front *Rukh* toward a moderate position. Its organizers, who stem disproportionately from West Ukraine, had earlier advanced programs for rapid cultural Ukrainization as well as church freedom and imminent independence. Events in the Donbass enabled the large contingent of literary dissidents from the 'Dnieper' lands (central Ukraine) to assume the leading role in *Rukh*. To them, it was evident that a program for economic gains and gradual movement toward independence would attract the greatest support. They also endorsed equal rights for all cultural groups, including use of Russian in parliament. Numerous Russian deputies, including a major parliamentary spokesman from Dnepropetrovsk, as well as several Jews and Poles, were endorsed by *Rukh*.

During 1990–91, the KGB continued to harass *Rukh* parliamentary deputies. Remarkably, however, deputies and ministers elected with the help of Communist party endorsements began to advance measures for Ukrainian economic autonomy. Restrictions (based on ration coupons issued to republic residents) were placed on the export of the bountiful Ukrainian harvests. In April 1991, the republic's Council of Ministers decreed that 'With the aim of carrying out the Declaration of the State Sovereignty of Ukraine and relevant legislative acts of Ukraine, it is stipulated that conscripts shall be sent to perform their service in military units located on the republic's territory. Citizens of the Ukrainian SSR may be sent beyond its borders for this purpose only with their voluntary written consents.[2]

Immediately after the failure of the August coup, the Ukrainian parliament declared independence. Strong cultural and religious ties connect a high proportion of residents of Ukraine to Russia; but disgust over failure of economic reform and fear of a new authoritarian centralism tipped the balance. A week later, however, Ukraine and the Russian republic signed a treaty pledging economic and military cooperation, while reserving the right to conduct separate foreign policies. If the present Ukrainian government under Leonid Kravchuk is sincere in its pursuit of independence, the status of Ukraine (and Belarus) as founding members of the United Nations could be crucial, for UN members are committed to support one another against overt aggression.

Ukraine's relatively compact territory and absence of climatic extremes makes transportation far easier than in the Russian republic. Although energy reserves are much smaller than Russia's, such minerals as manganese are plentiful. Above all, Ukraine has demonstrated that it can feed its population, not only because natural conditions are more favorable but because lengthy pre-Soviet experience prepared many of its rural people for individual farming by avoiding the common Russian practice of periodic redistribution of land among peasant families, which were thereby deprived of incentives for careful long-term land management. Traces of anti-urban ideology persist, but *Rukh* (drawing on the experience of its members in underground dissident cooperation) has made advances in overcoming antisemitism, which many Ukrainians now associate with extreme Russian nationalism.

A big problem—far greater than in most state nations—is recruitment and training of numerous competent, practical civil servants. Avoidance of ethnic discrimination and acceptance of capable, flexible holdovers from the Soviet economic and governmental administrations who had not been involved in acts of repression will be essential. Temporary employment of a small cadre of West European administrators to help introduce Western practices could provide a crucial balancing element. The biggest problem is development of a stable, orderly civil society to complement traditional Ukrainian love of liberty. In this respect, Ukraine's future is less secure than that of the East Central European northern tier. By far the strongest support for Ukrainian civil society would be membership in the European Community. Ukraine is, however, larger in population than any present member except Germany, Britain, Italy, and France. The EC, which apparently intends to delay membership for Poland, Czechoslovakia, and Hungary (all historical participants in the European international order) until the end of this decade, will be cautious about extending full membership to such a large, untried unit as Ukraine. However, informal West European counsel and cooperation can serve as a useful balance to economic cooperation with Russia.

Russia

It would be obtuse as well as ungenerous to exclude Russians from the prospect of eventual membership in a Europe from the Atlantic to the Urals— or, indeed, from the Atlantic to the Pacific. Cooperation as an equal with other former Soviet republics in a restricted association will notably enhance Russia's position in relation to Europe. The ultimate nature of the present Commonwealth is unclear. Even before its formation in December 1991, however, respected Russian voices questioned the wisdom of tight linkage between Russia and some other parts of the USSR. Solzhenitsyn, for one, contended that Russians must 'get rid of grand imperial thinking inherited from the Communists, the inflated "Soviet patriotism" that never really existed and takes such pride in "the great Soviet power".' He added: 'By the secession of 12 republics, Russia, with this seeming sacrifice, will liberate itself for precious inner development.'[3] Solzhenitsyn hoped the two smaller Slavic republics would remain with Russia, but appears to recognize their inherent right to secede. With some justification, he suggests that the northern districts of Kazakhstan, which have large Slavic majorities, should remain with Russia.

On the basis of Solzhenitsyn's reasoning, small Muslim autonomous republics in the North Caucasus ought to have the right to leave the Russian republic, perhaps entering some form of union with Azerbaijan. It is practically impossible to grant independence to the larger Tartar and Bashkir autonomous republics, which are ethnically intermixed with Russians and separated from other Muslim regions by extensive Slavic areas; but they deserve guarantees of complete cultural autonomy. In very exceptional cases, the principle of border adjustment (broached by Yel'tsin but renounced in favor of maintaining existing union–republic borders) might be extended to some anomalous border districts, although certainly not to Russian migrants in the urban centers of other republics.

Were Russia to demonstrate a determination to separate from the Central Asian and Transcaucasian republics (except for alliance arrangements where mutually agreeable), it would demonstrate Moscow's resolve to renounce its ostensible geopolitical capacity for adventures in the Middle East or South Asia. All erstwhile imperial powers (Solzhenitsyn points to Japan) profited from such renunciations—and only additional renunciations by the great powers can restore a truly multilateral world balance.

Russia would still stretch from St Petersburg to Vladivostok, but it would confront greater problems than most other East European nations. Although Russians did not invent them, anti-urban ideologies have repeatedly hindered employment of skilled foreigners and members of diasporas in Russia. Such thinking merges with remnants of communist populism, which 'rises up like a wall, blocking the way. "They'll make a fortune"—that is its chief objection to nonstate trade.'[4] Russians possess a great, though flawed, administrative tradition. Like Ukrainians, although to a lesser extent, Russian civil administration can profit from a temporary injection of administrative experts from Western Europe (which originally inspired the Russian administrative practice).

Although the tradition of individual farming is weaker in Russia than in Ukraine, the North Caucasus steppe and the Volga-Kursk black-earth zone can eventually produce an abundant grain supply. The grey-earth region from Smolensk to Nizhniy Novgorod with adequate drainage and fertilization could produce large potato crops. Perhaps Russia and Belarus could follow the example set when Germany leased extensive eastern tracts with similar drainage and soil problems to an experienced Dutch firm. Industrial renovation depends, as elsewhere, on plant modernization and speedy introduction of the market economy. Fortunately, Russia's huge oil and gas reserves, if exploited with the aid of foreign technology, could provide much of the capital required.

Everything depends on whether the Russians, like the Poles and many others, can endure the long wait for significantly improved living standards. In August 1991, Russian urbanites put the world in their debt with a demonstration of civic courage rarely seen in the last half century. Historically, though, Russian civic enthusiasm is often followed by withdrawal from active political participation. Coupled with the dissatisfactions arising from several more years of economic stagnation, the cycle of public opinion could make way for another attempt at dictatorship.

Overall Prospects

Recent events in Eastern Europe demonstrate that aroused public opinion can advance democracy even among populations accustomed to authoritarian rule. These events also undermine Metternichian ideas of an inviolable status quo beloved by Western chancelleries and by much of the media and scholarly world. New states are arising, borders are being altered, and even certain population transfers may be forthcoming. Present leaders—especially in Europe—are right to be concerned about the constant danger of violence during such changes, as the example of Yugoslavia demonstrates so tragically. Much depends on whether firm but prudent multilateral intervention can facilitate change without violence.

[. . .] Attainment of adequate living standards appears to be most likely in the northern-tier states of East Central Europe (with the possible exception of Poland), the Baltic states, and Ukraine. Prospects for Southeast European states, with the exception of Slovenia (if it is able to maintain independence) are jeopardized by ethnic strife; the same holds true for the Transcaucasus. Russia's prospects for sufficiently rapid economic growth are endangered by a combination of geographic limitations and the intensity and duration of communist rule. Muslim nations, while certainly not immune to consumer pressures, have considered adherence to ethno-religious lifestyles more important than the creation of modern economies.

The demand for stable ethno-religious communities and the spiritual values they foster that appears so strong among Muslims is somewhat less strong among Catholic nations headed by Poland, and among Orthodox groups like Georgians and Serbs. Predictably, the demand appears somewhat weaker overall in nations of mixed religious background—Czechoslovakia, Hungary, Ukraine, Russia, and Belarus.

Marginal tradeoffs may be feasible among demands for material improvement, ethno-religious community, and the third goal of responsive government, popular participation, and the rule of law. But abandonment of these prerequisites of democracy would mean a return to oppression, with no guarantee that the first two sets of demands would be met. For most East European nations, experience with democracy's complexities is too limited to make one confident that it will be retained in periods of economic stagnation or ethnic strife. Exceptions are Czechoslovakia, Hungary, the Baltic states, and possibly Poland, Armenia, and Slovenia. At the opposite pole are the formerly Soviet Muslim nations, which embody many democratic elements in their ethno-religious lifestyle, but consider significant aspects of Western democracy to be dispensable. Georgians and the antagonistic Southeast European nations also tend to treat democracy as secondary. If this analysis is correct, efforts to support recent democratic trends should be concentrated on the large Slavic nations—Poland, Ukraine, Russia—whose decisions for or against democracy are apt to determine the future of Eastern Europe.

I am cognizant of the temerity of an individual observer's attempt to specify alternative futures for such a vast, diverse region. We stand, however, at a rare moment of history when a large segment of the world map (one particularly significant for our own civilization) is being redrawn. The last time Western opinion had a chance to influence such a sweeping transformation was after World War I, when the Wilsonians' best intentions were thwarted in considerable measure by ignorance of the complexities of that same East European region. In preparing the preceding pages, I have been struck by the insights of such towering figures as Milosz, Solzhenitsyn, and John Paul II. If poets and popes feel called upon to point to a better future for their region, can the pedestrian observer trained throughout a lifetime for this moment refrain from endeavoring to fill in details of the prognosis?

['Nationalism in the Former Soviet Empire', *Problems of Communism*, 41/1–2 (Jan.–Apr. 1992), 129–33.]

Section VII

Beyond Nationalism?

INTRODUCTION

Can we envisage a world without nations or nationalism? To what extent has the concept of national identity been transformed in a global era? These issues are being debated vigorously in the light of the vast changes associated with economic, political, and cultural 'globalization' on the one hand, and the resurgence of ethnic nationalisms on the other. For Anthony Richmond, we are moving into a post-industrial society in which, beneath an overall allegiance to the main power blocs, denser networks using computerized technology and telecommunications are encouraging the proliferation of ethnic nationalism. Post-industrialism, rather than rendering nationalism obsolete, furnishes new bases for ethnic movements and cultures.

This is also a theme to be found in the broader historical analysis of William McNeill. He regards polyethnic hierarchy as the norm of civilized societies throughout history. Only in Europe between 1750 and 1920 did the aberrant ideology of national unity based on ethnic homogeneity hold sway, and even then only partially. With the decline of classical education, the rise of mass communications, the revulsion against racism, the massive influx of immigrants, and the internationalization of economic and military relations, specialized polyethnic hierarchy is once again replacing nationalism in an era of globalized economies.

This has entailed a profound change in our concepts of national identity. A number of scholars have drawn attention to the increasingly ambivalent, fragmented, and hybrid character of older and well-established national identities in the West; for Homi Bhabha and his associates, the influx of immigrants, minorities, and ex-colonized peoples has 'split' the pedagogical nationalist narrative from the everyday 'performative' reproduction of the people and redefined national identity in terms of 'the Other'. The entry of women into the national arena, as cultural and biological reproducers of the nation and as transmitters of its values, has also redefined the content and boundaries of ethnicity and the nation; the central role of women in ethnic and national culture is clearly demonstrated by Floya Anthias and Nira Yuval-Davis in their introduction to an influential volume on the relatively new and complex field of gender, ethnicity, and nationalism.

If the concept of 'national identity' is under scrutiny from within, it is also being transformed by external pressures and wider forms of association. This is the context of the often passionate debates about the project of European unification. An important issue here is whether a European cultural identity must resemble, and so challenge, existing national identities or become *sui generis*. For Philip Schlesinger, the idea of 'Europe' signifies a new cultural battlefield which is unlikely to supersede powerfully entrenched national, and ethnic, identities. Given the proliferation of intense national conflicts, it is difficult to foresee any transcendence of the nation or nationalism.

45 Ethnic Nationalism and Post-Industrialism

The central problem facing sociologists and political scientists has always been the problem of integration. Ever since the problem was first stated in Plato's *Republic*, two solutions have been expounded. The first represents societies as being held together by the coercive power of the dominant groups whose interests are, in the last resort, maintained through military force. This force is used to repel external sources of threat as well as for the maintenance of order within the society. The alternative view emphasizes the importance of a common value system which binds people together in a social contract or consensus concerning the necessity for order.[1] In practice, of course, both principles operate simultaneously and with varying degrees of emphasis. Even the most coercive regime must endeavour to translate naked force into legitimated authority, if all its energies and resources are not to be dissipated. Once achieved, a position of power can only be maintained if there is effective control over the agencies that disseminate information and influence human consciousness. The central value system must include legitimating principles that justify the existing differential distribution of economic status and political power. At the same time, varying degrees of economic division of labour and social differentiation give rise to mutual dependency which also contributes to the maintenance of social cohesion.[2]

The precise form of this relationship between economic and political power, on the one hand, and types of legitimation and social integration, vary with levels of technological and economic development. The abstract relationship is represented in Figure 1. Political power is exercised through control over the coercive forces, including the police and the military. The state is the supreme coercive power and those who control the armed forces ultimately exercise sovereignty. These forces are normally required to protect the territorial boundaries of the state but, in times of crisis, may also be used to quell internal threats to the ruling elites. However, in order to maintain their position, the elites must also exercise control over the agencies that legitimate their power and convert it into authority and the rule of law. The legitimating agencies include the judicial system, the education system and all those organizations concerned with the dissemination of information and the generation of belief systems containing core values. They are responsible for generating dominant ideologies which justify and sustain the existing distribution of political and economic power. These ideologies also rationalize and mobilize support for the use of coercion, for both external and internal purposes. There is a close link between the nature of the economic system, including the division of labour and the distribution of economic status, and the particular forms of social integration characteristic of the society in question. In the last resort the

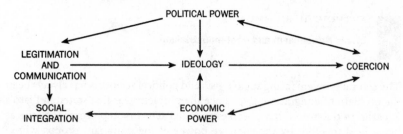

FIG. 1.   Power, legitimacy and social integration

economic elites also rely upon coercive measures to maintain the status quo but, in normal conditions, legitimating agencies such as education and the law are sufficient to maintain social order.

Figure 2 illustrates the relationship between economic and political power and the typical mode of social integration characteristic of a feudal economy and a theocratic state. Under these conditions there is a close alliance between Church and state in which the agencies of legitimation are dominated by the clergy, who also exercise direct political power. The King or other head of state rules by 'divine right' and is generally autocratic. The Church exercises effective control over both the judicial and the educational system. The dominant ideologies are those of the religion in question which sanctifies the use of military force in holy wars against the infidels. Internal rebellion will be coercively controlled by a ruler who is a 'defender of the faith'. Although such theocratic states have lasted to the present day they have their origins in a feudal type economy in which economic and social roles are essentially ascriptive. The characteristic form of social integration associated with such a system is that of a territorial community or 'Gemeinschaft'.[3] Such communities are comparatively small, often involving an extended kinship or tribal system with a restricted division of labour and little social differentiation. The value systems binding such a community together are those of the dominant religion, generally imposed by the priesthood through oral tradition on an often illite-

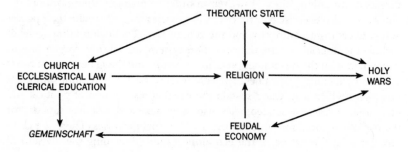

FIG. 2.   Power and legitimacy in a Gemeinschaft society

rate population. In such a system the law courts are ecclesiastical. Orthodoxy is maintained through inquisitions and harsh punishments. The classical form of the theocratic system was to be found in medieval Europe as it conducted its holy wars against Islam. Today some Islamic countries still exhibit the characteristics of such a theocratic state although their stability under conditions of rapid industrialization and social change is threatened.[4]

Figure 3 illustrates the relationship between political and economic power in the secular state that replaced the theocracies, following the decline of feudalism and the rise of the modern capitalist industrial system. The secular state retained many of the trappings of its predecessor but effective power shifted from autocratic monarchs to more democratic parliamentary institutions, and a generally independent judiciary. At the same time, control over the education system shifted from the Church to the state. A process of functional differentiation occurred between the various agencies of legitimation. Nevertheless, there was a general consensus on the dominant value system, whose central unifying principle was nationalism. In the industrialized countries the unity of Church and state was replaced by a unity of Nation and state. In fact those two concepts came to be linked in a way that is critical to our understanding of the emergence of ethnic nationalism in the later post-industrial societies. The nation-state in the industrial era was an assimilating agency. Majority groups and dominant elites were generally intolerant of ethnic variation within its boundaries. The internal cohesion and social integration of the nation-state depended upon an elimination of previous local, tribal or provincial attachments and the inculcation of loyalty to the larger territorial unit dominated by the secular state. Eighteenth- and nineteenth-century nationalism was a unifying force which brought together people of diverse backgrounds at the price of subordinating their ethnic loyalties to the larger entity. The dominant ideology was that of nationalism which idealized the state and deprecated the maintenance of any linguistic, religious or other sentiments that might conflict with loyalty to it.[5] The holy wars of an earlier era were replaced with the patriotic wars of the nineteenth and twentieth centuries which determined and maintained boundaries of these newly forged

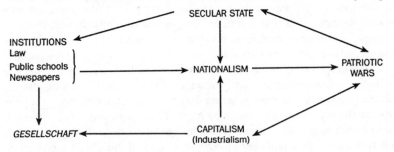

FIG. 3.   Power and legitimacy in a *Gesellschaft* society

nation-states. These countries also engaged in imperialist expansion outside Europe, in competing for access to raw materials in less developed regions. The agencies of legitimation were unified in support for patriotic wars against other nation-states. Ethnic loyalties, which sometimes transcended the boundaries of these states, were seen to be subversive and every attempt was made to suppress them.

The division of labour and the social differentiation that accompanied the rise of industrial capitalism created a new type of social integration, based upon economic and social interdependence, formal organizations, bureaucratic structures and *Gesellschaft*. As the economic system became more complex and technologically advanced, the franchise was extended to lesser property holders and eventually the adult population at large. A literate work force and electorate became essential. The public (state) school system became an important instrument of legitimation, an essential assimilating force in polyethnic societies, and the means of inculcating patriotic values. Nationalism in its most extreme forms glorified the state and, in its fascist manifestations, used genocidal policies to eliminate ethnic diversity.

The rise of capitalist industrialism also forged even stronger links between the economy and the military. Even under a feudal system the pursuit of holy wars had important economic and technological consequences. Taxation was never sufficient to pay for the wars in question, thus giving rise to inflationary pressures. However, these also provided an economic stimulus that reduced unemployment and created much profit for the craftsmen who made the armour and weapons used in the crusades and other religious wars. Later, the capitalist economic system became highly dependent upon the growth of an armaments industry whose enormous expenditures not only contributed to many technological advances but were a source of tremendous profit to the companies that manufactured the increasingly sophisticated weaponry. Wars, and the necessary preparation for them, were closely associated with the trade cycles of the nineteenth century. The rearmament that occurred in the mid-1930s provided the necessary anti-deflationary stimulus that brought Europe and America out of the great depression of that period. The capitalist system became increasingly dependent upon the exploitation of nationalism, not only in the advanced industrial countries but also in the Third World. Patriotic support for ever growing defense budgets led to a world-wide industry in new and second hand armaments that has now reached astronomical proportions.[6]

The concept of postindustrialism has been used to describe a variety of technological, economic and social changes that are currently taking place in advanced industrial societies, whether they are of the capitalist, free-enterprise type or the socialist, state-controlled form. There is evidence that these advanced industrial states are converging in their increasing interdependence as sub-systems within a global economy.[7] The roots of this global economy go back to the beginning of the industrial revolution and the mercantilism which established trade connections between Europe and the rest of the world.[8] The expanding nation-states of Europe established a colonial domination, involving economic exploitation backed by military force, in many parts of Africa, Asia and the New World. What distinguishes the global economy of the postindustrial era is the emergence of multinational companies whose capital investments take advantage of cheap labour supplies outside the already industrialized countries. This has given rise to a designation of the global economy into 'core' regions, 'semi-peripheral' and 'peripheral' areas, with varying degrees of dependency upon the metropolitan centres. In fact, the system is more complex than this trichotomy suggests, as the boundaries between core and periphery are constantly changing. Furthermore, the industrialized countries themselves are undergoing rapid economic change and do not constitute a unitary system. There is a global division of labour even among industrialized countries. However, these postindustrial developments and the emergence of a global economy have threatened the viability of the traditional nation-state. North America and the countries of Western Europe are clearly in transition, but the movement toward supranational states is threatening national sovereignty.[9]

Figure 4 illustrates the relationship between the economic and power structures of the emerging supranational states and corresponding forms of social integration. The ultimate coercive power rests with military alliances that transcend the boundaries of nation-states. The world is now divided by the confrontation of superpowers and by a precarious balance of nuclear terror. Each side has the capacity to totally annihilate the other and to destroy much of the rest of the world. Through the genetic damage which the use of nuclear weapons would entail, the destructive capacity extends into future generations of the whole human race. Under these conditions no nation-state, not even the largest and most powerful members of these opposing military alliances, can act independently.[10]

The power of the old nation-states is on the wane as they become more and more dependent upon military, economic, legal and social structures that transcend their territorial boundaries. In the case of Britain, and a growing

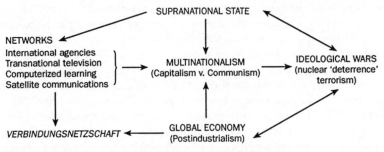

FIG. 4.   Power and legitimacy in a *Verbindungsnetzschaft society*

number of countries in Western Europe, the North Atlantic Treaty Organization (NATO), the Treaty of Rome and the European Common Market place severe restrictions upon their autonomy. New judicial agencies are emerging that restrict the freedom of nation-states and require conformity to international laws and agreements. Agencies such as the International Monetary Fund and the World Bank use powerful economic sanctions to demand conformity to economic and social policies that are against the interests of particular countries but maintain the global economic system. New bureaucratic structures are springing up which will eventually supersede those of the old nation-states. Similar developments are occurring in the Communist dominated countries although the struggle for independence from the Soviet Union continues, just as Western countries resent the growing domination of the United States. War, and the justification for military build up and nuclear deterrents, is no longer legitimated in terms of patriotic sentiments of a nationalistic type. Global confrontation is now expressed in terms of the overriding ideologies of Communism and anti-Communism.

The postindustrial era has been brought about by technological revolution. This revolution has been most evident in the spheres of computerization and automation, on the one hand, and in communications systems on the other. The full impact of this revolution has yet to be experienced. Previously labour-intensive industries, in both the manufacturing and the service sectors, will come to depend increasingly upon these new technologies. Already, world-wide telecommunications systems link individuals and organizations in complex networks of information exchange. Banks, insurance companies, stock markets and multinational companies, in every industrial sector, are now linked by these systems that permit instantaneous exchanges of information and the rapid movement of currency and capital from one country to another. At the domestic level our lives are being revolutionized by transnational radio and television networks aided by satellite communication systems. The education system is also being transformed by the use of television and various systems of computerized information storage and retrieval. Computerized learning systems are beginning to take over from traditional classroom instruction. Interactive computerized communication systems will remove the element of passivity which has characterized listening and viewing in the past.

A new principle of social organization has been introduced which will transform the social system of postindustrial societies. When the industrial revolution brought with it formal organizations of the *Gesellschaft* type it did not completely replace territorial communities of the *Gemeinschaft* type, but the former diminished in importance as people became more involved in transactional relationships and specialized economic and social roles. By the same token, the complex social and communication networks, the *Verbindung-snetzschaft*, that are characteristic of postindustrial societies will not entirely replace territorial communities or formal organizations. However, relationships based upon interpersonal, interorganizational, international and mass communication networks, will be the characteristic mode of social interaction in the future.[10]

The dominant ideologies of the postindustrial period are those which endeavour to rationalize and justify the activities of multinational companies, on the one hand, and multinational socialist regimes, on the other. In economic terms, the interests of national power elites are no longer aligned with the interests of nationally based economic organizations, whether under private enterprise or state socialism. Instead, the supranational power elites are aligned with the interests of multinational economic organizations, whether these are capitalist or socialist. The military-industrial complex is no longer an instrument of the nation-state for the pursuit of patriotic wars. It has become the instrument of the supranational state for the pursuit of ideological wars between the capitalist and communist superpowers. Even the civil wars within existing nation-states have become ideological rather than patriotic. They involve economic and military support from external supranational states. Insurgent movements, whether in the advanced industrial countries or the Third World, are linked through complex communication networks with each other and with the dominant suprastate agencies that encourage them. This is true whether the insurgent movements identify with the ideologies of Capitalism or Communism. Terrorism no longer operates within national boundaries but has become an international phenomenon involving bombing, hi-jacking and hostage taking in almost every country of the world.

The emergence of postindustrialism has profound implications for the future of ethnic consciousness, ethnic organizations and ethnic nationalist movements. In a theocratic state, variations in language, national identification and ethnic group formation are acceptable as long as all the sources of variation are subordinated to a single religious ideology. The ultimate power structure depends upon a close relationship between the religious, military and economic elites. There can be no religious toleration. Sectarian movements or competing religious faiths, including secular political philosophies, must be ruthlessly suppressed. Ethnic nationalism can survive under the conditions created by theocratic states as long as the ultimate power rests with the religious authorities. This was evident during the Catholic domination of Europe up to the Reformation and, to some extent, is characteristic of Islamic states today.

However, the theocratic structure of power was undermined as feudal economies gave way to industrialization. New power elites emerged that were no longer identified with the old religious order. The secular state, characteristic of industrialized countries, could afford religious toleration. The vestiges of established religions may have lingered on but religious reformist groups, new sects and widespread agnosticism or atheism were compatible with the new nationalist ideologies. However, the old link between Church and state was replaced by a link between nation and state. The process of industrialization was a powerful assimilatory force that compelled people to relinquish the *Gemeinschaft* attachments of the rural community in favour of the *Gesellschaft* relationships of the city. No matter how heterogeneous the ethnic origins of the city-dwelling industrial workers may have been, new loyalties were generated that ensured the solidarity of the new nation-state. The nineteenth century, and the first half of the twentieth century, in Europe and in North America, was a period during which old ethnic identities gave way to new nationalistic loyalties. Wars of religion were replaced by the Napoleonic era, and two world wars in which the patriotism of the linguistic and ethnic minorities within the nation-states was severely tested. The willingness to be conscripted into the military became a critical issue. Ethnic minorities that resisted conscription, or who were suspected of less than total loyalty to the nation at war, were subjected to severe penalties. In Britain the loyalty of Scottish and Welsh minorities was rarely in question but the Irish were less inclined to fight in the British cause. In Canada, there was a similar disinclination on the part of French-speaking Quebecers. In other parts of Canada, European immigrants and their children were often unjustly suspected of unpatriotic sentiments and behaviour. During the Second World War the Canadian treatment of Japanese Canadians is evidence of coercive assimilation and relinquishment of ethnic loyalties that was demanded. The McCarthy era in the United States was probably the last attempt to impose a single nationalistic ideology and to regard any non-conformity as evidence of 'un-American activities'. Already, the ideology of the new supranational state was emerging, that of anti-Communism.

Among first-generation immigrants in an industrialized society the maintenance of strong ethnic loyalties was seen as unpatriotic. In Europe, where changing boundaries of nation-states left many linguistic minorities politically isolated from those with whom they had cultural links, the incorporation of minorities into a single unit ready to fight in defence of the country concerned, became a major question in the nineteenth and twentieth centuries. At the same time, in the New World, waves of immigrants were to be incorporated as citizens of their new countries. In both the United States and Canada, the question of inculcating loyalty to the state continued to be an important political issue until after the Second World War. As the second and later generations, of various ethnic origins, established themselves in the countries concerned, they sought to overcome the prejudice and discrimination which previous generations had suffered.

The 'Black power' movement in the United States led the way and other ethnic groups followed in their attempt to gain recognition. In many cases, the ethnic minorities in industrialized countries identified closely with the independence movements in formerly colonized territories in the Third World. Political imperialism was replaced by economic imperialism within the framework of the global economy. Ethnic minorities within the indus-trialized countries began to regard themselves as having been exploited in the interests of dominant groups within the industrialized nation-states. Their situation has been interpreted as one of internal colonialism.[11] The second half of the twentieth century has seen a reaction against the assimi-latory pressures of industrialization and, at least among the elites within the ethnic populations concerned, a struggle for greater autonomy and even independence.

The emerging supranational states can afford to make concessions to the ethnic nationalist movements within industrialized countries as long as one overriding condition is fulfilled. That condition is an unswerving loyalty to the dominant ideology of the supranational state. In Western countries, this means unquestioning support for the economic philosophy of multinational-ism, Capitalism and anti-Communism. For countries within the Communist block the reverse is the case. Varying degrees of autonomy can be permitted for the constituent national groups as long as there is unswerving loyalty to the dictates of the Communist party. Any deviation from this is likely to be immediately suppressed, if necessary by military force.

It is not only ethnic groups which are geographically concentrated, and can establish an historical claim to particular territories, who will succeed in promoting their interests within the framework of the supranational state. The very nature of postindustrialism, with its technological advances in communi-cation networks, facilitates the maintenance of language and cultural differ-ences, even in remotely scattered populations. The immigrant minorities in countries such as Canada and Australia are already able to take advantage of multilingual radio and television channels. New developments in Pay TV and in satellite communications will further assist and promote the maintenance of linguistic and ethnic diversity. Mass communication networks will be sup-plemented by interpersonal networks, with kith and kin, maintained through rapid transportation and transnational telecommunications systems. Just as the emergence of the industrialized nation-state facilitated religious toleration, so the emergence of the postindustrial supranational state will facilitate the maintenance of ethnic diversity. However, those ethnic nationalist move-ments that identify themselves with the opposing ideology (multinational capitalism versus multinational communism) will be regarded as subversive and subject to coercive controls.

The transition from nationalism to multinationalism, and its associated multiculturalism, will not take place without a struggle between competing power elites. Already, the traditional power elites of the secular states are resisting incorporation into the new structures being created at the supra-national level. The growing threat of a nuclear war on a global scale must eventually overcome the resistance of the weaker units who depend for their defence upon larger and more powerful countries. However, encroachments on national sovereignty will continue to be resisted even as independence is undermined by the technological revolution of postindustrialism.

Meanwhile, within the old nation-states both ethnic and regional interests are asserting themselves. The emerging struggle for power has two major dimensions. The first is economic. Generally, it is a struggle for access to and control over natural resources, particularly those relating to energy. In this context, industrial and commercial elites will ally themselves with emerging ethnic or regional movements for autonomy and independence. In some cases, as in Scotland and Western Canada, the economic advantages of greater independence, and even separation, will be emphasized. Questions of mineral rights, export controls and taxation will be controversial. However, the economic elites may fail to gain popular support for their separatist policies which may not be perceived as in the best interests of the population as a whole.[12]

The second dimension of the struggle for power concerns the agencies of communication and legitimation. Specifically, the struggle focusses upon constitutional questions relating to devolution, the judicial system, the education system and the agencies of mass communication. The constitutional issues are fought out in the political arena through the electoral system and by the use of referenda. Again, the interests of regional and ethnic elites may not coincide with those of the electorate. The latter may be suspicious of the motives of the ethnic leaders; they may retain a lingering attachment to the larger nation-state, or they may consider that their economic interests will continue to be better served by remaining part of the wider society in its federal or other more centralized form. Much will depend upon the ability of the separatist movements to gain control of the socializing agencies that influence attitudes and public opinion. Teachers and journalists play an important part in this respect and are often among the strongest supporters of ethnic nationalism.

Next in importance to the legitimating function of the constitutional debates are those relating to the control of education. Where regional and ethnic interests converge, and are focussed on the maintenance of language and culture, the education system becomes a centre of controversy. In the earlier industrialized nation-states a single language of instruction was regarded as imperative and led, in some cases, to the use of coercive measures to eliminate ethnic languages in schools.[13] Now newly merging ethnic elites may adopt equally coercive means to impose their own language requirements. Bilingualism may be imposed upon members of the former dominant group, rather than being a functional prerequisite for an ethnic minority. In some cases the ethnic minority may succeed in imposing monolingual rules upon former majority group members, as in the case of recent Quebec legislation.[14] Where the ethnic minority groups do not have a territorial base they may, nevertheless, succeed in establishing the legitimacy of separate ethnic schools or bilingual instruction.

As the postindustrial revolution transforms the systems of communication in contemporary societies, a struggle for control of the networks also takes place. Access to and control over the instruments of mass communication becomes an important issue. Both child and adult socialization takes place through exposure to the information and the value systems transmitted through these networks. The school system itself becomes increasingly dependent upon televised and computerized learning systems. Some children actually spend more hours exposed to television viewing or video-terminals than they do in conventional classroom learning. Adults are also exposed increasingly to the flood of verbal and visual communications transmitted through the new technologies. At one time the number of channels was strictly limited. The effect was essentially assimilatory and homogenizing. Hence the resistance to American domination of mass communication networks in Canada. However, as the new technologies evolve a much greater variety of linguistic and cultural information will flow through these channels. Ethnic minorities will seek and generally obtain control over one or more television channels. This will permit the transmission of distinctive educational, informational, cultural and recreational programs in a variety of different languages.

Supranational states of the authoritarian or totalitarian type will have a special interest in controlling the mass communication networks and the educational systems. While some linguistic and cultural variation may be permitted, the networks will be the vehicle for transmitting a single dominant political ideology. In more democratically organized societies, there may be greater freedom of expression and more evidence of political discussion and dissent. However, ultimate control over licensing for broadcasting and reception is likely to rest with authorities who will not tolerate the use of the networks for active propaganda in favour of an opposing ideology. Nor will they permit the networks to be dominated by any one foreign source.

As the influence of *Verbindungsnetzschaft* replaces that of *Gemeinschaft* as a characteristic mode of social organization in postindustrial societies, the maintenance of ethnic identity will become less dependent upon either a territorial base or formal organizations. It will be possible for ethnic links to be maintained with others of similar language and cultural background throughout the world. Interpersonal networks may be sustained through videophones and other telecommunication links that will function much as the 'ham' radio networks have functioned in the past. Mass communication networks will also transcend the boundaries of former nation-states to link people of many different linguistic, cultural and national origins wherever they may be located throughout the world. International migration will still occur but it will no longer be necessary to compel immigrants to assimilate culturally to the majority group in the receiving society.

Ethnic nationalism will merge with the claims of other provincial and regional interest groups seeking greater economic and political influence, wherever numbers and territorial concentration make such an alliance advantageous. Even where ethnic minorities are widely dispersed they will still be able to maintain their links with others of similar ethnicity, wherever they may be. The complex communication networks of postindustrial societies will create the possibility of a new type of society, free of both religious and ethnic intolerance, by permitting great diversity within the structure of a supranational state. Reactionary movements, endeavouring to reassert national sovereignty and seeking to impose ethnic and cultural uniformity will likely occur. The transition from nationalism to multinationalism and from industrialism to postindustrialism will not take place without conflict. Eventually, a new era of ethnic and cultural diversity may be predicted. Its achievement will depend upon one overriding condition, namely, that the supranational states do not destroy themselves, and the rest of the world with them, in a nuclear conflagration precipitated by the combined forces of militarism and multinationalism.

['Ethnic Nationalism and Postindustrialism', *Ethnic and Racial Studies*, 7/1 (1984), 5–16.]

WILLIAM H. McNEILL
....

46 **Reasserting the Polyethnic Norm**

What happened? What explains such a reversal [of the trend to national homogeneity] of what once had seemed eternal verities? The question is perhaps better reversed by asking [. . .] what confluence of special factors sustained and fed ethnic unity in some parts of Europe in the late eighteenth and throughout the nineteenth century? For once we are conscious of those factors, it is easy to see how they have begun to weaken or disappear. In particular, ideas have altered, demography has altered, military organization has altered, and the continuing intensification of communications and transport, instead of favoring national consolidation, has begun to work in a contrary sense, inasmuch as its range transcends existing political and ethnic boundaries. Let me say a bit more about each of these changes.

First, ideas. Hitler's obsession with race and race purity discredited one important aspect of earlier European notions about national unity and its importance. In particular, his genocidal campaign against Jews and Gypsies, together with his intention of exterminating Slavs standing in the way of German *Lebensraum*, aroused intense horror and repulsion when the gruesome facts about Nazi death camps became known. The effect in postwar decades was twofold. On the one hand, it tainted advocacy of the ideal of ethnic unity within an existing state, since such sentiments smacked too much of Nazi doctrines. On the other, Jews in particular, and other ethnic minorities subsequently, began to abandon the ideal of assimilation to locally prevailing national groups. What had happened in Germany seemed to prove its futility, for German Jews had practiced a policy of assimilation longer and more enthusiastically than had been tried in any other European country, with the possible exception of France! Even before the French revolutionaries made religion a private matter, and removed all legal obstacles to the assimilation of Jews, similar ideas had taken root in Germany's cultivated circles, as the friendship of Moses Mendelssohn (1729–86) with Gotthold Lessing (1729–81) may remind us. But if assimilation merely provoked brutal backlash in the heartlands of European civilization, what use to pursue it elsewhere? Was it not better to accept or even accentuate differences? Or was migration to Israel preferable? But, ironically, the new Jewish homeland, after its establishment in 1947, instead of resolving religious–ethnic tensions between Jews and others, as the founders of Zionism had hoped, actually intensified such frictions, and internationalized them by creating a Palestinian refugee population that refused to acquiesce in its expulsion from lands seized by the Jews.

Other, previously quiescent minorities also awoke to a new sense of permanent, collective identity in the postwar decades. Conspicuously, the Blacks in the United States did so; but the French in Canada, and Flemings in Belgium, together with a small company of noisy Scottish and Welsh nationalists in Great Britain, all moved along parallel paths. If national uniformity was not a good to be treasured, it was not worth striving for; and since such striving required erasure of distinguishing cultural differences, the spokesmen for subordinated ethnic groups could appeal to emotionally vibrant symbols—language above all, but also religion, folkways, costume, and the like. Such things, remembered from childhood, had a potential for arousing strong nostalgia among dwellers in large cities, whose daily encounters with individuals of differing cultural and ethnic backgrounds were impersonal and cool at best, and easily degenerated into abrasive collision.

Before 1914, in Europe and many other parts of the world as well, peasants and country bumpkins, looking to the city for models of a better life, had been willing and even eager to assimilate as best they could to a middle-class, city-based national norm in language and manners. But city folk, born and bred in the streets, needed what rural folk inherited automatically and unthinkingly: a primary group to belong to—or leave behind, but against which personal choices and career success could always be measured. In a perverse way, the Nazi hypertrophy of nationalism and race-feeling expressed this urban yearning for membership in a primary community. Reaction against its catastrophic consequences for Europe and the world simply redirected that yearning from the nation as a whole towards a variety of subnational groupings.

Demography reinforced and inflamed these new tides in the climate of opinion. A sharp decline of birthrates in Europe (including Russia), and in lands of European settlement overseas, was matched by sustained high birthrates in poorer lands, while improved medical services accelerated population growth, reducing deaths from infectious diseases very markedly. In the western world deliberate birth control allowed economic expectations to become more and more decisive in fixing the number and timing of births. Some Europeans had been influenced by such considerations for many centuries; but until the 1880s and 1890s deliberate limitation of births had not been sufficiently widespread (except in France) to have much demographic effect. This had meant that even the meanest and most marginal occupations could be filled readily enough by migrants from the crowded countryside nearby.

The effect of the two great wars of the twentieth century on this traditional pattern was drastic. New attitudes and ideas were widely propagated by the prolonged exposure of millions of men to military sex practices which dated back to Old Regime armies, and involved quite effective prevention of births. Women's experiences of wartime employment in factories and offices were probably even more significant. Marriage and motherhood no longer appeared as the only possibility; and even in those parts of eastern Europe where peasant life had persisted into the 1930s with little change, the drastic upheavals of World War II broke down local village traditions everywhere except in Albania, and exposed young women to new experiences that made simple return to old patterns of life unacceptable.

On top of this, millions of Europeans were killed, so that when economic expansion got into high gear in the late 1950s, the local supply of underemployed rural youths, upon which west European cities had always counted to fill their meaner jobs, was inadequate. Communist countries prohibited emigration, since the governments wished to use their rural population as a labor reservoir for planned industrial expansion on the Soviet model. Yugoslavia, in this as much else, became exceptional in permitting its citizens to emigrate, as was also true of the poorer Mediterranean lands—southern Italy, Greece, Spain, and Portugal. These countries were able to supply west European cities (also Australia, Canada, and the United States) with low-skilled labor for a while. Such immigrants were, however, far more alien in their new environment than villagers from close by had been in earlier ages; and when recruitment expanded still further afield to attract Turks and Algerians, Indonesians, Pakistanis, West Africans, and others to the cities of western Europe, no one supposed that assimilation to the host society would or could occur, at least not in the foreseeable future.

In Germany and other central European countries, careful official regulation of immigration from Mediterranean and Moslem lands was intended to prevent exploitation and facilitate the matching of supply and demand for labor by allowing a stipulated number of alien workers to come temporarily. No doubt it did have that effect, defining minimum wage rates and conditions of labor. It also had the effect of separating the immigrants from the host society by giving them a distinct legal status as sojourners in an alien land, who were expected to maintain their native identity, pending return to their country of origin. Many conformed to official expectation by going home after some months or years abroad; but many others preferred to remain, even in periods of economic difficulty, when unemployment reared its ugly head. Moreover, humble jobs that had been filled by alien immigrants often seemed no longer fit for native-born citizens.

Such attitudes, if allowed to persist, would produce permanent differentiation between immigrants and native-born inhabitants. Official policy has not really come to grips with this prospect. It is, of course, impossible to say for sure what the future will bring, but as long as differential birthrates remain as great as they are between west European and nearby Moslem populations, the old-fashioned ethnically unitary nation is unlikely to be restored.

Even in Britain and France, where an indelible separate legal status was not pinned upon immigrants, the tacit liberal expectation of an eventual assimilation of newcomers to the national norm wilted rapidly in the postwar decades, especially for those groups who were readily distinguishable from the environing population, in physical appearance. The experience of the United States was important here, for in the 1950s Americans emphatically abandoned the ideal of assimilation in favor of a rather more strenuous ideal of somehow combining enduring ethnic multiplicity with legal and social equality for all. Public efforts to equalize income and status between Blacks and whites met with very limited success though some forms of racial discrimination were removed or diminished. In the 1950s and 1960s, the British and French were less exercised over their new minorities than were the Americans, partly because numbers were smaller and immigrants more timorous in asserting any sort of collective self-consciousness. More recently, Black and other visible minorities have become more assertive, at least in Britain; but what direction governmental policy will take remains unclear.

The long-term fate of American, French, and British experiments in polyethnic living remain just as problematic as is the future of the two-tiered society generated by the legal status of *Gastarbeiter* in Germany and Switzerland. Equality and freedom to be different are difficult to reconcile, especially when traditional cultural characteristics and patterns of education fit ethnic groups for some jobs and disqualify them for others. Moreover, even if the competing ideals of liberty and equality should achieve satisfactory resolution among the prevailing mix of ethnic groups, differential rates of population growth, and panic flight from political violence, can be counted on to generate new waves of migrants seeking entry to countries that are richer and freer than their homelands; and such migrants, if admitted, will bring new diversity and establish a still more complex ethnic hierarchy in western Europe and North America than anything that now exists.

Illegal immigrants who abound in the United States, coming mostly from Mexico and from some of the Caribbean islands, already demonstrate the dilemma confronting a country officially committed to equality and liberty.

Official efforts to prohibit or regulate migration can do much to control the magnitude and direction of these demographic tides, but cannot turn them on and off at will. Checking illegal migration into the United States, for example, would require an expansion of police power which many Americans are reluctant to accept; yet connivance in illegal immigration, such as now occurs, invites the sort of two-tiered society the Germans have inadvertently created with their *Gastarbeiter*, with the difference that American laws do not protect illegal immigrants from mistreatment as systematically as German regulations do.

These political and sociological dilemmas reflect improvements in communications and transport that continually nibble away at once formidable geographical obstacles to human interaction at a distance. In the nineteenth century and before, moving to a foreign country meant cutting close ties with the homeland for years if not forever. Modern conditions make it possible even for very humble immigrant workers to keep in touch with their place of origin by returning for vacations and telephoning relatives with news and gossip of the kind that used only to be exchanged locally. Such links mean that immigrants find it far easier to maintain their cultural identity in a strange land. Psychologically they remain at home even when away from home; or more exactly, they are able to inhabit two different worlds simultaneously, dealing part of the time with aliens and part of the time with familiars, even if some of their familiars happen to live in another country, many miles away.

Human communities, in other words, are becoming at least partially detachable from geography. This is an old phenomenon: as old as civilization perhaps, inasmuch as written texts allowed sacred truths to transcend both time and distance. But in earlier ages, only small elites participated actively in such communication, and ties among elites were slender since contacts at a distance had to overcome difficult obstacles. Such obstacles have now been reduced to the point that in the richer countries of the earth, at any rate, nearly everyone can keep in touch with kinfolk and friends at will, whether that means communicating across oceans and continents or simply down the road.

Large organizations, too, communicate at will around the globe. Multinational corporations can reallocate resources as seems best to their managers, seeking cheap labor or advantageous legal regulations wherever they are to be found. Such activity characteristically creates a rather different mingling of peoples, in which immigrants occupy the high-skill positions as managers and experts while locally recruited people fill the low-skilled jobs.

The military services of the two great powers, likewise, move across national borders with an ease and on a scale unknown before airplanes and electronic communications achieved their present capacities. Garrisons stationed permanently, or at least for an indefinite future, on foreign soil constitute another significant form of polyethnicity. Sometimes, military personnel are kept severely apart, as happens with Soviet forces stationed in eastern Europe. Sometimes encapsulation in a separate military society is far weaker, as for most American garrisons. But no matter what the legal and social barriers may be, foreign soldiers and host communities inevitably interact with each other in ways no one can fully control or foresee. [. . .]

Political resistance to intermingling of peoples and skills across state boundaries is therefore far from negligible, and may well increase in time to come as the difficulties of living in polyethnic societies become more widely apparent. The recent riots in Great Britain are a sample of what must be expected when different ethnic groups bring sharp cultural differences into immediate juxtaposition by migrating into city slums. Nothing assures that the assortment of migrants and their skills will fit smoothly into the host society. Indeed, market rhythms of boom and bust assure that periods of labor shortage will alternate with periods of labor surplus; and the groups most at risk in periods of economic downturn are usually the most recently arrived. Yet going back home is not always a feasible alternative for immigrants in times of hardship; and even the most carefully calculated public policies cannot foresee the future well enough to assure a smooth adjustment of supply and demand for labor by shuttling workers back and forth between host country and their native villages. People resist being herded about like sheep; and bureaucratic wisdom—not to say justice—is in too short supply to allow us to rely confidently on what would amount to a new, collectivized system of intermittent indentured labor. Yet private decisions, made on the basis of very imperfect information, confront the same uncertain future and have no chance of foreseeing the full consequences of a decision to emigrate or to stay home instead.

It would be silly to expect certainty or predictability in myriad human encounters provoked by modern transport and communications, acting in concert with the demographic dynamic of our time, and the tides of thought and feeling that run so tumultuously among us. It would be even more absurd to expect that ethnic unity within separate, sovereign national states would remain or, rather, become normal in such an interacting world. Yet, unexamined, our heritage inclines us to make that assumption. Mental inertia and the capacity we all have of seeing only what we wish to see and glossing over anything that contradicts our preferences may well continue to support pretense of ethnic unity within sovereign national states for some time to come. But the reality is otherwise and becoming more so with each decade. Polyethnic hierarchy is on the rise, everywhere.

[*Polyethnicity and National Unity in World History* (Toronto University Press: Toronto, 1986), 70–8, 81–2.]

47 Narrating the Nation

Nations, like narratives, lose their origins in the myths of time and only fully realize their horizons in the mind's eye. Such an image of the nation—or narration—might seem impossibly romantic and excessively metaphorical, but it is from those traditions of political thought and literary language that the nation emerges as a powerful historical idea in the west. An idea whose cultural compulsion lies in the impossible unity of the nation as a symbolic force. This is not to deny the attempt by nationalist discourses persistently to produce the idea of the nation as a continuous narrative of national progress, the narcissism of self-generation, the primeval present of the *Volk*. Nor have such political ideas been definitively superseded by those new realities of internationalism, multinationalism, or even 'late capitalism', once we acknowledge that the rhetoric of these global terms is most often underwritten in that grim prose of power that each nation can wield within its own sphere of influence. What I want to emphasize in that large and liminal image of the nation with which I began is a particular ambivalence that haunts the idea of the nation, the language of those who write of it and the lives of those who live it. It is an ambivalence that emerges from a growing awareness that, despite the certainty with which historians speak of the 'origins' of nation as a sign of the 'modernity' of society, the cultural temporality of the nation inscribes a much more transitional social reality. Benedict Anderson, whose *Imagined Communities* significantly paved the way for this book, expresses the nation's ambivalent emergence with great clarity:

The century of the Enlightenment, of rationalist secularism, brought with it its own modern darkness . . . [Few] things were (are) suited to this end better than the idea of nation. If nation states are widely considered to be 'new' and 'historical', the nation states to which they give political expression always loom out of an immemorial past and . . . glide into a limitless future. What I am proposing is that Nationalism has to be understood, by aligning it not with self-consciously held political ideologies, but with large cultural systems that preceded it, out of which—as well as against which—it came into being (p. 19).

The nation's 'coming into being' as a system of cultural signification, as the representation of social *life* rather than the discipline of social *polity*, emphasizes this instability of knowledge. For instance, the most interesting accounts of the national idea, whether they come from the Tory Right, the Liberal high ground, or the New Left, seem to concur on the ambivalent tension that defines the 'society' of the nation. Michael Oakeshott's 'Character of a modern European state' is perhaps the most brilliant conservative account of the equivocal nature of the modern nation. The national space is, in his view, constituted from competing dispositions of human association as *societas* (the acknowledgement of moral rules and conventions of conduct) and *universitas* (the acknowledgement of common purpose and substantive end). In the absence of their merging into a new identity they have survived as competing dogmas—*societas cum universitate*—'impos[ing] a particular ambivalence upon all the institutions of a modern state and a specific ambiguity upon its vocabulary of discourse'.[1] In Hannah Arendt's view, the society of the nation in the modern world is 'that curiously hybrid realm where private interests assume public significance' and the two realms flow unceasingly and uncertainly into each other 'like waves in the never-ending stream of the life-process itself'.[2] No less certain is Tom Nairn, in naming the nation 'the modern Janus', that the 'uneven development' of capitalism inscribes both progression and regression, political rationality and irrationality in the very genetic code of the nation. This is a structural fact to which there are no exceptions and 'in this sense, it is an exact (not a rhetorical) statement about nationalism to say that it is by nature ambivalent.[3]

It is the cultural representation of this ambivalence of modern society that is explored in this book. If the ambivalent figure of the nation is a problem of its transitional history, its conceptual indeterminacy, its wavering between vocabularies, then what effect does this have on narratives and discourses that signify a sense of 'nationness': the *heimlich* pleasures of the hearth, the *unheimlich* terror of the space or race of the Other; the comfort of social belonging, the hidden injuries of class; the customs of taste, the powers of political affiliation; the sense of social order, the sensibility of sexuality; the blindness of bureaucracy, the strait insight of institutions; the quality of justice, the common sense of injustice; the *langue* of the law and the *parole* of the people.

The emergence of the political 'rationality' of the nation as a form of narrative—textual strategies, metaphoric displacements, sub-texts and figurative strategems—has its own history. It is suggested in Benedict Anderson's view of the space and time of the modern nation as embodied in the narrative culture of the realist novel, and explored in Tom Nairn's reading of Enoch Powell's post-imperial racism which is based on the 'symbol-fetishism' that infests his febrile, neo-romantic poetry. To encounter the nation *as it is written* displays a temporality of culture and social consciousness more in tune with the partial, overdetermined process by which textual meaning is produced through the articulation of difference in language; more in keeping with the problem of closure which plays enigmatically in the discourse of the sign. Such an approach contests the traditional authority of those national objects of knowledge—Tradition, People, the Reason of State, High Culture, for instance—whose pedagogical value often relies on their representation as holistic concepts located within an evolutionary narrative of historical continuity. Traditional histories do not take the nation at its own word, but, for the most part, they do assume that the problem lies with the interpretation of 'events' that have a certain transparency or privileged visibility.

To study the nation through its narrative address does not merely draw attention to its language and rhetoric; it also attempts to alter the conceptual object itself. If the problematic 'closure' of textuality questions the 'totalization' of national culture, then its positive value lies in displaying the wide dissemination through which we construct the field of meanings and symbols associated with national life. This is a project that has a certain currency within those forms of critique associated with 'cultural studies'. Despite the considerable advance this represents, there is a tendency to read the Nation rather restrictively; either, as the ideological apparatus of state power, somewhat redefined by a hasty, functionalist reading of Foucault or Bakhtin; or, in a more utopian inversion, as the incipient or emergent expression of the 'national-popular' sentiment preserved in a radical memory. These approaches are valuable in drawing our attention to those easily obscured, but highly significant, recesses of the national culture from which alternative constituencies of peoples and oppositional analytic capacities may emerge—youth, the everyday, nostalgia, new 'ethnicities', new social movements, 'the politics of difference'. They assign new meanings and different directions to the process of historical change. The most progressive development from such positions takes 'a *discursive* conception of ideology—ideology (like language) is conceptualised in terms of the articulation of elements. As Volosinov said, the ideological sign is always multi-accentual and Janus-faced'.[4] But in the heat of political argument the 'doubling' of the sign can often be stilled. The Janus face of ideology is taken at face value and its meaning fixed, in the last instance, on one side of the divide between ideology and 'material conditions'. [. . .]

It is the project of *Nation and Narration* to explore the Janus-faced ambivalence of language itself in the construction of the Janus-faced discourse of the nation. This turns the familiar two-faced god into a figure of prodigious doubling that investigates the nation-space in the *process* of the articulation of elements: where meanings may be partial because they are *in medias res*; and history may be half-made because it is in the process of being made; and the image of cultural authority may be ambivalent because it is caught, uncertainly, in the act of 'composing' its powerful image. Without such an understanding of the performativity of language in the narratives of the nation, it would be difficult to understand why Edward Said prescribes a kind of 'analytic pluralism' as the *form* of critical attention appropriate to the cultural effects of the nation. For the nation, as a form of cultural *elaboration* (in the Gramscian sense), is an agency of *ambivalent* narration that holds culture at its most productive position, as a force for 'subordination, fracturing, diffusing, reproducing, as much as producing, creating, forcing, guiding'.[5]

I wrote to my contributors with a growing, if unfamiliar, sense of the nation as one of the major structures of ideological ambivalence within the cultural representations of 'modernity'. My intention was that we should develop, in a nice collaborative tension, a range of readings that engaged the insights of poststructuralist theories of narrative knowledge—textuality, discourse, enunciation, *écriture*, 'the unconscious as a language' to name only a few strategies—in order to evoke this ambivalent margin of the nation-space. To reveal such a margin is, in the first instance, to contest claims to cultural supremacy, whether these are made from the 'old' post-imperialist metropolitan nations, or on behalf of the 'new' independent nations of the periphery. The marginal or 'minority' is not the space of a celebratory, or utopian, self-marginalization. It is a much more substantial intervention into those justifications of modernity—progress, homogeneity, cultural organicism, the deep nation, the long past—that rationalize the authoritarian, 'normalizing' tendencies within cultures in the name of the national interest or the ethnic prerogative. In this sense, then, the ambivalent, antagonistic perspective of nation as narration will establish the cultural boundaries of the nation so that they may be acknowledged as 'containing' thresholds of meaning that must be crossed, erased, and translated in the process of cultural production.

The 'locality' of national culture is neither unified nor unitary in relation to itself, nor must it be seen simply as 'other' in relation to what is outside or beyond it. The boundary is Janus-faced and the problem of outside / inside must always itself be a process of hybridity, incorporating new 'people' in relation to the body politic, generating other sites of meaning and, inevitably, in the political process, producing unmanned sites of political antagonism and unpredictable forces for political representation. The address to nation as narration stresses the insistence of political power and cultural authority in what Derrida describes as the 'irreducible excess of the syntactic over the semantic'.[6] What emerges as an effect of such 'incomplete signification' is a turning of boundaries and limits into the *in-between* spaces through which the meanings of cultural and political authority are negotiated. It is from such narrative positions between cultures and nations, theories and texts, the political, the poetic and the painterly, the past and the present, that *Nation and Narration* seeks to affirm and extend Frantz Fanon's revolutionary credo: 'National consciousness, which is not nationalism, is the only thing that will give us an international dimension'.[7] It is this *inter*national dimension both within the margins of the nation-space and in the boundaries *in-between* nations and peoples that the authors of this book have sought to represent in their essays. The representative emblem of this book might be a chiasmatic 'figure' of cultural difference whereby the anti-nationalist, ambivalent nation-space becomes the crossroads to a new transnational culture. The 'other' is never outside or beyond us; it emerges forcefully, within cultural discourse, when we *think* we speak most intimately and indigenously 'between ourselves'.

Without attempting to précis individual essays, I would like briefly to elaborate this movement, within *Nation and Narration*, from the problematic unity of the nation to the articulation of cultural difference in the construction of an *inter*national perspective. The story could start in many places: with David Simpson's reading of the multiform 'body' of Whitman's American populism and his avoidance of metaphor which is also an avoidance of the problems of integration and cultural difference; or Doris Sommer's exploration of the language of love and productive sexuality that allegorizes and organizes the early historical narratives of Latin America which are disavowed by the later 'Boom' novelists; or John Barrell's exploration of the tensions between the civic humanist theory of painting and the 'discourse of custom' as they are drawn together in the ideology of the 'ornamental' in art, and its complex mediation of Englishness; or Sneja Gunew's portrayal of an Australian literature split between an Anglo-Celtic public sphere and a multiculturalist counter-public sphere. It is the excluded voices of migrants and the marginalized that Gunew represents, bringing them back to disturb and interrupt the writing of the Australian canon.

In each of these 'foundational fictions' the origins of national traditions turn out to be as much acts of affiliation and establishment as they are moments of disavowal, displacement, exclusion, and cultural contestation. In this function of national history as *Entstellung*, the forces of social antagonism or contradiction cannot be transcended or dialectically surmounted. There is a suggestion that the constitutive contradictions of the national text are discontinuous and 'interruptive'. This is Geoff Bennington's starting point as he puns (with a certain postmodern prescience) on the '*postal* politics' of national frontiers to suggest that 'Frontiers are articulations, boundaries are, constitutively, crossed and transgressed'. It is across such boundaries, both historical and pedagogical, that Martin Thom places Renan's celebrated essay 'What is a nation?'. He provides a careful genealogy of the national idea as it emerges mythically from the Germanic tribes, and more recently in the interrelations between the struggle to consolidate the Third Republic and the emergence of Durkheimian sociology.

What kind of a cultural space is the nation with its transgressive boundaries and its 'interruptive' interiority? Each essay answers this question differently but there is a moment in Simon During's exposition of the 'civil imaginary' when he suggests that 'part of the modern domination of the life-world by style and civility . . . is a process of the *feminisation* of society'. This insight is explored in two very different contexts, Gillian Beer's reading of Virginia Woolf and Rachel Bowlby's study of *Uncle Tom's Cabin*. Gillian Beer takes the perspective of the aeroplane—war machine, dream symbol, icon of the 1930s poets—to emphasize Woolf's reflections on the island race, and space; its multiple marginal significations—'land and water margins, home, body, individualism'—providing another inflection to her quarrels with patriarchy and imperialism. Rachel Bowlby writes the cultural history of readings of *Uncle Tom's Cabin*, that debate the feminization of American cultural values while producing a more complex interpretation of her own. The narrative of American freedom, she suggests, displays the same ambivalence that constructs the contradictory nature of femininity in the text. America itself becomes the dark continent, doubly echoing the 'image' of Africa and Freud's metaphor for feminine sexuality. George Harris, the former slave, leaves for the new African state of Liberia.

It is when the western nation comes to be seen, in Conrad's famous phrase, as one of the dark corners of the earth, that we can begin to explore new places from which to write histories of peoples and construct theories of narration. Each time the question of cultural difference emerges as a challenge to relativistic notions of the diversity of culture, it reveals the margins of modernity. As a result, most of these essays have ended up in another cultural location from where they started—often taking up a 'minority' position. Francis Mulhern's study of the 'English ethics' of Leavisian universalism pushes towards a reading of Q. D. Leavis's last public lecture in Cheltenham where she bemoans the imperilled state of that England which bore the classical English novel; an England, now, of council-house dwellers, unassimilated minorities, sexual emancipation without responsibility. Suddenly the paranoid system of 'English reading' stands revealed. James Snead ends his interrogation of the ethics and aesthetics of western 'nationalist' universalism with a reading of Ishmael Reed who 'is revising a prior co-optation of black culture, using a narrative principle that will undermine the very assumptions that brought the prior appropriation about'. Timothy Brennan produces a panoramic view of the western history of the national idea and its narrative forms, finally to take his stand with those hybridizing writers like Salman Rushdie whose glory and grotesquerie lie in their celebration of the fact that English is no longer an English language. This, as Brennan points out, leads to a more articulate awareness of the post-colonial and neo-colonial conditions as authoritative positions from which to speak Janus-faced to east and west. But these positions across the frontiers of history, culture, and language, which we have been exploring, are dangerous, if essential, political projects. Bruce Robbins' reading of Dickens balances the risks of departing from the 'ethical home truths' of humanistic experience with the advantages of developing a knowledge of acting in a dispersed global system. Our attention to 'aporia' he suggests, should be counterpointed with an intentionality that is inscribed in *poros*— practical, technical know-how that abjures the rationalism of universals, while maintaining the practicality, and political strategy, of dealing professionally with local situations that are themselves defined as liminal and borderline.

America leads to Africa; the nations of Europe and Asia meet in Australia; the margins of the nation displace the centre; the peoples of the periphery return to rewrite the history and fiction of the metropolis. The island story is told from the eye of the aeroplane which becomes that 'ornament' that holds the public and the private in suspense. The bastion of Englishness crumbles at the sight of immigrants and factory workers. The great Whitmanesque

sensorium of America is exchanged for a Warhol blowup, a Kruger installa-
tion, or Mapplethorpe's naked bodies. 'Magical realism' after the Latin American Boom, becomes the literary language of the emergent post-colonial world.
Amidst these exorbitant images of the nation-space in its transnational dimension there are those who have not yet found their nation: amongst them the
Palestinians and the Black South Africans. It is our loss that in making this book
we were unable to add their voices to ours. Their persistent questions remain
to remind us, in some form or measure, of what must be true for the rest of us
too: 'When did we become "a people"? When did we stop being one? Or are
we in the process of becoming one? What do these big questions have to do
with our intimate relationships with each other and with others?'[8]

['Introduction' to Homi K. Bhabha (ed.), *The Nation and Narration* (Routledge: London,
1990), 1–7.]

FLOYA ANTHIAS AND NIRA YUVAL-DAVIS

48 **Women and the Nation-State**

Women's link to the state is complex. On the one hand, they are acted upon as
members of collectivities, institutions or groupings, and as participants in the
social forces that give the state its given political projects in any particular
social and historical context. On the other hand, they are a special focus of state
concerns as a social category with a specific role (particularly human reproduction). It is important to note, however, that these roles cannot be understood
in relation to the state reproducing itself, or that any absolute control by the
state would be achievable, given women's incorporation at a number of other
social levels within civil society and in the economy.

A number of attempts[1] to conceptualise the link between women and the
state have focused on the central dimension of citizenship and how, far from
being gender-neutral, it constructs men and women differently. Thus the
feminist and socialist feminist critique of the state and state theorisation has
advanced from one which points to the way the state *treats* women unequally
in relation to men. There now exists a theoretical critique of the way the very
project of the welfare state itself has constituted the 'state subject' in a gen-
dered way, that is as essentially male in its capacities and needs. However,
different forms of the state and different states even within the same form,
involve the positing of a different constituency for 'citizenship'. The notion of
citizenship focuses on the way the *state* acts upon the *individual* and does not
address the problem of the way in which the state itself forms its political
project. Therefore it cannot on its own attend to the social forces and movements that are hegemonic within the state. This applies also to the state's
relationship to women. 'Citizenship', on its own, does not encapsulate adequ-

ately the relations of control and negotiation that take place in a number of different arenas of social life.

When we come to discuss the ways women affect and are affected by national and ethnic processes within civil society, and the ways these relate to the state, it is important to remember that there is no unitary category of women which can be unproblematically conceived as the focus of ethnic, national or state policies and discourses. Women are divided along class, ethnic and life-cycle lines and in most societies different strategies are directed at different groups of women. This is the case both from within the ethnic collectivity and from the state, whose boundaries virtually always contain a number of ethnicities.

While we have argued against the links between women, the state and ethnic/national processes taking any necessary form we can nevertheless locate five major (although not exclusive) ways in which women have tended to participate in ethnic and national processes and in relation to state practices. These are:

(a) as biological reproducers of members of ethnic collectivities;

(b) as reproducers of the boundaries of ethnic/national groups;

(c) as participating centrally in the ideological reproduction of the collectivity and as transmitters of its culture;

(d) as signifiers of ethnic/national differences—as a focus and symbol in ideological discourses used in the construction, reproduction and transformation of ethnic/national categories;

(e) as participants in national, economic, political and military struggles.

Different historical contexts will construct these roles not only in different ways but also the centrality of these roles will differ.

Before giving a further explication of the above categories, a word of caution is necessary in relation to the use of the term 'reproduction'. We consider this concept as problematic on more than one ground. First of all, its use in the literature includes many and indeed inconsistent meanings, from a definition of women's biological role to explanations of the existence of social systems over time.[2]

Even more importantly, the term 'reproduction' has been criticised as being tautological on the one hand, often implicitly assuming that 'reproduction' takes place, and static on the other hand, therefore unable to explain growth, decline and transformation processes (women act as both maintainers and modifiers of social processes). By retaining the term 'reproduction', however, in the depiction of some of the then central roles women play we wished to locate our work in relation to the literature which deals with human and social reproduction. Feminist literature on 'reproduction' has dealt with biological reproduction, the reproduction of labour power or state citizenship, but has generally failed to consider the reproduction of national, ethnical and racial categories.[3]

We shall now describe in more detail the range of policies and discourses which can be included in each of the five categories noted earlier.

(a) Various forms of population control are the most obvious policies which relate to women as biological reproducers of members of collectivities. The fear of being 'swamped' by different racial or ethnic groups has given rise to both individual state and interstate policies which are aimed at limiting the physical numbers of members of groups that are defined as 'undesirable'. One form these take is represented most clearly in immigration controls. More extreme measures are the physical expulsion of particular groups and even actual extermination of them (e.g. Jews and gypsies in Nazi Germany). A further strategy is to limit the number of people born within specific ethnic groups by controlling the reproductive capacity and activity of women. These range from forced sterilisation to the massive mobilisation of birth control campaigns. The other facet of such a concern is the active encouragement of population growth of the 'right kind', i.e. of the ethnic group dominant in the state apparatus. Calls for a 'White Australia' immigration policy or Jewish 'return' to Israel are supplemented at times of slack immigration or national crisis with active calls for women to bear more children so that no 'demographic holocaust' will take place. This encouragement is very often a question of using national and religious discourses about the duty of women to produce more children. (A popular Palestinian saying in Israel for example boasts that 'The Israelis beat us at the borders but we beat them in the bedrooms'.) However, in many cases, rather than relying on ideological mobilisation, the state establishes child benefit systems and other maternal benefits such as loans to this purpose. (The Beveridge Report for example cited fear for the fate of the 'British race' as the major reason for establishing child benefits in Britain.)

(b) Women are controlled not only by being encouraged or discouraged from having children who will become members of the various ethnic groups within the state. They are also controlled in terms of the 'proper' way in which they should have them—i.e. in ways which will reproduce the boundaries of the symbolic identity of their group or that of their husbands. In some cases (as until recently in South Africa) women are not allowed to have sexual relations with men of other groups. This particularly is the case for dominant-group women. Legal marriage is generally a condition if the child is to be recognised as a member of the group and very often religious and social traditions dictate who can marry whom so that the character as well as the boundaries of the group can be maintained from one generation to the other. In Israel, for example, it is the mother who determines whether or not the child will be considered Jewish. But if the mother is already married (or even divorced, but only by civil rather than by religious law) to another man, that child will be an outcast and not allowed to marry another Jew. In Egypt, on the other hand, a child born to a Muslim woman and a Copt Christian man will have no legal status.

(c) The role of women as ideological reproducers is very often related to women being seen as the 'cultural carriers' of the ethnic group. Women are the main socialisers of small children but in the case of ethnic minorities they are often less assimilated socially and linguistically within the wider society. They may be required to transmit the rich heritage of ethnic symbols and ways of life to the other members of the ethnic group, especially the young.

(d) Women do not only teach and transfer the cultural and ideological traditions of ethnic and national groups. Very often they constitute their actual symbolic figuration. The nation as a loved woman in danger or as a mother who lost her sons in battle is a frequent part of the particular nationalist discourse in national liberation struggles or other forms of national conflicts when men are called to fight 'for the sake of our women and children' or to 'defend their honour'. Often the distinction between one ethnic group and another is constituted centrally by the sexual behaviour of women. For example a 'true' Sikh or Cypriot girl should behave in sexually appropriate ways. If she does not then neither her children nor herself may be considered part of the community.[4]

(e) Finally, and probably the category that requires least explication is the role that women have come to play in national and ethnic struggles. Women's role in national liberation struggles, in guerilla warfare or in the military has varied, but generally they are seen to be in a supportive and nurturing relation to men even where they have taken most risks.[5] In addition, the way in which national liberation struggles have articulated issues concerning gender divisions and women's liberation is a consideration here.

The explication of some of the central roles that women play in relation to national and ethnic processes must bear in mind three important elements. The first relates to the link between national ethnic processes and the state. We have noted already that the relationship between collectivities and the state is complex and will vary in different historical and social contexts. Whilst only rarely exclusively so, customary and religious norms and legislation, which usually construct women as primarily biological reproducers, will often be incorporated and reinforced by state legislation, although contradictions can exist also between state and religious legislation. Thus the sphere of 'civil society' and the sphere of the 'state' can link hands in the construction of women in some ways although in others they might be in conflict. In addition, the political projects of the state are often the outcome of tensions and conflicts within civil society and are carried by social classes or other social forces.[6] In addition, the state will often identify and specify those groupings or social relations that it can legislate on but which it delineates as private and therefore essentially as an individual matter of choice or liberty in its specifics. Such is the case in relation to the family, for example. When we look at the role of women as markers of collective boundaries and differences and also as participants in national, political and economic struggles we often find a contradiction—women are constituted through the state but are also often actively engaged in countering state processes.

Secondly, the central role that women play should not lead us to the fallacy that women are attended to either only as women (i.e. in their 'difference' from men) or that all women, irrespective of class, age or family situation are attended to in the same way. Often there may indeed be tension between, on the one hand, treating women as 'different', say in certain of their capacities or potentialities, and treating them 'equally' in others (e.g. as workers). Also an 'equal' treatment by the state in any number of capacities will not necessarily lead to the destruction of a sexual division of labour in society more generally. Notions of what are specifically women's needs or duties often reassert themselves in very traditional ways even in revolutionary societies. This clearly requires the much wider discussion of gender relations. There is no space here to review some of the central positions taken in this regard but we argue elsewhere (Anthias & Yuval-Davis 1983) that gender divisions are irreducible to class or other divisions. Clearly, for the purpose of our argument here it is important to note that the state does not exclusively construct gender divisions nor can they be seen only in the context of any specific state mechanisms at any historical moment as they relate to the whole area of gender 'differentiation'.

In addition, we find it vitally important to emphasise that the roles that women play are not merely imposed upon them. Women actively participate in the process of reproducing and modifying their roles as well as being actively involved in controlling other women.

['Introduction' to F. Anthias and N. Yuval-Davis (eds.), *Woman—Nation—State* (Macmillan: London, 1989), 6–11.]

PHILIP SCHLESINGER

49 Europeanness: A New Cultural Battlefield?

The nation-state is a political configuration of modernity. But modernity is a curious condition, for in some respects it is characterised by flux and impermanence, what Baudelaire in his classic formulation identified as 'the transitory, the fugitive, the contingent'.[1] It is this aspect of modernity that has been emphasised in the recent vogue for 'postmodernity', whose proponents have been apt to think that the old collectivities may no longer confer identities that command special attention.

So, for instance, David Harvey[2] has argued that the present phase of capital accumulation results in a 'reterritorialisation' of social power which is part of the spatio-temporal disruption of an earlier social order. These globalising or universalising tendencies in contemporary capitalism, and the growth of post-

Fordist 'flexible accumulation' have placed 'a strong emphasis upon the potential connection between place and social identity'. Socialist, working class, racial and other groups opposing the reshaping of the world by capitalism find it easier to organise in given places but not where it counts—over space (i.e. globally). Such 'regional resistances' are inadequate to the task of creating alternative structures, although by way of interpreting 'a partially illusory past it becomes possible to signify something of a local identity and perhaps to do it profitably' (through, for instance, the heritage business). This offers a very slender basis for the construction of collective identities and, on this analysis, the nation-state does not even figure as a relevant framework.

Other theories of postmodernity have quite explicitly argued for the obsolescence of the nation-state and heralded this as opening up potential new spaces of tolerance for the 'stranger'.[3] Even on this analysis, however, the search for community goes on. The contemporary quest for shelter from the chill winds of ontological insecurity, of contingency, it has been argued, results in what Michel Maffesoli[4] has called 'neo-tribalism'. Such tribes, we are told, are formed 'as concepts rather than integrated social bodies—by the multitude of individual acts of self-identification. Such agencies as might from time to time emerge to hold the faithful together have limited executive power and little control over cooptation and banishment'.[5]

Such a view leads to the temptation to see national identity as on all fours with other forms of group identity. It is precisely this that has lately been encapsulated in the slogan of 'neo-tribalism'. In its most popular variants this, in some respects, acute perception of new forms of affiliation has degenerated into seeing all collectivities as choosable life-styles or sub-cultures.

In a neo-tribal world, on this account, if we don't like the company, we can opt out. Nothing like the cohesive tribes of old. While this might well account for many of the vagaries of everyday life in the advanced capitalist world, it does not give us much purchase upon what we are presently witnessing: namely 'the rebirth of history' in the former Soviet bloc and also in parts of the west (or perhaps, now, the centre)—the reunification of Germany being the most dramatic case in point.

In fact, some forms of collective identity are much more potent (and potentially stable) than others as Alberto Melucci[6] has argued. He observes that 'ethno-national mobilisation' understood as 'the formation, maintenance and alteration through time of a self-reflexive identity' arises from the contradictory realities of 'post-industrial democracies' in which there are both pressures to integrate and a need for identity-building. Like Bauman, Melucci argues that the nation-state system is exhausted, with decision-making moving to the global and local levels. However, Melucci sees ethnic identities as particularly powerful expressions of symbolic self-assertion, although as by no means reducible to a single form: for instance, they may express the desire within a given community to be recognised as legitimately different; alternatively they may have a territorial basis and reflect a desire to control a particular space. The first case suggests that of an ethnic community seeking rights within a wider social order. The latter comes closer to the ethnic basis of national identity, where autonomy or separatism might be on the order of the day, depending upon circumstances.

By contrast with the view that the multiplication of identities may offer scope for an end to xenophobia, Melucci rightly notes that such manifestations of diversity do carry inherent risks, as the pursuit of difference and the interests associated with this may become a source of conflict. The problem is then how the new rules of the game become established. That clearly depends upon the extent to which the conditions of genuine democracy and a civic culture are met—whether within a given state or between states, that is, internationally.

I would suggest that the present salience of national identity in European politics confutes the view that the grand narratives are *passé*, and that there are no compelling tales of solidarity to tell. Both the emergent nation-states of the old East, and the supranationalising European Community are heavily dependent upon convincing us that tales of solidarity within bounded communities are both plausible and desirable.

Clearly, the old model of national sovereignty will not do, given the reality of global interdependence. As William Wallace has pointed out, 'Inward and outward investment, multinational production, migration, mass travel, mass communications, all erode the boundaries that 19th century governments built between the national and the foreign'.[7] Alain Bihr[8] has similarly identified a crisis of the west European nation-state's capacity to manage its political-economic space that is due to the combined impact of economic internationalisation and decentralist demands from below. He argues that new 'systems of states' are emerging, with the EC as an alliance of capitalisms whose rival blocs are centred on the USA and Japan. However, it is precisely the decline in the state's capacity to manage *national* politics and guarantee the internal social order that has given rise to the search for new identities, based on ethnic, regional, religious and extreme nationalist perspectives. Étienne Balibar, from a different theoretical perspective, has come to a similar conclusion. He argues that the state in Europe today is neither national nor supranational and that the classic exercise of centralised power has disappeared: 'All the conditions are therefore present for a sense of *identity panic* to be produced and maintained. For individuals fear the state—particularly the most deprived and the most remote from power—but they fear still more its disappearance and decomposition'.[9]

Such macro- and micro-structural changes articulate with, and modify, any given national identity. Although the current situation in Europe is extremely confusing it is, nevertheless, too early to write off the nation-state and its relation to questions of collective identity. Despite being squeezed by the global and the local (as many have justly pointed out) it still remains a crucial point of reference. For Europeans, for around two centuries, this political form has offered an overarching normative ideal of collective identification and its time is not yet past, as the emergence of new nation-states in eastern and central Europe, and the internal strains in several western states amply testifies.

In Europe, as is well known, the nation-state has come into existence over a lengthy time-span and by quite distinct development paths. Following an established tradition of analysis, Anthony Smith has usefully distinguished between the Western model and the Eastern. The former, he characterises thus:

Historic territory, legal-political community, legal-political equality of members, and common civic culture and ideology; these are the components of the standard, Western model of the nation.[10]

This is contrasted with:

Genealogy and presumed descent ties, popular mobilisation, vernacular languages, customs and traditions: these are the elements of an alternative, ethnic conception of the nation, one that mirrored the different route of 'nation-formation' travelled by many countries in Eastern Europe and Asia and one that constituted a dynamic political challenge.[11]

Looked at from this point of view, the European Community's construction has something of the character of the administrative-bureaucratic mode of state-formation rather than the quest by an ethnic group to create a state for itself. The political classes of a group of nation-states (with varying degrees of popular support in different places) are in the process of trying to fashion an overarching political structure—in effect to create a state. Political union, a common economic space, a common defence identity . . . all of these point to the key appurtenances of statehood. The pluri-ethnic character of the emergent political formation, and the mixed legacy of nation-states (differently sedimented in their respective national cultures), poses a singular problem of collective identity formation. What can this Europe *mean*? What points of *identification* can it come to offer to its peoples?

Post-Maastricht, the euphemism 'ever closer union' may for some British politicians be a phrase more acceptable than 'federalism'. But however one finesses it, the *ultima ratio* of the current integration process surely eventually points to a central source of political legitimacy in the EC, ultimately disposing of a monopoly of the means of violence. If integration continues, we are talking about the eventual emergence of a new regime and source of sovereign authority. This is part of our modern understanding of the prerequisites for statehood. And the rather faltering steps taken towards a so-called European defence identity proclaim such a recognition, as does the oft-uttered trope that Europe should now acknowledge its superpower status in the world.

And yet, the ultimate boundaries of the Euro-state remain undefined—the eventual accession of the EFTA countries and the closer association of other states in the former communist bloc will ensure that this remains unresolved for the foreseeable future. It is worth saying that there is no good reason to suppose that the EC's politico-economic development path (fundamentally shaped by the realities of the Cold War) represents an ideal for the whole of Europe. Nor, as Helen Wallace[12] points out, should we assume that all parts of the continent require to be—or could be—integrated in precisely the same form given the very different needs and starting-points that are to be found.

So far as the question of collective identity is concerned, one question to be posed in relation to such future enlargement is whether we can plausibly conceive of talking of an eventual European nation-state? To be a 'European' is different from being a member of a 'European nation'. The latter, much more acutely than the former, raises an unavoidable cultural question about what the common basis of Euro-identity might be. It is telling to note the vagueness with which this question is commonly addressed. As Helen Wallace has recently noted, it is hard to characterise 'Europeanness'. She suggests that there are some 'core values', such as democracy, the rule of law, the military will to defend pluralism, a sense of political community, practices of consensus-building.[13] In similar vein, Pierre Hassner[14] has written of the countries of the former communist bloc reclaiming their European identity which he describes as 'adopting democratic and parliamentarian institutions, private property and the market, and expecting their standard of living to rise, in turn, to Western standards.' The list could be expanded or otherwise changed: without an adequate place for culture it does not add up to a convincing recipe for a collective identity.

This is precisely Anthony Smith's point, when he argues that the conditions for either a European super-state or super-nation have not been met. If there is a basis for transcending the nation-state in Europe, he argues, it is located in what he defines as the patterns of European culture:

the heritage of Roman law, Judeo-Christian ethics, Renaissance humanism and individualism, Enlightenment rationalism and science, artistic classicism and romanticism, and above all, traditions of civil rights and democracy, which have emerged at various times and places in the continent—have created a common European cultural heritage and formed a unique culture area straddling national boundaries and interrelating their different national cultures through common motifs and traditions.[15]

It is to this 'cultural heritage that creates sentiments of affinity between the peoples of Europe', it is argued, that we should look for the basis of a 'cultural Pan-European nationalism' which can overarch but 'not abolish individual nations'. Precisely how such cultural traits might be articulated into an identity is not specified: one can only assume that long-standing practice in the diverse nations, and the elaboration of shared institutional frameworks will produce affinity. But Smith precludes too much social engineering as likely to be counter-productive. Moreover, there are problems in producing such a list, since some of the items are highly disputable (for instance: What price the 'Judeo-Christian' hyphen, in the light of the Holocaust, and current anti-semitism? And what about the feebleness of civic and democratic traditions in many countries?). Besides, the distribution of these various traits across the European space is highly variable. Much of this complex of identifiers is *high* cultural too, and reflects the aspirations and perspectives of the intelligentsia. Even if we were to set these objections aside, current tendencies in Europe do not suggest that the potency of such a conception of European culture should be taken too seriously, in the short to medium term at least. In any case, Smith himself admits that Pan-nationalism can produce ethnic and nationalist reactions. Good intentions offer no escape.

To get the measure of the problem it is worth considering what is involved in talking about collective identities, that is, the means whereby collectivities construct and reconstruct a sense of themselves by reference to the signs provided by cultures.

Briefly, my position is this. First, the making of identities is an active process that involves inclusion and exclusion. To be 'us', we need those who are 'not-us'. Second, the imaginary process of creating traditions and of activating collective memories extends through time. The dark side of memory is amnesia; to shed light is also to throw shadows. Third, collective identities have a spatial referent, although this need not always conform to a model of territorial concentration and juridico-political integrity: you can belong to a religious diaspora or an ideocratic community (in Raymond Aron's phrase) such as the communist world and still identify with a given collectivity. In Europe, however, the primordial collective attachment does seem to be to a land or territory with defined boundaries.

Currently, the supranationalist quest of the European Community is compelling us to rethink the nature of the nation-state, a political, economic and cultural entity that is identity-conferring. European statehood—whatever concessions are made to 'subsidiarity'—will finally change the scope of contemporary conceptions of citizenship: the rights and duties of citizens will be redefined and the scope of allegiances shifted. They will need to become actively multifold. [. . .]

In the EC, there is no predominant cultural nation that can become the core of the would-be state's nation and hegemonise Euro-culture. It is difficult to conceive of engineering a collective identity—although this has been considered, particularly in respect of a mistaken view of what European television might produce. The production of an overarching collective identity can only seriously be conceived as the outcome of long-standing social and political practice. [. . .] Collective belief in the virtue of a civic order, however, does not seem to be the most compelling mobilising cry for Europe in the 1990s.

However, were such a conception—*demos* before *ethnos*—to have any chance of success, it is clear that broader active identification with the political construction of the European community could only come about if the so-called 'democratic deficit' were to be eliminated. [. . .] Amongst other things, this will involve recognising the potential and actual internal diversity of the existing nation-states within any larger supranational configuration.

The trick is a difficult one to turn as it involves the production of an overarching 'European' identity that can articulate with the official identities of existing nation-states and also with the emergent identities of regions. But it is not enough to define an identity from within, as it were; as I have suggested, it is also defined from without, interactively. [. . .]

Euro-integrationism, then, is one quest for ultimate statehood, with what results one can only presently conjecture. The possibility of constructing a European identity within the Community is rather slim, if we take as the model of *supra*-national identity the continuing powerful appeal of national identity as articulated by the official states of Community Europe. This model will not do, unless we suppose a substantial transfer of affect and identification to the supranational level. [. . .]

But there is also another level of possible contradiction. Within the boundaries of the EC, as indicated, there are stirrings of regionalisms with a nationalist potentiality. [. . .]

In one sense, then, processes of integration at the level of the EC could be said to be producing disintegration at the level of the nation-state, by way of the variable impact of the uneven development of capitalism at the level of the region. It is not clear how these pressures, in turn, will transform the present character of the nation-state—which is, after all, the present building-block of the EC. Whether these so-called neo-nationalisms turn into a separate quest for nation-statehood, fuelled by a sense of politico-cultural difference, remains to be seen. There is currently a vested interest on the part of central state governments and regionalists alike in fudging the issue. But it is reasonable to ask whether a Europe of the Regions is not ultimately in contradiction with a Europe of the Nation-States.

It is doubtless this perception, amongst others, that tips regionalists into being separatists. Nation-statehood, because of its institutional clout, offers two signal advantages within the present dispensation: first, it transforms regional status (i.e. virtual invisibility) into international recognition; second, it offers a greater measure of protection both against the former nation-state to which the separatists belonged and also against what might come to be seen as undesired features of Europeanisation. Statehood, under present rules, is a more effective vehicle for the articulation of interests than regionality. It therefore remains attractive, and might become even more attractive as new states (sometimes very small in population) clamour to join the EC. [. . .]

Nobody yet knows whether the EC will eventually constitute an umbrella framework for all European states. In the current metaphor the new architecture is still at the planning stage, although certain components of the European House—such as the EC, the WEU, EFTA, the CSCE, the Coucil of Europe—are already waiting on site. How these, and other elements (such as the Atlantic bridge at the heart of NATO), will be fitted together—or, indeed, whether they can be—is far from clear.

The debate about the 'deepening' or 'widening' of the EC is, of course, one about political economy and geopolitics. But in a generally unrecognised sense it is also one about culture. As the centre of the attraction of Europe, the EC represents the desirable future of 'Europeanism', however difficult that may be to define. Central to this representation, however, are the (social) market economy coupled with various forms of pluralistic democracy and civil society. Whatever the institutional realities, these stand as tokens of a level of civilisation or culture that represents both an aspiration for those who do not have it, and as a normative criterion for the haves with which to judge the credentials of the would-be aspirants. What Ernest Gellner has called the 'federal-cantonal' model of western European integration (if such it turns out to be) offers a potential way out of the ethnic hostilities that presently beset much of the old Eastern bloc. [. . .]

But how open is the door going to be to the nations of Central and Eastern Europe and the former Soviet empire? When there still Soviet Union, some proposed its exclusion on grounds of size, others on cultural grounds—namely that it was not European, but at best Eurasian. Which of the new republics will now pass the qualifying test and why? One must ask, because Central Europe's designation by Milan Kundera, almost a decade ago, as a kidnapped part of the West has its echoes in contemporary strategic thinking. With the collapse of communism, the formula has been recodified by asking where the writ of Roman Catholicism stops and where Orthodoxy begins. Thus religious resignation does the work of politico-cultural distinction. It does not seem far-fetched to argue, as does Michel Foucher, that the knew geopolitical lines in Europe could broadly follow those of the Great Schism of 1054 between Rome and Constantinople, with the Orthodox East coming second best to the recaptured Catholic West. [. . .]

If this is broadly correct, it somewhat complicates the arguments that Europe's Christian heritage (alongside political and economic designations) offers a coherent basis for the construction of common sentiments. Looked at from the inside, confessional devisions within Christendom remain, and these articulate with national questions in many cases. Looked at from the outside, however, whatever the considerable distortions involved, Christianity as a broad designation could be used to differentiate Europe from its neibours. Now that the godless Other of communism no longer functions as an ennemy there is something of a void. [. . .]

Islam has in some respects begun to fill the void brought about by the Soviet empire's collapse. It has been constructed both as an external threat in foreign policy terms and as an internal one by way of problematising the assimilability of

Muslims and by the demographic scare about migration from North and West Africa. The unacceptability of Turkey for EC membership because of its Muslim character periodically resurfaces in this connection. This links into the much broader issue of the position of Islamic minorities in Europe and obviously poses the question of the relations between being Muslim and being European. [. . .]

Turkey, it would seem, is seen ambivalently. On the one hand, as a 'secular' Muslim state it offers a development path contrary to that of 'fundamentalism', and thus its regional influence in the Turkic-speaking world may be seen as benign. On the other hand, as indicated, it is not 'European' enough. It is instructive to note, in this connection, that one evident motive behind Turkey's recognition of Bosnia-Herzegovina is that it has an officially designated Muslim population whose Europeannees cannot readily be denied, given that Yugoslavia has been long considered to be a European state. That 'Muslim' is now as much an ethnic as a religious designation is besides the point. The Ottoman legacy may continue to haunt Europe as much as does Byzantium.

Currently, despite the drive towards European unity in western Europe, counter-tendencies are only too much in evidence elsewhere. [. . .] The rebirth of history in the shape of the ethno-national reawakening of the old East is, with the demise of Yugoslavia and the USSR, leading to new configurations between nations and states, but in ways that are not yet clear-cut. The unresolved boundary questions between other states that cut through national groups—Hungary and Romania, for instance—or between component nationalities is an existing state—as in Czecho-Slovakia—raise many questions about the future of pacific conflict resolution in Europe. Especially so as nationalism, racism, and anti-semitism appear to be functioning as ideological replacements for official Marxism-Leninism in many of the post-communist states. [. . .]

This raises once again the relation between the crisis of the state form and crises of national identity. Clearly, if the valorisation of the nation-state and assertive nationalism become more deeply entrenched in post-communist Europe, this will pose a fundamental obstacle to an EC-style development path for the old East, because an overarching cultural Europeanism, one that in certain repects supersedes the national level, will eventually be indispensable (although I suspect that it is actually impossible). [. . .]

If we shift the focus again to the EC, fears of an incipient Fortress Europe appear to be borne out by current developments in terms of governmental concerns about the defence and policing of the outer frontiers as the inner ones become less salient. The extreme and often violent racist reaction to migration currently so much in evidence in Belgium, France, Italy and Germany makes one pose some further questions about how we might arrive at a transcendant 'Europeanism' that needs to embrace that vast diversity and complexity of this continent. For this is the supposedly pacific heartland of the nascent Euro-state. And such developments do also force a consideration of the links between forms of racism and nationalism when manifesting 'excess'. There is a case for saving, as does Balibar that such racism has deep roots in Europe, marked by the historical experiences both of colonialism abroad and of anti-semitism at home, and that the underlying, socially borne, propensity to discriminate comes to the surface in forms determined by the given political conjuncture. [. . .]

Current racism and anti-semitism in western Europe are to some extent the counterparts of the resurgent ethno-nationalism in the old East, and, as suggested earlier, may well reflect the crisis of the nation-state as a political instance. There is a justifiable fear that eastern nationalism may feed the nationalisms of the west and vice versa.

Characteristically, much of this new wave of nationalistic racism on both sides of the old Iron Curtain takes refuge in an essentialist conception of the nation: if your race or culture or religion do not fit the parameters, then you cannot belong. This poses a special danger to the EC project, for how can this western neo-nationalism—with its strong Nazi overtones—be squared with the professed expansive conception of Europeanness? It marks a rejection of pluri-culturalism and if this becomes a respectable political project— which it shows every sign of doing, paradigmatically in France, but also elsewhere—the prospects for building civic national identities will be seriously weakened. *Ethnos* threatens *demos*. Whatever the distinctive motivations and causes within each national context, the demand for pure identities within the major western nation-states would seem to manifest a desire for a simpler, more orderly, world, one that is purged of ambiguity—and therefore of the wrong kinds of people. Europe's current demographic panic, in which nervous eyes are cast to the Southern Mediterranean and towards the east of the German frontiers, is also part of this tendency.

My own perspective on the tensions that presently beset the nation-state in Europe compels me to note the paradoxical character of today's developments. On the one hand, the difficult search for a transcendent unity by the EC—one which must recognise component differences—throws the nation-state into question from above, arguably contributing to crises of national identity. The political and economic developments in the integration process, however, are out of phase with the cultural: what European identity *might be* still remains an open question. On the other hand, the ethno-nationalist awakenings in the former communist bloc and current developments within western Europe—whether neo-nationalist separatisms or racist nationalisms—tend to reaffirm the principle of the nation-state as a locus of identity and of political control.

Thus, Europe is simultaneously undergoing processes of centralisation and of fragmentation. These processes pass through the nation-state and are more and more throwing into relief questions of collective identity. Culture is therefore going to be one of the key political battlefields in the 1990s.

['Europeanness: A New Cultural Battlefield?', *Innovation*, 5/1 (1992), 12–18, 22.]

Notes

Extract 2

JOSEPH STALIN: *The Nation*

1. The abolition of serfdom in Georgia (1863–7).

Extract 3

MAX WEBER: *The Nation*

1. Organ of Prussian Junkers.
2. The text breaks off here. Notes on the manuscript indicate that Weber intended to deal with the idea and development of the national state throughout history. The following sentence is to be found on the margin: 'There is a close connection between the prestige of culture and the prestige of power.' Every victorious war enhances the prestige of culture (Germany (1871), Japan (1905), etc.). The question of whether war contributes to the 'development of culture' cannot be answered in a 'value neutral' way. Certainly there is no unambiguous answer (Germany after 1870!), not even when we consider empirical evidence, for characteristically German art and literature did not originate in the political centre of Germany. (Note of German editors.) The supplementary passage that follows is from Max Weber's comment on a paper by Karl Barth, *Gesammelte Aufsaetze zur Soziologie und Sozialpolitik* (Tubingen, 1924), 484–6.

Extract 4

KARL W. DEUTSCH: *Nationalism and Social Communication*

1. Cf. Max Huber, 'Swiss Nationality,' in Sir Alfred Zimmern (ed.), *Modern Political Doctrines* (Oxford University Press: London, 1939), 216–17.
2. Ernst Schuerch, *Sprachpolitische Erinnerungen* (Paul Haupt Verlag: Bern, 1943), 36–7.
3. This fundamental connection between a people and a community of mutual understanding seems to be reflected in some languages in the etymology of the terms involved. According to Karl Lamprecht, 'the word *Deutsch* is found already in the second half of the eighth century derived from the West-Aryan word root *diot*, "people", and its derivations *diutin*, "to adapt to the people" (*volksgemaess machen*) and *githiuti*, "intelligibility"; and this word *Deutsch* is developed in the meaning of "intelligible to the people" and applied to the language' (Karl Lamprecht, *Deutsche Geschichte*, 6th edn. (Weidmann: Berlin, 1920), i. 18–19). This development occurred first in border areas, where Germanic speech appeared as something common to different Germanic tribes, and in contrast to the Romance dialects of their neighbours (ibid. 18). Even in modern German the similarity between *Deutsch* and *deuten* (to point, to explain, to interpret), *deutlich* (clear, distinct), and *Deutung* (interpretation), seems suggestive. It seems to hint that there is an element of communication in the very concept of a people, and an element of social community in the very concepts of understanding and interpretation. For examples of

extreme overstatements of this view by Richard Wagner and others see Louis L. Snyder, *German Nationalism: The Tragedy of a People* (Stackpole: Harrisburg, Pa., 1952), 162–3, 171, with references.

4. Cf. J. K. Roberts and E. L. Gordy, 'Development', in C. Furnas (ed.), *Research in Industry, Its Organization and Management* (Van Nostrand: New York, 1948), 32–4.

5. Insufficient appreciation of this relationship often led to trouble. If attempts were made to suppress a nationality group, it would live on in the communicative characteristics of its individual members. If these individuals gained recognition for their rights, as in the Minorities Treaties after World War I, they would tend to act again as groups. 'It was individuals—nationals of a state who differed from the majority in "race, language or religion"—who were guaranteed against discrimination in linguistic and cultural as well as in their religious and civil rights. But the rights of language, education and culture are really *group* rights, requiring social institutions for their implementation and realization. Such institutions became the bulwark of a minority in the struggle to preserve its nationality and culture. Yet the minority *as a group was legally non-existent*, and could therefore exercise no effective control over its cultural agencies. The state, required by the Minorities Treaties to provide adequate educational facilities for the children of minorities, retained full control of the public schools. And the state, as the embodiment of the national–cultural aspirations of the majority, would naturally favor the dominant culture. In east-central Europe, with its heritage of forced assimilation, of which we must never lose sight, such a relationship was bound to result in strife.' Oscar I. Janowsky, *Nationalities and National Minorities* (Macmillan: New York, 1945), 132–3, with reference to the opinion rendered by a majority of the Permanent Court of International Justice in the Albanian Minority Schools case, *Judgment, Orders and Advisory Opinions*, Series A–B, Fascicule No. 64.

6. Or a somewhat lesser improbability of such a rise. In either case, the difference in vertical social mobility may become as important as the basic difference in the effectiveness of social communication.

7. For an elaboration of 'social processes' and organizations promoting face-to-face contacts and possible substitutions between members of different social classes, see W. Lloyd Warner and Paul S. Lunt, *The Status System of a Modern Community* (Yale University Press: New Haven, Conn., 1942), 5–66, particularly p. 20ff., and the chart on p. 17. It is striking that the only organization on this chart which offers vertical contacts throughout the authors' six social classes is a nationalistic organization, The American Legion.

Extract 5

CLIFFORD GEERTZ: *Primordial and Civic Ties*

1. See, for example, K. Deutsch, *Nationalism and Social Communication* (Wiley: New York, 1953), 1–14; R. Emerson, *From Empire to Nation* (Harvard University Press: Cambridge, Mass., 1960); J. Coleman, *Nigeria: Background to Nationalism* (University of California Press: Berkeley, Calif., 1958), 419ff.; F. Hertz, *Nationalism in History and Politics* (Oxford University Press: New York, 1944), 11–15.

2. Walter Z. Laqueur (ed.), *The Middle East in Transition: Studies in Contemporary History* (Praeger: New York, 1958).

3. Coleman, op. cit., 425–6.

4. Emerson, op. cit., 95–6.

5. I. Berlin, *Two Concepts of Liberty* (Oxford University Press: New York, 1958), 42.

6. E. Shils, 'Political Development in the New States', *Comparative Studies in Society and History*, 2 (1960), 265–92; 379–411.

7. E. Shils, 'Primordial, Personal, Sacred and Civil Ties', *British Journal of Sociology* (June 1957).

8. For a similar but rather differently conceived and organized listing, see Emerson, op. cit., chs. 6, 7, and 8.

Extract 6

ANTHONY GIDDENS: *The Nation as Power-Container*

1. Cf. S. B. Jones, *Boundary Making: a Handbook for Statesmen* (Carnegie Endowment for International Peace: Washington, DC, 1945).

2. T. R. V. Prescott, *Boundaries and Frontiers* (Croom Helm: London, 1978), 65.

3. A. Giddens, *A Contemporary Critique of Historical Materialism* (Macmillan: London, 1981), 190.

Extract 7

WALKER CONNOR: *A Nation is a Nation, is a State, is an Ethnic Group, is a . . .*

1. Jack C. Plano and Roy Olton, *The International Relations Dictionary* (Holt, Rinehart and Winston, Inc.: New York, 1969), 119, emphasis added.

2. Conrad Brandt, Benjamin Schwartz, and John Fairbank, *A Documentary History of Chinese Communism* (George Allen & Unwin Ltd.: London, 1952), 245, parenthetic material added.

3. Max Weber, *Economy and Society*, ed. Guenther Roth and Claus Wittich (Bedminster Press: New York, 1968) 395, notes that 'the concept of "nationality" (or "nation") shares with that of the "people" (*Volk*)—in the "ethnic" sense—the vague connotation that whatever is felt to be distinctively common must derive from common descent.' An old European definition of a nation, though intended to be humorous and derisive and which Karl Deutsch cites as such, hit almost the same mark: 'A nation is a group of people united by a common error about their ancestry and a common dislike of their neighbors' (*Nationalism and Its Alternatives* (Alfred A. Knopf: New York, 1969), 3).

4. A recent example of the loose manner in which 'nation' may be used is a work, published in the United States, entitled *Lesbian Nation*.

5. Raymond Williams, *Keywords: A Vocabulary of Culture and Society* (Oxford University Press: New York, 1976), 178.

6. Louis J. Halle, *Civilization and Foreign Policy* (Harper & Row: New York, 1952), 10. For another example of this practice of referring to states as nation-states, see Dankwart Rustow, *A World of Nations* (Brookings: Washington, DC, 1967), 30 for a reference to the United Kingdom and the Soviet Union as nation-states. Note also Rustow's concluding remarks (p. 282): 'More than 130 *nations*, real or so-called, will each make its contribution to the history of the late twentieth century. . .'. For other illustrations, see this writer's 'Ethnonationalism in the First World: The present in historical

perspective', in Milton Esman (ed.), *Ethnic Pluralism and Conflict in the Western World* (Cornell University Press: Ithaca, NY, 1977), particularly 20–1.

7. By a potential nation is meant a group of people who appear to have all of the necessary prerequisites for nationhood, but who have not as yet developed a consciousness of their sameness and commonality, nor a conviction that their destinies are interwound. They are usually referred to by anthropologists as ethno-linguistic groups. Such peoples' sense of fundamental identity is still restricted to the locale, extended family, clan, or tribe. The Andean states and South-western Asia offer several illustrations of such pre-national people.

8. A random survey of books, published within the United States and designed for college courses in global politics, will provide ample documentation of the impact this misuse of terminology has exerted upon the discipline. In addition to the host of titles consisting of or containing the expressions *International Relations* or *International Politics* are such well-known examples as *Politics Among Nations, The Might of Nations, Nations and Men, The Insecurity of Nations, How Nations Behave,* and *Games Nations Play.* Another illustration is offered by the American professional organiza-tion called the International Studies Association. Its official *raison d'être*, as set forth in the early issues of its Quarterly, notes that the organization 'is devoted to the orderly growth of knowledge concerning the impact of nation upon nation'.

9. Plano and Olton, op. cit. 119, 120.

10. Ibid. 120.

11. See G. de Bertier de Sauvigny, 'Liberalism, nationalism, and socialism: The birth of three words', *Review of Politics,* 32 (Apr. 1970), particularly 155–61.

12. A. Hitler, *Mein Kampf* (Reynal and Hitchcock: New York, 1940), 595.

13. For details, see this writer's 'The Political Significance of Ethnonationalism within Western Europe', in Abdul Said and Luiz Simmons (eds.), *Ethnicity in an International Context* (Transaction Books, Inc.: Edison, NJ, 1976), particularly 126–30.

14. George Theodorson and Achilles Theodorson, *A Modern Dictionary of Sociology* (Thomas Crowell and Co.: New York, 1969), 135. For a similar definition, see H. S. Morris's selection on 'Ethnic Groups' in *The International Encyclopedia of the Social Sciences* (Macmillan and Co., and The Free Press: New York, 1968).

15. Nathan Glazer and Daniel P. Moynihan, *Ethnicity: Theory and Experience* (Harvard University Press: Cambridge, Mass., 1975), 18.

16. See, for example, Peter Busch, *Legitimacy and Ethnicity* (D. C. Heath and Co.: Lexington, Mass., 1974), in which ethnicity refers to the breakdown of the popula-tion of Singapore into Chinese, Malay, and other such components, and in which nationalism refers to identity with the Singaporean state.

17. See, for example, Tomotshu Shibutani and Kian Kwan, *Ethnic Stratification: A Comparative Approach* (Macmillan and Co.: New York, 1965), 47, where an ethnic group is defined as composed of 'those who conceive of themselves as being alike by virtue of their common ancestry, real or fictitious, and who are so regarded by others'.

18. Weber, op. cit. 389.

19. See above, note 3.

20. Weber, op. cit. 923.

21. Ernest Barker, *National Character and the Factors in Its Formation* (Methuen: London, 1927), 173.

22. As Charles Winick, *Dictionary of Anthropology* (Philosophical Library: New York, 1956), 193 has observed with regard to an *ethnos*: 'A group of people linked by both nationality and race. These bonds are usually unconsciously accepted by members of the group, but outsiders observe the homogeneity.'

Extract 8

ELIE KEDOURIE: *Nationalism and Self-Determination*

1. The Rebbe's letter is reproduced and translated in I. Domb, *The Transformation*, pub. by the author (1958).

Extract 9

ERNEST GELLNER: *Nationalism and Modernization*

1. It is of course possible for nominally independent political units to exist in a kind of educationally parasitic way. But the present argument is not really undermined by the existence of Monaco or Andorra. Once, it used to be a cliché common in discussions of democracy, that democracy was easily conceivable in a state of the size of classical Athens or the Geneva remembered by Rousseau, but that it is hard to practise it in large modern territorial states. Suddenly, one no longer encounters this perception. It is sometimes said that Yoruba cities resemble those of classical Greece in their structure. The Nigerian Ministry of Education has sent no request for Professors of Classics, to act as technical advisers on how to reproduce a Periclean Age. It is hard to take a very passionate, practically relevant interest in what could or could not be done in old Athens or Geneva. Suddenly, it is taken for granted that a large, territorial modern state is a precondition of any kind of social order currently acceptable.

   The point is, of course, that apart from the slightly embarrassing matter of slavery, and the lower material standard of living (which one might accept), the Greek miracle was far too precarious to tempt emulation today. We might wish for the miracle, but not at the price of such precariousness. A modern society yearns for the security springing from the affluent contentment of its citizens. This is perhaps a weakness of a work such as Popper's *Open Society and Its Enemies*, in as far as *its* image of 'the transition' is too much inspired by the Greek miracle. There may have been many breakdowns of tribal societies, most of them not very fertile, and all precarious. They can hardly now provide us with our crucial myth.

2. It is interesting to highlight this point by reflecting on the notoriously unworkable constitution of post-independence Cyprus. What made it unworkable is the autonomy of the two communities, with their power of veto over changes. It is amusing to reflect that the running of an incomparably larger political unit, in the same region of the world—the Ottoman Empire—was perfectly possible on the basis not of two, but of even more autonomous cultural (religious) units, *milets*. Indeed, such units not merely presented no obstacle to the functioning of the state, they were the very basis of its functioning. What had changed? It is not that the Cypriots of today are more ferocious and intolerant than all other Middle Easterners, including their own grandfathers, had been in the past. It is rather that the role of a modern government and its pervasive and multiform activities, the radical changes it effects in daily life, are such that they are no longer compatible with autonomous sub-communities of the *milet* kind.

3. W. W. Rostow, *The Stages of Economic Growth* (Cambridge, 1960).
4. Germaine Tillion, *L'Algérie en 1957* (Paris, 1957).
5. Of course this model is merely the simplest case. More complex variants are possible. For one thing, the tidal wave can hit various groups at different times despite the fact that they are located in the same territory: the pre-existing culture and/or social organization of various groups makes some of them far more adaptable, far readier to profit from modernization or social change, than others. Or again, a group may have motives for secession, for hiving off or even for seeking a long-lost territory, not because it is less fitted to operate in a modern context, but because it is *more* fitted to do so. A minority group more successful in adaptation than the host majority, or the host political authority, may excite jealousy and covetousness, find itself the scapegoat in the crises which accompany social change, and have no option but to seek its security in a new nationalism, even if individual members of such a group have no economic incentive in this direction.

Extract 10
ERNEST GELLNER: *Nationalism and High Cultures*

1. G. W. F. Hegel, *Lectures on the Philosophy of World History*, trans. H. N. Nisbet (Cambridge, 1975), 134.
2. Yu. V. Bromley *et al.*, *Sovremennye Etnicheskie Protsessy v SSSR* (Contemporary Ethnic Processes in the USSR) (Moscow, 1975).

Extract 12
ERIC HOBSBAWM: *The Nation as Invented Tradition*

1. Eugene Weber, *Peasants into Frenchmen: The Modernization of Rural France, 1870–1914* (Stanford, Calif., 1976).
2. This was conclusively demonstrated in 1914 by the socialist parties of the Second International, which not only claimed to be essentially international in scope, but actually sometimes regarded themselves officially as no more than national sections of a global movement ('Section Française de l'Internationale Ouvrière').
3. Georges Duveau, *Les Instituteurs* (Paris, 1957); J. Ozouf (ed.), *Nous les Maîtres d'École: Autobiographies d'Instituteurs de la Belle Époque* (Paris, 1967).
4. Alice Gerard, *La Revolution Française: Mythes et Interpretations, 1789–1970* (Paris, 1970), ch. 4.
5. Charles Rearick, 'Festivals in modern France: The experience of the 3rd Republic', *Journal of Contemporary History*, 7/3 (July 1977), 435–60; Rosemonde Sanson, *Les 14 Juillet, Fête et Conscience Nationale, 1789–1975* (Paris, 1976), with bibliography.
6. For the political intentions of the 1889 one, cf. Debora L. Silverman, 'The 1889 Exhibition: The crisis of bourgeois individualism', *Oppositions, A Journal for Ideas and Criticism in Architecture* (Spring, 1977), 71–91.
7. M. Agulhon, 'La Statumanie et l'Histoire', *Ethnologie Française*, 3–4 (1978), 3–4.
8. M. Agulhon, 'Esquisse pour une Archéologie de la République: l'Allegorie Civique Feminine', *Annales ESC*, 28 (1973), 5–34.
9. Whitney Smith, *Flags through the Ages* (New York, 1975), 116–18. The nationalist black-red-gold appears to have emerged from the student movement of the post-Napoleonic period, but was clearly established as the flag of the national movement

in 1848. Resistance to the Weimar Republic reduced its national flag to a party banner—indeed the militia of the Social Democratic Party took it as its title ('Reichsbanner'), though the anti-republican right was divided between the imperial flag and the National Socialist flag, which abandoned the traditional tricolour design, possibly because of its associations with nineteenth-century liberalism, possibly as not sufficiently indicative of a radical break with the past. However, it maintained the basic colour scheme of the Bismarckian empire (black-white-red), while stressing the red, hitherto the symbol only of the socialist and labour movements. The Federal Republic and the Democratic Republic both returned to the colours of 1848, the former without additions, the latter with a suitable emblem adapted from the basic model of the Communist and Soviet hammer-and-sickle.

10. Hans-Georg John, *Politik und Turnen: die deutsche Turnerschaft als nationale Bewegung im deutschen Kaiserreich von 1871–1914* (Ahrensberg bei Hamburg, 1976), 41ff.

11. 'Fate determined that, against his nature, he should become a monumental sculptor, who was to celebrate the imperial idea of William II in giant monuments of bronze and stone, in a language of imagery and ever-emphatic pathos' (Ulrich Thieme and Felix Becker, *Allgemeines Lexikon der bildenden Künstler von der Antike bis zur Gegenwart* (Leipzig, 1907–50), iii. 185). See also, in general, entries under Begas, Schilling, Schmitz.

12. John, op. cit.; T. Nipperdey, 'Nationalidee und Nationaldenkmal in Deutschland im 19. Jahrhundert', *Historische Zeitschrift* (June 1968), 577ff.

13. J. Surel, 'La Première Image de John Bull, Bourgeois Radical, Anglais Loyaliste (1779–1815)', *Le Mouvement Social*, 56 (Jan.–Mar. 1979), 65–84; Herbert M. Atherton, *Political Prints in the Age of Hogarth* (Oxford, 1974), 97–100.

14. Heinz Stallmann, *Das Prinz-Heinrichs-Gymnasium zu Schöneberg, 1890–1945: Geschichte einer Schule* (Berlin, n.d. [1965]).

15. There was in fact no official German national anthem. Of the three competing songs, 'Heil Dir Im Siegerkranz' (to the tune of 'God Save the King'), being most closely associated with the Prussian emperor, roused least national fervour. The 'Watch on the Rhine' and 'Deutschland Uber Alles' were seen as equal until 1914, but gradually 'Deutschland', more suited to an expansionist imperial policy, prevailed over the 'Watch', whose associations were purely anti-French. Among the German gymnasts by 1890 the former anthem had become twice as common as the latter, though their movement was particularly keen on the 'Watch', which it claimed to have been instrumental in popularizing. John, op. cit. 38–9.

16. Stallmann, op. cit. 16–19.

17. R. E. Hardt, *Dir Beine der Hohenzollern* (E. Berlin, 1968).

Extract 13

PAUL R. BRASS: *Élite Competition and Nation-Formation*

1. Malcolm Yapp has contrasted the arguments of those theorists of nationalism who see it as a 'natural' phenomenon with those who see it as 'unnatural'. Judith A. Nagata has made a similar comparison between two groups of scholars of ethnicity whom she labels 'primordialists' and 'circumstantialists' in 'Defence of ethnic boundaries: The changing myths and charters of Malay identity', in Charles F. Keyes (ed.), 'Ethnic Change', unpublished manuscript submitted to University of

Washington Press. Joshua A. Fishman contrasts the work of those who approach the study of ethnicity from the subjective, internal point of view of the actors themselves with what he calls the 'objectivist, externalist' school in 'Social theory and ethnography: Neglected perspectives on language and ethnicity in Eastern Europe', in Peter Sugar (ed.), *Ethnic Diversity and Conflict in Eastern Europe* (Santa Barbara, CA: ABC-Clio, 1980). In this paper the two perspectives are referred to as 'primordialist' and 'instrumentalist'. The latter term refers to a perspective that emphasizes the uses to which cultural symbols are put by élites seeking instrumental advantage for themselves or the groups they claim to represent.

2. The quotations are, of course, from Clifford Geertz, 'The integrative revolution: Primordial sentiments and civil politics in the new states', in Clifford Geertz (ed.), *Old Societies and New States: The Quest for Modernity in Asia and Africa* (New York, 1967), 108–10, and 128.

3. Fishman, op. cit., takes this view. An extreme statement of the position may be found in Pierre L. van den Berghe, 'Race and ethnicity: A sociobiological look', *Ethnic and Racial Studies*, 1/4 (Oct. 1978).

4. See especially Fishman, op. cit.; Charles F. Keyes, 'Towards a New Formulation of the Concept of Ethnic Group', *Ethnicity* 3/3 (Sept. 1976), 202–13; and E. K. Francis, *Interethnic Relations: An Essay in Sociological Theory* (New York, 1976), 6–7.

5. See, for example, Joshua A. Fishman, 'Sociolinguistics and the language problems of the developing countries', in Joshua A. Fishman *et al.* (eds.), *Language Problems of Developing Nations* (New York, 1968), 3; and John J. Gumperz, 'Some remarks on regional and social language differences in India', and 'Language problems in the rural development of North India', in University of Chicago, The College, *Introduction to the Civilization of India: Changing Dimensions of Indian Society and Culture* (Chicago, 1957), 31–47.

6. All the situations mentioned in this paragraph have occurred among different language groups in North India. For details, see Paul R. Brass, *Language, Religion and Politics in North India* (London, 1974).

7. The conversion of untouchable Hindu castes in India to Buddhism is a case in point. See Owen M. Lynch, *The Politics of Untouchability: Social Mobility and Social Change in a City of India* (New York, 1969), ch. 5. Another well-known example is the Black Muslim movement in the United States.

8. Keyes, op. cit. 204–5, takes a rather different view on 'the facts of birth' than the one presented here.

9. See especially Geertz, 'The Integrative Revolution'.

10. Fishman, 'Social Theory and Ethnography', is especially insistent on this point. See also Keyes, op. cit. 210.

11. Fishman, 'Social Theory and Ethnography'. Even for the Jews, however, there have been important internal divisions of attitude and feeling towards some aspects of the core culture. For an interesting analysis of the ways in which the meanings of persistent Jewish cultural symbols have been reinterpreted at different times and in different cultural contexts, see Pearl Katz and Fred E. Katz, 'Symbols as charters in culture change: The Jewish case', *Anthropos*, 72 (1977), 486–96.

12. Even if, for example, one accepts Martin Kilson's view that 'black ethnicity' in the United States has 'lacked until recently the quality of authenticity—that is, a true and viable heritage, unquestionable in its capacity to shape and sustain a cohesive

identity or awareness', Blacks have, in fact, adopted or created new cultural symbols and used them to build a political cohesiveness and identity of greater strength than that of other groups with more 'authentic' cultural traditions ('Blacks and neo-ethnicity in American political life', in Nathan Glazer and Daniel P. Moynihan (eds.), *Ethnicity: Theory and Experience* (Cambridge, Mass., 1975), p. 243).

13. Nathan Glazer and Daniel P. Moynihan, 'Introduction', in ibid. 8.

14. Abner Cohen, 'Variables in ethnicity', in Keyes, op. cit.

15. Michael Banton, 'The direction and speed of ethnic change', in ibid.

16. Abner Cohen, *Two-Dimensional Man: An Essay on the Anthropology of Power and Symbolism in Complex Society* (Berkeley, Calif., 1974), 98–102 and 106–10.

17. I have contrasted these opposing points of view and presented my own in Brass, op. cit. ch. 3.

18. Francis Robinson, 'Nation formation: The Brass thesis and Muslim separatism', and Paul R. Brass, 'A reply to Francis Robinson', *Journal of Commonwealth and Comparative Politics* 15/3 (Nov. 1977), 215–34.

19. Francis Robinson, *Separatism Among Indian Muslims: The Politics of the United Provinces' Muslims, 1860–1923* (London, 1974), 13.

Extract 14

BENEDICT ANDERSON: *Imagined Communities*

1. The population of that Europe where print was then known was about 100,000,000 (L. Febvre and H.-J. Martin, *The Coming of the Book. The Impact of Printing, 1450–1800* (New Left Books: London, 1976), 248–9).

2. Emblematic is Marco Polo's *Travels*, which remained largely unknown till its first printing in 1559 (*The Travels of Marco Polo*, trans. and ed. William Marsden (Everyman's Library: London and New York, 1946), p. xiii).

3. Quoted in Elizabeth L. Eisenstein, 'Some conjectures about the impact of printing on Western society and thought: A preliminary report', *Journal of Modern History*, 40/1 (Mar. 1968), 56.

4. Febvre and Martin, op. cit. 122. The original text, however, speaks simply of 'par-dessus les frontières'.

5. Ibid. 187. The original text speaks of 'puissants' (powerful) rather than 'wealthy' capitalists.

6. 'Hence the introduction of printing was in this respect a stage on the road to our present society of mass consumption and of standardization', ibid. 259–60. The original text has 'une civilisation de masse et de standardisation', which may be better rendered 'standardized, mass civilization'.

7. Ibid. 195.

8. Ibid. 289–90.

9. Ibid. 291–5.

10. From this point it was only a step to the situation in seventeenth-century France where Corneille, Molière, and La Fontaine could sell their manuscript tragedies and comedies directly to publishers, who bought them as excellent investments in view of their authors' market reputations. Ibid. 161.

11. Ibid. 310–15.

12. Hugh Seton-Watson, *Nations and States: An Enquiry into the Origins of Nations and the Politics of Nationalism* (Westview Press: Boulder, Colo., 1977), 28–9; Marc Bloch,

Feudal Society, trans. I. A. Manyon (University of Chicago Press: Chicago, 1961), i. 75.

13. We should not assume that administrative vernacular unification was immediately or fully achieved. It is unlikely that the Guyenne ruled from London was ever primarily administered in Early English.
14. Bloch, op. cit., i. 98.
15. Seton-Watson, op. cit. 48.
16. Ibid. 83.
17. An agreeable confirmation of this point is provided by François I, who, as we have seen, banned all printing of books in 1535 and made French the language of his courts four years later!
18. It was not the first 'accident' of its kind. Febvre and Martin note that while a visible bourgeoisie already existed in Europe by the late thirteenth century, paper did not come into general use until the end of the fourteenth. Only paper's smooth plane surface made the mass reproduction of texts and pictures possible—and this did not occur for still another seventy-five years. But paper was not a European invention. It floated in from another history—China's—through the Islamic world. Febvre and Martin, op. cit. 22, 30, and 45.
19. We still have no giant multinationals in the world of publishing.
20. For a useful discussion of this point, see S. H. Steinberg, *Five Hundred Years of Printing*, rev. edn. (Penguin: Harmondsworth, 1966), ch. 5. That the sign *ough* is pronounced differently in the words although, bough, lough, rough, cough, and hiccough, shows both the idiolectic variety out of which the now-standard spelling of English emerged, and the ideographic quality of the final product.
21. I say 'nothing served . . . more than capitalism' advisedly. Both Steinberg and Eisenstein come close to theomorphizing 'print' *qua* print as the genius of modern history. Febvre and Martin never forget that behind print stand printers and publishing firms. It is worth remembering in this context that although printing was invented first in China, possibly 500 years before its appearance in Europe, it had no major, let alone revolutionary impact—precisely because of the absence of capitalism there.
22. Febvre and Martin, op. cit. 319. Cf. original text: 'Au XVIIᵉ siècle, les langues nationales apparaissent un peu partout cristallisées.'
23. Hans Kohn, *The Age of Nationalism* (Harper: New York, 1962), 108. It is probably only fair to add that Kemal also hoped thereby to align Turkish nationalism with the modern, romanized civilization of Western Europe.
25. Seton-Watson, op. cit. 317.

Extract 15
PIERRE VAN DEN BERGHE: *A Socio-Biological Perspective*

1. W. D. Hamilton, 'The genetical evolution of social behaviour', *Journal of Theoretical Biology*, 7 (1964), 1–52.
2. J. Maynard Smith, 'Group selection and kin selection', *Nature*, 201/4924 (1964), 1145–7.
3. R. Bigelow, *The Dawn Warriors* (Little Brown: Boston, 1969).
4. M. Sahlins, *The Use and Abuse of Biology* (University of Michigan Press: Ann Arbor, 1976).

5. M. Hechter, 'Ethnicity and industrialization', *Ethnicity*, 3/3 (1976), 214–24.

6. H. Hoetink, *Caribbean Race Relations* (Oxford University Press: London, 1967).

7. The classical historical anecdote is that of the massacre of French occupation forces by Flemings in 1302, in Bruges. The insurgent Flemings massacred their enemies at night in their beds. To make sure that no Flemings would be accidentally killed, the person was made to repeat a sentence 'schilde ende vriend', containing Dutch phonemes which are virtually unpronounceable for a native speaker of French. I daresay this kin-selection test was well over 99 per cent effective, and no physical trait could have come closer to it for reliability.

Extract 16

JOHN BREUILLY: *The Sources of Nationalist Ideology*

1. As in the English and French cases considered in John Breuilly, *Nationalism and the State* (Manchester, 1982), ch. 1.

2. Edmund Burke, *Reflections upon the French Revolution*, ed. Conor Cruise O'Brien (Harmondsworth, 1969), 152–5.

3. For Herder's views on language see J. G. *Herder on Social and Political Culture*, trans. and ed., with an Introduction, by F. M. Barnard (London, 1969), esp. 'Introduction', 17–32, and 'Essay on the origin of language', 117–77.

4. J. C. Herder, *Ideen zur Philosophie der Geschichte der Menschheit*, in *Sämmtliche Werke*, ed. Bernard Suphan (Berlin, 1887), xiii. 384.

5. See especially the fourth address in Fichte, *Addresses to the German Nation*, trans. R. T. Jones and G. H. Turnbull (Chicago and London, 1922).

6. Jomo Kenyatta, *Facing Mount Kenya* (London, 1938).

7. Terence Ranger, 'Rhodesia: The propaganda war', *New Statesman*, 97/2518 (22 June 1979), 922. Since I wrote Mr Mugabe has become Prime Minister of Zimbabwe. He now plays down his earlier emphasis on class division.

8. The Zionist Ahad Ha'am, for example, raised this sort of objection to the aim of achieving an independent state of Israel and stressed instead the need to develop an authentic cultural national identity.

9. Edward W. Said, *Orientalism* (London, 1980).

Extract 17

ANTHONY D. SMITH: *The Crisis of Dual Legitimation*

1. E. Gellner, *Thought and Change* (Weidenfeld and Nicolson: London, 1964), ch. 8.

2. An example of such enlightened despotism was the reformist monarch, Joseph II. On the general characteristics of absolutist states, see G. Poggi, *The Development of the Modern State* (Hutchinson: London, 1978), chs. 4–5, and for Germany, W. H. Bruford, *Germany in the Eighteenth Century* (Cambridge University Press: Cambridge, 1965).

3. On Baroque kings, see C. J. Friedrich, *The Age of the Baroque, 1610–1660* (Harper and Row: New York, 1962); also M. Beloff, *The Age of Absolutism, 1660–1815* (Hutchinson: London, 1954).

4. J. Lively (ed.), *The Enlightenment* (Longman: London, 1966); and R. Anchor, *The Enlightenment Tradition* (Harper & Row: New York, Evanston, and London, 1967).

5. G. Obeyesekere, 'Theodicy, sin and salvation in a sociology of Buddhism', in E. R.

Leach (ed.), *Dialectic in Practical Religion*, Cambridge Papers in Social Anthropology, 5 (Cambridge, 1968); for the philosophical arguments, see N. Pike (ed.), *God and Evil* (Prentice Hall: Englewood Cliffs, NJ, 1964).

6. For the traditional theodicies of Kharma, Zoroastrian dualism, and the predestination decree of the *deus absconditus*, see M. Weber, *From Max Weber, Essays in Sociology*, ed. H. Gerth and C. W. Mills (Routledge & Kegan Paul: London, 1947), 275, and id., *The Sociology of Religion*, trans. E. Fischoff (Methuen: London, 1965), 138–50; for the refusal to accept human suffering, see the figure of Ivan Karamazov in Dostoevsky's *The Brothers Karamazov* (Penguin: Harmondsworth, 1965), i. 287.

7. This is more fully discussed in A. D. Smith 'Modernity and evil: Some sociological reflections on the problem of meaning', *Diogenes*, 71 (1970), 65–80, and id., *Theories of Nationalism* (Duckworth: London, and Harper & Row: New York, 1971), ch. 10.

8. Poland is the obvious example, in the communist world; in Western societies, too, Ireland and the United States, and to some extent Holland and Greece, continue to manifest a vigorous public religious life and hierarchies. On these and other European cases, see D. Martin, 'The religious condition of Europe', in S. Giner and M. S. Archer (eds.), *Contemporary Europe, Social Structures and Cultural Patterns* (Routledge & Kegan Paul: London, 1978).

9. Examples were (and are) U Nu of Burma, Nyerere, Kaunda, Sukarno, Sadat, Muhammad Abduh, Iqbal, Roy, Blyden, and Martin Buber, each of whom, in their very different ways, worked out a personal synthesis of religious, national, and socially progressive motifs in varying proportions. On some of these syntheses in South-East Asia, see M. Sarkisyanz, 'On the place of U Nu's Buddhist Socialism in Burma's History of Ideas', in R. A. Sakai (ed.), *Studies on Asia* (University of Nebraska Press: Lincoln, Nebr., 1961), and, more generally, W. F. Wertheim, 'Religious reform movements in South and South-east Asia', *Archives de Sociologie des Religions*, 9 (1958), 53–62.

10. A. D. Smith, *Theories of Nationalism*, ch. 10, and id., *Nationalism in the Twentieth Century* (Martin Robertson: Oxford, 1979), ch. 2.

11. E. Kedourie, *Afghani and Abduh: An essay on Religious Unbelief and Political Activism in Modern Islam* (Cass: London and New York, 1966), and A. Hourani, *Arabic Thought in the Liberal Age, 1798–1939* (Oxford University Press: London and New York, 1970), ch. 5.

12. M. Adenwalla, 'Hindu concepts and the Gita in early Indian national thought', in Sakai, op. cit.; and K. Singh, *Prophet of Indian Nationalism* (Allen & Unwin: London, 1963). See also A. Embree, *India's Search for National Identity* (Knopf: New York, 1972), chs. 2–3.

13. Anchor, op. cit.: F. M. Barnard, *Herder's Social and Political Thought: From Enlightenment to Nationalism* (Clarendon Press: Oxford, 1965), ch. 1; P. Gay, *The Enlightenment: An Interpretation* (Wildwood House: London, 1973), ii., ch. 5.

14. E. Kedourie (ed.), *Nationalism in Asia and Africa* (Weidenfeld & Nicolson: London, 1971), Introduction; T. Hodgkin, 'The relevance of "Western" ideas in the derivation of African nationalism', in J. R. Pennock (ed.), *Self-government in Modernising Societies* (Prentice-Hall: Englewood Cliffs, NJ, 1964).

15. Smith, *Theories of nationalism*, ch. 10. For reformists in the Muslim, Hindu and Jewish worlds, see H. A. R. Gibb, *Modern Trends in Islam* (Chicago University Press: Chicago, 1947); C. Heimsath, *Indian Nationalism and Hindu Social Reform* (Princeton

University Press: Princeton, NJ., 1964); and A. Hertzberg (ed.), *The Zionist Idea: A Reader* (Meridian Books: New York, 1960), Introduction.

16. J. L. Blau, 'Tradition and innovation', in Blau *et al.* (eds.), *Essays in Jewish Life and Thought* (Columbia University Press: New York, 1959).

17. An excellent example of such a position occurs in Egypt at the turn of the century, especially in the writings of Rashid Rida and the *salafiyya* movement; see C. E. Dawn, 'From Ottomanism to Arabism: The origin of an ideology', *Review of Politics* 23 (1961), 379–400, and J. Abun-Nasr, 'The Salafiyya movement in Morocco: The religious bases of the Moroccan nationalist movement', in I. Wallerstein (ed.), *Social Change: The Colonial Situation* (Wiley: New York, 1966).

18. It is important to stress that these positions remain relevant and persistent options in the latter half of the twentieth century, as the Islamic revival today clearly illustrates. It is also relevant that, once ethnic nationalism has itself become a much-publicized and successful option, each of the three intellectual positions tends to reinforce the trend towards an ethnic historicism; so that, increasingly, for all their differences, the three positions operate within a definite and circumscribed political framework. This may also help to explain why individual thinkers and writers may cross over from one position to another, without too much difficulty, and why an ethnic nationalism of one sort may, under changing conditions, give way to that of another kind.

19. On the European case of perceiving diversity, see R. Nisbet, *Social Change and History* (Oxford University Press: Oxford, 1969), pt. II, and E. Kedourie, *Nationalism* (Hutchinson: London, 1960), ch. 4.

Extract 18

JOHN HUTCHINSON: *Cultural Nationalism, and Moral Regeneration*

1. J. G. Herder, *Reflections on the Philosophy of the History of Mankind*, ed. F. Manuel (Chicago, 1968), 50–60.

2. I. Berlin, *Vico and Herder: Two Studies in the History of Ideas* (London, 1976), 158–63.

3. F. M. Barnard, 'Culture and political development: Herder's suggestive insights', *American Political Science Review*, 63 (1969), 385–90.

4. Herder, op. cit. 117.

5. Ibid. 106.

6. Ibid. 172.

7. Berlin, op. cit. 26.

8. A. D. Smith, 'Ethnic myths and ethnic revivals', *European Journal of Sociology*, 25 (1984), 292–3.

9. The point of the distinction between imitation and emulation is that the former is a passive process, justified because the prophet embodies and teaches a truth that is final for all times and places. The nationalist teaches that only the spirit of its heroes can be followed, since the essence of humanity is its continuous progress. To be true to the past, therefore, is to creatively transcend it, just as former heroes did in their time. (See J. R. Levenson, *Liang Ch'I Cha'ao and the Mind of Modern China* (London, 1959), 122.)

10. Berlin, op. cit. 203–4.

11. W. A. Wilson, *Folklore and Nationalism in Modern Finland* (Bloomington, Ind., 1976), 37–42.
12. Herder, op. cit. 130.
13. Cf. W. J. Argyle, 'Size and scale as factors in the development of nationalist movements', in A. D. Smith (ed.), *Nationalist Movements* (London, 1976).
14. P. Brock, *The Slovak National Awakening* (Toronto, 1976), 22.
15. Barnard, op. cit. 390–4.
16. S. Z. Pech, 'The nationalist movements of the Austrian Slavs in 1848: A comparative sociological profile', *Social History*, 9/18 (1976), 343.
17. For a discussion of the latter case, see Argyle, op. cit. 42–3.
18. Pech, op. cit. 343.
19. Ibid. 347.
20. My discussion of the Shevchenko Society is based on S. M. Horak, 'The Shevchenko Scientific Society (1873–1973): Contribution to the birth of a nation', *East European Quarterly*, 7 (1973), 249–64; and I. L. Rudnytsky, 'The Ukrainian national movement on the eve of the First World War', *East European Quarterly*, 11 (1977), 141–54.
21. H. Kohn, *The Idea of Nationalism* (New York, 1946).
22. E. Gellner, *Nations and Nationalism* (Oxford, 1983).
23. Kohn, op. cit. 3–4.
24. Ibid. 329–41.
25. Ibid. 429–30.
26. Gellner, op. cit. 57–61.
27. Cf. M. Matossian, 'Ideologies of "delayed industrialization": Some tensions and ambiguities', in J. H. Kautsky (ed.), *Political Change in Underdeveloped Countries* (New York, 1962).
28. For an exposition of this historical vision, see B. T. McCully, *English Education and the Origins of Indian Nationalism* (New York, 1940), ch. 5.
29. C. Heimsath, *Indian Nationalism and Hindu Social Reform* (Princeton, NJ, 1964), 355.
30. Levenson, op. cit. 93–4.
31. R. W. July, *The Origins of Modern African Thought* (London, 1968), 215–19.

Extract 19

HUGH SETON-WATSON: *Old and New Nations*

1. At Paris were *nationes* of France, Picardy, Normandy, and Germany: the Norman included persons from various northern lands, the German at one time Englishmen. At Prague in the late fourteenth century were Bohemian, Bavarian, Saxon, and Polish *nationes*, but their composition too was rather mixed.

2. The Székély were a people from the steppes, originally distinct from the Hungarians (or Magyars), but culturally assimilated towards them in the course of time. The Saxons were Germans established by the kings of Hungary in the thirteenth cntury.

3. An exception was Hungarian, in which the distinct words *nemzet* and *nép* were assiduously preserved: this was a result of the long continued maintenance of political power of the nobility. A systematic comparative study of the evolution of the use and meaning of these words in Europe has yet to be done: it would be invaluable to historians and even to social scientists.

Extract 20

SUSAN REYNOLDS: *Regnal Sentiments and Medieval Communities*

1. A. D. Smith, 'Nationalism', *Current Sociology*, 21/3 (1973), 10.
2. R. Emerson, *From Empire to Nation* (Cambridge, Mass., 1960), 96.
3. Isidore of Seville, *Etymologiarum Libri*, ed. W. M. Lindsay (Oxford, 1911), 9. ii. 1, iv. 4–6; 15. ii. 1.

Extract 21

JOHN ARMSTRONG: *Nations before Nationalism*

1. Carlton J. H. Hayes, *Essays on Nationalism* (Macmillan: New York, 1933), 44. Cf. Hans Kohn, *The Idea of Nationalism: A Study in its Origins and Background* (Macmillan: New York, 1944), 17; and Friedrich Meinecke, *Cosmopolitanism and the National State*, trans. Robert B. Kimber (Princeton University Press: Princeton, NJ, 1970), 10.
2. See especially, Norbert Elias, *Ueber den Prozess der Zivilisation* (Haus zum Falken: Basle, 1939), i. 116. Cf. id. *Die höfische Gesellschaft* (Luchterhand: Neuwied, 1969); Hermann J. Bidermann, 'Die staatsrechtlichen Wirkungen der österreichischen Gesammtsstaatsidee', *Zeitschrift für das Privat- und Öffentliche Recht*, 21 (1894), 339–429; Fernand Braudel, *The Mediterranean and the Mediterranean World in the Age of Philip II*, trans. Sian Reynolds, 2 vols. (Harper: New York, 1972–3); Alfhons Lhotsky, *Das Zeitalter des Hauses Österreich* (Böhlau: Vienna, 1971), iv.; Perry Anderson, *Lineages of the Absolutist State* (NLB: London, 1974).
3. Fredrik Barth (ed.) *Ethnic Groups and Boundaries* (Universitetsforlaget: Bergen, 1969), 9–10. See also Robert A. LeVine and Donald T. Campbell, *Ethnocentrism: Theories of Conflict, Ethnic Attitudes and Group Behavior* (Wiley: New York, 1972), 82–3, 102.
4. Reinhard Wenskus, *Stammesbildung und Verfassung* (Böhlau: Cologne, 1961), 210, 252. Cf. Otto Jespersen, *Mankind, Nation and Individual from a Linguistic Point of View* (George Allen & Unwin: London, n.d.), 9; František Graus, 'Die Entstehung der mittelalterlichen Staaten in Mitteleuropa', *Historica*, 10 (1965), 60.
5. Georg Hüsing, 'Völkerschichten in Iran', *Mitteilungen der Anthropologischen Gesellschaft in Wien*, 46 (1916), 199.
6. Émile Benveniste, *Le Vocabulaire des Institutions Indo-Européennes*, 2 vols. (Éditions de Minuit: Paris, 1969), i. 368.
7. See Robert T. Anderson, *Traditional Europe: A Study in Anthropology and History* (Wadsworth: Belmont, Calif., 1971), on a separate peasant culture in medieval Europe. Cf. André Varagnac, *Civilisation Traditionnelle et Genres de Vie* (Michel: Paris, 1948), 21.
8. See especially Clifford Geertz, *The Interpretation of Cultures* (Basic Books: New York, 1973), 45, 209; Ernst Cassirer, *Language and Myth*, trans. Suzanne K. Langer (Harper: New York, 1945), 91; Raymond Firth, *Symbols: Public and Private* (George Allen & Unwin: London, 1973), 40; Harold D. Lasswell with Merritt B. Fox, *The Signature of Power* (Transaction Books: New Brunswick, NJ, 1979).
9. Suzanne K. Langer, 'On Cassirer's theory of language and myth', in Paul A. Schlipp (ed.), *The Philosophy of Ernst Cassirer* (Library of Living Philosophers: Evanston, Ill., 1949), 386; Max Weinrich, 'The reality of Jewishness versus the Ghetto Myth: The

Sociolinguistic Roots of Yiddish', in *To Honor Roman Jakobson* (Mouton: The Hague, 1967), iii. 2209.

10. Karl Brandi, 'Der Weltreichgedanke Karls V', *Ibero-Amerikanisches Archiv*, 13 (1913), 265; Friedrich Heer, *Die Trägödie des Heiligen Reiches* (Europa Verlag: Zurich, 1952), 218.

11. Claude Lévi-Strauss, *Structural Anthropology*, trans. Claire Jacobson and Brooke G. Schoepf (Basic Books: New York, 1963), 210. Cf. id., *The Savage Mind* (University of Chicago Press: Chicago, 1966), 254; Karl W. Deutsch, *Nationalism and Social Communication* (MIT Press: Cambridge, Mass., 1953).

12. Ramon d'Abadal i de Vinyals, 'A Propos du Legs Visigothique en Espagne', *Settimane di Studio del Centro Italiano di Studi sull' Alt. Mediovo*, 2 (1958), 584.

13. Eric Dardel, 'The Mythic: According to the ethnological works of Maurice Leenhardt', *Diogenes*, 7 (1954), 38.

14. Miroslav Hroch, *Die Vorkämpfer der Nationalenbewegung bei den kleinen Völkern Europas* (Universita Karlova: Prague, 1968), 30. For other pertinent discussions of symbolism and identity, see especially John A. Wilson, 'Egypt', in Henry Frankfort *et al.*, *Before Philosophy: The Intellectual Adventure of Ancient Man* (Penguin: London, 1963), 41; Julius Kaerst, *Die Antike Idee der Oekumene in ihrer politischen und Kulturellen Bedeutung* (Teubner: Leipzig, 1903), 7 ff.; Henry Corbin, *Terre Céleste et Corps de Résurrection: De l'Iran Mazdéen à l'Iran Shi'ite* (Buchet-Chastel: Paris, 1960), 39, 160; Giorgio Buccellati, *Cities and Nations of Ancient Syria* (University of Rome: Rome, 1967); Otto G. von Simson, *Sacred Fortress: Byzantine Art and Statecraft in Ravenna* (University of Chicago Press: Chicago, 1948).

15. Myriam Yardeni, *La Conscience Nationale en France pendant les Guerres de Religion (1559–1598)* (Nauwelaerts: Louvain, 1971), 5. Cf. Jan H. Huizinga, *Patriotisme en Nationalisme in de Europeesche Geschiedenis tot net Einde der 19ᵉ Eeuw* (Tjeenk Willenk: Haarlem, 1940), 23–32.

16. Bernard Lewis, 'Islam', in Denis Sinor (ed.), *Orientalism and History* (Heffer: Cambridge, 1954), 16.

17. Karl Vossler, *Aus der romanischen Welt* (Stahlberg: Karlsruhe, 1948), 399; Helen Flanders Dunbar, *Symbolism in Medieval Thought and its Consummation in the Divine Comedy* (Yale University Press: New Haven, Conn., 1929), 72, 132.

18. Walter Ullmann, *The Carolingian Renaissance and the Idea of Kingship* (Methuen: London, 1969), 100.

Extract 22

ANTHONY D. SMITH: *The Origins of Nations*

1. C. Burney and D. M. Lang, *The Peoples of the Hills: Ancient Ararat and Caucasus* (Weidenfeld & Nicolson: London, 1971), 86–126; K. A. Kitchen, 'The Philistines', in D. J. Wiseman (ed.), *Peoples of the Old Testament* (Oxford University Press: Oxford, 1973); H. W. F. Saggs, *The Might That Was Assyria* (Sidgwick & Jackson: London, 1984) 117–21.

2. A. S. Atiyah, *A History of Eastern Christianity* (Methuen: London, 1968); E. Ullendorff, *The Ethiopians*, 3rd edn. (Oxford University Press: Oxford, 1973), 54–92.

3. B. C. Keeney, 'Military service and the development of nationalism in England, 1272–1327', in L. Tipton (ed.), *Nationalism in the Middle Ages* (Holt, Rinehart & Winston: New York, 1972).

4. P. Corrigan and D. Sayer, *The Great Arch: English State Formation as Cultural Revolution* (Blackwell: Oxford, 1985).

5. H. Seton-Watson, *Nations and States* (Methuen: London, 1977), 22–31; L. Smith (ed.), *The Making of Britain: The Middle Ages* (Macmillan: London, 1985).

6. S. Reynolds, *Kingdoms and Communities in Western Europe, 900–1300* (Clarendon Press: Oxford, 1984), 250–331.

7. H. MacDougall, *Racial Myth in English History: Trojans, Teutons and Anglo-Saxons* (Harvest House: Montreal, 1982), 7–17.

8. Ibid., chs. 2–4.

9. Reynolds, op. cit. 276–89; M. Bloch, *Feudal Society*, 2 vols. (Routledge & Kegan Paul: London, 1961), ii. 431–7.

10. R. H. C. Davis, *A History of Medieval Europe* (Longmans: London, 1958), 298, 313; Archibald Lewis, *Knights and Samurai: Feudalism in Northern France and Japan* (Temple Smith: London, 1974), 57–70; John Armstrong, *Nations before Nationalism* (University of North Carolina Press: Chapel Hill, NC, 1982), 152–9.

11. Hans Kohn, *Prelude to Nation-States: The French and German Experience, 1789–1815* (Van Nostrand: New York, 1967); Engene Weber, *Peasants into Frenchmen: The Modernization of Rural France, 1870–1914* (Chatto & Windus: London, 1979). Again, the continuity is cultural, and indirect. It remained significant into the nineteenth century to claim descent from 'Franks' and even 'Gauls' for political purposes; the recovery of medieval French art and history also spurred this sense of ethnic identification. By the later Middle Ages, the claim to Frankish descent could hardly be substantiated; but again, it is claims within a cultural framework that count.

12. W. C. Atkinson, *A History of Spain and Portugal* (Penguin: Harmondsworth, 1960); S. Payne, 'Catalan and Basque nationalism', *Journal of Contemporary History*, 6/1 (1971) 15–51; D. Greenwood, 'Continuity in change: Spanish Basque ethnicity as a historical process', in M. Esman (ed.), *Ethnic Conflict in the Western World* (Cornell University Press: Ithaca, NY, 1977), 81–102.

13. These are discussed by Anthony D. Smith, *The Ethnic Origins of Nations* (Blackwell: Oxford, 1986), 47–68; and see Armstrong, op. cit.

14. S. W. Baron, *Modern Nationalism and Religion* (Meridian Books: New York, 1960), 213–48; J. Carmichael, *The Shaping of the Arabs* (Macmillan: New York, 1967); R. Patai, *The Arab Mind*, rev. edn. (Charles Scribner's Sons: New York, 1983).

15. H. Sharabi, *Arabic Intellectuals and the West: The Formative Years, 1875–1914* (Johns Hopkins Press: Baltimore, 1970); A. D. Smith, 'Nationalism and religion: The role of religious reform in the genesis of Arab and Jewish nationalism', *Archives de Sociologie des Religions*, 35 (1973), 23–43.

16. A. Hertzberg (ed.), *The Zionist Idea: A Reader* (Meridian Books: New York, 1960); D. Vital, *The Origins of Zionism* (Clarendon Press: Oxford, 1975), 3–20.

17. See the essays in P. Sugar and I. Lederer (eds.), *Nationalism in Eastern Europe* (University of Washington Press: Seattle, 1969), and more generally Smith, *The Ethnic Origins of Nations*, 129–52.

18. It is necessary to distinguish the educator-intellectuals proper from the wider stratum of the professional intelligentsia, on which see Alvin Gouldner, *The Rise of the Intellectuals and the Future of the New Class* (Macmillan: London, 1979), and Anthony D. Smith, *The Ethnic Revival in the Modern World* (Cambridge University Press: Cambridge, 1981), 87–107.

Extract 23
WALKER CONNOR: *When is a Nation?*

1. Eugene Weber cites a 1911 observer as noting that 'for peasants and workers, the mother tongue is patois, the foreign speech is French' (*Peasants into Frenchmen: The Modernization of Rural France, 1870–1914* (Chatto & Windus: London, 1979), 73). Earlier (p. 67), he offers data demonstrating that at least 25 per cent of the population could speak no French and that French was considered a foreign language by approximately half of the population who achieved adulthood between 1875 and 1900.

2. Ibid., 47.

3. Marc Bloch, *Feudal Society*, trans. L. A. Manyon (University of Chicago: Chicago, 1964), 436.

4. Johann Huizinga, *Men and Ideas: History, the Middle Ages, the Renaissance* (Free Press: New York, 1959), 21.

5. Sydney Herbert, *Nationality and its Problems* (Dutton: New York, 1919), 66–7.

6. This work was the co-ordinated effort of six of the United States' most distinguished scholars.

7. Albert Bushnell Hart (ed.), 'France: Historical outline', in *A Reference History of the World From the Earliest Times to the Present* (Merriam: Springfield, Mass., 1934), 131.

8. While the Yugoslav census recorded no people claiming Bulgarian descent within Macedonia, it did report the presence of such people immediately across the Macedonian border in Serbia, further feeding a suspicion that those within Macedonia claiming a Bulgarian descent were simply not recorded.

9. For a discussion of whether a single sense of national consciousness has transcended the highlander–lowlander division within Scotland, as well as a discussion of the relative weakness of an Italian consciousness, see W. Connor, 'From tribe to nation?', *History of European Ideas* (forthcoming).

10. Operating on a larger canvas, Alexandre Bennigsen was the best-known of a number of Central-Asian specialists who for some years maintained that the Central-Asian peoples of the Soviet Union shared a common Muslim identity that rendered insignificant an identity such as Kazakh, Uzbek, Turkman, etc. Supporting data for this thesis, which runs counter to the experiences of Islamic peoples elsewhere, have not been offered. Recent developments suggest that the individual ethno-national is stronger than the common religious bond.

11. For more details, see W. Connor, *The National Question in Marxist-Leninist Theory and Strategy* (Princeton University Press: Princeton, NJ, 1984) 128–71. Among the groups taking the position that the Croats, Serbs, etc. were merely tribal components of a single Yugoslav nation was the Yugoslav Communist Party. For example, a declaration of the Croatian Social Democrats of 1 May 1918 asserted that 'Slovenes, Croats, and Serbs are one and the same people, and that as a consequence they have all the attributes of one people, and especially in this respect . . . that they constitute an independent free state'. In a similar vein, the Serbian Social Democrats proclaimed in November of the same year: 'The Serbs, Croats, and Slovenes are one nation, for they have one language and identical remaining ethnic characteristics. They feel like one people and desire union. It follows that their union in one national state is a great, political, economic, and cultural need which is beyond any discussion.'

12. The magnitude of the cleavage is suggested by the following citation (*Nationalism: A Report by a Study Group of Members of the Royal Institute of International Affairs* (1939), 96): 'It was said of a Croat landowner of the 19th century that he would sooner have regarded his horse than his peasant as a member of the Croat nation. The same was true of most Polish and Magyar landowners of the period.' From this perspective, the so-called 'Polish Question' that occupied Europe's leaders from the late eighteenth century until the First World War could more accurately be described as an élite rather than a national question.

13. Rupert Emerson, *From Empire to Nation* (Beacon: Boston, 1960), 95–6.

14. An interesting illustration of the incompatibility between outcast group and nation is offered by the *burakumin* of Japan. Although these people are physically indistinguishable from the Japanese, the Japanese treat them as contaminated inferiors with whom all social intercourse is to be avoided. This treatment is justified by the popularly held conviction—all biological and historical evidence to the contrary notwithstanding—that *burakumin* are not of Japanese descent. A number of quite fanciful theories of the *burakumin*'s separate descent have been periodically promoted, because upon such myths depends the justification for perpetuating the social ostracism of these people, that is, for denying them membership of an extended family.

15. The case of France is somewhat different, since the system was much less stable, with non-democratic political regimes in power during much of the late eighteenth and early nineteenth centuries. However, the franchise was still extremely limited more than half a century after the French Revolution. According to Hall and Albion (*A History of England and the British Empire*, 2nd edn. (Ginn: Boston, 1946), 613) the Revolution of 1830 only extended the vote to one in every 200 adult males. Palmer and Cotton (*A History of the Modern World*, 4th edn. (Knopf: New York, 1971), 498) place the post-1830 French figure at one voter in every thirty adult males, as contrasted with a pre-1830 figure of one in every sixty male adults. Whatever the correct figure, it is evident that a highly élitist view of the nation prevailed at least until the upheavals of 1848.

16. E. M. Carr, *Nationalism and After* (Macmillan: London, 1967), 10, 18, 20.

17. For a contemporary case of such confusion by a Soviet author, see S. Dumin, 'Shlyakham ab'ektyunaga vyvuchennya', *Litaratura i mastatstva* (8 July 1988), as reported by Kathleen Mihalisko, 'Historian outlines revisionist view of Belorussia's past', *Radio Liberty, RL 415/88* (8 September 1988), 2. As reported by Kathleen Mihalisko, Dumin avers that Belorussian nationhood dates to the medieval era, although we have seen from the United States' migrant data that this sense of nationhood had probably not infected the masses as recently as the First World War.

18. For references to several such polls, see W. Connor, 'From a theory of relative economic deprivation toward a theory of relative political deprivation', paper presented at the *Conference of the International Sociological Association's Research Committee on Ethnic, Race and Minority Relations*, Amsterdam, 8–10 December 1988.

Extract 24

HANS KOHN: *Western and Eastern Nationalisms*

1. Israel Zangwill, *The Principle of Nationalities* (Watts: London, 1917), 39. Max Weber

defines (loc. cit.) nationality as 'a common bond of sentiment whose adequate expression would be a state of its own, and which therefore normally tends to give birth to such a state'. See also Alfred E. Zimmern, *Nationality and Government, and Other Wartime Essays* (Chatto & Windus: London, 1918), 52.

Extract 25
LIAH GREENFELD: *Types of European Nationalism*

1. Liah Greenfeld, *Nationalism: Five Roads to Modernity* (Harvard University Press: Cambridge, Mass., 1992), 3.

2. The concept comes to us from biology (see, for example, Samuel Alexander, *Space, Time and Deity* (Macmillan: London, 1920), and Michael Polanyi, 'Life's Irreducible Structure', *Science*, 160 (June 1968), 1308–12); and life is the paradigmatic example of emergence. Life cannot be reduced to the sum total of its inanimate elements, it cannot be explained by any of their properties; it is the relationship between the elements, unpredictable from these properties, which gives rise to it, and which in many ways conditions the behaviour of the elements the moment they become elements of the living matter. The mystery of life lies in that we do not know its unifying principle: we do not know why inanimate elements form a relationship which gives rise to life. Because of our systematic inability to solve this mystery, the best strategy in the study of life has been considered to put this question aside and be content with the study of the mechanisms and expressions of life. In many other areas of study this is not the best strategy. In the case of emergent social phenomena, which are structurally parallel to the phenomenon of life, we can answer the question of what brings elements together, and why, and can discover the unifying principle, if we choose to do so. A text, a simple sentence, is such an emergent phenomenon. A sentence is composed of certain elements which have definite grammatical, morphological, and phonetic properties. Yet, nothing in them can explain the existence of a sentence or why all these elements combine together to form it. This is explained by the idea of the author of the sentence, by what he or she wishes to express, by the significance of the sentence for him or her. Undoubtedly, the author is only able to construct a sentence within the boundary conditions formed by the grammatical, morphological, and other properties of the elements in a language he or she uses. But it is the idea which brings some of the elements together in a sentence and determines the role each of them is to play in it. It is the idea which creates out of existing elements a novel reality. Currents of culture, traditions, and ideologies are also emergent phenomena, though on a higher level of complexity. It was their emergent character that led Mannheim to refer to them as 'styles of thought'.

3. This political nature of nationalism does not necessitate statehood either as a reality or as an aspiration. It has to do with the definition of the ultimate source of authority which does not have to belong to the state, as religious believers among us so well know, although it may be in part delegated to it. As a result, nations without states of their own are in no way abnormal or incomplete, and the one-to-one correspondence between the two, while a fact or a desideratum in many cases, is not at all of essence in nationalism. In much of the scholarship on nationalism it is seen as such, however. (On the imperfect correspondence between

states and nations, see G. P. Nielsson, 'States and "nation-groups": A global taxonomy', in E. A. Tiryakian and R. Rogowski (eds.), *New Nationalisms of the Developed West* (Allen & Unwin: Boston, 1985), 27–56.)

4. For discussion of 'ethnicity', see Nathan Glazer and Daniel P. Moynihan (eds.), *Ethnicity: Theory and Experience* (Harvard University Press: Cambridge, Mass., 1975), especially the editors' introduction. A. D. Smith, *The Ethnic Origins of Nations* (Basil Blackwell: Oxford, 1986) emphasizes the role of ethnicity in nationalism.

5. The existence of a supra-societal system, or shared social space, was a necessary condition for the spread of nationalism from the very beginning of the process. Borrowing presupposed the existence of a shared model, and such a model could exist only for societies which were explicitly relevant for each other. It is probable that initially such shared social space was created by Christianity and, perhaps, the Renaissance. Parenthetically, this may explain why, while individual proto-nations—namely societies held together by solidarities remarkably similar to national, although not called 'nations'—were known in the ancient world, notably among the Jews and the Greeks, nationalism never spread beyond the borders of these individual societies. In distinction, Christianity did create in Europe the supra-societal social space which made such spread possible. This social space could contract or expand. The rise to dominance of the West continued the work of the Middle Ages, and ensured the expansion of this social space. The more it expanded, the more societies were drawn within the orbit of the influence of the 'nation canon', until, in our day, it became shared by virtually the whole world.

6. This means that 'reference societies' (Reinhard Bendix, *Kings or People* (University of California Press: Berkeley, Calif., 1978)) do not simply impose themselves, but are chosen as models by those whom they influence.

7. I use this concept in the sense it was originally defined by Durkheim in *The Division of Labor in Society* and in *Suicide*, and later developed by Robert K. Merton in 'Social Structure and Anomie', as denoting structural inconsistency, and specifically the inconsistency between values and other elements of social structure.

8. Friedrich Nietzsche, 'Genealogy of Morals' (1887), in *The Philosophy of Nietzsche* (The Modern Library: New York, 1927), 617–809; Max Scheler, *Ressentiment* (1912) (The Free Press: Glencoe, Ill., 1961).

9. Alexis de Tocqueville, *The Old Regime and the French Revolution* (1856) (Doubleday Anchor Books: Garden City, NJ, 1955); François Furet, *Interpreting the French Revolution* (Cambridge University Press: Cambridge, 1981). In some cases (for example, Germany) *ressentiment* was originally nurtured by the situation within the community that was to be defined as national, but the unsatisfactory internal situation was interpreted as the result of foreign influence, and a foreign country that had been the object of imitation became the focus of *ressentiment* all the same.

10. *Ressentiment*, which is a specific psychological state associated with the emergence of certain types of nationalism (ethnic, and to a lesser extent, collectivistic but civic), should not be equated with the psychological dimension of nationalism as such, which is much broader. A student of society cannot be oblivious to psychological processes. In the social process they perform the role of necessary conductors, mediating between social structures and cultural formations, and between social structures and cultural formations at different stages in social transformation. The final outcome at any stage is affected by the nature of the psychological processes

involved. Every social phenomenon is, therefore, also psychological, and national-ism is no exception. But, since this in no way defines it, in this book the psycholog-ical dimension of nationalism is treated as given. Even *ressentiment*, it should be noted, which plays a specific role in the formation of certain nationalisms, does not generate nationalism in and of itself. Only in certain structural conditions *may* it do so, and only in confluence with very specific ideas *can* it do so. In other conditions, and in conjunction with other ideas, the very same psychological state may trans-late into entirely different phenomena, as well as vainly spend itself and have no effect at all.

While there is no justification for interpreting nationalism as the product of specific psychological states or needs (possibly in distinction from identity in general), neither is there any for considering it a psychological state. As do many other stimuli, nationalism arouses psychological responses, and therefore has psy-chological manifestations. These manifestations are not specific to it: other ident-ities, as well as emotions of a totally different nature, may be similarly expressed. The specificity of nationalism (that which makes it what it is, a phenomenon *sui generis*) lies not in the specificity of the psychological responses it arouses, but in the specificity of the stimulus, which is cultural.

Extract 26

PETER SUGAR: *Nationalism in Eastern Europe*

1. The position taken by Arató in his chapter 'A magyar nacionalizmus . . .' is not unique, but reflects the approach of Eastern European historians since the Second World War to the problem of nationalism. It is with this approach, and not specifically with Arató, that this author disagrees.

2. Julius Moskolezy, *Ungarn in der Habsburger-Monarchie*, in Karl Eder, Hugo Hantsch, and Hans Kramer (eds.), *Wiener Historische Studien* (Herold: Vienna–Munich, 1959), v. 57–62.

3. Emil Franzel, *Der Donauraum im Zeitalter des Nationalitätenprinzips* (Dalp Taschen-bücher, A. Francke: Bern; Leo Lehnen: Munich, 1958), 69.

4. Edward Dicey, *The Peasant State: An Account of Bulgaria in 1894* (John Murray: London, 1894), coined the excellent phrase 'the peasant state', although his work leaves much to be desired.

Extract 27

ERIC HOBSBAWM: *The Rise of Ethno-Linguistic Nationalisms*

1. K. Renner, *Staat und Nation*, 89.

2. Ibid. 9.

3. M. Hroch, *Social Preconditions of the National Revival in Europe* (Cambridge Univer-sity Press: Cambridge, 1985).

4. See 'Report of the Commissioners appointed to inquire into the operation of the Sunday Closing (Wales) Act 1881' (*Parliamentary Papers*, HC, vol. 60 of 1890); K. O. Morgan, *Wales: Rebirth of a Nation, 1880–1980* (Clarendon Press: Oxford, 1982), 36.

5. Jean Finot, *Race Prejudice* (London, 1906), pp. v–vi.

Extract 28

MICHAEL HECHTER AND MARGARET LEVI: *Ethno-Regional Movements in the West*

1. M. Weber, *Economy and Society* (Bedminster Press: New York, 1968), 387.
2. M. Hechter, *Internal Colonialism: The Celtic Fringe in British National Development, 1536–1966* (Routledge & Kegan Paul: London, 1975).
3. See T. Nairn, *The Breakup of Britain* (NLB Books: London, 1977), 203.
4. Hechter, op. cit. 342–3.
5. Id. 'Group Formation and the cultural division of labor', *American Journal of Sociology*, 84/2 (1978), 293–318.
6. Nairn, op. cit. 202–4.
7. C. C. Herod, *The Nation in the History of Marxian Thought* (Martinns Nijhoff: The Hague, 1976).
8. A. Oberschall, *Social and Political Movements* (Prentice-Hall: Englewood Cliffs, NJ, 1973), 124.
9. M. Hechter, 'Language loyalty in theoretical perspective', *Language Problems and Language Planning*, 1/1 (1977), 1–9.
10. D. North and R. Thomas, *The Rise of the Western World* (Cambridge University Press: London, 1973), 99; and G. Ardant, 'Financial policy and economic infrastructure of modern states and nations', in C. Tilly (ed.), *The Formation of National States in Western Europe* (Princeton University Press: Princeton, NJ, 1975), 164–242.
11. J. McCarthy and M. Zald, 'Resource mobilization and social movements: A partial theory', *American Journal of Sociology*, 82 (1977), 1212–41; M. Olson, *The Logic of Collective Action* (Princeton University Press: Princeton, NJ, 1965); A. Stinchecombe, 'Social structure and organizations', in J. G. March (ed.), *Handbook of Organizations* (Rand-McNally: Chicago, 1965); C. Tilly, *From Mobilization to Revolution* (Addison-Wesley: Reading, Mass., 1978).
12. Tilly, op. cit. 228.
13. K. O. Morgan, *Wales in British Politics, 1868–1922* (University of Wales Press: Cardiff, 1963).
14. J. Hayward, *The One and Indivisible French Republic* (W. W. Norton: New York, 1973); E. Weber, *Peasants into Frenchmen* (Chatto & Windus: London, 1979).
15. S. Berger, *Peasants against Politics* (Harvard University Press: Cambridge, Mass., 1972), 50; J. Reece, 'Internal colonialism: The case of Brittany', *Ethnic and Racial Studies*, 2/3 (July 1979).
16. H. Machin, *The Prefect in French Public Administration* (St. Martin's Press: New York, 1977); also see F. Ridley and J. Blondel, *Public Administration in France* (Routledge & Kegan Paul: London, 1964); and S. Tarrow, *Between Center and Periphery* (Yale University Press: New Haven, Conn., 1977), 48–58.
17. E. Barker, *The Development of Public Services in Western Europe, 1660–1930* (Oxford University Press: New York, 1944); W. J. M. McKenzie and J. W. Grove, *Central Administration in Britain* (Longmans: New York, 1957), 262–75.
18. I. Duchacek, *Comparative Federalism: The Territorial Dimension of Politics* (Holt, Rinehart and Winston: New York, 1970), 212; also see D. Ashford, 'Are Britain and France "unitary"?', *Comparative Politics*, 9/4 (1977), 483–99.

19. S. Berger, 'Bretons and Jacobins', in M. Esman (ed.), *Ethnic Conflict in the Western World* (Cornell University Press: Ithaca, NY, 1977), 159–79.

20. V. Turner, *Dramas, Fields, and Metaphors* (Cornell University Press: Ithaca, NY, 1974), 231–71; C. Geertz, 'Deep play: Notes on the Balinese cockfight', in *The Interpretation of Cultures* (Basic Books: New York, 1973), 412–53.

21. E. Shorter and C. Tilly, *Strikes in France* (Cambridge University Press: New York, 1974).

22. Tilly, op. cit.

23. M. Duverger, *Political Parties* (John Wiley: New York, 1967).

24. S. Rokkan, *Citizens, Elections, Parties* (David McKay: New York, 1970).

25. S. M. Lipset and S. Rokkan, 'Cleavage structures, party systems, and voter alignments', in id. (eds.), *Party Systems and Voter Alignments* (The Free Press: New York, 1967), 31–2.

26. Olson, op. cit.; J. Q. Wilson, *Political Organizations* (Basic Books: New York, 1973).

27. M. Lipsky, 'Protest as a political resource', *American Political Science Review*, 6/2 (1968), 1144–58.

28. D. Ashford, 'French pragmatism and British idealism', *Comparative Political Studies*, 11 (1978), 231–54.

29. N. Frolich, J. Oppenheimer, and O. Young, *Political Leadership and Collective Goods* (Princeton University Press: Princeton, NJ, 1971).

30. Oberschall, op. cit. 160; for an analogous case see R. J. Brym, *The Jewish Intelligentsia and Russian Marxism* (Schocken: New York, 1978).

31. D. Bell, 'Ethnicity and Social Change?', in N. Glazer and D. P. Moynihan (eds.) *Ethnicity: Theory and Experience* (Harvard University Press: Cambridge, Mass., 1975), 141–74.

32. M. Levi, 'Poor people against the state', *Review of Radical Political Economics*, 6/2 (1974), 76–98.

33. Id. *Bureaucratic Insurgency* (Lexington Books: Lexington, Mass., 1977), 149–59.

Extract 29

BENEDICT ANDERSON: *Creole Pioneers of Nationalism*

1. G. Masur, *Simón Bolívar* (University of New Mexico Press: Albuquerque, 1948), 678.

2. Ibid. 19. Naturally these measures were only partially enforceable, and a good deal of smuggling always went on.

3. Ibid. 546.

4. See V. Turner, *The Forest of Symbols: Aspects of Nolembu Ritual* (Cornell University Press: Ithaca, NY, 1967), esp. the chapter 'Betwixt and between'. For a later, more complex elaboration, see his *Dramas, Fields, and Metaphors* (Cornell University Press: Ithaca, NY, 1974), chs. 5 and 6.

5. C. R. Boxer, *The Portuguese Seaborne Empire, 1415–1825* (Knopf: New York, 1969), 266.

6. Ibid. 253.

7. Rona Fields, *The Portuguese Revolution and the Armed Forces Movement* (Praeger: New York, 1975), 15.

8. L. Febvre and H.-J. Martin, *The Coming of the Book: The Impact of Printing, 1450–1800* (New Left Books: London, 1976), 208–11.

Extract 30

ELIE KEDOURIE: *Dark Gods and their Rites*

1. A prominent early exponent of Indian nationalism.
2. London, 1938.

Extract 31

PARTHA CHATTERJEE: *National History and its Exclusions*

1. Bhudeb Mukhopadhyay, 'Svapnalabdha bhrāratbarṣer itihās', in Pramathanath Bisi (ed.), *Bhūdeb racanā sambhār* (Mitra & Ghosh: Calcutta, 1969), 341–74.
2. Rabindranath Thakur, 'Grantha-samālocanā', in *Rabīndra racanābalā* (Government of West Bengal: Calcutta, 1961), 13: 484–7.
3. Ibid. 487.
4. I quote here from *Bankim racanābalī*, ed. J. Bagal (Sahitya Samsad: Calcutta, 1965), ii. 319–63.
5. Ibid. 332.
6. Ibid. 339. The word *renaissance* is in the original.
7. Ibid. 332.
8. Ibid. 326.
9. Ibid. 363.
10. Rajkrishna Mukhopadhyay, *Pratham śikṣā bāṅgālār itihās* (Calcutta, 1875), 61–2.
11. Krishnachandra Ray, *Bhāratbarṣer itihās, imrājdiger adhikārkāl*, 14th edn. (Sanskrit Press Depository: Calcutta, 1875), 245.

Extract 32

FRANCIS ROBINSON: *Islam and Nationalism*

1. P. R. Brass, *Language, Religion and Politics in North India* (London, 1974), 124.
2. S. F. Dale, 'The Islamic frontier in South-West India: The Shahid as a cultural ideal among the Mappillas of Malabar', *Modern Asian Studies*, 11/1: 41–56.
3. R. E. Miller, *Mappilla Muslims of Kerala: A study in Islamic trends* (Bombay, 1976), 176–83.
4. Ibid. 183.
5. G. Ram Reddy, 'Language, religion and political identity: The case of the Majlis-e-Ittehadul-Muslimeen in Andhra Pradesh', below pp. 125–6.
6. M. Mines, 'Labbai', in R. V. Weekes (ed.), *Muslim Peoples: A World Ethnographical Survey* (New Haven, Conn., 1978), 227–31.
7. M. Shakir and U. B. Bhoite, 'Maharashtrians', in ibid. 246–50.
8. C. L. Reimer, 'Maranao', in ibid. 267–72; and P. G. Gowing, 'The Muslim Filipinos', in P. G. Gowing and R. D. McAmis (eds.), *The Muslim Filipinos: Their History, Society, and Contemporary Problems* (Manila, 1974), 288–90.
9. R. Israeli, 'Muslims in China: The incompatibility between Islam and the Chinese order', paper delivered at the International Conference on Asian Islam, Hebrew University of Jerusalem, 1977, 25–6.
10. Ibid. 29. The 'Hundred Flowers relaxation of 1956' refers to Mao Zedung's policy of allowing many opinions to flourish.
11. C. S. Kessler, *Islam and Politics in a Malay State: Kelantan, 1838–1969* (Ithaca, NY, 1978), esp. 208–34.
12. I must reiterate that I cannot accept the significance Brass gives to social mobiliza-

tion (F. Robinson, 'Nation formation: The Brass thesis and Muslim separatism', *Journal of Commonwealth & Comparative Politics*, 15/3 (Nov. 1977), 218–21) and this position has recently been emphasized by the detailed research of Ian Talbot on the Muslim League's rise to power in the Punjab in the 1940s.

13. P. R. Brass, 'Élite groups, symbol manipulation and ethnic identity among the Muslims of South Asia', in op. cit. 39.

14. Ibid. 41.

Extract 33

MARY MATOSSIAN: *Ideologies of Delayed Development*

1. See Karl Mannheim, *Ideology and Utopia* (London, 1936).

2. Gamal Abdul Nasser, *Egypt's Liberation: The Philosophy of the Revolution* (Washington, DC, 1955), 27. See also Jawarharlal Nehru, *The Discovery of India* (London, 1946), 34.

3. Mohandas K. Gandhi, *Hind Swaraj* (Ahmedabad, 1946), 73.

4. Soetan Sjahir, *Out of Exile* (New York, 1949), 5.

5. Nehru, op. cit. 36.

6. Gandhi, op. cit. 45–6, 74.

7. Ibid. 72.

8. J. V. Stalin, *Problems of Leninism* (Moscow, 1947), 356.

9. Mustafa Kemal Ataturk, *Atatürk'ün Söylev ve Demeçleri* (Istanbul, 1945), i. 29.

10. Ibid. iii. 67–8, 87 (Ankara, 1954).

11. Gandhi, op. cit. 46. Gandhi's archaism went to incredible lengths. In the same work he indicts Western medicine (pp. 42–3).

12. As quoted by H. Finer, *Mussolini's Italy* (New York, 1935), 191.

13. Sun Yat-sen, *san Min Chu I* (Shanghai, 1927), 125–6.

14. Nehru, op. cit. 447.

15. Adam Ulam, 'The historical role of Marxism and the Soviet System', *World Politics*, 8/1, 20–45.

16. Sun Yat-Sen, op. cit. 12.

17. Ibid. 61–2.

18. Mohammed Naguib, op. cit. 149.

19. Alexander Gerschenkron, 'Economic backwardness in historical perspective', in Bert Hoselitz (ed.), *The Progress of Underdeveloped Areas* (Chicago, 1952), 22–5.

20. Rupert Emerson, 'Paradoxes of Asian nationalism', *Far Eastern Quarterly*, 13/2 (Feb. 1954), 140.

Extract 34

CRAWFORD YOUNG: *The Colonial Construction of African Nations*

1. Aidan Southall, 'The illusion of tribe', *Journal of Asian and African Studies*, 5/1–2 (Jan.–Apr. 1970), 36.

2. Elizabeth Colson, 'African society at the time of the scramble', in L. H. Gann and Peter Duignan (eds.), *The Rulers of Belgian Africa, 1884–1914* (Princeton University Press: Princeton, NJ, 1979), i. 31.

3. Raymond Apthorpe, 'Does tribalism really matter?', *Transition*, 7/6 (Oct. 1968), 18.

4. Marshall Segall and Martin Doornbos, *Becoming Ugandan: The Dynamics of Identity in a Multi-Cultural African State*, Foreign and Comparative Series No. 24 (Syracuse University: Syracuse, NY, 1976).

5. Ernest Gellner and Charles Micaud (eds.), *Arabs and Berbers: From Tribe to Nation in North Africa* (D.C. Heath: Lexington, Mass., 1972), 175–99.

Extract 35

BENYAMIN NEUBERGER: *State and Nation in African Thought*

1. Max Sylvius Handmann, in Louis Snyder (ed.), *The Meaning of Nationalism* (New Brunswick, NJ, 1964), 48.
2. Walker Connor, 'Self-determination: The new phase', *World Politics*, 20/1 (Oct. 1967), 50.
3. Elie Kedourie, *Nationalism* (New York, 1960).
4. Rupert Emerson, *From Empire to Nation* (Boston, 1969), 105–32.
5. C. J. Friedrich, *Man and His Government* (New York, 1963), 565 and 555.
6. Sékou Touré, *L'Afrique et la Révolution* (Paris, n.d.), 124.
7. Léopold Senghor, *On African Socialism* (New York, 1964), 25.
8. Obafemi Awolowo, *The People's Republic* (Ibadan, 1968), 118.
9. David Hume, 'Of national characters', in Snyder, op. cit. 57.
10. I. M. Lewis, *The Modern History of Somaliland* (New York, 1965).
11. Kenneth Kaunda, *A Humanist in Africa* (London, 1966), 82.
12. Ahmadou Ahidjo, interview in *Études Congolaises*, 2/3 (July–Sept. 1968), 115.
13. Senghor, op. cit. 25.
14. Sékou Touré, interview in *Jeune Afrique*, 30 June 1968.
15. Id., *Guinean Revolution and Social Progress* (Cairo, 1963), 126.
16. Yakubo Gowon, in A. Kirk-Greene (ed.), *Crisis and Conflict in Nigeria, 1966–1969* (London, 1971), i. 204–5.

Extract 38

ALFRED COBBAN: *The Rise of the Nation-State System*

1. Edmund Burke, *Annual Register*, Historical Section (1768), i. 2.
2. J.-J. Rousseau, *Political Writings*, ed. G. E. Vaughan (1915), i. 340–1.
3. C. A. Macartney, *National States and National Minorities* (London, 1934), 119. This translation is perhaps not quite fair to the nuances in the original.

Extract 40

MICHAEL HOWARD: *War and Nations*

1. L. B. Namier, *The Revolution of the Intellectuals* (Oxford, 1946), 88.

Extract 41

AREND LIJPHART: *Ethnic Conflict in the West*

1. Karl W. Deutsch, *Nationalism and Social Communication* (MIT Press: Cambridge, Mass., 1953), 99–100. Emphasis added.
2. Id., *Political Community at the International Level* (Doubleday: Garden City, NY, 1954), 33, 39–40.
3. Walker Connor, 'Nation-building or nation-destroying?', *World Politics*, 24 (Apr. 1972), 319–55.
4. Ernst B. Haas, 'Technocracy, pluralism and the new Europe', in Stephen R. Graubard (ed.), *A New Europe?* (Houghton Mifflin: Boston, 1964), 68.

5. Robert A. Dahl (ed.), *Political Oppositions in Western Democracies* (Yale University Press: New Haven, Conn., 1966), 400.
6. Samuel P. Huntington, 'Post-industrial politics: How benign will it be?', *Comparative Politics*, 6 (Jan. 1974), 191.

Extract 42

DONALD HOROWITZ: *The Logic of Secessions*

1. Immanuel Wallerstein, *Africa: The Politics of Independence* (Vintage: New York, 1961), 88. See also Peter Alexis Gourevitch, 'The re-emergence of "peripheral nationalisms" ', *Comparative Studies in Society and History*, 21 (July 1979), 303–22.

Extract 43

JAMES MAYALL: *Irredentist and Secessionist Challenges*

1. Martin Wight, *Systems of States* (Leicester University Press: Leicester, 1977), 167.
2. Ibid.
3. See, for example, M. Honeywell, J. Pearce *et al.*, *Falklands–Malvenas: Whose Crisis?* (Latin American Bureau: London, 1982), and *Millennium: Journal of International Studies*, special issue, *The Falklands Crisis: One Year Later*, 12/1 (1983).
4. Anthony S. Rayner, 'Morocco's international boundaries: A factual background', *Journal of Modern African Studies*, 1/3 (1963); Edouard Meric, 'Le Conflit Algero–Marocain', *Revue Française de Science Politique*, 15/4 (1965); also Patricia Berko Wild, 'The Organisation of African Unity and the Algerian–Moroccan border conflict', *International Organisation*, 20/1: 19.
5. Witness the difficulty which, in early 1985, the British and Spanish governments had in arriving at a formula which would allow the reopening of the border between Gibraltar and Spain without prejudicing possible future negotiations on the issue of sovereignty; and the difficulties of the British and Irish governments in finding a stable basis on which to discuss the Northern Irish problem.
6. See John Drysdale, *The Somali Dispute* (Pall Mall Press: London, 1964) and I. M. Lewis, *A Modern History of Somalia* (Longmans: London, 1980).
7. Vincent Thompson, 'Conflict in the Horn of Africa: A study of the Kenya–Somalia border problem, 1941–1948' (University of London, Ph.D. thesis, 1985).
8. Alistair Lamb, *The China–Indian Border: The Origins of the Disputed Boundaries* (Oxford University Press: London, 1964), ch. 3.
9. M. D. Donelan and M. J. Grieve, *International Disputes: Case Histories 1945–1970* (Europa Publications: London, 1973), 147–50.
10. The International Court of Justice was asked first, whether Western Sahara was a territory belonging to no one at the time of its colonization and secondly, if not, what legal ties existed between the territory, the kingdom of Morocco, and the 'Mauritanian Entity'. Its opinion was delivered on 16 October 1975. On the first count, by a vote of 13–3, the Court judged that the territory did not belong to anyone; on the second, by votes of 14–2 and 15–2 respectively, it found that only limited legal ties existed between the territory, the kingdom of Morocco, and Mauritania. The substantive passage of the opinion reads as follows: 'The Court's conclusion is that the material and information presented to it do not establish any tie of territorial sovereignty between the territory of Western Sahara and the

kingdom of Morocco. Thus the Court has not found legal ties of such a nature as might affect the application of General Assembly Resolution 1514 (XV) on the decolonisation of Western Sahara and, in particular, of the expression of self-determination through the free and genuine expression of the will of the peoples of the territory.'

11. Ernest Gellner, *Nations and Nationalism* (Blackwell: Oxford, 1983), 43–50.

12. On 10 July 1973 the Pakistan National Assembly passed a unanimous resolution authorizing President Bhutto to recognize Bangladesh 'at the appropriate time'. Diplomatic recognition was finally announced shortly before the opening of the Islamic Conference on 22 February 1974.

13. Selig F. Harrison, *In Afghanistan's Shadow: Baluch Nationalism and Soviet Temptation* (Carnegie Endowment for International Peace: New York, 1981), ch. 7.

14. L. C. Buchheit, *Secession, The Legitimacy of Self-Determination* (Yale University Press: New Haven, Conn., and London, 1978), p. 119.

15. Ibid. 98–9.

16. Ian Lustick, *State-building in British Ireland and French Algeria* (Berkeley, Institute of International Studies: University of California, 1985), 17–39 and 45.

17. A. D. Smith, *The Ethnic Revival in the Modern World* (Cambridge University Press: Cambridge, 1981), ch. 9.

Extract 44

JOHN ARMSTRONG: *Towards a Post-Communist World*

1. At the time of writing (late 1991).

2. Quoted in *Izvestiya*, 30 Apr. 1991, trans. in *CSDP* (29 May 1991), 27–8.

3. Alexander Solzhenitsyn, *New York Times* (19 Sept. 1990).

4. *Izvestiya*, 11 Mar. 1991, trans. in *CSDP* (10 Apr. 1991), 3.

Extract 45

ANTHONY H. RICHMOND: *Ethnic Nationalism and Post-Industrialism*

1. Talcott Parsons, *The Social System* (Tavistock: London, 1952); P. S. Cohen, *Modern Social Theory* (Heinemann: London, 1968).

2. E. Durkheim, *The Division of Labour in Society*, trans. George Simpson (The Free Press: Chicago, 1947); Max Weber, *Essays in Sociology*, trans. and ed. H. H. Gerth and C. W. Mills (Oxford University Press: London, 1946).

3. F. Tönnies, *Community and Society*, trans. and ed. L. P. Loomis (Michigan State University Press: East Lansing, Mich., 1957).

4. Gabriel Warburg, *Islam, Nationalism and Communism in a Traditional Society* (Cass: London, 1978).

5. Karl W. Deutsch, *Nationalism and Social Communication* (MIT Press: Cambridge, Mass., 1953).

6. A. Myrdal, *The Game of Disarmament: How the United States and Russia Run the Arms Race* (Pantheon Books: New York, 1976); A. Sampson, *The Arms Bazaar. The Companies, the Dealers, the Backers: From Vickers to Lockheed* (Hodder & Stoughton: London, 1977).

7. D. Bell, *The Coming of Post-Industrial Society* (Heinemann: London, 1973); J. K.

Galbraith, *The New Industrial State* (Houghton Mifflin: Boston, 1971); A. Touraine, *The Post-Industrial Society* (Random House: New York, 1971).

8. I. Wallerstein, *The Modern World-System* (Academic Press: New York, 1974); K. Kumar, *Prophecy and Progress: The Sociology of Industrial and Post-Industrial Society* (Penguin: Harmondsworth, 1978).

9. David Cameron (ed.), *Regionalism and Supranationalism* (Institute for Research on Public Policy: Montreal, 1981).

10. S. Nora and A. Mine, *The Computerization of Society* (MIT Press: Cambridge, Mass., 1978); S. Serafini and M. Andrieu, *The Information Revolution and its Implications for Canada* (Supply and Services Canada: Hull, Quebec, 1980); A. Toffler, *The Third Wave* (Bantam Books: New York, 1980).

11. Robert Blauner, 'Internal colonialism and the ghetto revolt', *Social Problems*, 16/4 (1969), 393–408.

12. A. Breton and R. Breton, *Why Disunity? An Analysis of Linguistic and Regional Cleavages in Canada* (Institute for Research on Public Policy: Montreal, 1980).

13. B. B. Khleif, *Language, Ethnicity and Education in Wales* (Mouton: The Hague, 1980).

14. Hubert Guindon, 'The modernization of Quebec and the legitimacy of the Canadian State', in D. Glenday, N. Guindon, and A. Turowetz (eds.), *Modernization and the Canadian State* (Macmillan: Toronto, 1978).

Extract 47

HOMI BHABHA: *Narrating the Nation*

1. M. Oakshott, *On Human Conduct* (Oxford University Press: Oxford, 1975), 201.

2. H. Arendt, *The Human Condition* (Chicago University Press: Chicago, 1958), 33–5 and *passim*.

3. T. Nairn, *The Breakup of Britain* (Verso: London, 1981), 348.

4. S. Hall, *The Hard Road to Renewal* (Verso: London, 1988), 9.

5. E. Said, *The World, The Text and The Critic* (Harvard University Press: Cambridge, Mass., 1983), 171.

6. J. Derrida, *Dissemination* (Chicago University Press: Chicago, 1981), 221.

7. F. Fanon, *The Wretched of the Earth* (Penguin: Harmondsworth, 1967), 199.

8. E. Said, *After the Last Sky* (Faber: London, 1986), 34.

Extract 48

FLOYA ANTHIAS AND NIRA YUVAL-DAVIS: *Women and the Nation-State*

1. C. Pateman, 'Feminism and participatory democracy', paper given to the American Philosophical Association, Missouri, May 1986; C. Saraceno, 'Gender in the construction of citizenship', paper given to workshop on women and the State, Berlin, 29 June–1 July 1987.

2. F. Edholm, O. Harris, and K. Young, 'Conceptualizing Women', *Critique of Anthropology*, 3/9 (1976), 101–30; B. Hindess and P. Hirst, *Pre-Capitalist Modes of Production* (Routledge & Kegan Paul: London, 1975).

3. See, for example, Edholm *et al.*, op. cit.; M. O'Brien, *The Politics of Reproduction* (Routledge & Kegan Paul: London, 1981); a notable exception has been WING, *Worlds Apart: Women under Immigration and Nationality Law* (Pluto: London, 1985). See also N. Yuval-Davis, 'The bearers of the collective: Women and religious

legislation in Israel', *Feminist Review*, 4 (1980), 15–27; id. 'National reproduction: Sexism, racism and the State', paper given to the British Sociological Association annual conference, April 1982; F. Anthias, 'Sexual divisions and ethnic adaptation', in A. Phizacklea (ed.), *One Way Ticket* (Routledge & Kegan Paul: London, 1983).

4. F. Anthias and N. Yuval-Davis, 'Contextualising Feminism: Gender, ethnic, and class divisions', *Feminist Review*, 15 (1983), 62–76.

5. N. Yuval-Davis, 'Front and rear: The sexual division of labour in the Israeli army', *Feminist Studies*, 2/3 (1985), 649–76.

6. M. Molyneux, 'Women in socialist societies: Theory and practice', in K. Young, C. Wolkowitz, and R. McCullagh (eds.), *Of Marriage and the Market* (CSE Books: London, 1985), 167–202; D. Kandiyoti, 'Emancipated but unliberated? Reflections on the Turkish case', *Feminist Studies*, 13/2 (1987), 317–88.

Extract 49

PHILIP SCHLESINGER: *Europeanness: A New Cultural Battlefield?*

1. Cf. Frisby, 1985.

2. David Harvey, *The Condition of Postmodernity* (Blackwell: Oxford, 1989), 302–3.

3. Cf. Zygmunt Bauman, 'Modernity and ambivalence', *Theory, Culture and Society*, 7/3 (1990), 239–60.

4. Michel Maffesoli, *Le Temps des Tribus: le Déclin de l'Individualisme* (Meridiens Klincksinck: Paris, 1988).

5. Zygmunt Bauman, *Modernity and Ambivalence* (Polity Press: Cambridge, 1991), 249.

6. Alberto Melucci, 'The voice of the roots: Ethno-national mobilizations in a global world', *Innovation*, 3/3 (1990), 335.

7. William Wallace, 'Foreign policy and national identity in the United Kingdom', *International Affairs*, 67/1 (1991), 66–7.

8. Alain Bihr, 'Malaise dans l'état-nation', *Le Monde Diplomatique*, 455 (Feb. 1992), 7.

9. Étienne Balibar, 'Es gibt keinen Staat in Europa: Racism and Politics in Europe today', *New Left Review*, 186 (Mar.–Apr. 1991), 17.

10. Anthony D. Smith, *National Identity* (Penguin: Harmondsworth, 1991), 11.

11. Ibid. 13.

12. Helen Wallace, 'The Europe that came in from the cold', *International Affairs*, 67/4 (Oct. 1991), 661–4.

13. Ibid. 654.

14. Pierre Hassner, 'Europe beyond partition and unity: Disintegration or reconstitution?', *International Affairs*, 66/3 (July 1990), 469.

15. Smith, op. cit. 174.

16. Ernest Gellner, *Nations and Nationalism* (Blackwell: Oxford, 1983).

Select Bibliography

General

DEUTSCH, KARL, *An Interdisciplinary Bibliography on Nationalism, 1935–53* (MIT Press: Cambridge, Mass., 1956).

SMITH, ANTHONY D., *Nationalism: A Trend Report and Annotated Bibliography, Current Sociology*, 21/3 (1973) (Mouton: The Hague and Paris, 1973).

KOHN, HANS, *Nationalism: Its Meaning and History* (Van Nostrand: Princeton, NJ, 1955).

SHAFER, BOYD, *Nationalism: Myth and Reality* (Harcourt, Brace: New York, 1955).

SNYDER, LOUIS (ed.), *The Dynamics of Nationalism: A Reader* (Van Nostrand: New York, 1964).

BARNARD, F. M., *Herder on Social and Political Culture* (Cambridge University Press: Cambridge, 1969).

BERLIN, SIR ISAIAH, *Vico and Herder* (Hogarth Press: London, 1976).

REX, JOHN, and MASON, DAVID (eds.), *Theories of Race and Ethnic Relations* (Cambridge University Press: Cambridge, 1986).

ALTER, PETER, *Nationalism* (Edward Arnold: London, 1989).

I. The Question of Definition

ZERNATTO, GUIDO, 'Nation: The history of a word', *Review of Politics*, 6 (1944), 351–66.

SNYDER, LOUIS, *The Meaning of Nationalism* (Rutgers University Press: New Brunswick, 1954).

BARON, SALO, *Modern Nationalism and Religion* (Meridian Books: New York, 1960).

KEMILAINEN, AIRA, *Nationalism: Problems concerning the Word, the Concept and Classification* (Kustantajat Publishers: Yvaskyla, 1964).

HAUGEN, EINAR, 'Language, dialect, nation', *American Anthropologist*, 68 (1966), 922–35.

RUSTOW, DANKWART, *A World of Nations* (Brookings Institution: Washington, DC, 1967).

FISHMAN, JOSHUA (ed.), *Language Problems in Developing Countries* (John Wiley: New York, 1968).

BARTH, FREDRIK (ed.), *Ethnic Groups and Boundaries* (Little, Brown and Company: Boston, 1969).

SHAFER, BOYD, *Faces of Nationalism: New Realities and Old Myths* (Harcourt, Brace, Jovanovich: New York, 1972).

CONNOR, WALKER, 'Nation-Building or Nation-Destroying?', *World Politics*, 24 (1972), 319–55.

KAMENKA, EUGENE (ed.), *Nationalism: The Nature and Evolution of an Idea* (Edward Arnold: London, 1976).

SCHLESINGER, PHILIP, 'On National Identity: Some Conceptions and Misconceptions Criticised', *Social Science Information*, 26/2 (1987), 219–64.

II. Theories of Nationalism

ZNANIECKI, FLORIAN, *Modern Nationalities* (University of Illinois Press: Urbana, Ill., 1952).

KAUTSKY, JOHN (ed.), *Political Change in Underdeveloped Countries* (John Wiley: New York, 1962).

DOOB, LEONARD, *Patriotism and Nationalism: Their Psychological Foundations* (Yale University Press: New Haven, Conn., 1964).

SMITH, ANTHONY D., *Theories of Nationalism* (1st edn., Duckworth: London, 1971); (2nd edn., Holmes and Meier: London and New York, 1983).

GELLNER, ERNEST, 'Scale and Nation', *Philosophy of the Social Sciences*, 3 (1973), 1–17.

GLAZER, NATHAN, and MOYNIHAN, DANIEL (eds.), *Ethnicity: Theory and Experience* (Harvard University Press: Cambridge, Mass., 1975).

HECHTER, MICHAEL, *Internal Colonialism: The Celtic Fringe in British National Development, 1536–1966* (Routledge & Kegan Paul: London, 1975).

VAN DEN BERGHE, PIERRE, *The Ethnic Phenomenon* (Elsevier: New York, 1979).

ORRIDGE, ANDREW, 'Uneven Development and Nationalism', *Political Studies*, 29/1–2 (1981), 1–15, 181–90.

CONNOR, WALKER, *The National Question in Marxist-Leninist Theory and Strategy* (Princeton University Press: Princeton, NJ, 1984).

—— 'Eco- or Ethno-Nationalism?', *Ethnic and Racial Studies*, 7/3 (1984), 342–59.

SMITH, ANTHONY D., 'The Myth of the "Modern Nation" and the Myths of Nations', *Ethnic and Racial Studies*, 11/1 (1988), 1–26.

III. The Rise of Nations

HAYES, CARLTON, *The Historical Evolution of Modern Nationalism* (Smith: New York, 1931).

HERTZ, FREDERICK, *Nationality in Politics and History* (Routledge and Kegan Paul: London, 1944).

EMERSON, RUPERT, *From Empire to Nation* (Harvard University Press: Cambridge, Mass., 1960).

BENDIX, REINHARD, *Nation-Building and Citizenship* (John Wiley: New York, 1964).

KOHN, HANS, *Prelude to Nation-States: The French and German Experience, 1789–1815* (Van Nostrand: Princeton, NJ, 1967).

TIPTON, LEON (ed.), *Nationalism in the Middle Ages* (Holt, Rinehart and Winston: New York, 1972).

FINLEY, MOSES, *The Use and Abuse of History* (Hogarth Press: London, 1986).

SMITH, ANTHONY D., *The Ethnic Origins of Nations* (Blackwell: Oxford, 1986).

KITROMILIDES, PASCHALIS, ' "Imagined Communities" and the Origins of the National Question in the Balkans', *European History Quarterly*, 19/2 (1989), 149–92.

MENDELS, DORON, *The Rise and Fall of Jewish Nationalism* (Doubleday: New York, 1992).

IV. Nationalism in Europe

KOHN, HANS, *Pan-Slavism: Its History and Ideology*, 2nd rev. edn. (Vintage Books: New York, 1960).

JELAVICH, BARBARA, and JELAVICH, CHARLES (eds.), *The Balkans in Transition* (University of California Press: Berkeley, Calif., 1963).

MOSSE, GEORGE, *The Crisis of German Ideology* (Grosset and Dunlap: New York, 1964).

BENTHEM VAN DEN BERGHE, G. VAN, 'Contemporary Nationalism in the Western World', *Daedalus*, 95 (1966), 828–61.

POLIAKOV, LEON, *The Aryan Myth* (Basic Books: New York, 1974).

PECH, STANLEY, 'The Nationalist Movements of the Austrian Slavs', *Social History*, 9 (1976), 336–56.

HOWARD, MICHAEL, *War in European History* (Oxford University Press: London, 1976).

ESMAN, MILTON (ed.), *Ethnic Conflict in the Western World* (Cornell University Press: Ithaca, NJ, 1977).

WEBER, EUGENE, *Peasants into Frenchmen: The Modernisation of Rural France, 1870–1914* (Chatto & Windus: London, 1979).

SMITH, ANTHONY D., *Nationalism in the Twentieth Century* (Martin Robertson: Oxford, 1979).

SUGAR, PETER (ed.), *Ethnic Conflict and Diversity in Eastern Europe* (ABC-Clio: Santa Barbara, 1980).

MITCHISON, ROSALIND (ed.), *The Roots of Nationalism: Studies in Northern Europe* (John Donald Publishers Ltd.: Edinburgh, 1980).

KREJCI, YAROSLAV, and VELIMSKY, VITESLAV, *Ethnic and Political Nations in Europe* (Croom Helm: London, 1981).

WILLIAMS, COLIN (ed.), *National Separatism* (University of Wales Press: Cardiff, 1982).

PEARSON, RAYMOND, *National Minorities in Eastern Europe, 1848–1945* (Macmillan: London, 1983).

HROCH, MIROSLAV, *Social Preconditions of the National Revival in Europe* (Cambridge University Press: Cambridge, 1985).

TIRYAKIAN, E., and ROGOWSKI, R. (eds.), *New Nationalisms in the Developed West* (Allen & Unwin: Boston, 1985).

RAMET, PEDRO (ed.), *Religion and Nationalism in Soviet and East European Politics* (Duke University Press: Durham and London, 1989).

COLLEY, LINDA, *Britons: Forging a Nation, 1707–1837* (Yale University Press: New Haven, Conn., and London, 1992).

BREMMER, IAN, and TARAS, RAY (eds.), *Nations and Politics in the Soviet Successor States* (Cambridge University Press: Cambridge, 1993).

TEICH, MIKULAS, and PORTER, ROY (eds.), *The National Question in Europe in Historical Context* (Cambridge University Press: Cambridge, 1993).

V. Nationalism outside Europe

HODGKIN, THOMAS, *Nationalism in Colonial Africa* (Muller: London, 1956).

LEVENSON, JOSEPH, *Liang Ch'i Ch'ao and the Mind of Modern China*, 2nd edn. (University of California Press: Berkeley, Calif., and Los Angeles, 1959).

HAIM, SYLVIA (ed.), *Arab Nationalism: An Anthology* (University of California Press: Berkeley, Calif., and Los Angeles, 1962).

HALPERN, MANFRED, *The Politics of Social Change in the Middle East and North Africa* (Princeton University Press: Princeton, NJ, 1963).

HUMPHREYS, R., and LYNCH, J. (eds.), *The Origins of Latin American Revolutions, 1808–26* (A. Knopf: New York, 1965).

MASUR, GERHARD, *Nationalism in Latin America: Diversity and Unity* (Macmillan: New York, 1966).

BELL, WENDELL (ed.), *The Democratic Revolution in the West Indies* (Schenkman Publishing Co.: Cambridge, Mass., 1967).

JULY, ROBERT, *The Origins of Modern African Thought* (Faber & Faber: London, 1968).

LEWIS, BERNARD, *The Emergence of Modern Turkey* (Oxford University Press: Oxford, 1968).

HOURANI, ALBERT, *Arabic Thought in the Liberal Age, 1798–1939* (Oxford University Press: London and New York, 1970).

ROTBERG, ROBERT, and MAZRUI, ALI (eds.), *Protest and Power in Black Africa* (Oxford University Press: New York, 1970).

GEISS, IMMANUEL, *The PanAfrican Movement* (Methuen: London, 1974).

BRASS, PAUL, *Religion, Language and Politics in North India* (Cambridge University Press: Cambridge, 1974).

YOUNG, CRAWFORD, *The Politics of Cultural Pluralism* (University of Wisconsin Press: Madison, Wis., 1976).

LEWIS, IOANN (ed.), *Nationalism and Self-Determination in the Horn of Africa* (Ithaca Press: London, 1982).

THOMPSON, LEONARD, *The Political Mythology of Apartheid* (Yale University Press: New Haven, Conn., and London, 1985).

NEUBERGER, BENJAMIN, *National Self-Determination in Post-Colonial Africa* (Lynne Rienner Publishers: Boulder, Col., 1986).

KAPFERER, BRUCE, *Legends of People, Myths of State* (Smithsonian Institution Press: Washington, DC, 1988).

Third World Quarterly, 11/4 (August 1989).

YOSHINO, KOSAKU, *Cultural Nationalism in Contemporary Japan* (Routledge: London and New York, 1992).

BROWN, DAVID, *The State and Ethnic Politics in Southeast Asia* (Routledge: London and New York, 1994).

VI. Nationalism and the International System

ANDERSON, CHARLES, VON DER MEHDEN, FRED, and YOUNG, CRAWFORD, *Issues of Political Development* (Prentice-Hall: Englewood Cliffs, NJ, 1967).

HINSLEY, F. H., *Nationalism and the International System* (Hodder & Stoughton: London, 1973).

LIJPHART, AREND, *Democracy in Plural Societies* (Yale University Press: New Haven, Conn., and London, 1977).

BEITZ, C., *Political Theory and International Relations* (Princeton University Press: Princeton, NJ, 1979).

TIVEY, LEONARD (ed.), *The Nation-State* (Martin Robertson: Oxford, 1980).

ENLOE, CYNTHIA, *Ethnic Soldiers* (Penguin: Harmondsworth, 1980).

BUCHEIT, LEE, *Secession: The Legitimacy of Self-Determination* (Yale University Press: New Haven, Conn., 1981).

MAYALL, JAMES (ed.), *The Community of States* (Allen and Unwin: London, 1982).

BERAN, HARRY, 'A Liberal Theory of Secession', *Political Studies*, 32, (1984), 21–31.

MAYALL, JAMES, 'Nationalism and the International Order', *Millennium: Journal of International Studies*, 14/2 (1985), 143–58.

JACKSON, ROBERT, *Quasi-States: Sovereignty, International Relations and the Third World* (Cambridge University Press: Cambridge, 1990).

Millennium: Journal of International Studies, 20/3 (Winter 1991).

HERACLIDES, ALEXIS, *The Self-Determination of Minorities in International Politics* (Frank Cass: London, 1991).

VII. Beyond Nationalism?

TONKIN, ELISABETH, MCDONALD, MARYON, and CHAPMAN, MALCOLM (eds.), *History and Ethnicity* (Routledge: London, 1989).

SAMUEL, RAPHAEL (ed.), *Patriotism: The Making and Unmaking of British National Identity*, 3 vols. (Routledge: London and New York, 1989).

FEATHERSTONE, MIKE (ed.), *Global Culture: Nationalism, Globalisation and Modernity* (Sage: London, 1990).

SMITH, ANTHONY D., 'The Supersession of Nationalism?', *International Journal of Comparative Sociology*, 31/1–2 (1990), 1–36.

—— *National Identity* (Penguin: Harmondsworth, 1991).

TOMLINSON, JOHN, *Cultural Imperialism* (Pinter Publishers: London, 1991).

SCHLESINGER, PHILIP, *Media, State and Nation: Political Violence and Collective Identities* (Sage Publications: London, 1991).

Biographical Notes

ANDERSON, B. Professor of International Relations at Cornell University, Benedict Anderson specializes in the politics of South-East Asia. His major work on nationalism, *Imagined Communities* (1983), has become one of the most cited texts in the field. Its focus on literary devices in narrating and representing the nation and its concepts of 'print-capitalism', 'empty, homogenous time', and 'imagined community' have illuminated the cultural sources of nationalism and have been especially influential for post-modernist analyses.

ANTHIAS, F. Floya Anthias is Senior Lecturer in Sociology at the University of Greenwich. She has conducted research on race and community in South-East London and on refugees in Cypriot society, and has written several important articles on sexual divisions and ethnic adaptations and on Greek–Cypriot relations in Britain.

ARMSTRONG, J. Emeritus Professor of Political Science at the University of Wisconsin, John Armstrong is a highly regarded specialist in East European politics and author of the classic *Ukrainian Nationalism* (1963). But his *magnum opus* in the field is his pioneering *Nations before Nationalism* (1982), in which his massive researches into the many factors that combined to produce a sense of ethnic identity in pre-modern Islamic and Christian civilizations are brought together through a phenomenological analysis of myths, symbols, and codes which owes much to Fredrik Barth's symbolic boundary approach.

BHABHA, H. Professor of English and Literary and Cultural Theory at the University of Chicago, Homi Bhabha has become a leading exponent of 'post-modernist' approaches to problems of national identity. The collection of essays that he edited, *Nation and Narration* (1990), has been influential in questioning the concepts used to explain the social context of cultural representations like the nation, and in bringing the insights of cultural studies to bear on problems of cultural location and national identity.

BRASS, P. Professor of Political Science and South Asian Studies at the University of Washington, Seattle, Paul Brass is internationally known for his studies of the politics of South Asia, especially *Language, Religion and Politics in North India* (1974), *The Politics of India since Independence* (1990), and *Ethnicity and Nationalism* (1991). Throughout he has argued the centrality of élite perceptions and actions in shaping the politics of ethnic identity, especially in South Asia; the present extract summarizes one of his main concerns.

BREUILLY, J. Reader in History at the University of Manchester, John Breuilly specializes in European and especially German history. His major work in the field, *Nationalism and the State* (1982), from which this extract is taken, puts forward an original theory of nationalism as a political strategy, and a persuasive historicist pseudo-solution to the alienation caused by the split between the modern state and society and the consequent loss of community.

CARR, E. Carr was one of the most distinguished British historians of his generation and the author of a multi-volume history of the Soviet Union. His interest in nationalism was stimulated by the survey conducted by the Royal Institute of International Affairs, which he chaired. His subsequent small book, *Nationalism and After* (1945), with its well-known stages and its attention to economic history, has exerted a strong influence on scholars in international relations and political science.

CHATTERJEE, P. A leading member of the *Subaltern Studies* collective, Partha Chatterjee is Professor of Political Science at the Centre for Studies in Social Sciences, Calcutta. He is well known for his analysis of colonial nationalist discourses in Asia in his *Nationalist Thought and the Colonial World: A Derivative Discourse* (1986). His recent book, *The Nation and its Fragments* (1993), explores these themes further in relation to the writing of Indian national history.

COBBAN, A. Professor of Modern History at the University of London. Alfred Cobban was one of the most respected historians of modern France. His penetrating studies of the French Revolution (*The Social Interpretation of the French Revolution*, 1965) and French history (*A History of Modern France*, 3 vols., 1957–63) went hand in hand with his concern for the often tragic consequences of national self-determination in the twentieth century. This extract from *The Nation-State and National Self-Determination* (rev. edn., 1969) summarizes his understanding of the stages of development of nationalism.

CONNOR, W. Reitemeyer Professor of Political Science at Trinity College, Hartford, Connecticut, Walker Connor is best known for his *The National Question in Marxist-Leninist Theory and Strategy* (1984) and especially for the series of seminal and hard-hitting articles on various aspects of ethnicity and nationalism, which have influenced scholars from several disciplines. In the first extract Connor argues the need for clear and unequivocal definitions of key concepts in the field; in the second he challenges prennialist accounts of the antiquity of the nation.

DEUTSCH, K. Professor of Political Science at MIT, Karl Deutsch has been one of the most influential of the communications theorists. To this approach, Deutsch added a socio-demographic analysis which enabled him to plot the growth of nations and regimes, especially in his well-known books *Nationalism and Social Communication* (1953) and *The Nerves of Government* (1963), which opened the way for the use of quantitative techniques in history and political science. The definitions come from chapter 4 of the former book.

GEERTZ, C. Professor of Anthropology at the University of Chicago, Clifford Geertz is a distinguished exponent of cultural anthropology and has published important studies of culture and society in Indonesia and Morocco, notably *The Interpretation of Cultures* (1973). His emphasis on cultural 'givens', the 'primordial ties' of religion, language, race, and territory, highlighted in this extract from his well-known edited collection of essays, *Old Societies and New States* (1963), has been influential in stimulating current debates on the nature of ethnic ties.

GELLNER, E. Formerly Professor of Philosophy with special reference to Sociology at the London School of Economics and then William Wyse Professor of Social Anthropology at Cambridge University, Ernest Gellner is one of the most wide-ranging and influential scholars in the social sciences. He put forward one of the few original theories of nationalism in *Thought and Change* (1964), arguing that nationalism is an inevitable product of modernization, which requires literate cultures to create homogenous societies of citizens. In his later *Nations and Nationalism* (1983) Gellner explored the material basis of the transition to literate 'high' cultures in industrial society.

GIDDENS, A.   Professor of Sociology at Cambridge University, Anthony Giddens is one of the most distinguished and prolific sociologists today. His many influential works include major studies like *Capitalism and Social Theory* (1971) and *The Nation-State and Violence* (1984), from which this extract is taken. His work emphasizes the revolutionary, global nature of modernity and the key role of the self-monitoring nation-state.

GREENFELD, L.   Liah Greenfeld is John L. Loeb Associate Professor of the Social Sciences at the University of Harvard. Her major work, *Nationalism: Five Roads to Modernity* (1992), is a detailed historical and sociological study of the rise of national identity in England, France, Germany, Russia, and America.

HECHTER, M.   Professor of Sociology at the University of Arizona, Michael Hechter is well known for his highly influential theory of 'internal colonialism' (*Internal Colonialism*, 1975), which illuminated the social conditions of ethnic persistence and change in modern Western Europe. Subsequently, Hechter moved to a 'rational choice' analysis of ethnic nationalism and secession movements, in which cultural and economic conditions form the basis for rational political strategies.

HOBSBAWM, E.   A distinguished historian of nineteenth-century Europe, Eric Hobsbawm is Emeritus Professor of Modern History at Birkbeck College, University of London. His many books include *Bandits* (1969), *The Age of Revolution* (1962), *The Age of Capital* (1975), and *The Age of Empire* (1987). In *The Invention of Tradition* (1983) Hobsbawm and his associates include the nation as one way of holding together societies endangered by mass mobilization, a theme continued in *Nations and Nationalism since 1780* (1990), with its critique of the many divisive and often fabricated ethno-linguistic nationalisms—as opposed to the earlier mass-democratic political nationalism of the West.

HOROWITZ, D.   Professor of Law, Public Policy Studies, and Political Science at Duke University, Donald Horowitz is a distinguished political scientist who has published in several fields, ranging from the law courts to the current political scene in South Africa. His books include *The Jurocracy* (1977), *Coup Theories and Officers' Motives* (1980), and his major work in the field, *Ethnic Groups in Conflict* (1985). The present extract is taken from his lucid and original typology of irredentist and secessionist movements, which seeks to balance the many economic, political, and cultural factors at work in ethnic conflicts in Asia and Africa.

HOWARD, M.   Michael Howard was Regius Professor of Modern History at the University of Oxford and is an eminent scholar of the history of war. He is the author of several major works, including *War in European History* (1976) and *The Lessons of History* (1991).

HUTCHINSON, J.   John Hutchinson is a Senior Lecturer in the Faculty of Humanities at Griffith University, Brisbane, where he teaches modern European history. He has specialized in the cultural and political history of Britain and Ireland, but his forthcoming book, *Modern Nationalism* (1994), explores a wide range of issues in the field of ethnicity and nationalism. The extract here comes from his influential *The Dynamics of*

Cultural Nationalism (1987), which demonstrated the separate role of cultural nationalism as a source of moral regeneration for subject communities.

JOHNSON, H. Harry Johnson was a distinguished monetary economist. Professor of Economics at Chicago and the London School of Economics, Johnson was interested in the applications of economic theory to a wide range of current problems. The extract here is taken from his seminal essay on the economics of nationalism in new states, with its emphasis on the psychic rewards of policies of nationalization.

KEDOURIE, E. The late Elie Kedourie was Professor of Government at the London School of Economics. His many interests included political philosophy and the modern history of the Middle East. His path-breaking work on nationalist ideas was in the conservative tradition of Lord Acton. In his classic works, *Nationalism* (1960) and *Nationalism in Asia and Africa* (1971), Kedourie combined a fierce denunciation of nationalism with an acute insight into its causes and operations both in Europe and outside, paying special attention to the pivotal role of marginalized intellectuals seeking millennial political solutions to their discontents.

KOHN, H. Professor of History at the City College of New York, Hans Kohn was the leading exponent of the history of nationalist ideologies in Western Europe, North America, Eastern Europe, and the Middle East. His major studies include *A History of Nationalism in the East* (1929), *PanSlavism* (1960), *The Mind of Germany* (1965), *Prelude to Nation-States* (1967), and particularly *The Idea of Nationalism* (1944: rev. edn. 1967), from which this extract is taken. In this and subsequent works Kohn put forward his influential distinction between a rational, civic nationalism of the 'West' and the authoritarian, organic, ethnic nationalism of the 'East'.

LEVI, M. Margaret Levi is Professor of Political Science at the University of Washington, Seattle, and author of *Bureaucratic Insurgency* (1977) and *Of Rule and Revenue* (1988).

LIJPHART, A. Professor of Political Science at the University of California, Arend Lijphart is an international authority on the politics of plural societies. He is particularly well known for his analysis of power-sharing in ethnically divided societies like Belgium, Holland, and Canada in his major work, *Democracy in Plural Societies* (1977). His work has inspired policy-oriented research into the conditions of civic nationalism in plural democracies. In this extract Lijphart dismisses a number of plausible explanations of the ethnic revival, and focuses on the expansion of the state, democratization, and the decline of the salience of class.

MCNEILL, W. William McNeill, Professor of History at the University of Chicago, is one of the most distinguished historians and the foremost exponent of the field of world history. He has made a special study of military technology and the role of disease in history. His best-known works are *The Rise of the West* (1963), *Plagues and Peoples* (1976), and *The Pursuit of Power* (1982). In the lectures from which this extract is taken, McNeill uses the themes of his earlier work to show the necessity of polyethnic hierarchy in any civilized society.

MATOSSIAN, M. A specialist on Soviet Armenia, Mary Matossian is Associate Professor of History at the University of Maryland. This extract is taken from an influential early essay on the ambivalence and archaism of nationalist ideologies among leaders of the new states of Asia in the wake of decolonization.

MAYALL, J.   Professor of International Relations at the London School of Economics, James Mayall is a specialist in the politics of the Horn of Africa and has written extensively on economic nationalism and liberalism. In his major work in the field, *Nationalism and International Society* (1990), from which this extract is taken, Mayall explores the social and political conditions of irredentism and ethnic secession movements and especially the interstate factors that facilitate their success.

NAIRN, T.   Tom Nairn has been an editor of *New Left Review* and now works as a journalist and writer and for BBC TV Scotland, researching nationalism in Scotland and Europe. His work on neo-nationalism has made an important contribution to the debates on national identity generally, as well as in the British Isles. This extract comes from his *The Breakup of Britain* (1977), which is at once a powerful critique of the Marxist failure to come to grips with the 'national question' and an original attempt to formulate a broadly neo-Marxian theory of nationalism.

NEUBERGER, B.   Associate Professor of Political Science at Tel Aviv University, Benjamin Neuberger is a specialist on nationalism in sub-Saharan Africa. He has written on nationalist ideology in ethnically plural societies outside Africa, but his main work, *National Self-Determination in Post-Colonial Africa* (1986), has illuminated the ideological and political problems of the post-colonial states of Africa in their attempts to modify and transpose western categories and concepts on to a very different social and political terrain.

RENAN, E.   A Breton by birth, Ernest Renan was an eminent French scholar of languages and history. A professor at the Sorbonne, he wrote a controversial life of the historical Jesus. His celebrated essay on the nation was written in 1882 in an atmosphere of French revanchism over the loss of Alsace-Lorraine to Germany in the Franco-Prussian War in 1870; the liberal and voluntarist approach illustrated in this extract is one of the very first scholarly statements in the field of nationalism.

REYNOLDS, S.   Formerly Fellow of Lady Margaret Hall, Oxford University, Susan Reynolds is a distinguished medieval historian who has worked widely on different forms of community in the medieval West. Her *Kingdoms and Communities of Western Europe, 900–1300* (1984), from which this extract is taken, demonstrates the many parallels and differences between medieval concepts and forms of identity and community and those of modern nations.

RICHMOND, A.   Professor of Sociology at York University, Toronto, Anthony Richmond is a well-known scholar of the sociology of education, culture, and race in plural societies. In the article from which this extract is taken, he advances a theory of the resurgence of ethnic nationalism in 'post-industrial' societies based on dense communications networks of ethnic groups and regions in technologically advanced states.

ROBINSON, F.   Professor of History at Royal Holloway and Bedford New College, Francis Robinson is a distinguished historian of the Indian sub-continent. The author of *Separatism among the Indian Muslims* (1974) and many important articles on Indian history, he takes issue here with Paul Brass about the weight to be given to pre-existing Muslim ties in shaping separatist movements among Indian Muslims.

SCHLESINGER, P.   Professor of Film and Media Studies at the University of Stirling and Director of the Stirling Media Research Institute. He is the author of *Putting 'Reality'*

Together (1987, 2nd edn.), *Media, State and Nation* (1991) and co-author of *Televising Terrorism* (1983), *Women Viewing Violence* (1992) and *Reporting Crime* (1994). An editor of the journal *Media, Culture & Society*, he is currently also a Professor in the Department of Media and Communication at the University of Oslo.

SETON-WATSON, H. One of the most eminent historians of Eastern Europe and Russia, the late Hugh Seton-Watson was Professor of Russian History in the University of London and Director of the School of Slavonic and East European Studies. His major works include *Neither War nor Peace* (1960), *The Russian Empire, 1801–1917* (1967), and *Nations and States* (1977), a magisterial survey of national consciousness in Europe and outside. The extract here summarizes the distinction between the 'old-continuous nations' of Western and Northern Europe and the later nations created by nationalist movements in Eastern Europe, Asia, and Africa, which serves to organize his rich survey.

SMITH, A. D. Professor of Sociology at the London School of Economics, Anthony D. Smith has specialized in the study of ethnicity and nationalism, especially the theory of the nation. He has published *Theories of Nationalism* (1971), *The Ethnic Revival* (1981), *The Ethnic Origins of Nations* (1986), and *National Identity* (1991). His work has focused especially on the historical and social origins of nations, departing from the current 'modernist' standpoints in favour of the view that we can only explain the character of modern nations in terms of their antecedent popular ethnic memories, myths, and symbols.

STALIN, J. As General Secretary of the Communist Party of the Soviet Union, Joseph Stalin was responsible for expelling Trotsky and purging the original leaders of the Bolshevik Party, and for murdering millions of Soviet citizens, especially in the Ukraine. The extract dates from 1913, when Stalin, at Lenin's request, made a study of the nationalities question in Eastern Europe, partly to discredit the rival Austro-Marxists and Jewish Bundists; the 'objectivist' definition that he employs became the canonical Marxist statement on the subject until the 1950s.

SUGAR, P. Professor of History at the University of Washington, Seattle, Peter Sugar is one of the foremost historians of Eastern Europe and the author of *The Industrialisation of Bosnia-Hercegovina, 1878–1918* (1963). He has edited two important volumes, *Ethnic Diversity and Conflict in Eastern Europe* (1980) and the earlier *Nationalism in Eastern Europe* (1969, with Ivo Lederer), from which this extract is taken; it documents the complex forms assumed by ethnic nationalisms in Eastern Europe.

TILLY, C. Professor of History at the New School for Social Research in New York, Charles Tilly is one of the most eminent historians of his generation. In his path-breaking *The Vendée* (1963) he pioneered the use of quantitative sociological techniques in history, a method which he continued in subsequent works. The substantial introduction and conclusion to the influential volume *The Formation of National States in Western Europe* (1975), from which this extract is taken, sets out his causal method for investigating the main political and social factors that produced the system of Western national states.

VAN DEN BERGHE, P. Professor of Sociology at the University of Washington, Seattle, Pierre van den Berghe has published several major studies of race relations, notably *Race and Racism* (1967). In the 1970s he embraced sociobiology and published

The Ethnic Phenomenon (1979), which offers a controversial sociobiological account of ethnicity and race in terms of concepts of individual reproductive success and inclusive fitness; the article included here summarizes his thesis.

WEBER, M.   Renowned for his breadth of scholarship and erudition, Max Weber became one of the founders of sociology. His 'interpretive method' was allied to a strong commitment to causal analysis and value neutrality. A convinced German nationalist, his main intellectual interest was in analysing the role of various factors—religious, economic, and political—which came to shape the unique civilization of the West. Though he never wrote the promised book on the formation of national states, Weber adopted a 'political' approach to ethnicity and national identity which has been highly influential.

YOUNG, C.   Professor of Political Science at the University of Wisconsin, Madison, Crawford Young is a leading exponent of the study of politics in the new states of sub-Saharan Africa. In his major works, *The Politics of Cultural Pluralism* (1976) and *Ideology and Development in Africa* (1982), as well as in some important articles, Young perceptively analyses the problems of decolonization and development in the plural societies of Black Africa; in this extract Young demonstrates the ways in which colonial states moulded ethnic self-definitions in Africa.

YUVAL-DAVIS, N.   Nira Yuval-Davis is Reader at the University of Greenwich and has specialized in the politics of ethnicity and feminism. She has published stimulating and important articles and volumes on gender and ethnicity, especially in the Middle East. In this extract from their introduction to *Woman—Nation—State* (1989) Yuval-Davis and Anthias set out the main areas of female participation in, and reproduction of, ethnic identities and national collectivities.

Acknowledgements

ANDERSON, BENEDICT, from *Imagined Communities* (Reprinted by permission of Verso, 1991).

ANTHIAS, F. and YUVAL-DAVIS, N., 'Introduction' from *Woman–Nation–State*, Yuval-Davis, Anthias, and Campling (1989). Reprinted by permission of Macmillan Ltd.

ARMSTRONG, J., from *Problems of Communism* (Jan.–April 1992). United States Information Agency.

ARMSTRONG, JOHN A., reprinted from *Nations Before Nationalism*, by John A. Armstrong. Copyright © 1982 by the University of North Carolina Press. Used by permission of the author and publisher.

BHABHA, HOMI, 'Introduction' from *The Nation and Narration*, ed. by H. Bhabha (Routledge, 1990).

BRASS, PAUL R., 'Élite Groups, Symbol Manipulation and Ethnic Identity Among the Muslims of South Asia', in *Political Identity in South Asia*, eds. D. Taylor and M. Yapp (Curzon Press, 1979).

BREUILLY, JOHN, from *Nationalism and the State* (1982). Reprinted by permission of Manchester University Press.

CARR, E. H., from *Nationalism and After* (Copyright © 1945 by E. H. Carr). Reproduced by permission of The Curtis Brown Group Ltd., London.

CHATTERJEE, PARTHA, from *The Nation and Its Fragments* (Copyright © 1993 by Partha Chatterjee). Reprinted by permission of Princeton University Press.

COBBAN, ALFRED, from *The Nation-State and Natural Self-Determination* (Fontana, 1969). Reprinted by permission of Harper Collins Publishers Limited.

CONNER, WALTER, 'A Nation is a Nation', from *Ethnic and Racial Studies*, vol. 1, no. 4, 1978. Reprinted by permission of Routledge.

CONNER, WALTER, 'When is a Nation', from *Ethnic and Racial Studies*, vol. 13, no. 1, 1992. Reprinted by permission of Routledge.

DEUTSCH, KARL, from *Naturalism and Social Communication*, 2nd edn. (MIT Press, 1966).

GEERTZ, CLIFFORD, reprinted with the permission of The Free Press, a member of Paramount Publishing from *Old Societies and New States: 'The Quest for Modernity in Asia and Africa'* by Clifford Geertz. Copyright © 1963 by The Free Press.

GELLNER, ERNEST, 'Nationalism', in *Thought and Change* (George Weidenfeld & Nicolson Limited, 1964).

GELLNER, ERNEST, from *Nations and Nationalism* (Blackwell Publishers, 1983).

GIDDENS, A., from *A Contemporary Critique of Historical Materialism, Vol. II* (Polity Press, 1985). Reprinted by permission of Blackwell Publishers.

GREENFELD, LEAH, reprinted by permission of the publishers from *Nationalism: Five Roads to Modernity* by Leah Greenfeld, Cambridge, Mass.: Harvard University Press, Copyright © 1992 by Leah Greenfeld.

HECHTER, MICHAEL and LEVI, MARGARET, 'The Comparative Analysis of Ethnoregional Movements', from *Ethnic and Racial Studies*, vol. 2, no. 3, 1979. Reprinted by the permission of Routledge.

HOBSBAWM, E. J., from *Nations and Nationalism since 1780* (Cambridge University Press, 1990).

HOBSBAWM, E. J., 'Mass-Producing Traditions: Europe 1870–1914' and 'Introduction: Inventing Traditions', in *The Invention of Tradition*, eds. E. Hobsbawm and T. Ranger (Cambridge University Press, 1983).

HOROWITZ, DONALD, from *Ethnic Groups in Conflict* (Copyright © 1985 The Regents of the University of California). Reprinted by permission of University of California Press.

HOWARD, MICHAEL, from *The Lessons of History* (Oxford University Press, 1991).

HUTCHINSON, JOHN, from *The Dynamics of Cultural Nationalism* (HarperCollins Publishers Limited, 1987).

JOHNSON, HARRY, 'A Theoretical Model of Economic Naturalism in New and Developing States', from *Political Science Quarterly*, 80 (June 1965): 176–80; 182–5.

KEDOURIE, ELIE, from *Nationalism*. Reprinted by permission of Blackwell Publishers 1993.

KEDOURIE, ELIE (ed.), 'Introduction', in *Nationalism in Asia and Africa* (George Weidenfeld & Nicolson Limited, 1971). Reprinted by permission of Mrs E. Kedouri.

KOHN, HANS, reprinted with the permission of Macmillan Publishing Company from *The Idea of Nationalism* by Hans Kohn. New York: Macmillan Publishing Company, 1945.

LIJPHART, A., reprinted from Milton J. Esman: *Ethnic Conflict in the Western World* (Copyright © 1977 by Cornell University). Used by permission of the publisher, Cornell University Press.

MCNEILL, WILLIAM H., from *Polyethnicity and National Unity in World History* (© 1990 by William H. McNeill). Reprinted by permission of University of Toronto Press Incorporated.

MATOSSIAN, MARY, from *Political Change in Underdeveloped Countries*, ed. by John H. Kautsky (Wiley, 1962). Originally published in *Economic Development and Cultural Change*, VI, No. 3, 1958. Reprinted by permission of the University of Chicago Press.

MAYALL, JAMES, from *Nationalism and International Society* (Cambridge University Press, 1990).

NAIRN, TOM, from *The Break-up of Britain: Crisis and Neo-Naturalism*, 2nd edn. New Left Books, 1977. Reprinted by permission of Verso.

NEURBERGER, BENJAMIN, 'State and Nation in African Thought' in *Journal of African Studies*, 4(2), 1977.

REYNOLDS, SUSAN, from *Kingdoms and Communities in Western Europe, 900–1300* (© Susan Reynolds 1984). Reprinted by permission of Oxford University Press.

RICHMOND, ANTHONY, 'Ethnic Nationalism and Postindustrialism' from *Ethnic and Racial Studies*, vol. 7, no. 1, 1984. Reprinted by permission of Routledge.

ROBINSON, FRANCIS, 'Islam and Muslim Separatism', in *Political Identity in South Asia*, eds. D. Taylor and M. Yapp (Curzon Press, 1979).

SCHLESINGER, PHILIP, 'Europeanness—A New Cultural Battlefield?', from *Innovation*, vol. 5, no. 1, 1992. Reprinted by permission of Carfax Publishing Company, PO Box 25, Abingdon, Oxfordshire ox14 3UE, U.K.

SETON-WATSON, HUGH, from *Nations and States* (1977), Westview Press, Boulder, Colorado and Methuen Co. Reprinted by permission of the publishers.

SMITH, ANTHONY D., 'The Origins of Nature', from *Ethnic and Racial Studies*, vol. 12, no. 3, 1989. Reprinted by permission of Routledge.

SMITH, ANTHONY D., from *The Ethnic Revival* (Cambridge University Press, 1981).

STALIN, JOSEPH, 'The Nation' in *Marxism and the Natural Question* from *The Essential Stalin: Major Theoretical Writings 1905–1952*, ed. Bruce Franklin (Croom Helm, 1973).

SUGAR, P. and LEDEVER, I. (eds.), from *Nationalism in Eastern Europe* (University of Washington Press, 1969).

TILLY, CHARLES, 'Western State-Making and Theories of Political Transformation', from *The Formation of National States in Western Europe* (Copyright © 1975 by Charles Tilly). Reprinted by permission of Princeton University Press.

VAN DEN BERGHE, PIERRE, 'Race and Ethnicity: A Sociological Perspective', from *Ethnic and Racial Studies*, vol. 1, no. 4 (Routledge, 1978).

WEBER, MAX, 'The Nation' from *Max Weber: Essays in Sociology*, translated and edited by H. H. Gerth and C. Wright-Mills (Routledge & Kegan Paul, 1948).

YOUNG, CRAWFORD, 'Ethnicity and the Colonial and Post-Colonial State in Africa', in *Ethnic Groups and the State*, ed. Paul Brass (Croom Helm, 1985).

Index

OXFORD**READERS**

An important new series that explores timeless global issues, drawing on history, philosophy, politics, art history, anthropology, and literature to provide students and general readers with an authoritative collection of primary and secondary sources.

Edited by experts, they bring together a wide range of texts that would otherwise be inaccessible to many students.

Oxford Readers available from 1994/5:

War *Edited by Lawrence Freedman*
Ethics *Edited by Peter Singer*
Nationalism *Edited by John Hutchinson and*
Anthony D. Smith
Class *Edited by Patrick Joyce*
Fascism *Edited by Roger Griffin*

Forthcoming titles:

Classical Thought
Feminism
Sexuality
Race in the Twentieth Century
The Enlightenment
Evolution
Aesthetics
Postmodernism
Gender

OXFORD**READERS**

War

Edited by Lawrence Freedman

What are the causes of war? Which strategic as well as moral principles guide its conduct, and how have these changed? Has total war become unthinkable? What is the nature of contemporary conflict? How is war experienced by those on the front line?

Drawing on sources from numerous countries and disciplines, with accounts by generals, soldiers, historians, strategists, and poets, covering conflicts from the Napoleonic Wars to Vietnam and Bosnia, this Reader examines key issues and illustrates the theory and the experience of war in its many guises.

Includes extracts by:

Raymond Aron	Basil Liddell Hart
André Beaufre	Helmuth von Moltke
Carl von Clausewitz	Napoleon I
Anthony Giddens	Wilfred Owen
Robert Gilpin	Herbert Read
Max Hastings	Field Marshal Rommel
Michael Howard	Mao Tse-tung
Morris Janowitz	Paul C. Warnke
Vladimir Lenin	John Yoder

Reviews:

'. . . readable, interesting and valuable . . . This prose anthology of war is a delight for specialists and general readers alike.'
Sir Anthony Parsons, *International Relations*

'Freedman has shrewdly picked out some of the pithiest and most disturbing passages, he has arrayed a marvellous variety of authors ranging from contemporary times to the Battle of Trafalgar, and ordered them with splendid effect.'
Foreign Affairs

OXFORD**READERS**

Ethics

Edited by Peter Singer

What is ethics? Where does it come from? Can we really hope to find any rational way of deciding how we ought to live? If we can, what would it be like, and how are we going to know when we have found it?

To capture the essentials of what we know about the origins and nature of ethics, Peter Singer has drawn on anthropology, history, observations of non-human animals, the theory of evolution, game theory, works of fiction, and moral philosophy. With some of the finest pieces of writing, old and new, in and about ethics, he conveys the intellectual excitement of the search for answers to basic questions about how we ought to live.

Includes extracts by:

Aquinas	Immanuel Kant
Aristotle	Karl Marx
Albert Camus	Thomas Nagel
Charles Darwin	Plato
F. M. Dostoevsky	John Rawls
Sigmund Freud	J.-J. Rousseau
Jane Goodall	Jean-Paul Sartre
David Hume	Voltaire
William James	Frans B. M. de Waal